W9-BLT-574

Writing Analytically

FOURTH EDITION

David Rosenwasser
Jill Stephen

Muhlenberg College

THOMSON

WADSWORTH

Australia Canada Mexico Singapore Spain United Kingdom United States

Writing Analytically, Fourth Edition
David Rosenwasser • Jill Stephen

Publisher: Michael Rosenberg
Senior Acquisitions Editor: Dickson Musslewhite
Development Editor: Karen R. Smith
Senior Technology Project Manager: Cara Douglass-Graff
Executive Marketing Manager: Carrie Brandon
Marketing Assistant: Dawn Giovanniello
Advertising Project Manager: Patrick Rooney
Project Manager, Editorial Production: Brett Palana-Shanahan
Manufacturing Manager: Marica Locke
Permissions Editor: Sarah Harkrader

Production Service: GEX Publishing Services
Text Designer: Meral Dabcovich
Photo Manager: Sheri Blaney
Cover Designer: Gina Petty
Cover Printer: Phoenix Color Corp.
Printer: Courier Corp.
Cover Art: Photographer: 1937: Bill Hedrich, Hedrich-Blessing HB-04414-D3, Edgar Kaufman residence, Fallingwater, Bear Run (Pa)-Chicago Historical Society; Architect: Frank Lloyd Wright Alterations have been made to the original copy, including cropping, tinting or detailing.

© 2006 Thomson Wadsworth, a part of The Thomson Corporation. Thomson, the Star logo, and Wadsworth are trademarks used herein under license.

ALL RIGHTS RESERVED. No part of this work covered by the copyright hereon may be reproduced or used in any form or by any means— graphic, electronic, or mechanical, including photocopying, recording, taping, Web distribution, information storage and retrieval systems, or in any other manner—without the written permission of the publisher.

Printed in the United States of America
2 3 4 5 6 7 09 08 07 06 05

Thomson Higher Education
25 Thomson Place
Boston, MA 02210-1202
USA

Asia (including India)
Thomson Learning
5 Shenton Way
#01-01 UIC Building
Singapore 068808

Australia/New Zealand
Thomson Learning Australia
102 Dodds Street
Southbank, Victoria 3006
Australia

Canada
Thomson Nelson
1120 Birchmount Road
Toronto, Ontario M1K 5G4
Canada

UK/Europe/Middle East/Africa
Thomson Learning
High Holborn House
50–51 Bedford Road
London WC1R 4LR
United Kingdom

Latin America
Thomson Learning
Seneca, 53
Colonia Polanco
11560 Mexico
D.F. Mexico

Spain (including Portugal)
Thomson Paraninfo
Calle Magallanes, 25
28015 Madrid, Spain

For more information about our products, contact us at:
Thomson Learning Academic Resource Center
1-800-423-0563
For permission to use material from this text or product, submit a request online at **http://www.thomsonrights.com**
Any additional questions about permissions can be submitted by email to **thomsonrights@thomson.com**

Library of Congress Control Number: 2005924653

Student Edition: ISBN 1-4130-1012-1
Instructor's Edition: ISBN 1-4130-1015-6

Credits appear on page C-1, which constitutes a continuation of the copyright page.

BRIEF CONTENTS

CONTENTS

CHAPTER 4   Reading: How to Do It and What to Do with It   109

CHAPTER 5   Linking Evidence and Claims: 10 on 1 versus 1 on 10   137

CHAPTER 9   Organization: Forms and Formats   241

CHAPTER 10   Style: Choosing Words   257

CHAPTER 11   Style: Shaping Sentences (and Cutting the Fat)   275

PREFACE

Writing *Analytically* is about how to have ideas and develop them in an academic setting and beyond. It offers a book-length treatment of analysis, a form of thinking and writing required in virtually all college courses but frequently overshadowed in writing texts and first-year composition courses by emphasis on argument (persuasion), expressive writing, or the traditional rhetorical modes.

The book is suitable for composition courses as a central text, and as a supplementary text for writing-intensive courses across the curriculum. It would also work well in more advanced expository writing courses, first-year seminars, and as a guide for writing center tutors and teachers. The book is really for anyone who wishes to learn how to use writing as a tool of thought.

The book proceeds on the assumption that there are certain elements of effective analytical writing common to all disciplines. Our experience teaching seminars to faculty across the curriculum has convinced us that the area of consensus about writing is larger and more significant than the differences. So, although the book respects disciplinary difference, it does not lead with difference. Instead, it attempts to forge a common language for talking about writing that does not over-rely on the technical jargon of any one discipline. In the many instances where discussion of disciplinary difference is clearly called for, we create spaces—labeled "Voices from Across the Curriculum"—for professors from various disciplines to write in their own words about their practices and preferences.

The text takes from the process approach to writing a concern with the stages that a writer goes through in composing an essay—emphasizing conceptual revision as an ongoing rather than a late-stage activity. It takes from the critical thinking movement a concern with such logical matters as reasoning back to premises and the careful analysis of evidence. It combines these two approaches to offer an inside-the-head guided tour of analytical thinking.

Writing Analytically is deeply committed to the concept of writing to learn—that is, to the notion that writing is a tool that can facilitate and enrich understanding. Thus, the book emphasizes ways of using writing to figure out what things mean. It encourages writers to assume an exploratory stance toward ideas and evidence: to delay their judgments in favor of understanding, to treat their ideas as hypotheses to be tested rather than as self-evident truths, and to share their thought processes with readers.

Writing Analytically offers alternatives to oversimplified thinking of the like/dislike, agree/disagree variety. It argues that an idea is not the same thing as an opinion and demonstrates how to respect the complexity of subjects where there is no single right answer.

The main discovery we made as we worked on this book is that none of the reading we'd done about thesis statements (the major claim in a piece of writing) seemed to match either our own practice as writers and teachers or the practice of published writers. Textbooks about writing tend to present thesis statements as the finished products of an act of thinking—as inert statements that writers should march through their papers from beginning to end. In practice, the relationship between thesis and evidence is far more fluid and dynamic. In most good writing, the thesis grows and changes in response to evidence, even in final drafts.

So, finding new ways to talk about what a thesis is and how it operates became the heart of our project. This led us, in turn, to see that much of what typically characterizes weak writing is the result of writers leaping too quickly to a generalization that would do as a thesis, and then treating evidence only as something to be mustered in support of that idea. Much weak writing, in other words, is prematurely and too narrowly thesis-driven precisely because people try to formulate the thesis before they have done much (or any) analyzing. They say, for example, that a given article was about the threat to democracy or about love or death or rebirth—all of which are not only hopelessly broad but generic and clichéd.

What strategies would work best, we wondered, to help writers keep a more open and responsive relationship between thesis and evidence? What methods would most effectively get in the way of a writer's rush to thesis, so that he or she could prolong the thinking stage and thereby get to a better idea, without feeling unmoored in the process?

The solution sounds easy but actually isn't easy to accomplish. As writers and thinkers, we all need to SLOW DOWN—to dwell longer in the open-ended, exploratory, information-gathering stage. This requires specific tasks that will reduce the anxiety for answers, impede the reflex move to judgments, and encourage a more hands-on, less passive engagement with materials. *Writing Analytically* supplies these tasks for each phase of the writing and idea-generating process—making observations, inferring implications, and making the leap to possible conclusions.

HOW TO USE THIS BOOK

The book is designed to be usable with a wide range of course contents and types of assignments. It does not require that a professor organize a course around it. Though the chapters form a logical sequence, each can also stand alone and be used in any order. The book assumes that most professors will want to supply their own subject matter for students to write about. The book does, however, contain writing exercises throughout that can be applied to a wide range of materials—print and visual, text based (reading) and experiential (writing from direct observation). In the text itself we suggest using newspapers, magazines, films, primary texts (both fiction and nonfiction), academic articles, textbooks, television, historical documents, places, advertising, photographs, political campaigns, and so on.

The book's writing exercises take two forms: end-of-chapter assignments that could generate papers, and informal writing exercises called "Try this" that are embedded inside the chapters near the particular skills they employ. Many of the "Try this" exercises could generate papers, but usually they are more limited in scope, asking you to experiment with various kinds of data gathering and analysis.

The best way to work with each chapter is to try out its particular writing techniques on something else you are studying. You are seeking to cultivate habits of mind that will make you a more observant and more insightful thinker. One of these habits of mind is to notice that interesting things to think about are all around you.

As noted above, the book differs the most markedly from other writing texts in its treatment of the "thesis" (a paper's governing idea). We argue that the problem with much writing of the sort that people are taught to do in school is that it arrives prematurely at an idea that the writer then "proves" by attaching it to a number of examples (a pattern we call 1 on 10; see Chapter 5). For the best quick hit on what the book has to say about thesis statements, start with the sections in Chapter 1 called "What It Means to Have an Idea" and "Moving from Idea to Thesis Statement: What a Good Thesis Looks Like."

If you are interested in argument, you should know that we believe writers should learn to analyze before concentrating on persuasive writing. The best arguments start from the best ideas, which are arrived at through careful analysis. You will find that the methods the book offers in its first two chapters, and especially in the third part of Chapter 3 ("Reformulating Binaries and Uncovering Assumptions"), are well suited to both analyzing and constructing arguments.

Some of the tools come later in the book than we would like. Such is the case with what we offer you on sentence style. It has become common in writing courses, for all sorts of good reasons, to delay attention to style. This is, at least in part, a reaction against a past imbalance when a course on writing inevitably meant a course on improving your grammar and style. Worrying about style while you are struggling to arrive at ideas can be a hindrance. On the other hand, style is related to thinking. Our three chapters on style (10, 11, and 14), like the other chapters in the book, are about thinking. We use them early in our writing courses, inviting students to perceive a writer's characteristic sentence shapes and words as useful windows on that writer's mind, his or her way of approaching the world.

Past readers of the book have asked if we could include in one place a brief annotated list of the various observation and idea-generating strategies that the book recommends.

You will find a brief glossary of these strategies—entitled "The Book's Heuristics: an Overview"—later in this preface. You can also gain quick access to the book's perspective on writing by browsing the "Try this" exercises, the short sections at the beginning of each chapter called "Quick Takes," as well as the guidelines that end each chapter.

WHAT'S NEW IN THIS EDITION

1. The book's first three chapters are extensively rewritten for tone and clarity but mostly to better integrate the book's observation and interpretive strategies. We have, for example, restored the "analytical moves" from the second edition and integrated "the Method" (looking for patterns of repetition and contrast), the primary heuristic introduced in the third edition, into them. (See Chapter 2.)

2. We have, in Chapter 1, integrated the So what? question (making the interpretive leap) into the observation strategies: Notice and focus and 10 on 1. The book's message is still that writers need to slow down and prolong the data-gathering stage before leaping to conclusions, but readers can now see the whole process of moving from observations to implications to conclusions in one chapter. (See Chapter 1.)

3. We have put the sections on uncovering assumptions and on reformulating binaries together, as they were in the second edition, providing what we think is an excellent means of teaching students to analyze and to write arguments. Our claim is that what really makes an argument persuasive is the quality of the ideas themselves and a writer's willingness to entertain complexity. And so our emphasis is on the analysis of an argument's assumptions rather than on persuasion. (See the third section of Chapter 3.)

4. We have responded to readers' requests for more examples of the book's writing and thinking strategies. See the analyses of a contemporary film (*Good Bye Lenin!*) at the end of Chapter 1 and in the thesis chapter, Chapter 6. See also the additional examples and more extended discussion of the Method in Chapter 2 and in the second section of Chapter 3.

5. We have responded to readers' requests for a glossary/overview of the book's various heuristics so that these can be easily reviewed and are easier to find. See this overview at the end of this preface.

6. We have restored guidelines to the ends of all chapters and now begin each chapter with a brief overview/sampling of the chapter's advice called a "Quick Take."

7. The "Try this" writing exercises are now numbered, have titles, and are more freestanding (like the "Applications" in the second edition), so that readers can more easily browse them as a convenient means of surveying the book's advice.

8. We have streamlined and relocated the discussion of counterproductive habits of mind so that it follows rather than precedes the book's introduction of observation strategies. The argument against leaping to judgments and generalizations remains strong, but it is now better integrated into a more positive and more hands-on opening chapter, which gets students involved in a range of group and individual observation exercises with an emphasis on attention to detail, word choice, and concrete description. (See Chapter 1.)

9. We have moved up the chapters on diction and sentence style so that they come before rather than after the chapters on research writing. We did this to better integrate attention to word choice and syntax with the book's other analytical strategies. A regular assignment for attending to syntax is now introduced in Chapter 1 in the context of students' analyzing the style of typical sentences in their own and others' descriptive writing.

10. The section on electronic research has been updated and rewritten.

THE BOOK'S HEURISTICS: AN OVERVIEW

As this book uses the term, a *heuristic*—from the Greek word for "discover"—is a formula for searching evidence to arrive at ideas. We think of our heuristics as "universal" topics because they can be applied to virtually any subject matter. They are topics of invention—fairly formulaic moves that you can make to notice more about a subject, to discover what you think about it, and to arrive at more sophisticated topics, which can then be developed further.

Here is a skeletal list of the book's primary heuristics, along with a brief description and a reference to the chapters in which they are discussed:

1. **Paraphrase × (times) 3** (See Chapters 1 and 4.)

   Paraphrasing inevitably discloses that what is being paraphrased is more complicated than it first appeared. When you recast a sentence or two—finding the best synonyms you can think of for the original language, translating it into a parallel statement—you are thinking about what the words mean. Do it three times to open a range of meanings. Paraphrase is not summary; it's a mode of inquiry and the first step toward interpretation. It also gives writers something to do with the reading besides simply recording it or agreeing/disagreeing with it.

2. **Notice and Focus + Ranking** (See Chapter 1.)

   The prompt here—What do you notice?—helpfully short-circuits the tendency to generalize. It redirects the writer's attention to the subject matter and thus delays the pressure to come up with answers prematurely. The second step has you focus by asking you to rank (create an order of importance for) the various features you have noticed in the subject.

3. **[What do you find most] "Interesting" or "Strange"?** (See Chapter 1.)

   These prompts can be integrated into other heuristics or used to get you thinking on the page, as in, "What I find most strange about *x* is . . . ." They offer alternatives to what we call the judgment reflex—a counterproductive habit of mind that approaches the world in terms of like/dislike, right/wrong, should/shouldn't. The prompts shift attention from pro/con argument to thinking aimed at *understanding* and theorizing about the nature of things. They invite writers to *defamiliarize*, rather than to normalize things out of our range of notice.

4. **Looking for Patterns of Repetition and Contrast (aka the Method)** (See Chapters 2 and 3.)

   This is the book's primary heuristic for the observation stage of analysis. It consists of data gathering in response to three basic questions: What do you notice? What repeats? What is opposed to what? Here are the steps:

   Step 1. List exact repetitions and the number of each (words, details).

   Step 2. List strands—groupings of same or similar kinds of words, details (for example, *polite, courteous, mannerly*). Be able to explain the strand's connecting logic with a label.

   Step 3. List organizing contrasts—binary oppositions (for example, *open/closed, gray/brown*). Start with what's on the page; then move to implied terms.

   Step 4. Select and list the two or three most significant repetitions, strands, and binaries.

   Step 5: Locate anomalies: exceptions to the pattern, things that seem not to fit. Then compose one healthy paragraph explaining your choice of one repetition, or strand, or binary as most significant.

5. **The Five Analytical Moves** (See Chapter 2.)

   These moves define the context within which Looking for Patterns and other heuristics operate. The moves establish the ground for having ideas.

   Move 1: Suspend judgment (understand before you judge).

   Move 2: Define significant parts and how they are related.

Move 3: Look for patterns of repetition and contrast and for anomalies (aka the Method).

Move 4: Make the implicit explicit (convert to direct statement meanings that are only suggested—make details "speak").

Move 5: Keep reformulating questions and explanations. (What other details seem significant? What else might they mean?)

6. **Asking So What?** (See Chapter 1.)

This question is our universal prompt for spurring the leap to interpretation. It is shorthand for such questions as these:

Why does this observation matter? Where does it get us?

What ideas are implicit in it?

How can we begin to generalize from the observation to the larger subject?

Asking So what? presses writers to move beyond the patterns and emphases they've been observing in the data and make some kind of claim. The So what? question should be posed all of the time, not just at the end of the thinking process, and not just once about an observation.

7. **Freewriting & Passage-Based Focused Freewriting** (See Chapters 1 and 4.)

The central question to ask in improving one's ability to read critically is What is the single sentence that I think it is most important for us to discuss and why? This heuristic works on the assumption that readers will have a better appreciation of how the whole works when they've seen how a piece works. A freewrite should target key phrases and paraphrase them, ask So what? about the details, and address how the passage is representative of broader issues in the reading.

8. **Finding "Go To" Sentences** (See Chapter 11.)

What are the two or three sentence structures that reveal the tendency any given writer has to shape his or her thought—the characteristic ways he or she uses language? Because the way that a sentence is structured reveals a way of thinking, identifying a writer's typical sentence structure—the form he or she "goes to" when the writing matters most—can be revelatory. Then ask yourself in what ways this type of sentence reveals how the writer thinks.

9. **"Seems to Be about *X*, but Could Also Be (or Is 'Really') about *Y*"** (See Chapter 3.)

This prompt is based on the conviction that understandings are rarely simple and overt, but rather, complexly embedded in particular contexts. Completing the formula by supplying key terms for *x* and *y*, writers get practice in making the implicit explicit and accepting the existence of multiple plausible meanings for something. (Note: *Really* aims not to suggest a single hidden right answer but to prompt a range of less obvious landing sites for interpretive leaps.) "Seems to be about *x*" is especially useful when considering the *rhetoric* of a piece: its complex and various ways of targeting and appealing to an audience. It's also useful for "reading against the grain"—seeking out what something is about that it probably does not know it's about.

10. **Doing 10 on 1** (See Chapters 1 and 5.)

This heuristic encourages analyzing in depth. The phrase *10 on 1* is shorthand for the principle that it is better to make ten observations or points about a single representative issue or example (10 on 1) than to make the same basic point about ten related issues or examples (1 on 10). (The number 10 is arbitrary, standing for "a lot.") Doing 10 on 1 helps writers narrow their focus and draw out as much meaning as possible from their best examples. It operates to locate a range of possible meanings suggested by the evidence. It will also prevent you from jumping to a thesis prematurely, while your thinking is still too general.

11. **A Template for Organizing Papers Using 10 on 1** (See Chapter 5.)

Here is a pared-down version of a formula for organizing a paper by doing 10 on 1. It is an alternative to more rigid models, such as five-paragraph form, which tends to stunt rather than promote thinking.

1. In the introduction, note a pattern or tendency in the evidence and explain why you find it potentially significant and worth looking at (a working thesis about what this pattern might reveal or accomplish).
2. Zoom in on your representative example, some smaller part of the larger pattern. Argue for the example's representativeness and usefulness in coming to a better understanding of your subject.
3. Do 10 on 1 on this example, sharing your observations and tentative conclusions (answers to the So what? question). Then use complicating evidence to refine your claims.
4. In a short paper, move to conclusion, offering a qualified version of your thesis and brief commentary on the ways your analysis has illuminated the larger subject.
5. In a longer paper, begin "constellating"—that is, exploring the connections among several representative 10-on-1 examples. The first of these is used as a lens for examining the others, which in turn further qualify and develop the claim (with conclusion to follow).

12. **Applying a Reading as a Lens** (See Chapter 4.)

This heuristic models how to compare two readings without just listing similarities and differences. It suggests how to focus on the way a reading uses its point of view as a lens—a way of looking at or understanding something else (another subject or another reading). The key move is for the reader to assume that the match between lens A and subject B won't be exact, and therefore he or she should focus on how A both fits and does not fit B. The writer then uses the differences to develop the analysis.

13. **[Looking for] Difference Within Similarity and Similarity Despite Difference** (See Chapter 5.)

This heuristic seeks to make the standard "comparison and contrast" move more analytical—not just a mechanical matching exercise ("A does this; B does that," and so on). The formula is this:

- Identify fundamental similarity. Account for its significance by answering the question, So what that A and B have this similarity?

- Then, given the similarity, locate the most important difference, and again ask So what? When A and B are obviously similar, look for unexpected difference. When A and B are obviously different, look instead for unexpected similarity.

These steps will prevent a conclusion such as "Thus, we see there are many similarities and differences between A and B."

14. **Six Steps for Making a Thesis Evolve (through Successive Complications)** (See Chapter 6.)

This heuristic offers the book's primary model for developing complex ideas on a subject and then organizing a paper around this process. It emphasizes using evidence that complicates the major claim, to make the claim more supple and accurate.

1. Formulate an idea about your subject—a working thesis.
2. See how far you can make this thesis go in accounting for (confirming) evidence.
3. Locate complicating evidence that is not adequately accounted for by the thesis.
4. Make explicit the apparent mismatch between the thesis and selected evidence, asking and answering So what?
5. Reshape your claim to accommodate the evidence that hasn't fit.
6. Repeat steps 2, 3, 4, and 5 several times.

In contrast to debate-style argument, this format has the advantage of trying neither to hide nor to ignore evidence that doesn't fit the claim. That is because it approaches evidence as more than "the stuff that proves I'm right." The evolving thesis seeks to account fully and accurately for what is there.

15. **Conversing with Sources** (See Chapter 12.)

This is less a single heuristic than a governing idea for how to approach secondary materials in ways that get beyond using them as answers or disagreeing with the experts. The various ways of conversing share the approach of using the source as a point of departure. Here is a brief list of how to use sources in this way:

- Make as many points as you can about a single representative passage from your source, and then branch out from this center to analyze other passages that "speak" to it in some way.
- Build upon the source's point of view, extending its implications.
- Apply the idea in the source to another subject.
- Agree with most of what the source says but take issue with one small part that you want to modify.
- Identify a contradiction in the source and explore its implications, without necessarily arriving at a solution.

ABOUT THE AUTHORS

David Rosenwasser and Jill Stephen are Professors of English at Muhlenberg College in Allentown, Pennsylvania, where they have co-directed a Writing Across the Curriculum (WAC) program since 1987. They began teaching writing to college students in the early 1970s—David at the University of Virginia and then at the College of William and Mary, and Jill at New York University and then at Hunter College (CUNY). *Writing Analytically* has grown out of their undergraduate teaching and the seminars on writing and writing instruction that they have offered to faculty at Muhlenberg and at other colleges and universities across the country.

ACKNOWLEDGMENTS

This book first came into being primarily because of the insight and patience of one person, our original developmental editor, Karl Yambert, then at Harcourt. We remain grateful to Karl for starting our education (still under way) on how to write a decent "how to" book for writers. Similar thanks go to his successor, Michell Phifer, who made the revision and production phases of the second and third editions a pleasure, and to our former acquisitions editors, John Meyers, who taught us about getting a book out of the hands of the publisher and into the hands of readers, and Julie McBurney, who brought the second edition into being. We now have the good fortune to work with Karen R. Smith, developmental editor at Thomson, who has consistently offered her encouragement, patience, and good advice on the evolution of this fourth edition. We are grateful to Dickson Musslewhite, senior acquisitions editor at Thomson, who saw us into the book's third edition and now into its fourth and has fortified us with his humor, intelligence, good will, and first-rate fiction. Finally, Michael Rosenberg, publisher at Thomson, has been gracious with his ideas, both for this and for subsequent writing projects.

Our debts to our teaching and writing friends are very great. Christine Farris has been a great friend of the book since its early days. She and John Schilb and their colleagues at Indiana University—especially Matthew Johnson and Ted Leahy—kept us in touch with the ideas and problems that first brought the book into being. Our friend Dean Ward at Calvin College has been a source of inspiration and good conversation on writing for many years. Paul Heilker of Virginia Tech has long been a friend and supporter who doesn't allow us to forget our original aims. Thanks as well to Georgina Hill at Western Michigan, to her former student Matt Hollrah at the University of Kansas, and to our friends at the National Writing Project: Richard Louth and Lin Spence.

The book and the workshops that we do at campuses where it is used have brought us into contact with many truly inspirational teachers and administrators. Over the past two years, we have been fortunate to come to know Wendy Hesford and Eddie Singleton of

Ohio State University. In a number of respects this new edition was inspired by them and their students at Ohio State.

We are also, of course, deeply indebted to our students at Muhlenberg College, who have shared their writing and their thinking about writing with us. Chief among these (lately) are Sarah Kersh, Robbie Saenz di Viteri, Laura Sutherland, Jessica Skrocki, and Jake McNamara. Thanks also go to all the students who have allowed us to use their writing in our book, most recently, Rachel Breckman, Thomas Prevete, Liz McNierney, Kim Schmidt, Pete Lankarge, and Wendy Eichler.

Among our colleagues at Muhlenberg, we are especially grateful to reference librarian Kelly Cannon for his section on library and Internet research in Chapter 13. Special thanks as well to James Peck, Mark Sciutto, and Jeremy Teissere for sharing with us their insight and generous advice as we embarked on this new edition. Our thanks also go to other Muhlenberg colleagues for their good counsel, their teaching materials, and for writing the "Voices from Across the Curriculum" boxes that appear throughout the book: Barri Gold, Linda Miller, Jim Bloom, Tom Cartelli, Grant Scott, Karen Dearborn, Anna Adams, John Malsberger, Jack Gambino, Ted Conner, Joseph Eliot, Fred Norling, James Marshall, Bruce Wightman, Rich Niesenbaum, Alan Tjeltveit, Laura Snodgrass, Robert Milligan, and our good friend Alec Marsh, with whom we argue endlessly about writing. Carol Proctor in the English Department looks out for us and casts a sympathetic eye on our organizational deficiencies. We also thank Muhlenberg College, especially its provost, Marjorie Hass, for continuing to support our participation at national conferences.

We would also like to thank the many colleagues who reviewed the book; we are grateful for their insight:

Derede Arthur, *University of California, Santa Cruz*

Barbara Bird, *Taylor University*

Margaret D. Bonesteel, *Syracuse University*

David W. Bottorff, *Brandeis University*

James Bryant-Trerise, *Clackamas Community College*

Stephen M. Byars, *University of Southern California*

Diane Chin, *University of Illinois, Chicago*

Rachel Clark, *The Ohio State University*

Allan R. Cook, *Marygrove College*

Melanie Culbertson, *University of Evansville*

Kevin Degnan, *The Ohio State University*

Abby M. Dubisar, *The Ohio State University*

Christine Elliott, *The Ohio State University*

Allison Fisher, *The Ohio State University*

Andrew Green, *University of Miami*

Wendy Hesford, *The Ohio State University*

Mary G. Jackson, *St. Mary's University, San Antonio*

Justin A. Joyce, *University of Illinois, Chicago*

Erick Kelemen, *Columbia College*

Doug Kirshen, *Brandeis University*

Charlene Kiser, *Milligan College*

Mary Klages, *University of Colorado, Boulder*

Joshua Kronenberg, *University of Illinois, Chicago*

Linda Krumholz, *Denison University*

Theresa A. Kulbaga, *The Ohio State University*

Mary B. Lindsey, *University of Illinois, Urbana-Champaign*

Kelly Lowe, *Mount Union College*

Michael Lueker, *Our Lady of the Lake University*

April Mann, *University of Miami*

Kim Martin, *Fort Lewis College*

Tom Moss, *University of Illinois, Chicago*

Christine Mueri, *The Ohio State University*

Jamil Mustafa, *Lewis University*

Stacy O. Nicklow, *Southern Illinois University, Carbondale*

Rolf Norgaard, *University of Colorado, Boulder*

Anne-Marie Obilade, *Southern Illinois University, Carbondale*

Scott Payne, *University of Findlay*

Susan Reeve, *Dickinson College*

Juliet Rodeman, *University of Missouri, Columbia*

John M. Rybnik, *La Salle University*

Andy Scahill, *The Ohio State University*

Andrea Scarpino, *The Ohio State University*

Gina Victoria Shaffer, *University of California, Los Angeles*

Rosemarie Shields, *Milligan College*

Shannon Thomas, *The Ohio State University*

Ben Thompson, *University of California, Los Angeles*

Shirley Thompson, *George Washington University; University of Maryland, College Park*

David M. Weed, *Washburn University*

Ayana Wilson, *The Ohio State University*

James M. Wilson, *Flagler College*

Angie Wong-Hayes, *Winona State University*

Daniel Worden, *Brandeis University*

Elizabeth Zimmerman, *The Ohio State University*

Finally, thanks to our spouses (Deborah and Mark) and our children (Lizzie, Lesley, and Sarah) for their love and support during the many hours that we sit immobile at our computers.

CHAPTER 1

Seeing Better: The Analytical Habit of Mind

"See better, Lear." – William Shakespeare

"Reserving judgements is a matter of infinite hope." – F. Scott Fitzgerald

Quick Take

T his book is interested in ideas: what they are, how they operate in a piece of writing, and how they happen. Our primary claim about ideas is that they are the product of minds habituated to focusing sustained attention on details: the analytical habit of mind. Central to this habit of mind is a writer's willingness to use description as an analytical tool.

People who have ideas are not necessarily smarter or more creative than the rest of us, and they may not even work harder. People who are struck more often by the thing we call inspiration have method on their side, whether they are aware of this fact or not. This chapter introduces many of the book's idea-generating strategies, including Notice and focus, 10 on 1, paraphrase × 3, and asking "So what?"

The chapter is divided into four sections. The first section emphasizes description as an analytical tool—a means of attending more closely to evidence. It is all about learning to see more when we observe things.

The second section seeks to open things up in your writing. It proposes the value of tolerating uncertainty and of becoming more aware of counterproductive habits of mind that can close thinking down prematurely.

Those of you who wish to get to the heart of the book's analytical method could move directly to Sections 3 and 4 of this first chapter. These include "What It Means to Have an Idea" and the book's basic strategies for observing, uncovering implication, and pushing observations to conclusions. Section 4 is an extended example of student writing using these strategies. In Section 4 you will also learn how to mark up a draft to find opportunities for developing its ideas.

We hope that you find the book's writing exercises enjoyable as well as useful, and that they help you cultivate confidence in your own writing process. Writing, like most worthwhile human activities, works best if powered, at least in part, by joy.

SECTION 1: SEEING THE DETAILS

Although much of this first section is about description, and thus might seem to be geared more to the needs of the fiction or memoir writer than to people learning to write analytically, we believe that good analytical writing (and thinking) depends upon the same skills that energize all good writing: attention to concrete detail. If you can afford to spend some time on the description exercises, especially Hemingway's five finger exercise in this first section of the chapter, before you move on to more strictly analytical writing, your work will benefit.

NOTICING (AND THE DEADENING EFFECT OF HABIT)

Some people, perhaps especially the very young, are good at noticing details. They see things the rest of us don't see or have ceased to notice. But why is this? Is it just that people become duller as they get older? The poet William Wordsworth, among others, argued that we aren't the victims of declining intelligence but of habit. That is, as we organize our lives so that we can function more efficiently, we condition ourselves to see in more predictable ways and to screen out things that are not immediately relevant to our daily needs.

You can test this theory by considering what you did and did not notice this morning on the way to work or class. Getting where we need to go, following a routine for moving through the day, can be done with minimal engagement of either the brain or the senses. Our minds are often, as we say, "somewhere else." As we walk along, our eyes wander a few feet in front of our shoes or stare blankly in the direction of our destination. Moving along the roadway in cars, we periodically realize that miles have gone by while we were driving on automatic pilot, attending barely at all to the road or the car or the landscape. Arguably, even when we try to focus on something we want to consider, the habit of not really attending to things stays with us. We glide over the top. We go for rapidly acquired impressions and then relax our attention and forget the rest.

People tend to remember their reactions and impressions. The dinner was dull. The house was beautiful. The music was exciting. But they forget the specific, concrete causes of these impressions (if they ever fully noticed them). As a result, we deprive ourselves of material to think with—the data that might allow us to reconsider our initial impressions and to share them with others. A premise of this book is that frequent writing trains people to become more observant, better able to remember the details of an experience, and thus much more likely to have ideas.

People tend to remember their reactions but forget the cause.

The deadening effect of habit on seeing and thinking has long been a preoccupation of artists as well as philosophers and psychologists. Some people have even defined the aim of art as "defamiliarization." "The essential purpose of art," writes the novelist David Lodge, "is to overcome the deadening effects of habit by representing familiar things in unfamiliar ways." The man who coined the term *defamiliarization*, Victor Shklovsky, wrote, "Habitualization devours works, clothes, furniture, one's wife, and the fear of war. . . . And art exists that one may recover the sensation of life" (David Lodge, *The Art of Fiction*. New York: Penguin, 1992, p.53). This claim takes us to the chapter's first and most fundamental exercise, tracing impressions back to causes.

TRACING IMPRESSIONS BACK TO CAUSES

To become more aware—which is key to becoming a better writer—we have to train ourselves to notice more: both our impressions of things and how these impressions are formed. The single best piece of advice we know on this subject can be found in the counsel the writer Ernest Hemingway offered to a young man who had come to him for guidance on becoming a writer. You can try this advice yourself in the box below.

> ### Try this 1.1: Hemingway's Five Finger Exercise
>
> Read the passage by Ernest Hemingway below and then start practicing the five finger exercise that he recommends. Practice it at least once a day for a week in a notebook that you set aside for trying out the writing exercises in this book. Each five finger exercise will probably be about a paragraph, or at most a page in length. At the end of the week, type your two best five finger exercises. If possible, read them aloud to a class or smaller group of people who also have been doing the exercise.
>
> Throughout the passage Hemingway refers to experiences on a day of deep sea fishing.
>
> Watch what happens today. If we get into a fish, see exactly what it is that everyone does. If you get a kick out of it while he is jumping, remember back until you see exactly what the action was that gave you the emotion. Whether it was the rising of the line from the water and the way it tightened like a fiddle string until drops started from it, or the way he smashed and threw water when he jumped. Remember what the noises were and what was said. Find what gave you the emotion; what the action was that gave you the excitement. Then write it down, making it clear so the reader will see it too and have the same feeling you had. That's a five finger exercise.
>
> After you've done some writing, go back over what you have said and select the most significant details. A good description is not an undifferentiated catalogue, the verbal equivalent of a photograph. Good description is highly selective. Build a descriptive paragraph around these details. We like the term *telling details* for those you think are most revealing in sharing with readers the essential character and feel of an experience. Your goal is to cause a person who reads your paragraph to think and feel as you did. Achieve this without telling your readers how you thought and felt. Let the details do the telling. Show rather than tell.

WHAT WE DO WHEN WE DESCRIBE THINGS

The passage from Hemingway offers not only a useful exercise but also an opportunity to consider just what it is that we do—and why—when we describe things. Describing consists of a combination of three activities, all of which are illustrated in the following sentence, which describes a bullfighter's way of walking: "The gypsy was walking out toward the bull again, walking heel-and-toe, insultingly, like a ballroom dancer." Let's consider what this sentence does and then compare it with the way Hemingway handles description in the five finger exercise.

The three things that people typically do in description are

1. **offer concrete detail**—that is, details that allow others to share the writer's sensory experience ("walking heel-and-toe");
2. **make comparisons** that allow readers to understand something unfamiliar in terms of something they might be expected to know better ("like a ballroom dancer"); and
3. **name the experience** in some way (for example, happy, sad, confusing), often through the use of evaluative adjectives and adverbs ("insultingly").

A good description is not an undifferentiated catalogue, the verbal equivalent of a photograph. Good description is highly selective.

► Try this 1.2: Looking at What We Do When We Describe

Look back at Hemingway's five finger exercise above and consider which of the three descriptive activities he relies on the most. Find the comparisons, the concrete detail, and any direct naming or evaluating of the experience of the sort that we see with the word *insultingly* in the sentence about the gypsy. Look also at the parts of speech Hemingway uses. Does he seem to prefer any particular parts of speech—nouns, for example, or adjectives, or verbs? What is the role of nouns relative to adjectives? You will notice that Hemingway doesn't use many adjectives. Why might this be, and what is the effect of leaving adjectives out?

EVALUATIVE AND ABSTRACT VERSUS CONCRETE WORDS

It is useful to consider that adjectives and adverbs can be divided into two basic types: those that offer concrete information, something we can actively imagine and visualize, such as walking heel-to-toe, and those that offer judgments (good, bad, pretty, ugly, depressing, exciting). Evaluative adjectives and adverbs don't actually tell readers very much about the subject itself, only about the impact that the subject had on the writer. Evaluative adjectives, the ones that offer judgments rather than concrete detail, don't really describe. Instead they simply label. They tell us how the writer responded, but they don't share the causes of that response with the reader. It is this problem, among others, that the five-finger exercise addresses.

Consider the difference for a reader in being told, "The lecture was boring" or being offered the following rendering of the same thing in concrete detail: "The professor leaned forward on the podium, fixing his eyes on his notes. As the minutes ticked by, the professor's eyes moved from the notes to some spot high on the ceiling at the back of the room and then back to the notes again. Sentence after sentence rolled out, with nothing more to mark its passing than these slight shifts in the professor's eyes, never once stopping to alight on his students."

You can best address the evaluative adjective problem by sharing with your readers the actual data, the concrete detail that made you respond as you did. This shift from evaluative adjectives and explicit statement to concrete detail is called showing versus telling. Concrete detail allows you to share your data—the grounds of your convictions—with your readers. Evaluative adjectives and abstractions shut the reader out of your thinking process.

A concrete detail is one that allows us to visualize (see in our mind's eye) or hear or touch or smell the particulars of an experience. The opposite of *concrete* is *abstract*. The word *democracy* is abstract. It is a concept—an idea. We know what it means, but we cannot see it, taste it, hear it, or smell it. The red handle on the lever that closes the curtain in a voting booth and the many little boxes with names next to them are concrete details, the stuff of democracy as an experience. (For an extended discussion of concrete versus abstract words, see Chapter 10, "Choosing Words.")

Try this 1.3: Distinguishing Abstract from Concrete Words

Make a list of the first ten words that come to mind and then arrange them from most concrete to most abstract. Then repeat the exercise by choosing key words from a page of something you have written recently.

Try this 1.4: Distinguishing Evaluative from Nonevaluative Words

The dividing line between evaluative and nonevaluative words is often much harder to see in practice than you might assume. Categorize each of the terms in the following list as judgmental or nonjudgmental, and be prepared to explain your reasoning: monstrous, delicate, authoritative, strong, muscular, automatic, vibrant, tedious, pungent, unrealistic, flexible, tart, pleasing, clever, and slow.

SHOWING VERSUS TELLING

The act of describing, of showing rather than telling, is just as important to analytical writing—in fact to all kinds of writing—as it is to the writing of poems or fiction. Browse through, for example, a history book—even a history textbook—the newspaper, or any collection of essays, including some on scientific subjects, and you will find description (and narrative as well, since the two so often go hand in hand). Description is essential to writing. We simply cannot think well without it. Although the various academic disciplines differ in the kinds of description they employ and in the ways that description may be used, they all call for keeping thinking in touch with telling detail.

▶ Try this 1.5: Showing versus Telling: an Evocative Place

Pick a place, either from memory or from your current experience, that appeals to your senses, a place that makes you take notice of your surroundings. Describe this place in a way that will cause another person to experience it as you do. Avoid evaluative adjectives and descriptions of your feelings. Write the piece without telling your readers your reactions to the place or the reasons for them. Offer instead the concrete details that shape your response to the place. You can include action and people other than yourself in your description if you like.

As we have already noted, this kind of writing is not the sole province of short-story writers, novelists, and poets. All kinds of writing depend on the writer's ability to use words to re-create experience. Weak writing tends to offer the writer's conclusions without sharing his or her experience of the evidence with readers. Your goal as a writer is to let your readers think with you. This means that you have to give them the stuff that made you think as you do, to risk letting them think along with you rather than just imposing your views. Good writing offers not only a writer's conclusions, but the thinking about particulars that produced the conclusions.

Another piece of Hemingway's conversation with the young writer offers us some useful thinking on the relation between judgments (evaluation) and understanding.

> Then get in somebody else's head for a change. Don't just think who is right. . . . As a writer you should not judge. You should understand.

> When people talk, listen completely. Don't be thinking what you're going to say. Most people never listen. Nor do they observe. You should be able to go into a room and when you come out know everything that you saw there and not only that. If that room gave you any feeling, you should know exactly what it was that gave you that feeling. Try that for practice. When you're in town stand outside the theater and see how the people differ in the way they get out of taxis and motor cars. There are a thousand ways to practice.

Notice that in his advice here, Hemingway concentrates not only on activities—observing and remembering—but on habits of mind that get in the way of observing and remembering. Judging, as we discuss at more length later in this chapter, is the habit of mind most likely to shut down our powers of observation. This is so because once a judgment has been made, we tend to screen out anything that runs counter to it. Judgments cause us to fall back on evaluative adjectives rather than doing the more difficult job of tracing our judgments back to causes. When we don't trace our judgments back to causes, we deprive ourselves of the data necessary for reconsidering our response. It is through this process that our responses to the world harden into the kinds of automatic judgments that we call opinions.

> ### Try this 1.6: Observation Fieldwork
>
> Station yourself somewhere on campus, such as the entrance to the student union or any place where people tend to gather. Go there every day for at least five days and write a neutral description of what you see and hear. Don't include judgments or conclusions about your scene. Just collect detail that strikes you as particularly telling. You will find that it is surprisingly difficult to leave out your reactions, though you should recognize that the details you choose to record are already reactions because it is you and your orientation toward the world that have selected them.
>
> When you are finished, put together a one- to two-page account that tells by showing—that is, your account should be made up entirely of telling detail rather than your interpretations of the significance of that detail. Your goal is to provide readers of your account with a window on the world, but one that is, of course, highly selective, because writing does not operate like a camera eye. Writing is inevitably and necessarily more selective. Keep revising your account until you have a rendering of your "data"—the observed details—that will cause your readers to think and feel as you do about the scene.

Description as a Form of Analysis Virtually all forms of description are implicitly analytical. When you choose what you take to be the three most telling details about your subject, you have selected significant parts and used them as a means of getting at what you take to be the character of the whole. This is what analysis does: it goes after an understanding of what something means, its nature, by zeroing in on the function of significant detail.

What follows are two short descriptive passages from personal essays written by students. Analyze the different kinds of descriptive work that goes on in each: explicit telling, especially with evaluative adjectives; showing, through the use of concrete detail; and making comparisons. What seems to you to be the most important telling detail in each? What does this detail "say"?

Notice, by the way, that the distinction between evaluative adjectives and concrete ones is not always entirely clear. *Blurry*, for example, as used in the second piece, is both an evaluation and a concrete detail. As an evaluation it means "not clear." As a concrete detail, it suggests the actual experience of memory in which images are present but are dim and jumbled and ill defined.

For your consideration of word choice in the passages, let us add another interesting category—the kind of adverbs known as intensifiers. Like adjectives and adverbs that merely name evaluative conclusions (such as *boring*), intensifiers

offer little or no information about the subject. An intensifier is a verbal exclamation point. You can greatly improve your writing by systematically cutting out
the intensifiers (*very*, *really*, *terribly*, etc.). Spot the intensifier in our last sentence.
Sometimes intensifiers are good for purposes of emphasis—but a little bit goes a
long way.

Two Examples of Description as a Form of Analysis

First student description

22 Green Hill Road was the most beautiful house I had ever seen. The
bricks a light brown, and the ivy growing along the sides reflected the sun with
such perfection every afternoon. Everything about it was magnificent, but the
best part about it was how it never changed—even from the moment I moved
in when I was three, the house itself had always been there for me to come
back to.

It was junior year in high school and I was visiting 22 Green Hill Road to
pick up a few things, when I noticed something different under the clock that
wasn't there when I moved out with my mom months earlier. It was a frame
filled with pictures of a woman in the process of rolling down a luscious light
green hill. I couldn't stop staring at her: her hair was dark brown and her jeans
were a size too big. I had never met her before, and she certainly did not
belong in my kitchen—the kitchen that was once so familiar I could recall
every detail on every wall. My father walked in.

I turned to him. "Who . . . is this?" I asked him. It took him a while to figure out what to say. He sighed and answered, "That's my friend Beth." He had
an ultimate innocence in his voice that never went away; I could never stay
mad at him for long.

"Oh," I replied. Then I asked what I wished I had not for a long time afterward. "Did you take this?" He backed away from me.

Whenever I stopped by, from that moment on, he turned the frame
around so I could not see the images of a strange yet now so familiar woman
in what used to be my kitchen.

Second student description

I wish I could tell you more about that night, but it's kind of blurry. What
do I remember? My father's voice, "Mommy passed away." I know I cried,
but for how long I don't remember. My boyfriend was there; he only heard
my end of the conversation. He drove me home from college. I guess that
took a couple of hours. There was a box of tissues on my lap, but I didn't use
any. He smoked a cigarette at one point, and opened up a window. The
black air rushed in and settled on me like a heavy cloak.

Try this 1.7: Finding the Implicit Analysis in Description

In addition to noting the different kinds of descriptive activities and descriptive words that appear in the two passages above, you could think about what it is that each writer is analyzing through the use of description. Which sentences and which details reveal the implicit analysis contained in the description? Consider for example what thinking is implicit in the following two sentences: "It was a frame filled with pictures of a woman in the process of rolling down a luscious light green hill. I couldn't stop staring at her: her hair was dark brown and her jeans were a size too big." Why these details rather than others the writer might have selected? Why the word *luscious*? In the second descriptive passage, what implicit analysis does the sentence about the box of tissues reveal?

A NOTE ON MATCHING SENTENCE SHAPES TO SUBJECTS

The management of sentence style—syntax—is as important to the effect of both of these descriptive pieces, especially the second one, as the word choice is. In our chapter on sentence style (Chapter 11) we discuss a useful concept we learned from a colleague: the "go to" sentence. The "go to" sentence is the sentence type, the particular way of ordering words, that each of us habitually goes to. The "go to" sentence is actually a feature of who we are, because it embodies how we characteristically respond to the world.

All of us have "go to" sentences that we fall back on in daily life—in speaking as well as writing. Our choice of sentence shape is influenced by how we think, but it varies according to the subjects we are writing and talking about. The matching of sentence shape to subject matter is especially interesting in the second descriptive passage above.

The "go to" sentence is actually a feature of who we are, because it embodies how we characteristically respond to the world.

The second passage tends to go to sentences that offer flat, largely unembellished declarative statements, as in "He drove me home from college" or "He smoked a cigarette at one point, and opened up a window." If you know something about how to analyze the shapes of sentences, you might profitably spend a little time trying to figure out the relation between the kinds of sentences the writer typically uses in the second description and the content of that passage. It will help if you know the difference between coordinate sentences, in which everything is treated at one level of importance, and subordinate sentences, in which some things depend upon and are set up as less important than other things. (See the glossary in Chapter 14.)

WRITING THE SELF AS AN INTRODUCTION TO ANALYSIS

All writing is, in a sense, personal, since there is an "I" doing the thinking and selecting the details to consider. But most analytical writing done in the academic disciplines is about some subject other than the self. Writing about the self, about one's own memories and defining experiences, is, however, a useful way to stimulate our thinking about words (evaluative and abstract versus concrete, for example) and about the role of detail in shaping our ideas about things.

And so, we offer the following assignment for a personal essay. It treats the writer's self as the subject of an analysis and calls for the writer to conduct that analysis through the careful selection and arrangement of telling detail. It helps in thinking about this kind of writing to assume that we all have various versions of ourselves to offer to others—and to ourselves. In other words, writing the self inevitably means constructing a version of yourself, not just writing what "is."

► Try this 1.8: Writing the Self

Write a brief (two-page) descriptive piece about yourself that you would be willing to read out loud to others engaged in the same exercise. Do this by offering a narrative of some revealing and representative "moment"—perhaps a kind of moment that tended to recur—in your life. Sometimes the most telling moments, those that play a significant role in how we come to be who we are, are subtle, small moments, rather than "big" life-changing experiences. Some of these small but significant moments are barely remembered until we start looking for them with writing. Thus, they engage readers in the writer's process of discovery, which is what good writing should do.

Your piece will necessarily be a blend of showing and telling, of description and more explicit analysis, but make sure not to substitute telling readers how you felt for re-creating the experience that made you feel as you did. Offer your experience of a revealing moment to your readers. Avoid evaluative (empty of detail, judgmental) adjectives. Insofar as judgments are being made in your piece, let them be implied rather than overtly stated, as the author of the descriptive piece on the picture of a strange woman in her kitchen does. We learn a lot in that piece about how the writer thinks and the kinds of judgments she was making, but she does not dwell on her thinking or her judgments. She lets us see these through her choice of detail.

One of us does a version of this assignment with the following direction: talk about a single event in your life that most people don't know about, and if we did, we'd understand you better.

Two Examples of Writing the Self

Here are two excerpts from longer personal essays that students eventually developed from this short assignment. The first is an opening paragraph. It offers less concrete detail than the other examples, but there is a lot of thought-provoking work and implicit analysis going on in the writer's word choice. The second is a paragraph from a piece in which we learn about the writer—as she learns about herself—in the context of her relationship with a best friend who was, in a way, her opposite.

Memoir 1

I was still young enough to be in elementary school, and my siblings were newly initiated teens, when my parents brought home one day, strapped to the back of my mother's GMC Suburban, a behemoth on wheels. Upon further inquisition and speculation, we discovered that this three-dimensional, trapezoidal structure was hospitable and meant to house individuals for lengths of time—a home on wheels. My family was from then on in possession of a trailer, one that had to be dragged across miles of circuitous highways and man-made, pothole-studded campgrounds before returning to the driveway of our little ranch house in the town my siblings and I refer to today as a branch of white-trash suburbia.

Memoir 2

She used to come to me for advice on relationships. She was the science geek and I was her public relations advisor. We were supposed to stick to our roles. After that night, though, we were playing her game. She was the referee just waiting for me to foul so she could blow the whistle. The more we saw of each other, the worse it got. Instead of sitting on our comfy pedestals, sizing up the rest of the world, now we were both at our own separate podiums, ready for debate.

SECTION 2: OPENING THINGS UP: NEGATIVE CAPABILITY, PARAPHRASE × 3, FREE-WRITING, AND COUNTERPRODUCTIVE HABITS OF MIND

This section of the chapter seeks to open things up in your writing. It proposes the value of tolerating uncertainty—a stance toward experience for which we like the poet John Keats's concept of "negative capability." We introduce two primary strategies for opening things up rather than closing them down: paraphrase × 3 and freewriting in its various forms. The section concludes with a more theoretical discussion of counterproductive habits of mind that cause us to short-circuit our thinking. These are judging, generalizing, personalizing, and confusing opinions with ideas. By becoming more self-conscious about the ways you think, you can become more comfortable with uncertainty and thus remain more open to evidence and the ideas it invites you to have.

NEGATIVE CAPABILITY: LOCATING AN AREA OF UNCERTAINTY

Most of us learn early in life to pretend that we understand things even when we don't. Rather than ask questions, and risk looking foolish, we nod our heads. Soon, we even come to believe that we understand things when really we don't, or not nearly as well as we think we do. This understandable but problematic human trait means that, to become better thinkers, most of us will have to cultivate a more positive attitude toward not knowing. Prepare to be surprised at how difficult this can be.

Start by trying to accept that uncertainty—even its more extreme version, confusion—is a productive state of mind, a precondition to allowing yourself to have ideas. The poet John Keats coined a memorable phrase for this productive habit of mind. He called it negative capability.

> I had not had a dispute but a disquisition with Dilke, on various subjects; several things dovetailed in my mind, & at once it struck me, what quality went to form a Man of Achievement especially in Literature & which Shakespeare possessed so enormously—I mean *Negative Capability*, that is when man is capable of being in uncertainties, Mysteries, doubts, without any irritable reaching after fact & reason.
>
> —Letter to George and Thomas Keats, December 1817

The key phrases here are "capable of being in uncertainties" and "without any irritable reaching." Keats is not saying that facts and reason are unnecessary and therefore can be safely ignored. But he does praise the kind of person who can remain calm (rather than becoming irritable) in a state of uncertainty. His is a praise for a way of being that is capable of staying open to possibilities for longer periods of time than most of us are comfortable with.

Try to accept that uncertainty is a productive state of mind, a precondition to allowing yourself to have ideas.

Another nineteenth-century poet, Emily Dickinson, writes in the same vein as Keats's concept of negative capability in her poem that begins "Perception of an object/Costs precise the object's loss." When we leap prematurely to our perceptions about a thing, we place a filter between ourselves and the "object," shrinking the amount and kinds of information that can get through to our minds and our senses. The point of the Dickinson poem is a paradox—that the ideas we arrive at actually deprive us of material with which to have more ideas. So we have to be careful about leaping to conclusions, about the ease with which we move to generalization, because if we are not careful, such moves will lead to a form of mental blindness—loss of the object.

By training yourself to be more comfortable with not knowing, you give yourself license to start working with your material, the data, *before* you try to decide what you think it means. The problem with convincing ourselves that we have the answers is that we are thus prevented from *seeing the questions*, which are usually much more interesting than the temporary stopping points we have initially elected as answers.

PARAPHRASE × 3: OPENING UP THE MEANING OF WORDS

Paraphrasing is an extremely valuable activity in analysis—and in all kinds of thinking. Our term for looking closely at evidence is *descriptive paraphrase*. What does this mean? Too often when people look at words they summarize—that is, they produce a general overview of what the words say. Paraphrasing stays much closer to the actual words than summarizing. The word *paraphrase* means to put one phrase next to ("para") another phrase. When you paraphrase a passage, you cast and recast its key terms into near synonyms.

Descriptive paraphrasing calls for careful restatement. We call it paraphrase × 3 because usually only one paraphrase—one synonym—is not enough. Take a sentence you want to understand better and recast it into other language three times. This will banish the problematic notion that the meaning of words is self-evident, and it will stimulate your thinking.

Why is paraphrasing useful? The answer has to do with words—what they are and what we do with them. When we read, it is easy to skip quickly over the words, assuming we know what they mean. Yet when people start talking about what they mean by particular words—the difference, for example, between *assertive* and *aggressive* or the meaning of ordinary words such as *polite* or *realistic* or *gentlemanly*—they usually find less agreement than they expected.

Most words mean more than one thing and mean different things to different people. Words matter. They are our primary means of negotiating the space between ourselves and others, and of figuring out our relation to the world. Yet most of us go through our days assuming that the meaning of the words we use—and those spoken to us by others—is obvious.

The next time you find yourself staring at something and saying to yourself, "I don't understand this" or "I don't know what I would say about this," try paraphrasing. Ideas will come.

Try this 1.9: Paraphrase versus the Transparent Theory of Language

Consider that meaning is not separable from the language in which it appears; what you say is inescapably a product of how you say it. This is to say that language doesn't merely "reflect" reality; in a sense, it invents it. What we see as reality is shaped by the words we use. This idea is known as the constitutive theory of language. It is opposed to the so-called "transparent" theory of language, which implies that we can see through words to some meaning that exists beyond and is independent of them.

In a famous essay called "Politics and the English Language," George Orwell points out that our ability to think clearly about important matters is greatly reduced by the human tendency to settle for abstractions, rather than more concrete words, and to unthinkingly plug in prefabricated—which is to say, clichéd—language in place of fresher words that still have the power to provoke thought. In this context, political conflicts can be seen as a war of words. This is nowhere more evident than in the language we use to talk about war. Consider, for example, the effect and possible purpose of referring to bombs as *ordinance*.

You might profitably spend a week noting the different words that two different political orientations—for example, Democrats and Republicans—use for the same thing. You might also spend a week collecting clichés. This too is useful for becoming more self-conscious about the relation between words and thinking. What is the problem with clichés, especially given that the ideas they offer are typically reasonable and even well said?

▶ Try this 1.10: Looking at Gendered Language

Another excellent way to start looking at words and stop assuming that their meaning is self-evident is to consider the way our language encodes and quietly invites us to accept value assumptions about gender (masculinity and femininity—as opposed to the biological fact of being male or female). What words do we have in English for unmarried men, for example? What words do we use for unmarried women? What words do we use for men who are sexually active with more than one person? What words do we use for women who are sexually active with more than one person?

The words we use to describe men versus women change with social norms on what constitutes ideal male or female behavior. This process is often interestingly local, which is to say that it occurs inside particular discourse communities (groups sharing a common language). If you are reading this book on a college campus, you might spend a week collecting words that encode changing attitudes toward idealized forms of masculinity and femininity. What, for example, has happened to the word *geek* as a word for describing a particular kind of male? Is *geek* used as often to describe women? If not, why not?

THE IMPORTANCE OF EXPLORATORY WRITING

This book has a lot to say about exploratory writing. We believe that most writing courses and writing texts, although they advocate attention to the process rather than just to the products of writing, include way too little exploratory writing and practically no specific procedures for the exploration stage. A revealing feature of supposedly process-oriented writing texts is their use of the word *prewriting*. Exploratory writing is writing. Exploratory writing precedes a finished draft, but it is not something that comes *before* writing, nor is it something that the final form of the writing needs to entirely exclude.

> *The problem with convincing ourselves that we have the answers is that we are thus prevented from seeing the questions, which are usually much more interesting than the temporary stopping points we have initially elected as answers.*

Among practiced writers, the similarities between exploratory writing and "finished" (revised and polished) writing are significant. This is not because writers stop doing exploratory writing and manage to go straight to finished drafts. Instead, the finished form of the writing behaves more in the meditative and searching way that good exploratory writing behaves.

This is not to say that we think writers should care only about process and not about product, or that they should substitute freewriting and inconclusive thinking for carefully organized finished drafts. Instead we argue that revising the final or next to final draft would be much easier if the writer had spent more time doing various kinds of exploratory writing before moving to the final draft stage. We also argue that good writing, at whatever stage, should have an exploratory feel, that it should share its discovery process with the reader. To a significant extent, especially in analytical writing, the final draft of an essay re-creates for the reader the writer's experience of arriving at his or her key ideas.

FREEWRITING: HOW TO DO IT AND WHAT IT'S GOOD FOR

The writer Anne Lamott writes eloquently (in *Bird by Bird*) about the internal censor we all hear as a nasty voice—actually a collection of nasty voices—in our heads that keep us from writing. These are the internalized voices of past critics whose comments have become magnified to suggest that we will never get it right. Freewriting allows us to tune out these voices long enough to discover what we might think.

In freewriting, you write *without stopping* for a predetermined period of time, usually ten or fifteen minutes. There aren't many rules to freewriting, just that it is important to keep your pen (or fingers on the keyboard) moving. Don't reread as you go. Don't pause to correct things. Don't cross things out. Just keep writing. To get to good writing, we first have to tolerate some chaos. In freewriting, especially if you engage in it frequently, you will often surprise yourself with the quality of your own thinking, with the ideas you didn't really know you had and the many details you hadn't really noticed until you started writing. For a good example of what can be done with a freewrite, see "Doing 10 on 1: An Example from Student Writing" near the end of this chapter.

Some Forms of Freewriting

There are many forms of freewriting, but they are all premised on the belief that the act of writing is not just a way of recording what you think, but of discovering what you think. Unlike a finished essay, in which the sentences follow logically as you unfold your central idea, freewriting encourages you to leap associatively from idea to idea as they arise.

One of the advantages of this less structured, less sequential kind of writing is that it effectively reduces anxiety. Rather than worrying about what you can find to say, you start saying things. Not everything you come up with will be worthy of developing into a paper, but you will often be surprised at the connections you make and the workable starting points you discover when prewriting.

1. *Freewrites* are the loosest form of exploratory writing, requiring only that you write more or less continuously—and usually without much premeditation—for a specified period of time (usually somewhere between ten and twenty minutes). Try to keep moving. Don't pause to edit or correct or bite your pen, or stare into space; just write.

2. *Focused freewrites* follow the same procedure as freewrites, except that you attempt to stay within a more narrowly defined subject. Often you will take your best idea from a previous freewrite and then explore it on the page for ten minutes or so without stopping. Or you might put a single word or idea at the top of the page and write continuously about that.

3. *Writer's notebooks (journals)* are unlike a personal diary in which you keep track of your days' activities and recount the feelings these occasioned; journals are for generating and collecting ideas and for keeping track of your ongoing interactions with course materials. A journal can be, in effect, a collection of focused freewrites that you develop in response to the reading and lectures in a course.

The best way to get a journal to work for you is to experiment. You might try, for example, copying and commenting on statements from your reading or class meetings that you found potentially illuminating. Use the journal to write down the ideas, reactions, and germs of ideas you had during a class discussion or that you found running around in your head after a late night's reading. Use the journal to retain your first impressions of books or films or music or performances or whatever, so that you can then look back at them and trace the development of your thinking.

If possible, write in your journal every day. As with freewriting, the best way to get started is just to start, see what happens, and take it from there. Also as with freewriting, the more you write, the more you'll find yourself noticing and thus the more you'll have to say.

► **Try this 1.11:** Descriptions from Everyday Life

Descriptive freewriting is an especially fruitful activity for training think-ing and observation skills. Spend a week describing things that you can observe in your everyday environment—whatever interests you on a particular day, or the same kind of thing over a period of days. Get the detail of what you are describing on the page. If judgments and general-izations come out, let them come, but don't stay on them long. Try to get back to the narration of detail as quickly as you can. At the end of the week you could write a piece called either "What I learned in a week of looking at . . ." or come up with your own shaping title. See if you can turn your freewrites into an essay—either descriptive or analytical.

COUNTERPRODUCTIVE HABITS OF MIND

We began this chapter with an emphasis on noticing details (our discussion of Hemingway's five finger exercise). We have been arguing that cultivating an attitude of uncertainty improves your ability to really see and think about the world: indeed, the best ideas often start with something puzzling rather than with something you are sure that you already understand. And we have spoken of the importance of tracing impressions back to causes, because people so readily remember how they felt but fail to register the details that caused them to feel that way. What follows is a glossary of counterproductive habits of mind.

Generalizing   What it all boils down to is . . .What this adds up to is . . .The gist of her speech was . . . Generalizing is not always a bad habit. Reducing complex events or theories or books or speeches to a reasonably accurate summarizing statement requires practice and skill. We generalize from our experience because this is one way of arriving at ideas. The problem with generalizing as a habit of mind is that it deflects attention—usually much too swiftly—from the data that produced the generalization in the first place.

Generalizations are just as much a problem for readers and listeners as they are for writers. Consider for a moment what you are actually asking others to do when you offer them a generalization such as "His stories are very depressing." Unless the recipient of this observation asks a question—such as "Why do you think so?"—he or she is being required to take your word for it: the stories are depressing because you say so.

What happens instead if you offer a few details that caused you to think as you do? Clearly, you are on riskier ground. Your listener might think that the details you cite are actually not depressing or that this is not the most interesting or useful way to think about the stories. He or she might offer a different generalization, a different reading of the data, but at least conversation has become possible. There is something available to think with: the actual stuff of experience from which further generalizations can be made.

Vagueness and generality are major blocks to learning because, as habits of mind, they allow you to dismiss virtually everything you've read and heard except the general idea you've arrived at. Often the generalizations that come to mind are so broad that they tell us nothing. To say, for example, that a poem is about love or death or rebirth, or that the economy of a particular emerging nation is inefficient, accomplishes very little, since the generalizations could fit almost any poem or economy. In other words, your generalizations are often sites where you stopped thinking prematurely, not the "answers" you've thought they were.

The simplest antidote to the problem of generalizing is to train yourself to be more self-conscious about where your generalizations come from. Remember to trace your general impressions back to the particulars that caused them. This tracing of attitudes back to their concrete causes is the most basic—and most necessary—move in the analytical habit of mind. It will help you go through the world in less of a haze. Deciding to be more conscious of our own responses to the world and their causes is also an antidote to the inevitable numbing, the desensitizing, that takes place as habit takes control of our daily lives. Choose to notice more and to keep noticing.

Here's another strategy for bringing your thinking down from high levels of generality. Think of the words you use in terms of an *abstraction ladder.* The more general and vague the word, the higher its position on the abstraction ladder. "Mammal," for example, is higher on the abstraction ladder than "cow." You might try using "Level 3 Generality" as a convenient tag phrase reminding you to steer clear of the higher reaches of abstract generalization, some so high up the ladder from the concrete stuff that produced them that there is barely enough air to sustain the thought.

Why "Level 3" instead of "Level 2"? There aren't just two categories, abstract and concrete: the categories are the ends of a continuum, a sliding scale. And too often when writers try to concretize their generalizations, the results are still too general: they change "animal" to "mammal," but they need "cow" or, better, "black angus."

The Judgment Reflex   Much of what passes for thinking—in the press, on television, in everyday conversation—is actually not thinking but reflex behavior, reaction rather than thinking: right/wrong, good/bad, loved it/hated it, couldn't relate to it, boring.

It would be impossible to overstate the mind-numbing effect that the judgment reflex has on thinking. Why? Consider what we do when we judge something and what we ask others to do when we offer them our judgments. "Ugly," "realistic," "pretty," "boring," "wonderful," "unfair," "crazy." Notice that the problem with such words is a version of the problem with all generalizations—lack of information. What have you actually told someone else if you say that X is ugly or boring or realistic?

FIGURE 1.1 The problem with generalizing diagram

THE PROBLEM

leaps to
data (words, images, other detail) ---------> broad generalization

leaps to
data -----------> evaluative claims (like/dislike; agree/disagree)

The Judgment Reflex

In its most primitive form—most automatic and least thoughtful—judging is like an on/off switch. When the switch gets thrown in one direction or the other—good/bad, right/wrong, positive/negative—the resulting judgment predetermines and overdirects any subsequent thinking we might do. Rather than thinking about what X is or how X operates, we lock ourselves prematurely into proving that we were right to think that X should be banned or supported.

The psychologist Carl Rogers has written at length on the problem of the judgment reflex. He claims that our habitual tendency as humans—virtually a programmed response—is to evaluate everything and to do so very quickly. Walking out of a movie, for example, most people will immediately voice their approval or disapproval, usually in either/or terms: I liked it *or* didn't like it; it was right/wrong, good/bad, interesting/boring. The other people in the conversation will then offer their own evaluations plus their judgments of the others' judgments: I think that it was a good movie and that you are wrong to think it was bad. And so on.

This kind of reflex move to evaluation closes off thinking with likes and dislikes and instant categories. The fact that you liked or didn't like a movie probably says more about you—your tastes, interests, biases, and experiences—than it does about the movie. What makes a movie boring? That it doesn't have enough car chases? That its plot resembles half the plots on cable channels? That the leading man is miscast or the dialogue too long-winded? At the least, in such cases, you'd need to share with readers your *criteria* for judgment—your reasons and your standards of evaluation.

When people leap to judgment, they usually land in the mental pathways they've grown accustomed to traveling, guided by family or friends or popular opinion. If you can break the evaluation reflex and press yourself to analyze before judging a subject, you will often be surprised at how much your initial responses change. As a general rule, you should seek to understand the subject you are analyzing before moving to a judgment about it. Try to figure out what your subject means before deciding how you feel about it.

> *Try to figure out what your subject means before deciding how you feel about it.*

This is not to say that all judging should be avoided. Obviously, our thinking on many occasions must be applied to decision making—deciding whether we should or shouldn't vote for a particular candidate, should or shouldn't eat french fries, or should or shouldn't support a ban on cigarette advertising.

A writer needs to take into account how the judgment has been affected by the particular situation (context) and to acknowledge how thinking about these details has led to restricting (qualifying) the range of the judgment: X is *sometimes* true in these particular circumstances; Z is *probably* the right thing to do *but only when* A and B occur. Ultimately, in other words, analytical thinking does need to arrive at a point of view—which is a form of judgment—but analytical conclusions are usually not phrased in terms of like/dislike or good/bad. They disclose what a person has come to understand about X rather than how he or she imperiously rules on the worth of X.

In some ways, the rest of this book consists of a set of methods for blocking the ever-present judgment reflex in favor of more thoughtful responses. For now, here are two things to try in order to short-circuit the judgment reflex and begin replacing it with a more thoughtful, more patient, and more open-mindedly curious habit of mind. First, try the cure that Carl Rogers recommended to negotiators in industry and government. Do not assert an agreement or disagreement with another person's position until you can repeat that position in a way the other person would accept as fair and accurate. This is surprisingly hard to do because we are usually so busy calling up judgments of our own that we barely hear what the other person is saying.

Second, try eliminating the word "should" from your vocabulary for a while, since judgments so often take the form of recommendations. The analytical habit of mind is characterized by the words "why," "how," and "what." Analysis asks the following: What is the aim of the new law? Why do laws of this sort tend to get passed in some parts of the country rather than in others? How does this law compare with its predecessor? Judgments take the form of *should statements*. We *should* pass the law. We *should* not consider putting such foolish restrictions into law.

You might also try eliminating evaluative adjectives—those that offer judgments with no data. "Green" is a descriptive, concrete adjective. It offers something we can experience. "Beautiful" is an evaluative adjective. It offers only judgment.

Debate-Style Argument   People are customarily introduced to writing arguments through the debate model. They are taught to argue pro *or* con on a given position or issue, with the aim of defeating an imagined opponent and convincing

VOICES FROM ACROSS THE CURRICULUM
Habits of Mind

Readers should not conclude that the "Counterproductive Habits of Mind" presented in this chapter are confined to writing. Psychologists who study the way we process information have established important links between the way we think and the way we feel. Some psychologists such as Aaron Beck have identified common "errors in thinking" that parallel the habits of mind discussed in this chapter. Beck and others have shown that falling prey to habits of mind is associated with a variety of negative outcomes. For instance, a tendency to engage in either/or thinking, overgeneralization, and personalization has been linked to higher levels of anger, anxiety, and depression. Failure to attend to these errors in thinking chokes off reflection and analysis. As a result, the person becomes more likely to "react" rather than think, which may prolong and exacerbate the negative emotions.

—*Mark Sciutto, Professor of Psychology*

an audience of the rightness of one side of the argument. To its credit, the debate model teaches writers to consider more than a single viewpoint, their opponent's as well as their own.   ⦁

But unfortunately, it can also train them, even if inadvertently, to see the other side only as the opposition and to concentrate their energy only on winning the day. The problem with this approach is that it overemphasizes the bottom line—aggressively advancing a claim for *or* against some view—without *first* engaging in the exploratory interpretation of evidence that is so necessary to arriving at thoughtful arguments.

Thus, debate-style argument produces a frame of mind in which defending positions matters more than taking the necessary time to develop ideas worth defending. And, very possibly, it nourishes the mudslinging and opinionated mind-set—attack first—that proliferates in editorials and television talk shows, not to mention the conversations you overhear in going about your life. We are not saying that people should forget about making value and policy decisions and avoid the task of persuading others. We are saying that too many of the arguments we all read, hear, and participate in every day are based on insufficient analysis.

> *Debate-style argument produces a frame of mind in which defending positions matters more than taking the necessary time to develop ideas worth defending.*

The remedy, we suggest, is the temporary suspension of the pro/con, debate-style habit of mind. Argument and analysis are profoundly connected, but their stances toward subject matter and audience differ so much that most people need to learn them separately before being able to put them back together. And because the argumentative habit of mind is so aggressively visible in our culture, most people never get around to experimenting with the more reflective and less combative approach that analysis embraces. Thus, this book asks you to turn off the argument switch, not forever, but for as long as it takes for you to cultivate other habits of mind that argument might otherwise overshadow.

Although analysis and argument proceed in essentially the same way, they differ in the kinds of questions they try to answer. Argument, at its most dispassionate, asks "What can be said with truth about X or Y?" In common practice, though, the kinds of questions that argument more often answers are more committed, directive, and should-centered, such as "Which is better, X or Y?," "How can we best achieve X or Y?," and "Why should we stop doing X or Y?"

Analysis, by contrast, asks "What does X or Y mean?" In analysis the evidence (your data) is something you wish to understand, and the claims are assertions about what that evidence means. The claim that an argument makes—for example, readers should or shouldn't vote for bans on smoking in public buildings, or they should or shouldn't believe that gays can function effectively in the military—is often an answer to a "should" question. The writer of an analysis is more concerned with discovering how each of these complex subjects might be defined and explained than with convincing readers to approve or disapprove of them.

Overpersonalizing (Naturalizing Our Assumptions) The assumption that what seems true to me must be obviously and self-evidently true to everybody else is known as naturalizing your assumptions. The word *naturalize* in this context means you are representing—and seeing—your own assumptions as part of the universal scheme of things. The term *common sense* often accompanies naturalized assumptions, as in, "Oh, that's just common sense"—which means that my point of view doesn't need defending or even explaining, because any sensible person would think in this way. What is common sense—"natural"—for one person and so not even in need of explaining can be quite uncommon and not so obviously sensible to someone else.

The problem with "the personal" really has to do with how that term is commonly (mis)understood. It is usually located as one half of a particularly vicious binary that might be schematized thus:

subjective	objective
personal expression	impersonal analysis
passionately engaged	detached
genuinely felt	heartless

Like most vicious binaries, the personal/impersonal, heart/head binary overstates the case and obscures the considerable overlap of the two sides.

Most effective analytical prose has a strong personal element—the writer's stake in the subject matter. As readers, we want the sense that a writer is engaged with the material, cares about what he or she says about it, and is sharing what he or she finds interesting about it.

But in another sense, no writing is strictly personal. As contemporary cultural theorists are fond of pointing out, the "I" is not a wholly autonomous free agent who writes from a unique point of view. Rather, the "I" is always affected by forces outside the self—social, cultural, educational, historical, and so forth—that shape the self. The extreme version of this position allots little space for what we like to think of as individuality at all: the self is a site through which dominant cultural ways of understanding the world (ideologies) circulate. That's a disarming notion, but one worth pondering.

From this perspective we are like actors who don't know that we're actors, reciting various cultural scripts that we don't realize are scripts. This is, of course, an extreme position. A person who believes that civil rights for all is an essential human right is not necessarily a victim of cultural brainwashing. The grounds of his or her belief, shaped by participation in a larger community of belief (ethnic, religious, family tradition, and so forth) are, however, not merely personal.

▶ Try this 1.12: Looking for Naturalized Assumptions

Start listening to the things people say in everyday conversation. Read some newspaper editorials with your morning coffee (a pretty disturbing way to start the day in most cases). Watch for examples of people naturalizing their assumptions. You will find examples of this everywhere. Also, try paraphrasing the common complaint "I couldn't relate to it." What does being able to "relate" to something consist of? What problems would follow from accepting this idea as a standard of value?

One telltale sign of an overpersonalizing writer is his or her tendency to let personal narratives substitute for careful consideration of a subject. When we substitute personal narrative for analysis, our own experiences and prejudices tend to become an unquestioned standard of value. Your disastrous experience with a health maintenance organization (HMO), for example, may predispose you to dismiss a plan for nationalized health care, but your writing needs to examine in detail the holes in the plan, not simply evoke the three hours you lingered in some doctor's waiting room.

This is not to say that there is no learning or thinking value in telling our experiences. Storytelling has the virtue of offering concrete experience—not just the conclusions the experience may have led to. Personal narratives can take us back to the source of our convictions. The problem comes when "relating" to someone's story becomes a habitual substitute for thinking through the ideas and attitudes that the story suggests.

The antidote to the overpersonalizing habit of mind is to become more self-conscious about it. If we keep in mind that the "I" we tend to lead with is not simply a free agent but also a product of cultural influences, we will be more likely to notice our first responses and become curious about them. Ask yourself, Is this what I really believe? Asking that question is a healthy habit to cultivate and one that can often help you see the logic of other possible responses to the position you've initially taken.

Opinions (versus Ideas)   Consider for a moment the often-heard claim "I'm entitled to my opinion." This claim is worth exploring. What is an opinion? How is it (or isn't it) different from a belief or an idea? If I say that I am entitled to my opinion, what am I asking you to do or not do?

Many of the opinions people fight about are actually clichés, pieces of much-repeated conventional wisdom. For example, "People are entitled to say what they want. That's just my opinion." But, of course, this assertion isn't a private and personal revelation. It is an exaggerated and overstated version of one of the items in the U.S. Bill of Rights, guaranteeing freedom of speech. Much public thinking has gone on about this private conviction, and it has thus been carefully qualified. A person can't, for example, say publicly whatever he or she pleases about other people if what he or she says is false and damages the reputation of another person—at least without threat of legal action.

Our opinions are learned. They are products of our culture and our upbringing—not personal possessions. It is okay to have opinions, but not to give too many of our views and opinions protected-species status, walling them off into a reserve, not to be touched by reasoning or evidence.

> *Our opinions are learned. They are products of our culture and our upbringing—not personal possessions.*

Some things, of course, we have to take on faith. Religious convictions, for example, are more than opinions, though they operate in a similar way: we believe where we can't always prove. But even our most sacred convictions are not really harmed by thinking. The world's religions are constantly engaged in interpreting and reinterpreting what religious texts mean, what various traditional practices mean, and how they may or may not be adapted to the attitudes and practices of the world as it is today.

SECTION 3: THE BASIC ANALYTICAL STRATEGIES: FROM OBSERVATIONS TO IDEAS

This part of the chapter offers an observation exercise (Notice and focus, plus interesting and strange), another version of this exercise (10 on 1), and a verbal prompt for pushing observations to conclusions: the So what? question. This sequence of activities is our basic analytical formula. Spend some time practicing these moves and continue to use them with other exercises in this book.

THE DOGFISH PROBLEM: PREMATURE LEAPS TO THESIS

Often, it is not just carelessness or a judgmental cast of mind that closes down the information-gathering stage. People sometimes have unreasonable expectations of themselves when it comes to having ideas. They think that they should get to ideas right away, that arriving at a "thesis" is a necessary starting point for analysis. We like calling this "idea-first—look-later" anxiety *the dogfish problem* (a term coined by the writer Walker Percy in his essay about ways of knowing called "The Loss of the Creature"). For our purposes, the dogfish problem sets up an analogy between writing and other forms of analysis. A writer trying to start with a thesis before looking openly (with negative capability) at the evidence is like a scientist trying to theorize about the nature of dogfish with no more than a cursory look at one.

Our discussion of what it means to have an idea (below) is premised on avoidance of the dogfish problem in favor of negative capability (discussed in Section 2). Having ideas is dependent on allowing yourself to notice things in your subject that you want to better understand rather than glossing over things with a quick and too easy understanding. This relates, of course, to what we have said so far about how attending to conclusions but not their causes prevents us from thinking and seeing. The main point in the following discussion of ideas is that you need to start with something that is puzzling rather than with things that you think are clearly and obviously true.

WHAT IT MEANS TO HAVE AN IDEA

As a general rule, analytical topics privilege live questions over inert answers. Thinking, as opposed to reporting or reacting, should lead you to ideas. But what does it mean to have an idea? This question lies at the heart of our book.

Some years ago, while teaching a writing seminar for faculty in the writing across the curriculum program at our college, we were taken aback by faculty response to the suggestion that they should be expecting their students to arrive at ideas. "Ideas!" one professor of psychology exclaimed. "Do you mean like a PhD thesis?" We were unprepared for this reaction, because our seminars had taught us that faculty across the curriculum, regardless of discipline, shared similar expectations of their students' writing. Faculty told us they wanted not passive summary, not issue-oriented argument, and not personal "reaction" papers, but analysis. And yet they were dubious about accepting that their undergraduate students could arrive at ideas, which is the aim of analysis.

Clearly, a writer in the early stages of learning about a subject can't be expected to arrive at an idea so original that, like one in a PhD thesis, it revises complex concepts in a discipline. But the opposite expectation seems to us to be just as clearly wrong—that undergraduates are simply too inexperienced in the various academic disciplines to do anything but absorb information.

And so, we began looking at ideas—in our own writing, in our colleagues' writing, in our students' writing. Our primary discovery was that ideas are usually much smaller in scope, much less grand, than people seem to expect them to be. We also discovered that it is easiest to understand what ideas are by considering what ideas do and where they can be found. Here is a partial list:

- An idea answers a question; it explains something that needs to be explained or provides a way out of a difficulty that other people have had in understanding something.
- An idea usually starts with an observation that is puzzling, with something you want to figure out rather than something you think you already understand.
- An idea may be the discovery of a question where there seemed not to be one.
- An idea may make explicit and explore the meaning of something implicit—an unstated assumption upon which an argument rests, or a logical consequence of a given position.
- An idea may connect elements of a subject and explain the significance of that connection.
- An idea often accounts for some *dissonance*—that is, something that seems to not fit together.
- An idea provides direction; it helps you see what to do next.

Analysis places you in a situation where there are problems to resolve and competing ideas for you to bring into some kind of alignment. The starting point for analysis is a situation where there is something for you to negotiate, where you are required not just to list answers but to ask questions, make choices, and engage in reasoning about the meaning and significance of your evidence.

WHAT'S AN IDEA?

An idea usually starts with an observation that is puzzling, with something you want to figure out.

- Something *smaller* than most people suspect
- A subtle distinction
- A qualification
- An unearthed connection between two positions not previously linked
- Discovery of a question where there seemed not to be one
- *Something that accounts for some dissonance, what seemed not to fit together*

COMMON MISCONCEPTIONS ABOUT IDEAS

- Something large and global, and usually contentious
- Like a PhD thesis?

Try this 1.13: Researching Ideas Across the Curriculum

As you go through your education, you may find it interesting to think about how different disciplines seem to define what an idea is, what it does, and how you recognize one. Visit a professor in a discipline you find interesting and interview him or her about what constitutes an idea in that discipline. Ask for one or two single-sentence statements of ideas that the professor may have seen lately in a journal in his or her field, or may be working on in his or her research. You might also ask the professor to share with you a couple of good ideas that past students have arrived at in his or her courses. Write an account of your interview, including an example of what your interviewee considered a good idea and why.

MOVING FROM IDEA TO THESIS STATEMENT: WHAT A GOOD THESIS LOOKS LIKE

There are considerable misunderstandings about thesis statements among students—and among many teachers. The most disabling misunderstanding for students is that a writer needs to have a thesis before he or she begins writing. Good thesis statements are the product of writing, not its precursor. Worrying about having a thesis statement too early in the writing process will just about guarantee papers that support overly general and often obvious ideas. Arriving prematurely at claims also blinds writers to complicating evidence (that which runs counter to the thesis) and so—as we argue at length in Chapter 6, "Making a Thesis Evolve"—deprives writers of their best opportunities to arrive at better ideas.

Another disabling assumption is that good writing must include, preferably in the first or second paragraph, a single-sentence (at most, two-sentence) statement of a governing idea that the paper will go on to support. This sentence is typically meant to appear at the end of the introductory paragraph, although the location of a paper's primary claim differs across the academic disciplines and according to whether the paper is deductively or inductively organized.

The fact is that the main idea of most analytical writing is too complex to be asserted as a single-sentence claim—at least one that would be understood at the beginning of the paper. Nevertheless, it is also true that a writer has not moved from the exploratory writing phase to the writing of a paper until he or she has discovered an idea around which his or her thinking can cohere. Without a governing idea to hold on to, readers will not understand why you are telling them what you are telling them. For a paper to make sense to readers, a thesis, or, in the case of inductively organized papers, a thesis "trail" (some sense of the issues and questions that are generating the paper's forward momentum) must be evident.

The best way to learn about thesis statements is to look for them in published writing. When you start doing this, you will find that the single-sentence thesis statement as prescribed in writing textbooks is a rather rare specimen. It is most common in argument, wherein a writer has a proposition that he or she wants readers to either adopt or dismiss. In analytical writing, the thesis is more likely to become evident in phases. Sometimes, for example, as much as the first third of a paper will explore an idea that the rest of the paper will subsequently replace with a different, though not necessarily opposing, perspective. If you look closely, however, you will see the markers—the trail—that lets readers anticipate a shift from one possible way of seeing things to another.

This point—about the pressure of one way of seeing things against another—allows us to define what a good thesis in an analytical paper looks like. It is important to remember that a thesis is an idea. It is a thought that you have arrived at about your evidence, rather than something you can expect to find, ready-made, in whatever it is you are studying.

Good writing, especially good analytical writing, begins with something puzzling that the writer wishes to understand better. The pursuit of understanding is exploratory. "Good" thesis statements enable exploration. "Bad" thesis statements disable it by closing things down way too tightly at the outset.

A strong thesis comes from carefully examining and questioning your subject to arrive at a theory about its meaning and significance that would not have been immediately obvious to your readers. A weak thesis either makes no claim or makes a claim that doesn't need proving, such as a statement of fact or an opinion with which virtually all of your readers would most likely agree before reading your essay (for example, "Exercise is good for you").

> "Good" thesis statements enable exploration. "Bad" thesis statements disable it by closing things down way too tightly at the outset.

Here are two characteristics that an idea needs to have to work as a thesis:

1. The thesis of an analytical paper is an idea about what some feature or features of your subject *means*.
2. A thesis should be an idea that is in need of argument, which is to say it should not be a statement of fact or an idea with which most readers would already agree.

Below are six examples of good thesis statements, which is to say good translations of ideas into forms that could direct the development of an essay. None of these appeared in the first paragraph of the paper for which they served as the "driver." But each was clearly led to by a "thesis trail," and each emerged fairly early in the essay as the writer's explanation of the particular phenomenon he or she had noticed that served as a launching pad for the essay.

Let's consider how these statements, as good examples of what a thesis should look like, relate to the defining characteristics of ideas as explained in the section above, "What It Means to Have an Idea." The first thing you should notice about all these thesis statements is *the presence of tension*—the pressure of one idea against another idea, of one potentially viable way of seeing things against another viable, but finally less satisfactory way of seeing things.

Try this 1.14: Spotting the Tension in Good Thesis Statements

A quick review of our list of things that ideas do will reveal that good ideas usually take place with the aid of some kind of back pressure, by which we mean that the idea takes shape by pushing against (so to speak) another way of seeing things. This is not the same as setting out to overturn and completely refute one idea in favor of another. More often what happens is that the thesis statement's primary idea emerges as some kind of clarification of another idea. Both ideas remain, but the forward momentum of the thesis comes from playing the newer idea off the older one, wherein the newer idea clarifies and builds upon the older one.

Look at the thesis statements below, all of which are taken from published analytical essays. Find the tension in each, which is to say the defining pressure of one idea against another possibility. In the first thesis sentence, for example, the primary idea is that the new advertising campaign for Dockers trousers is radical. The back pressure against which this idea takes shape is that this new campaign may not seem radical. The writer will demonstrate the truth of both of these claims, rather than overturning one and then championing the other. The same can be said of the parts of the second thesis statement. One part of the thesis makes claims for the benefits of cosmetic surgery. The forward momentum of the thesis statement comes from the back pressure of this idea against the idea that cosmetic surgery will also make life worse for everyone. Notice that the thesis statement does not simply say, "Cosmetic surgery is bad."

1. It may not seem like it, but "Nice Pants" is as radical a campaign as the original Dockers series.
2. If opponents of cosmetic surgery are too quick to dismiss those who claim great psychological benefits, protesters are far too willing to dismiss those who raise concerns. Cosmetic surgery might make individual people happier, but in the aggregate it makes life worse for everyone.
3. The history of thought in the modern era of history of thinking about the self may be an exaggeration, but the consequences of this vision of a self set apart have surely been felt in every field of inquiry.
4. We may join with the modern builders in justifying the violence of means—the sculptor's hammer and chisel—by appealing to ends that serve the greater good. Yet too often modern planners and engineers would justify the creative destruction of habitat as necessary for doubtful utopias.
5. The derogation of middlebrow, in short, has gone much too far. It's time to bring middlebrow out of its cultural closet, to hail its emollient properties, to trumpet its mending virtues. For middlebrow not only entertains, it educates—pleasurably training us to appreciate high art.
6. There is a connection between the idea of place and the reality of cellular telephones. It is not encouraging. Places are unique—or at least we like to believe they are—and we strive to experience them as a kind of engagement with particulars. Cell phones are precisely the opposite.

If you have been taught to write in five-paragraph form in school (which is just about the only place that this oversimplified organizational scheme can be found), you will initially have some difficulty writing thesis statements of the sort you have just seen. This is because the typical three-part thesis of five-paragraph form offers a short list of broadly stated topics (rather than well-defined claims about the topics) and then offers examples of each part in the body paragraphs. This form invites listing rather than the articulation of ideas.

There is nothing wrong with partitioning the development of a subject into manageable parts (the best thing about five-paragraph form). There is a lot wrong with a thesis that makes no claim or an overly general and obvious claim such as "Television causes adolescents to become violent, lazy, and ill read." All of these general claims may be true, but nothing much of substance can be said about them in a short paper that is trying to cover all three. And notice the lack of tension in this sample thesis statement. Try writing a better thesis statement—one that has tension—about the effect of some aspect of television on teenagers. (See Chapter 7 for more on good and bad thesis statements.)

NOTICE AND FOCUS (RANKING)

So far this chapter has offered three strategies for getting past generalizations—tracing impressions back to causes (Hemingway's five-finger exercise), freewriting (various forms of exploratory writing), and paraphrase × 3 (a means of fighting the tendency to think that the meaning of words is self-evident). The next technique—Notice and focus—is aimed at helping you dwell longer with the data before feeling compelled to decide what the data means. Observation and interpretation go hand in hand, but it helps greatly to allow yourself a distinct observation stage and to prolong this beyond what most people find comfortable. The more you allow yourself to notice—the longer you allow yourself to dwell with the data before searching after a "point" about it—the richer and more rewarding your interpretation of the evidence will ultimately be.

Notice and focus is governed by repeatedly returning to the question "What do you notice?" As we have been arguing in the chapter so far, most people's tendency is to generalize and thus to rapidly move away from whatever it is they are looking at. The question What do you notice? redirects attention to the subject matter itself and delays the pressure to come up with answers, with a closing off of the experience.

So, the **first step** is for you to repeatedly answer the question What do you notice? Be sure to cite actual details of the thing being observed rather than moving to more general observations about it. (Note that this is more difficult than it sounds.) This phase of the exercise should produce an extended and unordered list of details—features of the thing being observed—that call attention to themselves for one reason or another.

The **second step** is the focusing part in which you *rank* (create an order of importance for) the various features of your subject you have noticed. Answer the question "What three details (specific features of the subject matter) are most interesting (or significant or revealing or strange)?" The purpose of relying on *interesting* or one of the other suggested words is that these will help to deactivate the like/dislike switch of the judgment reflex, and replace it with a more analytical perspective.

The **third step** in this process is to say why the three things you selected struck you as the most interesting (or revealing or significant or strange). This prioritizing of your observations triggers interpretive leaps to the meaning of whatever it is that you find most interesting in your observations.

Remember to start by noticing as much as you can about whatever it is you are studying. Narrow your scope to a representative portion of your evidence, and then dwell with the data. Record what you see. Don't move to generalization, or worse, to judgment. What this procedure will begin to demonstrate is how useful description is as a tool for arriving at ideas. Stay at the description stage longer (in that attitude of uncertainty we recommend), and have better ideas. Training yourself to notice will improve your memory and your ability to think.

Try this 1.15: Doing Notice and Focus with Words and Places and Images

Begin practicing this technique with visual detail. List a number of details about a place, for example, or about a magazine advertisement or some other visual image. Once you have allowed yourself to notice a number of things about the place or the image, choose the details that you think are most important for understanding its character. In both the noticing and focusing stages, use the four words suggested above—*interesting, significant, revealing,* or *strange.* In our classes we invite student thinking by advising them to keep completing the sentence "What I find interesting about this is . . . ."

Next, try this exercise with other subjects—a photograph, a cartoon, an editorial, conversations overheard around campus, looking at people's shoes, political speeches, and so forth. Make Notice and focus a habit of mind.

PROMPTS: INTERESTING AND STRANGE

Consider the verbal prompts *interesting, strange, revealing,* and *significant.* What do these do? First, they offer alternatives to the judgment reflex (like/dislike, right/wrong, and should/shouldn't). The prompts shift attention from pro/con argument to thinking aimed at understanding, at theorizing about the nature of things. The same words also press you to notice more and to stay more aware of the connections between your responses and the particulars that gave rise to them.

What does it mean to find something "interesting"? Often we are interested by things that have captured our attention without our clearly knowing why. Interest and curiosity are near cousins. Interest is also related to negative capability. When you can allow yourself to think that you don't have to have all the answers immediately, you can trust yourself to dwell with questions, a primary characteristic of good thinking.

The word *strange* is a useful prompt because it gives us permission to notice oddities, the things we called anomalies. *Strange* invites us to *defamiliarize* (notice what is strange—unfamiliar) about things within our range of notice.

RULES OF NOTICE & HABITS OF MIND
WORDS MATTER

- Not "What do you think?" &
- Not "What do you like or dislike?"

     but

- "What do you notice?"

     A few prompts:

- What do you find most INTERESTING?
- What do you find most STRANGE?
- What do you find most REVEALING?

Strange, in this context, is not a judgmental term but one denoting features of a subject or situation that aren't readily explainable. Where you locate something strange, you have something to interpret—to figure out what makes it strange and why.

Along similar lines, the words *revealing* and *significant* work by requiring you to make choices that can lead to interpretive leaps. If something strikes you as revealing, even if you're not yet sure why, you will eventually have to produce some theories on what it reveals. If something strikes you as significant, you will motivate yourself to come up with some things that it might signify or "say."

Try this 1.16: A Noticing Exercise on Conversation

Listen in on some conversations, writing down as much seemingly relevant detail (exact words and probably the physical actions that accompany them) as you can. Don't worry about order. Just keep recording what you hear and asking yourself what you notice. You will be able to shape the piece later in a way that you think best represents what you heard. After you have done the work of recording, say to yourself, What did I learn? What was especially *interesting, or revealing, or strange* about what I heard? Respond to these questions with freewriting, preferably in more than one freewriting session. Then produce two pieces of revised (shaped and ordered) writing: One should be the show-versus-tell "recording" of what you heard, the one that you hope will communicate by re-creating—without your explicitly telling—the effect that the talk had on you. The other should be a blend of empirical detail (showing) and analysis (your interpretation). Analyze rather than judge. Don't tell your readers what you liked or disliked. Tell them instead what was interesting and revealing and why.

PUSHING OBSERVATIONS TO CONCLUSIONS: ASKING SO WHAT?

The prompt for making the move from observation to implication and ultimately interpretation is: So what? The question is shorthand for questions such as the following:

Why does this observation matter? What does it mean?

Where does this observation get us?

How can we begin to generalize about the subject?

Asking, So what? is a calling to account, which is why, in conversation, its force is potentially rude. That is, the question intervenes rather peremptorily with a "Why does *this* matter?" It is thus a challenge to make meaning through a creative leap—to move beyond the patterns and emphases you've been observing in the data to tentative conclusions on what these observations suggest.

The peremptoriness of the So what? question can, we think, be liberating. Okay, take the plunge, it says. Start laying out possible interpretations. And, when you are tempted to stop thinking too soon, asking So what? will press you onward.

At the least, consider asking and answering So what? at the ends of paragraphs. And then, if you ask So what? again of the first answer you've offered, you'll often tell yourself where your thinking needs to go next.

For example, let's say you make a number of observations about the nature of e-mail communication—it's cheap, informal, often grammatically incorrect, full of abbreviations ("IMHO"), and ephemeral (impermanent). You rank these and decide that its ephemerality is most interesting. So what? Well, that's why so many people use it, you speculate, because it doesn't last. So what that its popularity follows from its ephemerality? Well, apparently we like being released from the hard-and-fast rules of formal communication; e-mail frees us. So what? Well, . . .

The repeated asking of this question causes people to push on from and pursue the implications of their first responses; it prompts people to reason in a chain, rather than settling prematurely for a single link.

In Chapter 6, "Making a Thesis Evolve," we have more to say about what to do when your answer to So what? calls to mind conflicting data or an opposing idea, and thus interferes with the forward flow of your thinking. For now, start experimenting with asking So what?

Asking So What?: An Example   The following is the opening paragraph of a talk given by a professor of Politial Science, Dr. Jack Gambino, at our college on the occasion of a gallery opening. Study this piece of writing for the various methods of observation and interpretation it uses. Start by noticing the particular details that the writer has chosen to notice. Then look for places where he goes after implication (makes the details speak) by deciding what is interesting or strange or revealing about particular details. Finally, try putting question marks at the places where it seems to you that the writer has asked himself So what?

If you look closely at Camilo Vergara's photo of Fern Street, Camden, 1988, you'll notice a sign on the side of a dilapidated building:

Danger: Men Working

W. Hargrove Demolition

Perhaps that warning captures the ominous atmosphere of these very different kinds of photographic documents by Camilo Vergara and Edward Burtynsky: "Danger: Men Working." Watch out—human beings are at work! But the work that is presented is not so much a building-up 'as it is a tearing-down— the work of demolition. Of course, demolition is often necessary in order to construct anew: old buildings are leveled for new projects, whether you are building a highway or bridge in an American city or a dam in the Chinese countryside. You might call modernity itself, as so many have, a process of creative destruction, a term used variously to describe modern art, capitalism, and technological innovation. The photographs in this exhibit, however, force us to pay attention to the "destructive" side of this modern equation. What both Burtynsky and Vergara do in their respective ways is to put up a warning sign—they question whether the reworking of our natural and social environment leads to a sustainable human future. And they wonder whether the process of creative destruction may not have spun recklessly out of control, producing places that are neither habitable nor sustainable. In fact, a common element connecting the two photographic versions is the near absence of people in the landscape. While we see the evidence of the transforming power of human production on the physical and social environment, neither Vergara's urban ruins nor Burtynsky's industrial sites actually show us "men working." Isolated figures peer suspiciously out back doors or pick through the rubble, but they appear out of place. It is this sense of displacement—of human beings alienated from the environments they themselves have created—that provides the most haunting aspect of the work of these two photographers.

NARROW YOUR SCOPE BY DOING 10 ON 1

One sure way to notice more is to narrow your scope. The wider your scope, and the more ground you try to cover, the less you will be able to say in any sort of depth about your subject.

The term *10 on 1* is shorthand for the principle that it is better to make ten observations or points about a single representative issue or example (10 on 1) than to make the same basic point about ten related issues or examples (1 on 10). Doing 10 on 1 teaches writers to narrow their focus and then analyze in depth, drawing out as much meaning as possible from their best examples.

Ten, in this case, is an arbitrary number. We offer it to you as a reminder that the best writing comes when writers engage in prolonged scrutiny of a single telling piece of evidence rather than shutting down their thinking with a premature leap to the first idea that might serve as a thesis (the tendency we labeled earlier as the dogfish problem). A paper that has evolved from detailed analysis of what the writer takes to be his or her single most telling example is far more likely to arrive at a good idea than a paper that settles prematurely for one idea and applies it mechanically to each piece of evidence it encounters.

What exactly are the "1" and the "10," and how do you go about finding them? In the case of 10 on 1, the 1 is a representative example, an opportunity to narrow your focus to the point where you could consider your subject in more detail, drawing out observations and implications (10). The 10 are the observations you make about your representative example—ten things you notice about it, some combination of observations and implications. The practice of doing 10 on 1 is the opposite of attaching a single observation or implication to ten examples.

The shift from making one observation about ten examples to making ten possible observations about your single best example is the aim of the exercise. If you can keep the number ten in mind, it will prod you to keep asking yourself questions rather than stopping the observation process too soon. What do I notice? What else do I notice? What might this imply? What else might it imply?

How then should you go about selecting the example that you will analyze in depth? In many cases, your thinking process will start with a version of 1 on 10 as a preliminary step—locating some single trait or set of traits that a number of examples in your subject seem to share. Then you can narrow your scope to one of these ten examples that seems interestingly representative, thereby creating a space for in-depth analysis.

For extended discussion of doing 10 on 1, see Chapter 5, "Linking Evidence and Claims: 10 on 1 versus 1 on 10." We include brief mention of 10 on 1 in this chapter in order to better integrate it with our other observational strategies, such as Notice and focus, which it builds upon.

SECTION 4: HOW TO MARK UP A DRAFT

This last section of the chapter opens with a student freewrite and then offers a technique for analyzing a freewrite to better see its thinking and how this thinking might be developed.

DOING 10 ON 1: AN EXAMPLE FROM STUDENT WRITING

Freewrite on a scene from the film Good Bye Lenin!

By Sarah Kersh

The movie shows us Alex and Lara's first date, which is to a sort of underground music club where the performers wear costumes made of plastic tubing and leather, and play loud hard-core rock music. At first, the musicians look surreal, as though they are part of a strange dream from which, at any moment, Alex will awake. The Western rock is real, though, as are the sci-fi costumes, and the scene moves forward to show Alex and Lara climbing a stairway out onto what looks like a fire escape and then through a window and into an apartment.

Here, Alex and Lara settle down into conversation. The young couple sits, hand in hand, and gazes together into the night sky; yet, as the camera pans away, we see that the apartment where the two have retreated is missing its façade. Inside, three walls are still decorated, complete with furniture, wallpaper, and even working lamps; yet, the two sit on the ledge of the fourth wall, which has crumbled away completely.

On the surface, I think the movie invites us to read this as a visual representation of the new lives Alex, Lara, and the other characters face now that the wall has fallen. As a Westerner, at first I read this scene as a representation of the new relationship between Lara and Alex. In other words, I imagined the movie's placement of the couple on the ledge of a domestic space as a representation of where their lives were going together—toward some shared domestic life, toward living together, toward becoming a family. I also thought this was a clever representation of the collapse of communism—this wall has also fallen down.

I don't think, however, that the movie lets us entertain this one romanticized reading of the scene for long—the image is too frightening. As the camera pans away, we see that this isn't a new Westernized apartment; this is an East German flat decorated in much the same way as Alex's home was only months before. The image is alarming; the wall here has been ripped down, and we are forced to ask, did the fall of communism violently blow apart domestic and daily living of East German people?

The movie allows us this dichotomy and, I think, fights to sustain it. On one hand, Alex and Lara would not be on this date if the wall hadn't come down, and yet the scene is more than just another representation of East Germany torn between Communism and the new Westernization. The movie tries hard to remind us that the rapid Westernization of East Germany devastated while it liberated in other ways. This scene uses space to represent Alex and Lara's (and East Germany's) dilemma: Alex and Lara gaze out at the night sky but only because the wall has been blown apart. The exposed apartment is uninhabitable and yet the lights still work, the pictures are still hung, and a young couple leans against one another inside.

HOW TO ANALYZE A FREEWRITE FOR IDEAS: AN EXAMPLE

The student freewrite on a scene from the film *Good Bye Lenin!* is an opportunity to practice some text marking and freewriting strategies that can help you make better use of your own freewriting. These strategies will also help you see that freewrites can be smart and thoughtful.

One of our colleagues invites her students to do their freewriting on the word processor and then to go back either in the same writing session or later—in a different type font—to places where the writer seems to have hit upon something interesting that he or she hadn't completely figured out. As an aid in finding such places in the freewrite, the sentence "The part I liked best was . . ." can serve to get things started. The result of these different-font insertions into the original freewrite is a form of what we call focused freewriting. Similar to but not the same as revising an essay draft, focused freewrites pick up at places where the original freewrite gave up too soon. In practice, a series of focused freewrites—each one starting from some promising but underdeveloped starting point in the previous freewrite—can lead to an essay draft.

Instructions: Look at the student freewrite on *Good Bye Lenin!* and nominate one place she might profitably return to for a different-font "look again/expansion."

The same colleague who uses this technique of focused freewriting also has students look at each other's freewrites in small groups to consider the movement and types of thinking that the freewrites contain. In the small groups, students collaboratively mark up each freewrite as follows:

- **Mark things that are interesting but not yet fully thought out with an asterisk in the margin.** These are potential sites for subsequent freewrites. Try to explain what has been left unsaid.

- **Mark claims—assertions made about the evidence—with the letter** C. Claims are ideas that the evidence seems to support. An example of a claim in the student freewrite is "I don't think, however, that the movie lets us entertain this one romanticized reading of the scene for long." Another claim is "I think the movie invites us to read this as a visual representation of the new lives Alex, Lara, and the other characters face now that the wall has fallen."

- **Underline evidence.** The evidence is the freewrite's pool of primary material (data)—details from the film, rather than the writer's ideas about it. An example of evidence in the freewrite is, "As the camera pans away, we see that this isn't a new Westernized apartment; this is an East German flat decorated in much the same way as Alex's home was only months before." Another example of evidence in the freewrite is "The young couple sits, hand in hand, and gazes together into the night sky; yet, as the camera pans away, we see that the apartment where the two have retreated is missing its façade." This second piece of evidence is the 1 of the 10 on 1 that this freewrite is. In effect, the whole freewrite goes after the range of possible implications that may be inferred from the image of the young couple sitting at the edge of an apartment that is missing one of its walls, presumably a result of war damage.

- **Circle complications.** Complications can be found both in the evidence a writer cites and in the claims a writer makes about it. Complicating evidence is evidence that does not fit the claims the writer has been making. The complication of a claim is a statement that qualifies and finds problems in (problematizes) the original claim.

An example of complicating evidence in the freewrite is "As the camera pans away, we see that this isn't a new Westernized apartment; this is an East German flat decorated in much the same way as Alex's home was only months before. The image is alarming; the wall here has been ripped down." This evidence causes the writer to reconsider her earlier claim: "I imagined the movie's placement of the couple on the ledge of a domestic space as a representation of where their lives were going together—toward some shared domestic life, toward living together, toward becoming a family."

We see the writer articulating the resulting complication of her claim when she writes, "and we are forced to ask, did the fall of communism violently blow apart domestic and daily living of East German people?" Notice that the writer doesn't just notice the complication, concede how it might complicate her thinking, and then go back to her claims about the scene as a sign of Lara and Alex's happy domestic future. She uses contradictory evidence to complicate her claim, but doesn't stop there. Look at the freewrite for places where the writer moves through successive complications—that is, where she complicates a previous claim that was itself a complication.

- **Mark potential thesis statements with a** Th **in the margin.** This freewrite seems to have arrived at what we call in Chapter 6 ("Making a Thesis Evolve") a working thesis. A working thesis is a claim of sufficient scope and significance to launch a paper's exploration process. The working thesis (in most academic disciplines) usually appears at or near the end of an essay's first paragraph. The potential thesis in the freewrite is "the scene is more than just another representation of East Germany torn between Communism and the new Westernization. The movie tries hard to remind us that the rapid Westernization of East Germany *devastated while it liberated* in other ways. This scene uses space to represent Alex and Lara's (and East Germany's) dilemma: Alex and Lara gaze out at the night sky but only because the wall has been blown apart."

Something really interesting has happened here. The phrase in italics is the heart of this potential working thesis. It meets all the requirements of a good analytical thesis. It is in need of argument (that is, its meaning is not self-evident); it is not a fact or something most readers would already agree with; and it has tension, that is, it has the necessary back pressure of one idea against a competing possibility that would give the essay forward momentum. Good thesis statements are often the result of qualifying (limiting, modifying) an overstated, insufficiently complicated claim, which is why tension is a defining characteristic of good thesis statements.

Overall, we see that the writer has succeeded in finding something puzzling rather than settling for her first response (happy domestic future). She has made the most important move in using writing to arrive at ideas—starting with questions, with something she wants to understand better, rather than with answers. When the writer arrives at tentative answers, she tests them rather than just adding more evidence to prove that she is right.

An exciting thing about this freewrite is that it contains fruitful starting points for a subsequent draft that the writer may not yet fully recognize. In studying her freewrite, she will enable herself to see them and follow through on where they might lead. Has the writer yet realized the implications of her own observations in the last sentence of the freewrite? What are the implications of that last sentence? What might the writer discover if she began her different-font freewrite there?

Rules of Thumb for Handling Complexity

1. **Reduce scope.** Whenever possible, drastically reduce the range of your inquiry. Resist the temptation to try to include too much information. Even when an assignment calls for broader coverage of a subject, you will usually do best by covering the ground up front and then analyzing one or two key points in greater depth.

2. **Don't trust your first responses.** If you settle for these, the result is likely to be superficial, obvious, and overly general. A better strategy is to examine your first responses for ways in which they are inaccurate and then develop the implications of these overstatements (or errors) into a new formulation. In many cases, writers go through this process of proposing and rejecting ideas ten times or more before they arrive at an angle or approach that will sustain an essay. A first response is okay for a start, as long as you don't stop there.

3. **Begin with questions, not answers.** You are usually better off to begin with something that you don't understand very well and want to understand better. Begin by asking what kinds of questions the material poses.

4. **Write all the time about what you are studying.** Don't wait to start writing until you think you have an idea you can organize a paper around. Ideally, you should be formulating possible topics long before an actual topic is assigned. By writing informally—as a matter of routine—about what you are studying, you can acquire the habits of mind necessary to having and developing ideas. Similarly, by reading as often and as attentively as you can, and writing spontaneously about what you read, you will accustom yourself to being a less passive consumer of ideas and information, and will have more ideas and information available to think actively with and about.

5. **Accept that interest is a product of writing—not a prerequisite.** The best way to get interested is to expect to become interested. Writing gives you the opportunity to cultivate your curiosity by thinking exploratively. Rather than approaching topics in a mechanical way, or putting them off to the last possible moment and doing the assignment grudgingly, try giving yourself and the topic the benefit of the doubt. If you can suspend judgment and start writing, you will often find yourself uncovering interests where you had not seen them before.

6. **Use the "back burner."** In restaurants, the back burner is the place that chefs leave their sauces and soup stocks to simmer while they are engaged in other, more immediately pressing, and faster operations on the front burners. Think of your brain as having a back burner—a place where you can set and temporarily forget (though not entirely) some piece of thinking that you are working on. A good way to use the back burner is to read through and take some notes on something you are writing about—or perhaps a recent draft of something you are having trouble finishing—just before you go to sleep at night.

   Writers who do this often wake up to find whole outlines and whole strings of useful words already formed in their heads. Keep a notebook by your bed and record these early-morning thoughts. If you do this over a period of days (which assumes, of course, that you will start your writing projects well in advance of deadlines), you will be surprised at how much thinking you can do when you didn't know you were doing it. The back burner keeps working during the day as well—periodically insisting that the front burner, your more conscious self, listen to what it has to say. Pretty soon, ideas start popping up all over the place.

◀ ASSIGNMENT: Doing 10 on 1: A Sample Assignment

As we discuss at more length in Chapter 5, "Linking Evidence and Claims: 10 on 1 versus 1 on 10," doing 10 on 1 is a productive alternative to the shallow analysis of evidence encouraged by organizational schemes such as five-paragraph form, which typically attach evidence to predetermined ideas and provide very little analysis of either. When you do 10 on 1, you have the space to analyze your evidence and to pursue a range of possible implications. If you were writing a short paper about a film, for example, you might spend most of your paper laying out the implications of telling details in a scene that you find especially interesting and revealing, as in the student freewrite on *Good Bye Lenin!* In a longer paper, you would then use your analysis of this scene to open up interestingly related moments from elsewhere in the film and arrive at some conclusions.

- Pick a single scene from a film (or a single photograph from a collection of a photographer's photographs, or some other single example that is interestingly representative of a larger subject). Do 10 on 1 with your scene or other representative example. Notice as much as you can about it. What details repeat? What is opposed to what? (See the heuristic "Looking for Patterns of Repetition and Contrast" in Chapter 2.)

- Make details speak. What do the details "say"? What are some of the things that the film seems to say in this way? Do 10 on 1 in pursuit of implications.

- If time and space allow, pick another scene that is interestingly related to the first one and do 10 on 1 with it. How are the two scenes related, and so what?

We use the word *constellating* to describe a paper that is organized by drawing connections among interestingly related examples, each of which is analyzed using 10 on 1. This strategy works well as an organizational scheme in both exploratory and more polished drafts. For a fuller discussion of constellating as an organizational strategy for papers employing 10 on 1, see the template on pg. 160 in Chapter 5, "Linking Evidence and Claims: 10 on 1 versus 1 on 10." ▶

GUIDELINES FOR SEEING BETTER

1. Trace impressions back to causes.

2. Attend to details; most of us aren't in the habit of noticing details.

3. Narrow your scope in order to notice more.

4. Notice at least ten things in your evidence before you start to have ideas; keep your mind open longer to detail before deciding what it means.

5. Pay attention to the words you choose to describe your evidence; description leads to interpretation because claims are implicit in what you notice.

6. Push yourself to interpretive leaps by asking yourself, So what? This question is shorthand for What are we to make of this? Another version of the same question would be And so?

7. Keep taking your ideas (answers to the repeated application of the So what? question) back to their causes, the details that made you think as you do. Good thinking stays grounded in the evidence.

8. In sum, to have better ideas stay open longer to the data and to a range of possible ideas about the data.

CHAPTER 2

What Is Analysis and How Does It Work?

Quick Take

To analyze something is to ask what that something means. It asks how something does what it does or why it is as it is. Analysis is a form of detective work that begins not with the views you already have, but with something you are seeking to understand. As we said in the discussion of "What It Means to Have an Idea" in Chapter 1, analysis typically pursues something puzzling; it finds questions where there seemed not to be any; and it makes connections that might not have been evident at first.

People analyze all the time, but they don't always realize that this is what they're doing. A first step, then, toward becoming a better analytical thinker and writer is to become more aware of your own thinking processes, building on skills you already possess and eliminating habits that get in the way. Toward this end, here are five moves to practice, five activities people engage in when they analyze. The remainder of the chapter explains and offers examples of these moves as analytical activities.

- Move 1: Suspend Judgment (understand before you judge)
- Move 2: Define Significant Parts and How They're Related
- Move 3: Look for Patterns of Repetition and Contrast and for Anomaly
- Move 4: Make the Implicit Explicit (convert to direct statement meanings that are suggested indirectly)
- Move 5: Keep Reformulating Questions and Explanations

The first of these five moves, *suspending judgment*, is really more a precondition than an actual activity, but because it takes an act of will to suspend judgment and substitute other ways of thinking, we include it as an analytical move.

The second two activities—*defining significant parts and how they're related*, and *looking for patterns of repetition and contrast*—are the primary ways of looking at evidence analytically. The two are related. Looking for patterns is your best means of deciding which parts of a subject to focus on and how best to relate these to each other and to your subject as a whole.

The last two moves, *making the implicit explicit* and *repeatedly reformulating questions and explanations*, are the steps that push observations toward conclusions (the "So what?" part of the process, as explained in Chapter 1).

This chapter has a lot to say about implication, because a primary definition of analysis is that it makes the implicit explicit. The chapter offers exercises for recognizing the difference between an implication and a hidden meaning. The hidden meaning theory of interpretation ("reading *between* the lines") misinterprets analysis as a fanciful imposition of a writer's feelings and opinions onto a subject ("reading *into* the subject"). Analysis, the chapter argues, is a systematic and logical way of reading the lines themselves rather than the white space that lies between them.

The chapter ends by illustrating the importance of selecting and defending the appropriateness of an *interpretive context* as a means of legitimizing a writer's theory about what something means. We illustrate the concept of interpretive context with two short examples and one longer one—a student paper analyzing a perfume advertisement. Chapter 3 offers three more examples of analytical writing, each illustrating the role of the five analytical moves and the concept of interpretive context.

A. FIVE ANALYTICAL MOVES

Analysis is the search for meaningful pattern. In Chapter 1 we talked about the analytical habit of mind: the habit of attending to detail, of tracing impressions back to causes, of searching out questions rather than rushing to answers. That chapter, you'll recall, recommended locating yourself in an area of uncertainty, where there is something to figure out. Overall, the chapter defined the analytical habit of mind as an exploratory stance toward experience.

The first chapter's various thinking and writing practices—Hemingway's five-finger exercise, showing versus telling, freewriting, paraphrase × 3, Notice and focus, asking So what?, and 10 on 1—all share the goal of opening up rather than closing down a subject and the writer's thinking about it.

This chapter, in addition to offering further definitions of analysis—as a process—will provide you with an additional technique for making observations about evidence. This technique, looking for patterns of repetition and contrast ("the Method"), is a sequence of steps for noticing meaningful patterns in whatever it is you are studying.

MOVE 1: SUSPEND JUDGMENT

We discussed this essential move in some detail in Chapter 1, so we'll just restate it briefly here. Suspending judgment is a necessary precursor to thinking analytically because our habitual tendency to evaluate tends to shut down our ability to see and to think. It takes considerable effort to break the habit of responding to everything with likes and dislikes, with agreeing and disagreeing. Just listen in on a few conversations to be reminded of how pervasive this phenomenon really is. Even when you try to suppress them, judgments tend to come.

In the last chapter we suggested that you could get around this reflex move to judgment in several ways. One is to trace impressions back to causes, rather than just settling into and accepting the judgment. Another is to remember that judgments usually say more about the person doing the judging than they do about the subject. The determination that something is "boring" is especially revealing in this regard. Yet people typically roll their eyes and call things boring, as if this assertion clearly said something about the thing they are reacting to but not about the mind of the beholder.

> Judgments usually say more about the person doing the judging than they do about the subject. The determination that something is "boring" is especially revealing in this regard.

Consciously leading with the word *interesting* (as in "What I find most interesting about this is . . .") tends to deflect the judgment response into a more exploratory state of mind, one that is motivated by curiosity and thus better able to steer clear of approval and disapproval. The phrase *naturalizing your own assumptions* helps too. It can be used as a kind of mantra to help you notice when you are slipping into the assumption that what feels right and "natural" for you is self-evidently true, right, and natural for others too.

MOVE 2: DEFINE SIGNIFICANT PARTS AND HOW THEY'RE RELATED

Whether you are analyzing an awkward social situation, an economic problem, a painting, a substance in a chemistry lab, or your chances of succeeding in a job interview, the process of analysis is the same:

- divide the subject into its defining parts, its main elements or ingredients, and
- consider how these parts are related, both to each other and to the subject as a whole.

One common denominator of all effective analytical writing is that it pays close attention to detail. We analyze because our global responses—to a play, for example, or a speech or a social problem—are too general. The move from generalization to analysis, from the larger subject to its key components, is characteristic of good thinking. To understand a subject, we need to get past our first, generic, evaluative response to discover what the subject is "made of," the particulars that contribute most strongly to the character of the whole.

If all analysis did, however, was take subjects apart, leaving them broken and scattered, the activity would not be worth very much. The student who presents a draft of a paper to his or her professor with the words, "Go ahead; rip it apart," reveals a disabling misconception about analysis—that, like dissecting a frog in a biology lab, analysis takes the life out of its subjects. Clearly, analysis means more than breaking a subject into its parts. When you analyze a subject, you ask not just what it is made of, but also how the parts contribute to the meaning of the subject as a whole.

VOICES FROM ACROSS THE CURRICULUM

Science as a Process of Argument

I find it ironic that the discipline of science, which is so inherently analytical, is so difficult for students to think about analytically. Much of this comes from the prevailing view of society that science is somehow factual. Science students come to college to learn the facts. I think many find it comforting to think that everything they learn will be objective. None of the wishy-washy subjectivity that many perceive in other disciplines. There is no need to argue, synthesize, or even have a good idea. But this view is dead wrong.

Anyone who has ever done science knows that nothing could be further from the truth. Just like other academics, scientists spend endless hours patiently arguing over evidence that seems obscure or irrelevant to laypeople. There is rarely an absolute consensus. In reality, science is an endless process of argument, obtaining evidence, analyzing evidence, and reformulating arguments. To be sure, we all accept gravity as a "fact." To not do so would be intellectually bankrupt, because all reasonable people agree to the truth of gravity. But to Newton, gravity was an argument for which evidence needed to be produced, analyzed, and discussed. It's important to remember that a significant fraction of his intellectual contemporaries were not swayed by his argument. Equally important is that many good scientific ideas of today will eventually be significantly modified or shown to be wrong.

—*Bruce Wightman, Professor of Biology*

MOVE 3: LOOK FOR PATTERNS OF REPETITION AND CONTRAST AND FOR ANOMALY (THE METHOD)

We have been defining analysis as understanding parts in relation to each other and to a whole. But how do you know which parts to attend to? What makes some details in the material you are studying more worthy of your attention than others? Here are three procedures for selecting significant parts of the whole. First, we'll briefly discuss the three procedures. Then we will restate them in the form of an observation strategy (the Method) for locating meaningful patterns.

Look for a pattern of repetition (exact repetitions and strands). In virtually all subjects, repetition is a sign of emphasis. In a symphony, for example, certain patterns of notes repeat throughout, announcing themselves as major themes. In a legal document, such as a warranty or lease, a reader quickly becomes aware of words that are part of a particular idea or pattern of thinking, as in, for instance, disclaimers of accountability.

The repetition may not be exact. In Shakespeare's play *King Lear*, for example, references to seeing and eyes call attention to themselves through repetition. A reader of the play would do well to look for various occurrences of words and other details that might be part of this pattern. Let's say you notice that references to seeing and eyes almost always occur along with another strand of language having to do with the concept of proof. How might noticing these two strands lead to an idea? You might start by inferring from the two patterns that the play is concerned with ways of knowing (proving) and with seeing as opposed to other ways of knowing, such as faith or intuition.

Look for binary oppositions and organizing contrasts. Repetition of the same or similar type of word or detail (strands) almost always causes you to notice contrasts (opposing words and details) as well. A strand having to do with eyes and seeing may be contrasted with another strand having to do with its opposite: blindness and ways of accessing experience other than through the eyes. You will find a number of oppositions in virtually anything you study. These usually appear as what are called binary oppositions.

A binary opposition is a pair of elements (words, details, concepts, etc.) in which the two members of the pair are more or less direct opposites. The word *binary* means "consisting of two." We say more below and in subsequent chapters (especially the last section of Chapter 3, "Analyzing an Argument by Reformulating Binaries and Uncovering Assumptions") about the value of searching out binary oppositions. For now, we ask you to begin noticing the oppositions that occur in things that you look at and read.

Through noticing binaries and then casting and recasting the words you use to name them, you enable yourself to discover what is at stake in whatever you are looking at or reading. Writing, as we argue in more detail in our chapter on reading, is virtually always attempting to address some problem or issue. Until you can find the problem, until you can see how the issue is defined, you will not fully understand what you are reading. This is why the process of noticing binaries is valuable.

Look for anomalies—things that seem unusual, that seem not to fit. An anomaly (*a* = not, and *nom* = name) is something that is hard to name, what the dictionary defines as a deviation from the normal order. Along with looking for pattern, it is fruitful to attend to anomalous details—those that seem not to fit the pattern. Anomalies help us revise our stereotypical assumptions. A recent TV commercial for a baseball team, for example, featured its star player reading a novel by Dostoyevsky in the dugout during a game. In this case, the anomaly, a baseball player who reads serious literature, is being used to subvert (question, unsettle) the stereotypical assumption that sports and intellect don't belong together.

Anomalies are important because noticing them often leads to new and better ideas. Most advances in scientific thought, for example, have arisen when a scientist has observed some phenomenon that does not fit with a prevailing theory. Just as people tend to leap to evaluative judgments, they also tend to avoid information that challenges (by not conforming to) opinions they already hold. The result is that they ignore the evidence that might lead them to a better theory. (For much more on this process of using potentially contradictory and seemingly anomalous evidence to evolve an essay's main idea, see Chapter 6, "Making a Thesis Evolve.")

We will now recast the process of looking for repetition and contrast into a series of steps that we call the Method (for short).

Looking for Patterns of Repetition and Contrast (The Method) Looking for patterns of repetition and contrast (the Method) is a universal assignment, by which we mean that it works with all kinds of materials—a political speech, an essay, a film or scene from a film, a place, a book of poems, a photograph, your own essay drafts that you seek to revise—and with a wide range of purposes. The method of looking for patterns works through a series of steps. Hold yourself initially to doing the steps one at a time and in order. List what you notice for each step as thoroughly as you can before moving on. As you get adept at using this procedure, you will be able to record your answers under each of the three steps simultaneously. This analytical method can be applied to virtually anything.

Step 1. *Locate exact repetitions*—identical or nearly identical words or details—and note the number of times each repeats.

> For example, if the word *seems* repeats three times, write "seems × 3." Consider different forms of the same word—*seemed, seem*—as exact repetitions. Similarly, if you are working with images rather than words, the repeated appearance of high foreheads would constitute an exact repetition.

> Concentrate on substantive words, although sometimes seemingly unimportant words such as *and* become interesting when they begin to repeat a lot. If you are working with a longer text, such as an essay or book chapter or short story, limit yourself to recording the half-dozen or so words that call attention to themselves through repetition.

Step 2. *Locate repetition of the same or similar kind of detail or word (strands) and name the connecting logic.* A strand is a grouping of the same or similar kinds of words or details. (For example, *polite, courteous, mannerly* and *accuse, defense, justice, witness* are strands.)

> Simply listing the various strands that you find in your evidence will go a long way toward helping you discover what is most interesting and important for you to address. But to use the discovery of strands as an analytical tool, you have to do more than list. You have to <u>name</u> the common denominators that make the words or details in your list identifiable as a strand. Naming and renaming your strands will trigger ideas; it is itself an analytical move. And again, when working with longer pieces, try to locate the half-dozen strands that seem to you most important.

Step 3. *Locate details or words that form or suggest binary oppositions, and select from these the most important ones, which function as organizing contrasts.*

> Sometimes patterns of repetition that you begin to notice in a particular subject matter will be significant because they are part of a contrast—a basic opposition—around which the subject matter is structured. To find these oppositions, ask yourself, *What is opposed to what?*

> When looking for binary oppositions, start with what's on the page. List words and details that are set in opposition to other words and details. Gradually move to implied binaries, but keep these close to the data. Images of rocks and water, for example, might suggest the implied binary permanence/impermanence or the binary unchanging/changing.

> One advantage of detecting binary oppositions and elements of them that repeat is that this process will lead you to discover *organizing contrasts*, which are key in helping you locate central issues and concerns in the material you are studying. Organizing contrasts unify and give structure to the whole. Some examples that we encounter frequently are nature/civilization, city/country, public/private, organic/inorganic, and voluntary/involuntary.

Step 4. *List what you take to be the* **two** *most important exact repetitions,* **two** *most important strands, and* **two** *most important binaries.* Usually you will find that strands work in opposition to other strands.

At this point you are ready to use *ranking* (selecting some items from your lists as more important, more interesting than others) as a means of moving toward interpretive leaps. We ask you to choose the two most important kinds of repetition from each of your three kinds of lists so that you don't cut out too much data too soon. Your most important binaries might be a pair of opposed terms and/or ideas, but each might also be a strand that is opposed to another strand.

Step 5. *Write one healthy paragraph—half a page or so—in which you explain your choice of one repetition or one strand or one binary as most important for understanding whatever it is that you have been observing.*

Anomaly

After you have produced your three lists, selected the most important items from each, and written a paragraph explaining your ranking, you are ready to add a step to the process of looking for patterns. Along with looking for patterns, it is fruitful to attend to anomalous details—those that seem not to fit the pattern.

Like searching out binary oppositions, searching out anomalies often takes you to those places in your subject matter where something is going on—where some kind of breaking out of an old pattern or some attempt at "re-seeing" is beginning.

Why add anomalies as a separate activity? Anomalies become evident only after you have begun to discern a pattern, so it is best to locate repetitions, strands, and organizing contrasts—things that fit together in some way—before looking for things that seem not to fit. Once you see an anomaly, you will often find that it is part of a strand you had not detected, a strand that may be the other side of a previously unseen binary. In this respect, looking for anomalies is great for shaking yourself out of potentially limited ways of looking at your evidence and getting you to consider other possible interpretations. See an example of the use of anomaly in the essay on Ovid later in the chapter, as well as in the student essay on a dance performance toward the end of the chapter.

"The Method": What It Is and Why It Works

Think of this method of analysis as a form of mental doodling, which is actually what it is. The major advantage of this kind of doodling is that it encourages the attitude of *negative capability* that we spoke of in Chapter 1. Rather than worrying about what you are going to say, or about whether or not you understand, you instead get out a pencil and start tallying up what you see. Engaged in this process, you'll soon find yourself gaining entry to the logic of your subject matter.

While you are involved in the kinds of observing and listing activities that this method involves, you will be allowing your mind to range freely over the data. The activities of circling, underlining, and listing cause you to get physical with your data, and thus to come down from abstractions into the realm of concrete detail.

The Method shares aims with the observation strategies introduced in Chapter 1, but its approach to evidence differs in interesting ways. The primary observation strategy of Chapter 1, Notice and focus, tends to cut through to individual details. It acts like a laser beam to target something interesting and often anomalous (strange) that allows a writer to economically capture the character of the whole through a representative part. Because it relies on what you happen to notice or find interesting, Notice and focus is more intuitive and more reliant on fortuitous discoveries than the method of looking for patterns.

Looking for patterns, by contrast, is more comprehensive. It goes for the whole picture, involving methodical application of a matrix or grid of observational moves upon a subject. Although these are separate moves, they also work together and build cumulatively to the discovery of an infrastructure, a blueprint of the whole.

Strands, Binaries, and the Writing (and Revision) Process

What is the value of looking for strands—groups of the same or similar kinds of details (or words)? The presence of strands in written or visual texts has much to do with the way we arrive at ideas, the way we go about finding out what we think. When you write a paper or a letter or a story or a poem, or when you compose some kind of picture, your thinking (at the semiconscious and subconscious, as well as the conscious levels) moves not just forward, in a straight line, but sideways and in circles.

LOOKING FOR PATTERNS OF REPETITION AND CONTRAST (THE METHOD)

- Do the steps (in writing) one at a time and in order.
- Resist the urge to leap to conclusions; dwell with the data first.

Step 1. List all details (or words) that repeat exactly and the number of repetitions of each.

Step 2. List strands—groupings of the same or similar kinds of words, details.

(for example: *polite, courteous, mannerly*)

Be able to explain the strand's connecting logic; name it.

Think carefully about what goes with what.

Step 3. List organizing contrasts—binary oppositions.

(for example, open/closed, round/pointed)

Start with what's on the page.

Gradually move to implied binaries but stay close to the data.

List as many binaries as you can.

Step 4. Select and list the two most significant repetitions, the two most significant strands, and the two most significant binaries.

Step 5. Select and list the one repeated detail, *or* one strand, *or* one binary that you take to be the most significant for arriving at ideas about what the image communicates. Write one paragraph explaining your choice.

can combine, not just limited to one).

This is to say that much of the thinking that we do as we write and as we read happens through a process of association, which is, by its very nature, repetitive. In associative thinking, thoughts develop as words, and details suggest other words and details that are like them. As you habituate yourself to looking for patterns of repetition and contrast, you will be surprised at how much repetition (of various kinds) goes on in any piece of communication.

> *When you write a paper or a letter or a story or a poem, or when you compose some kind of picture, your thinking (at the semiconscious and subconscious, as well as the conscious levels) moves not just forward, in a straight line, but sideways and in circles.*

Revision is the process of consciously recognizing and clarifying patterns of repetition and contrast in your drafts. Recognizing patterns of repetition and contrast helps writers and artists come to see what they wish to say; the same process of recognition produces readers' and viewers' understanding of the things they read and see. In this sense, writing (making something out of words) and reading (arriving at an understanding of someone else's words) operate in much the same way.

▶ Try this 2.1: Doing the Method on a Poem

Use the Method on the following student poem. Write up the lists called for in steps 1–4 of the Method, and then write the healthy paragraph called for in step 5 in which you explain your choice of one exact repetition, one strand, or one binary as most significant. We have done this for you below in the section called "Doing the Method: An Example." If you can make up your own lists and write your own paragraph before looking at ours, you'll learn more. There is, however, another "Try this" later in this chapter that we do not analyze for you.

Brooklyn Heights, 4:00 A.M.
Dana Ferrelli

sipping a warm forty oz.
Coors Light on a stoop in
Brooklyn Heights. I look
across the street, in the open window;
Blonde bobbing heads, the
smack of a jump rope, laughter

of my friends breaking
beer bottles. Putting out their
burning filters on the #5 of
a hopscotch court.
We reminisce of days when we were
Fat, pimple faced—

> look how far we've come. But tomorrow
> a little blonde girl will
> pick up a Marlboro Light filter, just to play.
> And I'll buy another forty, because
> that's how I play now.
> Reminiscing about how far I've come

Doing the Method on a Poem: Our Analysis

1. *Words that repeat exactly*: forty × 2, blonde × 2, how far we've (I've) come × 2, light × 2, reminisce, reminiscing × 2, filter, filters × 2, Brooklyn Heights × 2

2. *Strands:* jump rope, laughter, play, hopscotch (connecting logic: childhood games representing the carefree worldview of childhood)

   Coors Light, Marlboro Light filters, beer bottles (drugs, adult "games," escapism?)
   Smack, burning, breaking (violent actions and powerful emotion: burning)

3. *Binary oppositions:* how far we've come/how far I've come (a move from plural to singular, from a sense of group identity to isolation, from group values to a more individual consideration)

   Blonde bobbing heads/little blonde girl
   Burning/putting out
   Coors Light, Marlboro Lights/jump rope, hopscotch
   How far I've come (two meanings of *far*?, one positive, one not)
   Heights/stoop
   Present/past

4. *Two most important repetitions:* forty, how far we've/I've come

   Two most important strands: jump rope, laughter, play, hopscotch
   Coors Light, Marlboro Light filters, beer bottles
   Two most important binaries: jump rope, laugher, play, hopscotch versus
   Coors Light, Marlboro Light filters, beer bottles;
   Burning/putting out

5. *Write one healthy paragraph in which you explain your choice of* **one** *repetition or* **one** *strand or* **one** *binary as most important for understanding whatever it is that you have been observing.*

This is a poem about growing up—or failing to grow up, both being subjects about which the poem expresses mixed emotions. The repetition of *forty* (forty-ounce beer, forty cigarettes) is interesting in this context. It signals a certain weariness—perhaps with a kind of pun on forty to suggest middle age and thus the speaker's concern about moving toward being older in a way that seems stale and flat. The beer, after all, is warm—which is not the best state for a beer to be in, once opened, if it is to retain its taste and character. Forty cigarettes, forty ounces of beer—"supersizing"—suggest excess.

This reading of forty as excess along with the possible allusion to middle age takes us to what is, in our reading of the poem, the most important (or at least most interesting) binary opposition: *burning versus putting out*. We are attracted to this binary because it seems to be part of a more intense strand in the poem, one that runs counter to the weary prospect of moving on toward a perhaps lonely ("how far *I've* come") middle-aged feeling. Burning goes with breaking and the smack of the jump rope, and even putting out, if we visualize putting out not just as fire extinguished but in terms of putting a cigarette out by pushing the burning end of it into something (the number 5 on the Hopscotch court). The poem's language has a violent and passionate edge to it, even though the violent words are not always in a violent context (for example, the smack of the jump rope).

This is a rather melancholy poem in which, perhaps, the poetic voice is mourning the passing, the "putting out" of the passion of youth ("burning"). In the poem's more obvious binary—the opposition of childhood games to more "adult" ones—the same melancholy plays itself out, making the poem's refrain-like repetition of "how far I've come" ring with unhappy irony. The little blonde girl is an image of the speaker's own past self (since the poem talks about reminiscing), and the speaker mourns that little girl's (her own) passing into a more uncertain and less carefree state. It is 4:00 A.M. in Brooklyn Heights—just about the end of night, the darkest point perhaps before the beginning of morning, and windows in the poem are open, so things are not all bad. The friends make noise together, break bottles together, revisit hopscotch square 5 together, and contemplate moving on.

Analysis of Our Analysis   The point of tallying repetitions and strands and binaries and then selecting the most important and interesting ones is to trigger ideas. The hope is that the discipline of having to look closely at and notice patterns in the language will produce more specific, more carefully grounded conclusions than you otherwise might notice.

Virtually everything in our three paragraphs moves from the repeated words and patterns we noticed in the evidence. We didn't go outside the poem to generalities, nor did we take some single item out of context (looking for pattern helps prevent you from doing that) and produce an interpretation that might not be true to the rest of the poem.

We couldn't, by the way, find any anomalies in the poem—things that seemed not to fit. Of course, it is often the case that what at first seems to be an anomaly is actually part of a pattern you haven't yet fully noticed. For good examples of writers making use of anomalies in their evidence, see the Ovid example and the student paper on dance later in the chapter.

▶ Try this 2.2: Doing the Method on a Speech

Here is a speech that no doubt all readers of this book will know. Many of you may even have committed it to memory at some point. Try looking for patterns of repetition and contrast in it. See what this method allows you to notice about what is already a familiar piece of prose. Later, after you read our chapter on sentence style, you could come back to this speech and see what you notice in it if you look for pattern in terms of Lincoln's syntactical choices. This exercise could also serve as a model for further practice in looking for patterns of repetition and contrast in speeches. Speeches by various presidents, for example, are easy to find on the Internet. Your aim in doing the Method on speeches is to arrive at conclusions about the speech that get beyond the obvious and the general. What does doing the Method on this speech cause you to notice that you may not have noticed before?

The Gettysburg Address

Nov. 19, 1863

Fourscore and seven years ago our fathers brought forth on this continent a new nation, conceived in liberty and dedicated to the proposition that all men are created equal.

Now we are engaged in a great civil war, testing whether that nation or any nation so conceived and so dedicated can long endure. We are met on a great battlefield of that war. We have come to dedicate a portion of it as a final resting place for those who died here that the nation might live. This we may, in all propriety do. But in a larger sense, we cannot dedicate, we cannot consecrate, we cannot hallow this ground. The brave men, living and dead who struggled here have hallowed it far above our poor power to add or detract. The world will little note nor long remember what we say here, but it can never forget what they did here.

It is rather for us the living, we here be dedicated to the great task remaining before us—that from these honored dead we take increased devotion to that cause for which they here gave the last full measure of devotion—that we here highly resolve that these dead shall not have died in vain, that this nation shall have a new birth of freedom, and that government of the people, by the people, for the people shall not perish from the earth.

Start by listing words that repeat exactly. Then list repetitions of the same or similar kinds of words (strands). Then list words that fall into opposition to each other—binary oppositions. As you start listing, you will find that strands begin to suggest other strands that are in opposition to them. And you may find that words you first took to be parts of a single strand are actually parts of different strands and are, perhaps, in opposition. This process of noticing and then relocating words and details into different patterns is the part of doing the Method that pushes your analysis to possible interpretations.

A Note on the Importance of Finding Binaries

Let's think further about what binaries are and what they reveal. Binaries are deeply engrained in the ways that we think. Thinking is not possible without them. But the discovery of binaries is not an end unto itself. Why is it useful to find binary oppositions (binaries)? And why isn't this search for binaries a problem, like approaching the world as though everything in it could be divided into only two possibilities (either/or thinking)?

When you run into a binary opposition in your thinking, it is like a fork in the road, a place where two paths going in different directions present themselves and you pause to choose the direction you will take. Binary oppositions are sites of uncertainty, places where there is struggle among various points of view. As such, binaries are the breeding ground of ideas.

Binary oppositions are sites of uncertainty, places where there is struggle among various points of view.

When you find a binary opposition in an essay, a film, or a political campaign, you locate the argument that the film, essay, or campaign is having with itself, the place where something is at issue. You avoid the rigidifying and reductive habit of mind called either/or thinking when you allow yourself to notice binaries, but immediately begin to ask questions about and complicate them. To "complicate" a binary is to discover evidence that unsettles it and to formulate alternatively worded binaries that more accurately describe what is at issue in the evidence.

As a general rule, analysis favors live questions—where something remains to be resolved—over inert answers, places where things are already pretty much nailed down and don't leave much space for further thinking. Finding binaries will help you find the questions around which almost anything is organized. This is why we ask you to select those binary oppositions in your subject matter that seem to you to be "organizing contrasts." Much analytical thinking, whether you are aware of doing it or not, involves determining which of a number of opposing elements is the most fundamental, the most important for understanding how something operates as a whole. Think of an organizing contrast as the structural beam that gives conceptual shape to a piece. (See Chapter 3, Section C).

There is usually no single "right" answer about which of a number of binary oppositions is the primary organizing contrast. This is because analytical thinking involves interpretation. Interpretive conclusions are not matters of fact, but theories. It is in the nature of theories to be tentative and open to alternative readings of the same information. This is why good analytical thinking takes time and is inevitably open-ended.

Analysis at Work: An Example (a Student Draft on Ovid's Metamorphoses*)*
This preliminary draft of a paper on Ovid's *Metamorphoses*, a collection of short mythological tales dating from ancient Rome, exemplifies a writer in the process of discovering a workable idea. She begins with a list of similar examples. As the examples accumulate, the writer begins to make connections and formulate trial explanations. We have not included enough of this excerpt to get to the tentative thesis the draft is working toward, although it is already beginning to emerge. What we want to emphasize here is the writer's willingness to accumulate data and to locate it in various patterns of similarity and contrast.

The draft begins with two loosely connected observations about Ovid's stories: that males dominate females, and that many characters in the stories lose the ability to speak and thus become submissive and dominated. In the excerpt, the writer begins to connect these two observations and speculate about what this connection means.

We have included annotations in the draft to suggest how the writer's ideas evolve as she looks for pattern, contrast, and anomaly. Notice in particular how the writer manages to remain open to reformulation.

There are many other examples in Ovid's *Metamorphoses* that show the dominance of man over woman through speech control. In the Daphne and Apollo story, Daphne becomes a tree to escape Apollo, but her ability to speak is destroyed. Likewise, in the Syrinx and Pan story, Syrinx becomes a marsh reed, also a life form that cannot talk, although Pan can make it talk by playing it. [The writer establishes a pattern of similar detail.]

Pygmalion and Galatea is a story in which the male creates his rendition of the perfect female. The female does not speak once; she is completely silent. Also, Galatea is referred to as *she* and never given a real name. This lack of a name renders her identity more silent. [Here the writer begins to link the contrasts of speech/silence with the absence/presence of identity.]

Ocyrhoe is a female character who could tell the future, but was changed into a mare so that she could not speak. One may explain this transformation by saying it was an attempt by the gods to keep the future unknown. [Notice how the writer's thinking expands as she sustains her investigation of the overall pattern of men silencing women: here she tests her theory by adding another variable: prophecy.]

However, there is a male character, Tiresias, who is also a seer of the future and is allowed to speak of his foreknowledge, thereby becoming a famous figure. (Interestingly, Tiresias during his lifetime has experienced being both a male and a female.) [Notice how the Ocyrhoe example has spawned a contrast based on gender in the Tiresias example. The pairing of the two examples demonstrates that the ability to tell the future is not the sole cause of silencing, since male characters who can do it are not silenced—though the writer pauses to note that Tiresias is not entirely male.]

Finally, in the story of Mercury and Herse, Herse's sister, Aglauros, tries to prevent Mercury from marrying Herse. Mercury turns her into a statue; the male directly silences the female's speech.

The woman silences the man in only two stories studied. [Here the writer searches out an anomaly—women silencing men—that grows in the rest of the paragraph into an organizing contrast.] In the first, "The Death of Orpheus," the women make use of "clamorous shouting, Phrygian flutes with curving horns, tambourines, the beating of breasts, and Bacchic howlings" (246) to drown out the male's songs, dominating his speech in terms of volume. In this way, the quality of power within speech is demonstrated: "for the first time, his words had no effect, and he failed to move them [the women] in any way by his voice" (247). Next the women kill him, thereby rendering him silent. However, the male soon regains his temporarily destroyed power of expression: "the lyre uttered a plaintive melody and the lifeless tongue made a piteous murmur" (247). Even after death, Orpheus is able to communicate. The women were not able to destroy his power completely, yet they were able to severely reduce his power of speech and expression. [The writer learns, among other things, that men are harder to silence; Orpheus's lyre and his severed head continue to sing after his death.]

The second story in which a woman silences a man is the story of Actaeon, in which the male sees Diana naked, and she transforms him into a stag so that he cannot speak of it: "he tried to say 'Alas!' but no words came" (79). This loss of speech leads to Actaeon's inability to inform his own hunting team of his true identity; his loss of speech leads ultimately to his death. [This example reinforces the pattern that the writer had begun to notice in the Orpheus example.]

Thinking Recursively: Reformulating Binaries

For the purposes of using the Method, recursive thinking is essential. Working with strands is an inherently recursive activity because you'll tend to first think that one set of words or details fits together as a strand and then you'll find yourself regrouping—reformulating your strands as new patterns begin to strike you. As you begin to notice repetitions, they tend to suggest strands, and strands tend to beget organizing contrasts.

Thinking is not simply linear and progressive, moving from point A to point B to point C like stops on a train. Careful thinkers are always retracing their steps, questioning their first—and second—impressions, assuming that they've missed something. All good thinking is *recursive*—that is, it repeatedly goes over the same ground, reformulating ideas and rethinking connections.

Nowhere is it more important to *reformulate* than in working with organizing contrasts. This is because the habit of mind called binary (either/or) thinking can retard thought through oversimplification—through a tendency toward rigidly dichotomized points of view. But finding binary oppositions as a means of locating what is at issue and then using the binaries to *start* rather than end your thinking process is not reductive. Notice how in the Ovid example the writer keeps reformulating her ways of categorizing her data.

Let's consider a brief example in which a writer starts with the binary: was the poet Emily Dickinson psychotic, or was she a poetic genius? This is a useful, if overstated, starting point for prompting thinking. Going over the same ground, the writer might next decide that the opposing terms *insanity* and *poetic genius* don't accurately name the issue. He or she might decide, as the poet Adrienne Rich did, that poetic genius is often perceived as insanity by the culture at large and, thus, it's not a viable either/or formulation. This move, by the way, is known as *collapsing the binary:* coming to see that what had appeared to be an opposition is really two parts of one complex phenomenon.

Perhaps the insanity/poetic genius binary would be better reformulated in terms of conventionality/unconventionality—a binary that might lead the writer to start reappraising the ways in which Dickinson is not as eccentric as she at first appears to be.

Regrouping Strands and Binaries as a Method of Analysis: An Example

Although the steps of the Method are discrete and modular, they are also consecutive; they entail a kind of narrative logic. Each step leads logically to the next and then to various kinds of regrouping (which is actually rethinking). Let's run through a hypothetical example of this way of thinking with repetition, strands, and binaries.

The first step, the discovery of repetition, reveals what a piece of writing is about. If, for example, a piece of reading reveals numerous repetitions of the word *duty*, you would then know that (whatever the piece might think about duty) it is clearly, at the most factual level, *about* duty.

The repetition of *duty* might alert you to look for other related words that will begin to suggest themselves as part of a strand—at which point you would begin to educe and construct a *discourse* of duty, a strand of related words that your observation of repetitions of the word *duty* illuminated. You might then notice *guilt, responsibility, shame, obligation, task*, and so on as a *discursive strand* that further reveals what the piece is about. At this point of strand formation, you have already made an interpretive leap (observation has blended into interpretation). You would need to follow this up consciously by *articulating the logic of the strand*. In this case, it might be "words that suggest the writer's worries about performing certain acts."

Note that what the text thinks of the duty strand—what it is inviting us to think of duty, and how it resolves the problem or issue or question associated with duty—requires a step beyond noticing that the text is about duty because that word repeats. The formulation of a primary strand, which reveals what the text is about and interested in, usually leads to a next step: what the text is worried about, anxious about, trying to resolve. The formulation of a strand is thus usually one half of an organizing contrast.

> *The formulation of a primary strand, which reveals what the text is about and interested in, usually leads to a next step: what the text is worried about, anxious about, trying to resolve.*

So we should ask ourselves, What is duty in tension with here? To what is it opposed? Often the answer will turn out to be another term in the strand—let's say *shame*. And so we come to see, as our analysis evolves, that two words we had first grouped together, and rightly so, can also be separated into an organizing contrast, with each as the key term in its own strand. If you look back at our analysis of the poem above, you can see this happening.

The *duty* strand might retain *task, responsibility, work, reward*, and others from the original strand, which would now be "the upside of doing what is expected." The opposing *shame* strand might include *guilt* and other words that the discovery of this new strand would start to illuminate, say, *fear, humble, revulsion*. If the *duty* strand is the "upside," then the *shame* and *guilt* strand is the "downside," that which the text is worried and potentially anxious about.

The writer's consideration of how the text mediates the tension made apparent by this reward/revulsion, duty/guilt contrast would be the primary culminating business of the analysis, which might issue in a thesis such as "Although the American tobacco industry repeatedly pays lip service to the guilt it feels for making a profit on the lungs of its citizenry, ultimately it flees the shame in the name of corporate responsibility to serving its shareholders their slice of the American dream."

▶ **Try this 2.3:** Apply the Method to Something You Are Reading

Try the Method on a piece of reading that you wish to understand better, perhaps a series of editorials on the same subject, an essay, one or more poems by the same author (since the Method is useful for reading across texts for common denominators), a collection of stories, a political speech, and so on. You can work with as little as a few paragraphs or as much as an entire article or chapter or book. By focusing on repetition (exact repetitions and strands), contrast (binary oppositions), and anomalies, you press yourself to get closer to your data—to become more aware of what the subject is made of, rather than generalizing broadly about it.

This exercise can produce fruitful results with almost any kind of material. It offers, for example, a very useful way of accessing and characterizing the mental habits of particular authors. It is also particularly useful with complex theoretical arguments, as it allows you to gradually discover what the argument is made of rather than allowing yourself to become daunted by the scope and difficulty of the material. For more suggestions on working with difficult theoretical readings, see the sections on paraphrase × 3 in Chapter 1, "the pitch and the complaint" in Chapter 4, and our example of uncovering assumptions in a reading, which appears at the end of Chapter 3.

MOVE 4: MAKE THE IMPLICIT EXPLICIT

A definition of analytical writing to which this book repeatedly returns is that it makes explicit (overtly stated) what is implicit (suggested but not directly stated) in both your subject and your own thinking. This process of converting suggestions into direct statements is essential to analysis, but it is also the feature of analyzing that is least understood by inexperienced writers. They fear that, like the emperor's new clothes, implications aren't really "there," but are instead the phantasms of an overactive imagination. "Reading between the lines" is the common and telling phrase that expresses this anxiety. The implication is that analysis makes something out of nothing—the spaces between the lines—rather than what is there in black and white. Another version of this anxiety is implied by the term *hidden meanings*.

Some people fear that, like the emperor's new clothes, implications aren't really "there," but are instead the phantasms of an overactive imagination. "Reading between the lines" is the common and telling phrase that expresses this anxiety.

Implication versus Hidden Meanings

The problem some people have with this analytical move—making the implicit explicit—is that it focuses on a "part" of the whole that is not overtly (materially) present, but rather is something that some part of the whole suggests. Making the implicit explicit is an interpretive move and not simply a matter of observation. This aspect of analytical thinking is the least understood by people who are easily put off by analysis. Such people invariably jeer at analysis for allegedly picking things apart (which we call defining significant parts in relation to the whole) and finding "hidden meanings" (which we call making the implicit explicit).

Implications are not hidden, but neither are they completely spelled out so that they can be simply extracted. The word *implication* comes from the Latin *implicare*, which means "folded in." The word *explicit* is in opposition to the idea of implication. It means "folded out."

This etymology of the two words, *implicit* and *explicit*, suggests that meanings aren't actually "hidden," but neither are they opened to full view. An act of mind is required to take what is folded in and fold it out for all to see. What follows is a brief exercise on implication consisting of a series of observations for which you are asked to supply implications. On the basis of this activity, we then ask you to theorize the difference between an implication and a hidden meaning.

Try this 2.4: Inferring Implications from Observations

Do this exercise along with other people if you can, because part of its aim is to determine the extent to which different people infer the same implications. Write a list of as many plausible implications as you can think of for each of the items below.

1. The sidewalk is disappearing as a feature of the American residential landscape. New housing developments have them only if a township requires them of the developer.
2. New house designs are tending increasingly toward open plans in which the kitchen is not separated from the rest of the house. New house designs continue to have a room called the living room, usually a space at the front of the house near the front door, but many (not all) also have a separate space called the family room, which is usually in some part of the house farther removed from the front door and closer to the kitchen.
3. "Good fences make good neighbors."—Robert Frost
4. In the female brain, there are more connections between the right hemisphere (emotions, spatial reasoning) and the left hemisphere (verbal facility). In the male brain, these two hemispheres remain more separate.
5. An increasing number of juveniles—people under the age of eighteen—are being tried and convicted as adults, rather than as minors, in America, with the result that more minors are serving adult sentences for crimes they committed while still in their teens.
6. Neuroscientists tell us that the frontal cortex of the brain, the part that is responsible for judgment and especially for impulse control, is not fully developed in humans until roughly the age of twenty-one. What are the implications of this observation relative to observation 5?

7. Linguists have long commented on the tendency of women's s'
rising inflection at the end of statements as if the statements '
tions. An actual command form—Be home by midnight!—thus
question instead. What are we to make of the fact that in recent yea.
younger men (under 30) have begun to end declarative statements and
command forms with rising inflections?

8. Shopping malls and grocery stores rarely have clocks.

After you have made your list of implications for each item, consider
how you arrived at them. On the basis of this experience, how would
you answer the following questions? What is the difference between an
idea being "hidden" and an idea being implied? What, in other words,
is an implication? To what extent do you think most people would
arrive at the same implications that you did?

Having done the preceding exercise with inferring implications, you could
now make up your own list of observations and pursue implications. Make some
observations, for example, about the following, and then suggest the possible
implications of your observations.

- changing trends in automobiles today
- what your local newspaper chooses to put on its front page (or editorial page)
  over the course of a week
- shows (or advertisements) that appear on network television (as opposed to
  cable) during one hour of evening prime time
- advertisements for scotch whiskey in highbrow magazines

We end this discussion of the fourth analytical move, making the implicit
explicit, with a quick summary of the steps that analysis typically takes from
observations to conclusions. These steps may be charted as follows:

Observation (description) → Implications → Conclusions (So what?)

In *step 1* of this process, you describe your evidence, paraphrasing key language and looking for interesting patterns of repetition and contrast.

In *step 2* you begin querying your own observations by making what is implicit
explicit.

In the *final step* you push your observations and statements of implications to
interpretive conclusions by asking, So what?

As we have argued in this chapter and in Chapter 1, the analytical process
requires certain critical shifts in your attention. In Chapter 1, with the exercise
called Notice and focus, we noted that writers need to start by asking themselves
not "What do I think?" but "What do I notice?"

A similar shift that is conducive to inferring implication is:

Not What do I think?

but

What does it say?

MOVE 5: KEEP REFORMULATING QUESTIONS AND EXPLANATIONS

Analysis, like all forms of writing, requires a lot of experimenting. Because the purpose of analytical writing is to figure something out, you shouldn't expect to know at the outset exactly where you are going, how all your subject's parts fit together, and to what end. The key is to be patient and to know that there are procedures—in this case, questions—you can rely on to take you from uncertainty to understanding.

The following groups of questions (organized according to the analytical moves they're derived from) are typical of what goes on in an analytical writer's head as he or she attempts to understand a subject. These questions will work with almost anything you want to think about. As you will see, they are geared toward helping you locate and try on explanations for the meaning of various patterns of details.

Which details seem significant? Why?

What does the detail mean?

What else might it mean?

(Moves: Define Significant Parts; Make the Implicit Explicit)

How do the details fit together? What do they have in common?

What does this pattern of details mean?

What else might this same pattern of details mean? How else could it be explained?

(Move: Look for Patterns of Repetition and Contrast)

What details don't seem to fit? How might they be connected with other details to form a different pattern?

What does this new pattern mean? How might it cause me to read the meaning of individual details differently?

(Moves: Look for Anomalies, Keep Reformulating Questions)

The process of posing and answering such questions—the analytical process—is one of trial and error. Learning to write well is largely a matter of learning how to frame questions. One of the main things you acquire in the study of an academic discipline is knowledge of the kinds of questions that the discipline typically asks. For example, an economics professor and a sociology professor might observe the same phenomenon, such as a sharp decline in health benefits for the elderly, and analyze its causes and significance in different ways. The economist might consider how such benefits are financed and how changes in government policy and the country's population patterns might explain the declining supply of funds for the elderly. The sociologist might ask about attitudes toward the elderly and about the social structures that the elderly rely on for support.

Whatever questions you ask, the answers you propose will often produce more questions. Like signposts on a trail, details (data) that initially seem to point in one direction may, on closer examination, lead you someplace else. Dealing with these realities of analytical writing requires patience, but it will also make you a more confident thinker, because you'll come to know that your uncertainty is a normal and necessary part of writing.

Using Exploratory Writing to Find Workable Questions

The process of having ideas rarely moves steadily forward, traveling in an uninterrupted line from point to point like a connect-the-dots picture. Instead, thinking and writing are *recursive* activities, which means that we move forward by looking backward, by repeatedly going over the same ground, looking for wrong turns, uncovering signposts we may have missed, and reinterpreting signposts passed earlier because of what we later discovered.

A good paper is essentially the answer to a good question, an explanation of some feature or features of your subject that need explaining. If you don't take the time to look for questions, you might end up writing a tidy but relatively pointless paper. Spend some time simply recording what you notice about your subject without worrying about where these observations might lead. By opening up your thinking in this way, you will discover more data to think with, more possible starting points from which to develop an idea. And you will be less likely to get trapped into seeing only those features of your subject that support the first conclusion you come to.

> A good paper is essentially the answer to a good question, an explanation of some feature or features of your subject that need explaining. If you don't take the time to look for questions, you might end up writing a tidy but relatively pointless paper.

When you shift from exploratory writing to writing a first draft, you may not—and most likely will not—have all the answers, but you will waste significantly less time chasing ill-focused and inadequately considered ideas than might otherwise have been the case. Even as you write this draft, however, a good phrase to keep in mind is *Share your thought processes with the reader*. If readers can't see how you got to the position you are offering them, they have little reason to accept it, no matter how smooth the sentence style, grammar, paragraphing, and organization may be.

B. SOME COMMON CHARGES AGAINST ANALYSIS

Once you accept the challenge of thinking and writing analytically—the careful, recursive, and nonjudgmental observation of your subject and of your own thoughts—you can expect to encounter another obstacle. Although analysis is an activity we call on constantly in our everyday lives, many people are deeply suspicious of it. "Why can't you just enjoy the movie rather than picking it apart?" they'll say. Or, "Oh, you're just making that up!" You may even be accused of being unfeeling if you adopt an analytical stance, because it is typical of the anti-intellectual position to insist that feeling and thinking are separate and essentially incompatible activities. Some people fear that trusting our intellects will make us less feeling and sensitive. With this fear goes the opposite one—that trusting our feelings will necessarily render us incapable of thinking. Both of these suspicions about analysis have long histories.

Though among the most astutely analytical of thinkers, the famous nineteenth-century English Romantic poet William Wordsworth wrote that "we murder to dissect," thus giving voice to the still common anxiety that analysis takes the life out of things. This attitude arose in reaction against an equally extreme position from the eighteenth century (the so-called Age of Reason or Enlightenment), known for its indictment of emotion as the enemy of rationality.

In response to the eighteenth century's elevation of reason over all other human faculties, the nineteenth century sought to correct the imbalance by elevating the faculties of feeling and imagination. Few thinkers of either century really adhered to these positions in such extreme forms, but suffice it to say that analysts of human beings seem always to have been perplexed about how our various capacities fit together into a functional whole. One aim of this book is to demonstrate that taking refuge in either side of the opposition between thinking and feeling is not only counterproductive but unnecessarily reductive.

CHARGE 1: "ANALYSIS KILLS ENJOYMENT"

Why should enjoyment and understanding be incompatible? At the root of the analysis-kills-the-fun complaint is the idea that analysis is critical—in the sense of disapproving and negative. From this point of view, the basic activity of analysis (asking questions), along with its deliberate delaying of evaluation, seems skeptical, uncommitted, and uncaring. But raising questions and working out the possible meanings of significant details is not necessarily negative, nor does it require a complete absence of feeling.

In fact, analytical thinkers tend to be more dedicated than most people to understanding, and thus to being sensitive to rather than attacking a subject. Understanding is not the enemy of enjoyment, at least not for people who enjoy thinking. In any case, the global "I like it/I don't like it" move is less common to people who have learned to think analytically because they are more likely to make careful distinctions—deciding to like some features of a subject (for well-explained reasons) while disliking others.

CHARGE 2: "ANALYSIS FINDS MEANINGS THAT ARE NOT THERE"

What about the charge that analysis "reads into" a subject things that aren't there ("reading between the lines")? What does the charge mean, and why do people make it? The phrase *reading between the lines*, as we noted in our discussion of making the implicit explicit, implies that we are actually reading not the words on the page but the white space between the sentences. This implication suggests that analytical conclusions are merely fanciful and "made up," because white space offers evidence, presumably, of nothing.

The related term, *hidden meaning*, implies an act of conspiracy on the part of either an author, who chooses to deliberately obscure his or her meaning, or on the part of readers, who conspire to "find" things lurking below the surface that other readers don't know about and are unable to see. People who think it a good idea to look for "hidden meanings" assume that such meanings are there and are worth looking for. People who use the term derisively assume either that such meanings are not "there" (not real, but imagined) or that, if they are "there," they should not be hidden, thus sparing readers the trouble of looking for them. A further assumption is that people probably know what they mean most of the time but, for some perverse reason, are unwilling to come out and say so.

Proponents of these views of analysis are, in effect, committing themselves to the position that everything in life means what it says and says what it means. This position posits another related one: that meanings are always obvious and understood in the same way by everyone, and thus don't require interpretation (which is an example of "naturalizing our own assumptions" as discussed in Chapter 1). People who use the expressions *hidden meanings* and *reading between the lines* generally don't recognize that these phrases imply theories of interpretation, but they do.

It is probably safe to assume that most writers try to write what they mean and mean what they say. That is, they try to control the range of possible interpretations that their words could give rise to, but there is always more going on in a piece of writing (as in our everyday conversation) than can easily be pinned down and controlled. It is, in fact, an inherent property of language that it always means more than and thus other than it says. (See further discussion of this matter in the section "Reading With and Against the Grain" in Chapter 4.)

The hidden meaning theory is an exaggeration, an overextension of the idea of implication and a denial of the possibility that the implications of, say, a campaign slogan or a new fashion trend or a new tax law can be worked out rationally. The fact that ideas can be suggested rather than directly stated doesn't make such ideas "hidden."

Meanings and Social Context

You can easily test some of these assertions as you go through an ordinary day. What, for example, does the choice of wearing a baseball cap to a staff meeting or to a class "say"? Note, by the way, that a communicative gesture such as the wearing of a hat need not be premeditated to communicate something to other people. The hat is still "there" and available to be "read" by others as a sign of certain attitudes and a culturally defined sense of identity—with or without your intention. Things communicate meaning to others whether we wish them to or not, which is to say that the meanings of most things are socially determined.

Berets and baseball caps, for example, carry different associations because they come from different social contexts. Baseball caps convey a set of attitudes associated with the piece of American culture they come from. They suggest, for example, popular rather than high culture, casual rather than formal, young—perhaps defiantly so, especially if worn backward—rather than old, and so on. The social contexts that make gestures like our choice of hats carry particular meanings are always shifting, but some such context is always present.

We can, of course, protest that the "real" reason for turning our baseball cap backward is to allow more light in, making it easier to see than when the bill of the cap shields our faces. This practical rationale makes sense, but it does not explain away the social statement that the hat and a particular way of wearing it might make. As a certain practice becomes increasingly common, its character as a social signal becomes less pronounced. Like all complex social behaviors, our choices in clothing and the messages they send are constantly changing.

Because meaning is, to a significant extent, socially determined, we can't entirely control what our clothing, our manners, our language, or even our way of walking communicates to others. This is one of the reasons that analysis makes some people suspicious and uneasy. They don't want to acknowledge that they are sending messages in spite of themselves, messages they haven't deliberately and overtly chosen.

It helps to remember that interpretive leaps—conclusions arrived at through analysis—about what some gesture or word choice or clothing combination or scene in a film means, follow certain established rules of evidence. One such rule is that the conclusions of a good analysis do not rest on details taken out of context, but instead test and support claims about the details' significance by locating them in a pattern of similar detail. (See the previous section on the five analytical moves.) In other words, analytical thinkers are not really free to say whatever they think, as those who are made uneasy by analysis sometimes fear.

Reading What's Left Out

We should acknowledge, with respect to the reading-between-the-lines charge, that analysis sometimes does draw out the implications of things that are not there, because they have been deliberately omitted. Usually we recognize such omissions because we have been led to expect something that we are not given, making its absence conspicuous.

An analysis of the Nancy Drew mysteries, for example, might attach significance to the absence of a mother in the books, particularly in light of the fact that biological mothers, as opposed to wicked stepmothers, are pretty rare in many kinds of stories, such as fairy tales, that involve female protagonists (for example, "Hansel and Gretel," "Cinderella," and "Snow White"). Taking note of the absent mothers as a potentially significant omission could lead to a series of analytical questions, such as the following: How might this common denominator of certain kinds of children's stories be explained? What features of the stories' social, psychological, historical, economic, and other possible contexts might offer an explanation? As this example suggests, things are often left out for a reason, and a good analysis should therefore be alert to potentially meaningful omissions.

Try this 2.5: Reading What's Missing

Consider what you might make of a cigarette advertisement that includes a line of laughing young men and women in unisex attire holding one of their number across their outstretched arms, but does not include cigarettes or any sign of smoking. What might the omission of smoking in the picture mean, since its sponsor no doubt wishes to encourage the activity? What does this omission imply about the nature of the advertisement's message and its means of influencing viewers?

Try doing the same exercise with a political speech or a piece of public relations writing or coverage of the same situation in two different newspapers or magazines (in which case you would consider the implications of one periodical leaving out what the other chose to include). In what other kinds of communication might attention to what has been left out be especially revealing?

CHARGE 3: "SOME SUBJECTS WEREN'T MEANT TO BE ANALYZED"

The preceding examples, Nancy Drew mysteries and cigarette ads, raise the argument that it is foolish to analyze subjects that were meant only to entertain (like science-fiction movies) or to serve some practical need (like shopping malls or blue jeans). Should analytical thinkers steer clear of subjects that supposedly weren't meant to be analyzed, such as bowling and late-night television? This is a complex question because it runs into people's prejudices about so-called "highbrow" versus "lowbrow" activities. If asked to name highbrow subjects, most of us would come up with the same kind of list. Mozart's string quartets, for example, or foreign movies with subtitles are highbrow. The World Wrestling Entertainment (as seen on TV) is lowbrow. Highbrows are meant to stick to their own turf. To the extent that analytical thinking is labeled a highbrow activity, people are offended by its presuming to intrude on lowbrow terrain. It's okay to analyze Mozart or art films but not romance novels or popular entertainments.

The question of intention—what was and what wasn't "meant" to be analyzed—is, at least in part, an extension of the highbrow/lowbrow divide. The makers of tough-guy movies may not have intended to promote the value of rugged individualism and may even have produced completely different statements of their intentions. What the makers of a particular product or idea intend, however, is only a part of what their work means; intention does not finally control the implications that a work possesses.

A Sample Student Paper: A Close Reading of a Performance

The following student paper is an example of a close reading, which is the kind of attention to evidence this book is inviting you to make habitual. A close reading

VOICES FROM ACROSS THE CURRICULUM

Taking the Pressure Off

When writing about dance, the primary evidence is the dance itself and the theatrical accompaniments enhancing the work (sets, costumes, music, narrative, lights, etc.). Seeing and understanding how and what dance communicates is the main task of the dance writer. Because dance is often abstract and purposely open to multiple interpretations, students are usually terrified at the prospect of finding and interpreting evidence in support of a thesis. Typical first responses to analysis include

"I enjoy watching dance, but I have never looked for meaning or message."

"I don't know enough about dance to understand it."

My responses include, "Sit back, relax, and enjoy the dance—save analysis for later. Start your analysis by pretending you are discussing the performance with a friend who did not see it. As you tell him or her about the performance, you will naturally begin to gather evidence and analyze."

—Karen Dearborn, Professor of Dance

explicates; that is, it unfolds an interpretation by making explicit selected features of a subject that otherwise might not be readily recognized or understood. A close reading moves beyond the obvious, but it does not leap to some hidden meaning that is unconnected to the evidence. Rather, it stays close to and follows logically from the evidence: the meaning is implicit in the details, waiting to be brought out by the writer careful enough to look closely and questioningly.

Try this 2.6: Tracking the Moves in a Student Paper

The student paper exemplifies the five analytical moves around which this chapter is organized: suspending judgment, defining parts and how they are related, looking for patterns of repetition and for anomaly, making the implicit explicit, and asking questions. It also should prompt you to further consider the common charges against analysis, especially the charge that analysis finds meanings that are not there.

As you read the student paper, look for the five moves and how the writer uses evidence.

- What elements of the paper seem to be factual reporting—that is, description rather than interpretation of details in the dance?
- Locate those places in the paper where the student writer arrives at conclusions about what the details of the dance mean.
- Where has the writer made the move from implicit to explicit?
- This paper makes interesting use of anomaly. Find the anomaly.
- Look for places where the writer specifies one or more interpretive contexts. Consider, for example, the paper's opening sentence. We'll have more to say about interpretive contexts in the chapter's final two examples.

Hua dan: The Dance of Values in the Beijing Opera

[1] Lanfang says in his autobiography that "The beautiful dance movements created by past artists are all based on gestures in real life, synthesized and accentuated to become art ..." (36). In this quote Lanfang emphasizes a representation of life through "beautiful" movement. As he is a product of his culture, he is describing what his culture deems "beautiful." The female roles in the Beijing Opera, particularly the *Hua dan*, convey their own set of cultural values about femininity in Chinese culture.

[2] There is much posing and holding of shapes within the *Hua dan* role. There is a gentle, poised focus in these moments. This allows the viewers time to take in the elegance of the shape, costumes, makeup, music, and artistry of the performer. The fruit of these efforts becomes evident and framed by the pausing. The work the performers put in is valued in the pause.

[3] All the movements are very clear in their choices between making angles and using the full extension of the limbs, particularly the arms. The angular shapes give a sharp contrast to the extension of the arms

and legs. Circular formations of the arms are seamlessly round and often repeated to emphasize their distinctness. This exactness and clarity emphasizes the importance and power of the body. By paying such attention to particulars it gives greater emphasis to the powers held in making these shapes.

[4] There is much repetition and opening and closing in the movement. Repetition can represent the large amount of time females spend on such activities. It can also give a sense of the time it actually takes for such actions in real life, such as sewing. The women do spend much time sewing, and this time is represented. It also takes consistency and dedication to complete such tasks multiple times, so these become valued characteristics.

[5] Rhythm is also an element of the very controlled female walking consisting of small, even, steps. The feet barely leave the floor and don't extend into kicks or jumps, as do some of the male roles. Even in the *Hua dan* demonstration in the "Aspects of Peking Opera" video when a bounce was in the character's step and the eyes were alive, the flow of the walk remained consistent. The smallness of the steps could represent the female's place in society. They are petite and not flashy in their maneuvers. They complete their tasks without much fanfare. Keeping the feet low also limits the opening of the legs. Such protection and withholding represents a value in itself—the absence of overt sexual suggestion. Although the male characters may be more likely to overtly demonstrate their strength and power, it takes a great amount of control and focus for the women to execute their walks, so this convention is demonstrating the value of women keeping their struggles and work hidden.

[6] Although my viewing of Peking Opera is limited, it caught my eye to see the *Hua dan*'s shoulders finally move in a flirtation demonstration in the "Aspects" video. This isolation and interruption of flow seemed out of character to all other demonstrated acts. All other actions were focused on creating lines and full range of motion. Breaking typically occurs only at the elbows and wrists. These shoulder shrugs break not only the lines but the flowing rhythm. Making flirtation stand out suggests that in the context of the opera, such coquettish moments are important for the audience both in terms of character and life off the stage. It also reminds the viewers that there are even more areas of the body that have not been used but are present within the character and performer.

[7] What are the recurring themes in all these observations? They lie in control, value of movement, and repetition. The "beauty" lies not only in the quality of the movement but in what it represents. The dainty representation of females, their modesty and strong work ethic, and care in their activities are of great importance, but so too is the slight pleasure in restricted flirtation. When combined, these qualities of movement create a carefully crafted portrayal of a polished female. It serves to represent not only a clear character but a beautiful and desirable female figure.

▶ **Try this 2.7:** Casting a New Thesis Using Anomaly

The student paper on dance is a promising draft. Let's consider what she might do to make it even better by taking better advantage of some seemingly anomalous details. At one point the writer notes features of the dance that she describes as seeming "out of character." In Chapter 1 in the section called "What It Means to Have an Idea," we said that ideas often try to account for some kind of dissonance. We have also said that anomaly is useful for prompting good thinking because it causes you to complicate your initial formulations and evolve them into more carefully qualified, better-developed ideas.

Look at the anomaly paragraph ([6]) and then at the paper's concluding paragraph. Then try casting a thesis statement that takes the anomaly more fully into account. See the section called "Moving from Idea to Thesis Statement" in Chapter 1.

Specifying an Interpretive Context

We spoke earlier in this chapter about things that seemingly are or are not "meant" to be analyzed. Writers sometimes resist analysis on the grounds that some things were not intended to mean anything outside a limited context, such as entertainment, and so should not be analyzed from any other point of view. Barbie dolls are toys intended for young girls. Should the fact that the makers of Barbie intended to entertain children rule out analysis of Barbie's characteristics (built-in earrings and high-heeled feet), and thus what the doll "says" about different ideals of femininity?

What the makers of a particular product or idea intend is only part of what that product or idea communicates. The urge to cordon off certain subjects from analysis on the grounds that they weren't meant to be analyzed unnecessarily excludes a wealth of information—and meaning—from your range of vision. It is, however, right to be careful about the interpretive contexts we bring to our experience. Looking to an author's statements of intention as a key to the meaning of his or her work is not necessarily wrong. It is, in fact, a useful and interesting thing to do. But it can be limiting and misleading. What you want to avoid is defining your choice of interpretive contexts too narrowly.

Notice how in the following analysis the student writer's interpretation relies on his choice of a particular interpretive context, post–World War II Japan. Had he selected another context, he might have arrived at some different conclusions about the same details. Notice also how the writer perceives a pattern in the details and queries his own observations (asking So what?) to arrive at an interpretation.

"Kamaitachi" in Post-war Japan

The series entitled "Kamaitachi" is a journal of [Japanese photographer Eikoh] Hosoe's desolate childhood and wartime evacuation in the Tokyo countryside. He returns years later to the areas where he grew up, a stranger to his native land, perhaps likening himself to the legendary Kamaitachi, an invisible sickle-toothed weasel, intertwined with the soil and its unrealized fertility.

"Kamaitachi #8" (1956), a platinum palladium print, stands alone to best capture Hosoe's alienation from and troubled expectation of the future of Japan. [Here the writer chooses a biographical approach as his interpretive context.]

The image is that of a tall fence of stark horizontal and vertical rough wood lashed together, looming above the barren rice fields. Straddling the fence, half-crouched and half-clinging, is a solitary male figure, gazing in profile to the horizon. Oblivious to the sky above of dark and churning thunderclouds, the figure instead focuses his attentions and concentrations elsewhere. [The writer selects and describes significant detail.]

It is exactly this *elsewhere* that makes the image successful, for in studying the man we are to turn our attention toward him and away from the print. He hangs curiously between heaven and earth, suspended on a makeshift man-made structure, in a purgatorial limbo awaiting the future. He waits with anticipation—perhaps dread?—for a time that has not yet come; he is directed away from the present, and it is this sensitivity to time that sets this print apart from the others in the series. One could argue that in effect this man, clothed in common garb, has become Japan itself, indicative of the postwar uncertainty of a country once-dominant and now destroyed. What will the future (dark storm clouds) hold for this newly humbled nation? [Here the writer notices a pattern of "in-between-ness" and locates it in a historical context to make his interpretive leap.]

Remember that regardless of the subject you select for your analysis, you should directly address not just What does this say? but also, as this writer has done, What are we invited to make of it, and in what context? Here is yet another shift that can help you prompt analytical thinking:

Not What do I think about it? **but** What am I being invited to think and by what means?

When you consider how your response is being shaped by whatever it is you are looking at, you are engaged in *rhetorical analysis*.

C. RHETORICAL ANALYSIS

We will end this chapter with discussion of a particular kind of analysis—rhetorical analysis. To analyze the rhetoric of something is to determine how that something persuades and positions its readers or viewers or listeners. Rhetorical analysis is an essential skill because it reveals how particular pieces of communication seek to enlist our support and shape our behavior. Only then can we decide whether or not we should be persuaded to respond as we have been invited to respond.

Everything has a rhetoric: classrooms, churches, speeches, supermarkets, department store windows, Starbucks, photographs, magazine covers, your bedroom, this book. Intention, by the way, is not the issue. It doesn't matter whether the effect of a place or a piece of writing on its viewers (or readers) is deliberate and planned or not. What matters is that you can notice how the details of the thing itself encourage or discourage certain kinds of responses in the "consumers" of whatever it is you are studying. What, for example, does the high ceiling of a Gothic cathedral invite in the way of response from people who enter it? What do the raised platform at the front of a classroom and the tidy rows of desks secured to the floor say to the students who enter there?

Everything has a rhetoric: classrooms, churches, speeches, supermarkets, department store windows, Starbucks, photographs, magazine covers, your bedroom, this book.

If you are reading this book in a first-year college writing course, you may be asked to write a rhetorical analysis, often of a visual image of some kind, early in the semester. What follows is an exercise in rhetorical analysis that will help you better understand the aims and methods of this kind of analysis. We think it is easiest to start with analysis of visual rhetoric—the rhetoric, for example, of a typical classroom.

Try this 2.8: Rhetorical Analysis of a Place

Go someplace: the foyer of a campus building, the center of a campus quadrangle, a classroom, a coffee shop, a waiting room, someone's office or workstation (other than your own) at work, a courthouse or town hall, or any other place that you find interesting or frequent regularly. Study the details of the place and make a list of what you see. Description, as we repeatedly argue in this book, is essential to analysis and actively encourages interpretive leaps. Want to know more about something you are studying? Write a description of it and see what happens in the process. Description is the best antidote to writer's block.

After you gather your data, ask yourself the questions below. These questions overlap somewhat, which is to say that they go after the same kind of thinking in slightly different ways. Concentrate on the question or questions that work best for you.

- In what ways and by what means does this space shape the way I feel and think and behave?
- What does this space say to its occupants about how they should think and feel and behave in the space?
- What assumptions did the makers of this space seem to have about the people who would occupy it?

RHETORICAL ANALYSIS OF A PLACE: A BRIEF EXAMPLE

To get you started on a rhetorical analysis of a place, here is the beginning of one on the layout of our college campus. It was written as a freewrite and could serve as the basis for further observation.

The campus is laid out in several rows and quadrangles. It is interesting to observe where the different academic buildings are, relative to the academic departments they house. It is also interesting to see how the campus positions student housing. In a way, the campus is set up as a series of quadrangles— areas of space with four sides. One of the dormitories, for example, forms a quadrangle. Quadrangles invite people to look in—rather than out. They are enclosed spaces, the center of which is a kind of blank. The center serves as a shared space, a safely walled-off area for the development of a separate community. The academic buildings also form a quadrangle of sorts, with an open green space in the center. On one side of the quadrangle are the buildings that house the natural and social sciences. Opposite these—on the other side of a street that runs through the center of campus—is the modern brick and glass structures that house the arts and the humanities....

RHETORICAL ANALYSIS OF AN ADVERTISEMENT: AN EXAMPLE

Our final example is a student's rhetorical analysis of a perfume advertisement that appeared in a magazine aimed at young women. The analysis, which offers the writer's thinking on secondary sources as well as on the advertisement itself, was written in a course called Introduction to Communication. The writer's aim is not only to tell her readers what the advertisement "says," but to locate it in a social context. The student uses her secondary sources to provide an interpretive context (a lens) through which to see the rhetoric of the ad—its means of persuasion.

The visual imagery of advertisements offers instructive opportunities for rhetorical analysis because advertising is a form of persuasion. Advertisers attend carefully to rhetoric by carefully targeting their audiences. This means advertisements are well suited to the questions that rhetorical analysis typically asks: How is the audience being invited to respond and by what means (in what context)? You'll notice that in the rhetorical analysis of the magazine ad, the writer occasionally extends her analysis to evaluative conclusions about the aims and possible effects (on American culture) of the advertisement.

Marketing the Girl Next Door: A Declaration of Independence?

[1] Found in *Seventeen* magazine, the advertisement for "tommy girl," the perfume manufactured by Tommy Hilfiger, sells the most basic American ideal of independence. Various visual images and text suggest that purchasing tommy girl buys freedom and liberation for the mind and body. This image appeals to young women striving to establish themselves as unbound individuals. Ironically, the advertisement uses traditional American icons as vehicles for marketing to the modern woman. Overall, the message is simple: American individualism can be found in a spray or nonspray bottle.

[2] Easily, the young woman dominates the advertisement. She has the look of the all-American "girl next door." Her appeal is a natural one, as she does not rely on makeup or a runway model's cheekbones for her beauty. Freckles frame her eyes that ambitiously gaze skyward; there are no limits restricting women in capitalist America. Her flowing brown hair freely rides a stirring breeze. Unconcerned with the order of a particular hairstyle, she smiles and enjoys the looseness of her spirit. The ad tells us how wearing this perfume allows women to achieve the look of self-assured and liberated indifference without appearing vain.

[3] The second most prevalent image in the advertisement is the American flag, which neatly matches the size of the young woman's head. The placement and size of the flag suggest that if anything is on her cloudless mind, it is fundamental American beliefs that allow for such self-determination. The half-concealed flag is seemingly continued in the young woman's hair. According to the ad, American ideals reside well within the girl as well as the perfume.

[4] It is also noticeable that there is a relative absence of all land surrounding the young woman. We can see glimpses of "fruited plains" flanking the girl's shoulders. This young woman is barely bound to earth, as free as the clouds that float beneath her head. It is this liberated image Americans proudly carry that is being sold in the product.

[5] The final image promoting patriotism can be found in the young woman's clothing. The young woman is draped in the blue jean jacket, a classic symbol of American ruggedness and originality. As far as we can see, the jacket is spread open, supporting the earlier claim of the young women's free and independent spirit. These are the very same ideals that embody American pride and patriotism. The ad clearly employs the association principle in linking the tommy girl fragrance with emotionally compelling yet essentially unrelated images of American nationalism and patriotism.

[6] A final obvious appeal to American nationalism is the tagline of the advertisement, the underlying message being "a declaration of independence." The young woman has already declared her independence, and now it is your turn. Doesn't every young woman want to be in that green field, hair blowing in the wind, wearing a confident look outlined against an American flag and clean, carefree, endless blue sky?

[7] Lastly, the advertisement utilizes several implicit arrows that point to the actual product of tommy girl perfume. The white writing against the dark blue jean jacket catches the eye first, encouraging the reader to continue in the traditional, left to right order. When the writing stops, we are naturally pointed toward the product. In addition, the young woman's hair, seen earlier as an extension of the American flag, is flurrying out and somewhat downward. We follow the hair to its end, where it seemingly kisses the product's cap. All visual indications of direction in the advertisement lead the viewer to an inevitable end: the irresistible scent of tommy girl perfume.

[8] But we might also look beyond the ad's overt messages, and examine its effects on the viewer and our society as a whole. Returning to the ad's portrayal of the young woman, we are shown a girl with a natural beauty, free of worries or cares about conforming to the pressures of society as a female. Jean Kilbourne (2003) argues that countless ads tell women to search for freedom and independence through being thin, as echoed in the ad's skinny and attractive young woman. Kilbourne actually refers to another tommy girl ad that uses the same tagline: "'A declaration of independence,' proclaims an ad

for perfume that features an emaciated model, but in fact the quest for a body as thin as the model's becomes a prison for many women and girls" (p. 263). She argues that ads encouraging a search for feminine independence often promote the worship of the thinness ideal, as well as the dilemma of being a successful and powerful woman while remaining "feminine" and unthreatening (pp. 262–264).

[9] Additionally, the ad for tommy girl perfume is also effective because it "takes on the trappings of a movement for social justice," according to Thomas Frank (1997, p. 187). Frank describes how advertisers constantly link products with the rebellious, revolutionary political and social movements of the past in order to conjure the vehement emotions associated with their resounding emotional content. The tommy girl ad emphasizes typical patriotic American images—like the American flag and denim clothing—as well as the phrase *a declaration of independence,* which explicitly creates a connection between the perfume and the American colonists' revolutionary pursuit of liberty in their beliefs and behavior during the American Revolution.

[10] Yet in reality, this marketing of liberation is paradoxical; although this freeing message promotes rebellion and nonconformity, it actually supports the market economy and feeds into capitalism and conformity. When advertisers employ political protest messages to be associated with products, they imply that buying the product is a form of political action.

[11] But lastly, the ad gives another paradoxical message with the portrayal of the beauty of the American, unspoiled, natural environment. Another typical American image is of the untouched landscapes, green pastures, and cloudless blue skies of the open frontier, which serves as the ad's backdrop. The ad's clear blue sky with the American flag flying freely in the wind encourages the viewer to link the beauty of the natural American landscape with the purchase of tommy girl. Sut Jhally, editor of the video *Advertising and the End of the World* (1998), would argue that the ad's purpose—the consumption of the product—is paradoxically putting the environment at risk. Our "freedom" to buy all of what we need (and especially, what we don't need) is essentially spoiling the natural surroundings that we romanticize. And so the viewers are simply left to decide: Does this tommy girl ad truly portray a declaration of independence, or of *dependence?*

References

Frank, T. (1997). Liberation marketing and the culture trust. In E. Barnouw et al. (Ed.), *Conglomerates and the media* (pp. 173–190). New York: The New Press.

Jhally, S. (Ed.). (1998). *Advertising and the end of the world* [Videotape]. Northampton, MA: Media Education Foundation.

Kilbourne, J. (2003). The more you subtract, the more you add: Cutting girls down to size. In G. Dines & J. Humez (Eds.), *Gender, race and class in media* (pp. 258–267). Thousand Oaks, CA: Sage.

Try this 2.9: Commenting on a Draft

Throughout this book we provide discussions of student texts in bracketed comments located at the ends of paragraphs. Usually these perform descriptive paraphrasing of what the piece of writing *does* (rather than what it says), along with pointing out how it exemplifies general procedures of analytical writing that we have been discussing. Do these two tasks for "Marketing the Girl Next Door: A Declaration of Independence?" Describe what the writer does paragraph by paragraph and locate her use of the various analytical moves presented in this chapter. (For an example, see "'Kamaitachi' in Postwar Japan" at the end of the previous section.)

ASSIGNMENT: Making the Implicit Explicit and Pushing Observations to Conclusions

1. Locate any magazine ad that you find interesting. Ask yourself, What is this a picture of? Use the preceding paper as a kind of model for rendering the implicit explicit. Don't settle for just one or even three answers. Keep answering the question in different ways, letting your answers grow in length as they identify and begin to interpret the significance of telling details. Attend to your choice of language, because your word choice as you summarize details will begin to suggest to you the ad's range of implication.

   If you find yourself getting stuck, rephrase the question as, "What is this ad really about, and why did the advertiser choose this particular image or set of images? Your repeated answering of the first question should eventually lead you to answer the second question.

2. Write an essay in which you make observations about some cultural phenomenon, some place and its social significance, or an event (in terms of its significance in some context of your choice) and then push these observations to tentative conclusions by repeatedly asking, So what?

   Be sure to query your initial answers to the So what? question with further So what? questions, trying to push further into your own thinking and into the meaning of whatever it is you have chosen to analyze. Trends of some sort are good to work with. Marketing trend? So what? Trends in movies about unmarried women or married men or . . . So what? And so forth.

   Since the chapter offers sample analyses of paintings and advertisements, you might choose one of these. Cartoons are interesting subjects too. Here you would really have to think a lot about your choice of interpretive context. Gender? Politics? Humor? Family life? American stereotypes? Remember that the guiding questions of rhetorical analysis are What are we invited to make of this, by what means, and in what context?

GUIDELINES FOR HOW ANALYSIS WORKS

1. As you analyze a subject, ask not just "What are its defining parts?" but also "How do these parts help me to understand the meaning of the subject as a whole?"

2. When you describe and summarize, attend carefully to the language you choose, since the words themselves will usually contain the germs of ideas.

3. Always note repetitions in your subject. There is no surer means of discovering what it is about.

4. Simply listing the various strands that you find in your evidence will go a long way toward helping you discover what is most interesting and important for you to address. Then make sure to name each strand. Naming and renaming strands is itself an analytical move that will trigger further ideas.

5. Finding binaries will help you find the questions around which a film or an essay or a speech or a poem—almost anything—is organized. Through noticing binaries and then casting and recasting the words you use to name them, you enable yourself to discover what is at stake in whatever you are looking at or reading. To find these oppositions, ask yourself, *What is opposed to what?*

6. Always keep an eye out for anomalous details—those that seem not to fit the pattern. Anomalies help us revise our stereotypical assumptions.

7. Don't assume that all meanings are overt and ready-made, waiting to be found. Most of the time, they are implicit—not the same as *hidden*—and an act of mind is required to take what is folded in and convert the suggested meanings of particular details into overt statements.

8. Remember that regardless of the subject you select for your analysis, you should directly address not just What does this say? but also, What are we invited to make of it, and in what *context*?

9. As a general rule, analysis favors live questions—where something remains to be resolved—over inert answers, places where things are already pretty much nailed down and don't leave much space for further thinking.

10. The process of posing and answering questions—the analytical process—is one of trial and error. Learning to write well is largely a matter of learning how to frame questions. Whatever questions you ask, the answers you propose will often produce more questions.

CHAPTER 3

Putting Analysis to Work: Three Extended Examples

This chapter applies and further explores the approaches to analytical writing offered in Chapters 1 and 2. The first two extended examples—an analysis of a painting and an analysis of a magazine cover—illustrate the move from description to interpretation. The third extended example—analysis of an argument—illustrates the processes of reformulating binaries and uncovering unstated assumptions (reasoning back to premises).

The first of the extended examples, the analysis of a painting, differentiates summary from analysis, applies the five analytical moves detailed in Chapter 2, and takes up the issue of what we call the *fortune cookie* versus the *anything goes* theories of interpretation.

The second example, an analysis of a magazine cover, applies one of the five analytical moves—looking for patterns of repetition and contrast (the Method)—and then addresses the issue of multiple meanings by demonstrating the *process of choosing and applying multiple interpretive contexts.*

The third extended example—an editorial that analyzes other editorials on a social issue (a set of guidelines governing sexual conduct at Antioch College)—picks up Chapter 2's discussion of *binary oppositions* and adds to it the process of *locating unstated assumptions in an argument.* This section of the chapter is our best advice on analyzing and constructing arguments.

A. EXTENDED EXAMPLE 1: MOVING FROM DESCRIPTION TO INTERPRETATION

What is the difference between a description or a summary and analysis? And, at what point does analysis become interpretation? What we have suggested thus far is that analysis implies a search for meaning, and that analysis and interpretation are inseparable. The process of noticing, of recording selected details and patterns of detail (analysis) is already the beginning of interpretation. But, once the move from observation to conclusions begins, writers need to make explicit and defend the appropriateness of the interpretive context in which this leap takes place.

DIFFERENTIATING ANALYSIS FROM SUMMARY

Summary differs from analysis, because the aim of summary is to recount—in effect, to reproduce someone else's ideas. But summary and analysis are also clearly related and usually operate together. Summary is important to analysis, since you can't analyze a subject without laying out its significant parts for your reader. Similarly, analysis is important to summary, because summarizing is more than just copying someone else's words. We offer both our description/summary and our analysis of a painting—*Whistler's Mother*—to demonstrate the difference between the two ways of approaching subjects. You will see, however, that our analysis would not be possible without the description that allowed us to see which patterns of detail in the painting to attend to.

FIGURE 3.1 *Arrangement in Grey and Black: The Artist's Mother*
        by James Abbott McNeill Whistler, 1871.

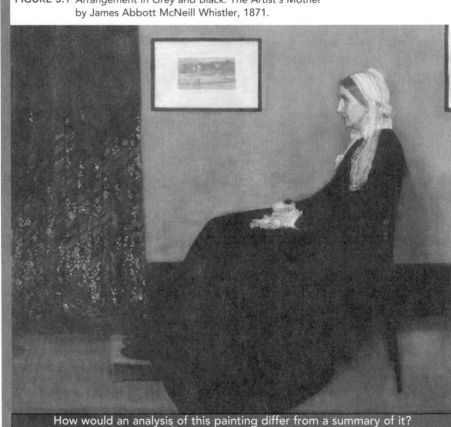

How would an analysis of this painting differ from a summary of it?

Try this 3.1: Analyzing *Whistler's Mother*

You will be better able to make use of our analysis of the picture if you try to do your own analysis of it first. Start with the steps of the observational strategy "looking for patterns of repetition and contrast" (the Method). What details repeat in the picture? What patterns of similar detail (strands) can you find? What details and patterns of detail seem to fall into organizing contrasts? Compile your three lists in writing; then rank the top two in each category, and write a paragraph on why you would choose one of these as most important.

A primary aim of this book's observation strategies, as you will recall, is to shift your attention from premature generalizing about a subject to recording detail that actually appears in it. Description is the best antidote to what we call in Chapter 1 the dogfish problem—trying to start with an idea about your subject without first really looking at it. This book's basic formula can be stated as follows:

- **What do you notice?**
- **What repeats?**
- **What is opposed to what?**
- **So what?**

Try applying this formula to the painting.

Summary, like analysis, is a tool of understanding and not just a mechanical task. But a summary stops short of analysis because summary typically makes much smaller interpretive leaps. A summary of the painting popularly known as *Whistler's Mother*, for example, would tell readers what the painting includes, which details are the most prominent, and even what the overall effect of the painting seems to be. A summary might say that the painting possesses a certain serenity, and that it is somewhat spare, almost austere. This kind of language still falls into the category of focused description, which is what a summary is.

An analysis would include more of the writer's interpretive thinking. It might tell us, for instance, that the painter's choice to portray his subject in profile contributes to our sense of her separateness from us and of her nonconfrontational passivity. We look at her, but she does not look back at us. Her black dress and the fitted lace cap that obscures her hair are not only emblems of her *self-effacement*, disguising her identity like her expressionless face, but also the tools of her *self-containment* and thus of her power to remain aloof from prying eyes. What is the attraction of this painting (this being one of the questions that an analysis might ask)? What might draw a viewer to the sight of this austere, drably attired woman, sitting alone in the center of a mostly blank space? Perhaps it is the very starkness of the painting, and the mystery of self-sufficiency at its center, that attracts us. (See Figure 3.1.)

Observations of this sort go beyond describing what the painting contains and enter into the writer's ideas about what its details imply, what the painting invites us to make of it and by what means.

Notice in our analysis of the painting how intertwined the description (summary) is with the analysis. Laying out the data is key to any kind of analysis, not simply because it keeps the analysis accurate but because, crucially, it is in the act of carefully describing a subject that analytical writers often have their best ideas.

You may not agree with the terms by which we have summarized the picture, and thus you may not agree with such conclusions as "the mystery of self-sufficiency." Nor is it necessary that you agree, because *there is no single, right answer to what the painting is about.* The absence of a single right answer does not, however, mean that anything goes.

As we discuss in more detail below (under the heading "The Limits on Interpretation"), your readers' willingness to accept an analytical conclusion is powerfully connected to their ability to see its *plausibility*—that is, how it follows from both the supporting details that you have selected and the language you have used in characterizing those details. The writer who can offer a plausible (not necessarily or obviously true, but believable) description of a subject's key features is likely to arrive at conclusions about possible meanings that others would share. Often the best that you can hope for with analytical conclusions is not that others will say, "Yes, that is obviously right," but "Yes, I can see where it might be possible and reasonable to think as you do."

FIGURE 3.2 Summary and analysis of *Whistler's Mother* diagram

Data	Method of Analysis	Interpretive Leaps
subject in profile, not looking at us	make implicit explicit (speculate about what the detail might suggest)	figure strikes us as separate, nonconfrontational, passive.
folded hands, fitted lace cap, contained hair, expressionless face	locate pattern of same or similar detail; make what is implicit in pattern of details explicit	figure strikes us as self-contained, powerful in her separateness and self-enclosure self-sufficient?
pattered curtain and picture versus still figure and blank wall; slightly frilled lace cuffs and ties on cap versus plain black dress	locate organizing contrast; make what is implicit in the contrast explicit	austerity and containment of the figure made more pronounced by slight contrast with busier, more lively, and more ornate elements and with little picture showing world outside.
slightly slouched body position and presence of support for feet	anomalies; make what is implicit in the anomalies explicit	These details destabilize the serenity of the figure, adding some tension to the picture in the form of slightly uneasy posture and figure's need for support: she looks too long, drooped in on her own spine.

Summary and Analysis of *Whistler's Mother*

Here are two general rules to be drawn from this discussion of analysis and summary:

1. **Describe with care.** The words you choose to summarize your data will contain the germs of your ideas about what the subject means.
2. **In moving from summary to analysis**, look consciously at the language you have chosen, asking, "Why did I choose this word? What ideas are implicit in the language I have used?"

DIFFERENTIATING ANALYSIS FROM EXPRESSIVE WRITING

In expressive writing, your primary subject is yourself, with other subjects serving as a means of evoking greater self-understanding. In analytical writing, your reasoning may derive from personal experience, but it is your reasoning and not you or your experiences that matter. Analysis asks not just the expressive question, "What do I think?" but "How good is my thinking? How well does it fit the subject I am trying to explain?"

We don't mean to suggest that expressive writing cannot be analytical or that analytical writing cannot be expressive. Expressive (writer-centered) writing is analytical in its attempts to define and explain a writer's feelings, reactions, and experiences. And analysis is a form of self-expression, since it inevitably reflects the ways a writer's experiences have taught him or her to think about the world.

Although observations like those offered in the preceding interpretive leaps column go beyond simple description, they don't move from the picture into autobiography. They stay with the task of explaining the painting, rather than moving to private associations that the painting might prompt, such as effusions about old age, or rocking chairs, or the character and situation of the writer's own grandmother. Such associations could well be valuable unto themselves as a means of prompting a searching piece of expressive writing. They might also help a writer interpret some feature of the painting that he or she was working to understand. But the writer would not be free to use pieces of his or her personal history as conclusions about what the painting communicates unless these conclusions could also be reasonably inferred from the painting itself.

Let's say, for example, that a writer believed that the woman is mourning the death of a son or is patiently waiting to die. In support of these theories, the writer might cite the black dress, the woman's somber expression, and the relative darkness of the painting. This selection of details might be sufficient to support some kind of interpretation concerning sadness or loss, but would clearly not support a leap to an implied narrative about a dead son. To make such a leap would be to substitute a personal narrative for analysis, to arrive at implications that are not sufficiently grounded in the evidence.

Because darkness and dark clothing need not operate as symbols of death, and because the woman's expression is not unquestionably grief-stricken (she looks expressionless to us), a writer might well need more evidence to jump to a narrative about the feelings and situation of the mother (a kind of jump that personal/expressive writing can be quick to make because it typically seeks shared feeling and experience). If, for example, part of a coffin were showing from behind the curtain, or if there were an hourglass somewhere in the painting, a reader might more plausibly conclude that mourning and mortality are governing contexts.

A few rules are worth highlighting here:

1. The range of associations for explaining a given detail or word must be governed by context.
2. It's fine to use your personal reactions as a way to explore what a subject means, but take care not to make an interpretive leap stretch further than the actual details will support.
3. Because the tendency to transfer meanings from your own life onto a subject can lead you to ignore the details of the subject itself, you need always to be asking yourself, "What other explanations might plausibly account for this same pattern of detail?"

THE LIMITS ON INTERPRETATION

Where do meanings come from? The first thing to understand about meanings is that they are *made*, not ready-made in the subject matter. They are the product of a transaction between a mind and the world, between a reader and a text or texts. That is, the making of meaning is a process to which the observer and the thing observed both contribute. It is not a product of either alone.

If meanings aren't ready-made, there to be found in the subject matter, what's to prevent people from making things mean whatever they want them to—say, for example, that *Whistler's Mother* is a painting about death, with the black-clad mother mourning the death of a loved one, perhaps a person who lived in the house represented in the painting on the wall? There are in fact limits on the meaning-making process.

- Meanings must be reasoned from sufficient evidence if they are to be judged plausible. Meanings can always be refuted by people who find fault with your reasoning or can cite conflicting evidence.
- Meanings, to have value outside one's own private realm of experience, have to make sense to other people. The assertion that Whistler's mother is an alien astronaut, for example, her long black dress concealing a third leg, is unlikely to be deemed acceptable by enough people to give it currency. This is to say that the relative value of interpretive meanings is socially (culturally) determined. Although people are free to say that things mean whatever they want them to mean, saying doesn't make it so.

MULTIPLE MEANINGS AND INTERPRETIVE CONTEXTS

In the last section we demonstrated that there are certain limits on interpretation, chiefly that interpretation has to follow the rules of evidence. It is useful and reassuring to know that a person can't just make up meanings and say they are true simply because he or she says so. But it is also necessary to recognize that meanings are multiple. Very few things in life are so simple as to communicate only one thing.

Evidence usually will support more than one plausible interpretation. Consider, for example, a reading of *Whistler's Mother* that a person might produce if he or she began with noticing the actual title, *Arrangement in Grey and Black: The Artist's Mother*. From this starting point, a person might focus observation on the disposition of color exclusively and arrive at an interpretation that *Arrangement* is a painting about painting (which might then explain why there is also a painting on the wall). The figure of the mother then would have meaning only insofar as it contained the two colors mentioned in the painting's title, black and gray, and the painting's representational content (the aspects of life that it shows us) would be ignored. This is a promising and plausible idea for an interpretation. It makes use of different details from previous interpretations we've suggested, but it would also address some of the details already targeted (the dress, the curtain) from an entirely different context, focusing on the use and arrangement of color.

To generalize: two equally plausible interpretations can be made of the same thing. It is not the case that our first reading, focusing on the profile view of the mother and suggesting the painting's concern with mysterious separateness, is right, whereas the aesthetic view, building from the clue in the title, is wrong. They operate within different contexts. An interpretive context is a lens. Depending on the context you choose—preferably a context suggested by the evidence itself—you will see different things.

> An interpretive context is a lens. Depending on the context you choose—preferably a context suggested by the evidence itself—you will see different things.

Regardless of how the context is arrived at, an important part of getting an interpretation accepted as plausible is to *argue for the appropriateness of the interpretive context you use*, not just the interpretation it takes you to.

AUTHOR'S INTENTION AS AN INTERPRETIVE CONTEXT

Let's turn now to an interpretive context that frequently creates problems in analysis: authorial intention. People relying on authorial intention as their interpretive context typically assert that the author—not the work itself—is the ultimate and correct source of interpretations. The work means what its author says it means, and even without his or her explicit interpretation, we are expected to guess at it.

Let's say that an enterprising person discovered that after Whistler did the painting, he wrote a letter to a friend in which he commented upon his intention, saying that because his mother had been needling him about painters never amounting to anything, he had deliberately painted her unflatteringly in somber puritanical tones as an act of revenge.

Armed with such a statement of the artist's intention, an interpretation of the painting as an act of revenge might be considered plausible, but the artist's stated intention would not necessarily require us to give this interpretation privileged status over the others we have suggested. Whatever an author thinks he or she is doing is often a significant part of the meaning of what he or she creates, but it

FIGURE 3.3 *The Dancers* by Sarah Kersh. Pen-and-ink drawing, 6" x 13.75".

does not outrank or exclude other interpretations. It is simply another context for understanding.

Why is this so? In our earlier discussion of personalizing ("Naturalizing Your Own Assumptions" in Chapter 1), we suggested that people are not entirely free agents, immune to the effects of the culture they inhabit. It follows that when people produce writing and works of art, they are inevitably affected by the culture, sometimes in ways they are aware of and sometimes in ways they don't stop to think about.

It is interesting and useful to try to determine from something you are analyzing what its makers might have intended. But, by and large, you are best off concentrating on what the thing itself communicates as opposed to what someone might have wanted it to communicate. As a rule, intention does not finally control the implications that an event, a text, or anything else possesses. (For a fuller discussion of this issue see "Reading with and against the Grain" in Chapter 4, our chapter on reading.)

Look at the drawing titled *The Dancers* above. What follows is the artist's statement about how the drawing came about and what it came to mean to her.

> This piece was created completely unintentionally. I poured some ink onto paper and blew on it through a straw. The ink took the form of what looked like little people in movement. I recopied the figures I liked, touched up the rough edges, and ended with this gathering of fairy-like creatures. I love how in art something abstract can so suddenly become recognizable.

In this case, interestingly, the artist initially had no intentions beyond experimenting with materials. As the work evolved, she began to arrive at her own interpretation of what the drawing might suggest. Most viewers would probably find the artist's interpretation plausible, but this is not to say that the artist must have the last word and that it is somehow an infraction for others to produce alternative interpretations.

But suppose the artist had stopped with her first two sentences. Even this explicit statement of her lack of intention would not prohibit people from interpreting the drawing in some of the ways that the she later goes on to suggest. The artist's initial absence of a plan doesn't require viewers to interpret *The Dancers* as only ink on paper.

Where do meanings come from? In the maker? In the thing itself? Although it is interesting and useful to infer from the material itself what a creator might have been trying to accomplish, the maker's personal intentions don't control meaning.

> *Where do meanings come from? In the maker? In the thing itself?*

THE FORTUNE COOKIE SCHOOL OF INTERPRETATION

The theory of interpretation that we call the Fortune Cookie School believes that things have a single, hidden, "right" meaning, and that if a person can only "crack" the thing, it will yield an extractable and self-contained "message." There are several problems with this conception of the interpretive process.

First, the assumption that things have single hidden meanings interferes with open-minded and dispassionate observation. The thinker looks solely for clues pointing to *the* hidden message and, having found these clues, discards the rest, like the cookie in a Chinese restaurant once the fortune has been extracted. The fortune cookie approach forecloses on the possibility of multiple plausible meanings, each within its own context. When you assume that there is only one right answer, you are also assuming that there is only one proper context for understanding and, by extension, that anybody who happens to select a different starting point or context and who thus arrives at a different answer is necessarily wrong.

Most of the time, practitioners of the fortune cookie approach aren't even aware that they are assuming the correctness of a single context, because they don't realize a fundamental truth about interpretations: they are always limited by contexts. In other words, we are suggesting that claims to universal truths are always problematic. Things don't just mean in some simple and clear way for all people in all situations; they always mean within a network of beliefs, from a particular point of view. The person who claims to have access to some universal truth, beyond context and point of view, is either naïve (unaware) or, worse, a bully—insisting that his or her view of the world is obviously correct and must be accepted by everyone.

> *Things don't just mean in some simple and clear way for all people in all situations; they always mean within a network of beliefs, from a particular point of view.*

THE "ANYTHING GOES" SCHOOL OF INTERPRETATION

At the opposite extreme from the single-right-answer Fortune Cookie School lies the completely relativist Anything Goes School. The problem with the anything goes approach is that it tends to assume that *all* interpretations are equally viable, that meanings are simply a matter of individual choice, irrespective of evidence or plausibility. Put another way, it overextends the creative aspect of interpretation to absurdity, arriving at the position that you can see in a subject whatever you want to see.

As we suggest throughout this book, it is simply not the case that meaning is entirely up to the individual. Some readings are clearly better than others: the aesthetic or separateness readings of *Whistler's Mother* are better than the mourning or, especially, alien astronaut interpretations. The better interpretations have more evidence and rational explanation of how the evidence supports the interpretive claims—qualities that make these meanings more public and negotiable.

In the field of logic there is a principle known as parsimony. This principle holds that "no more forces or causes should be assumed than are necessary to account for the facts" (*The Oxford English Dictionary*). In other words, the explanation that both explains the largest amount of evidence (accounts for facts) and is the simplest (no more than necessary) is the best. There are limits to this rule as well: sometimes focusing on what appears to be an insignificant detail as a starting point can provide a revelatory perspective on a subject. But as rules go, parsimony is a useful one to keep in mind as you start sifting through your various interpretive leaps about a subject.

SEEMS TO BE ABOUT X BUT COULD ALSO BE (IS "REALLY") ABOUT Y

This book's opening chapters have focused your attention on three prerequisites to becoming a more perceptive analytical thinker:

- Training yourself to observe more fully and more systematically—dwelling longer with the data before leaping to generalizations, using Notice and focus (ranking), the Method, looking for anomalies, and reformulating binaries.
- Pushing yourself to make interpretive leaps by describing carefully and then querying your own observations by repeatedly asking, So what?
- Getting beyond common misconceptions about where meanings come from— that meanings are hidden, that they are "read into" something but are really "not there" (reading between the lines), that there are single right answers or that anything goes, that meanings ought to be controlled by a maker's intentions, that some things should not be analyzed because they weren't meant to be, and so forth.

A useful verbal prompt for acting on these principles is Seems to be about *x* but could also be (or is "really") about *y*. Here's why the formula works. Frequently, the nominal (in name only) subject matter—what a book or speech *appears* to be about, what it says it is about—is not what the book or speech *is actually most interested in*. The nominal subject, in other words, is a means to some other end; it creates an opportunity for some less overtly designated matter to be put forward.

Consider the following example:

A recent highly successful television ad campaign for Nike Freestyle shoes contains sixty seconds of famous basketball players dribbling and passing and otherwise handling the ball in dexterous ways to the accompaniment of court noises and hip-hop music. The ad seems to be about x (basketball or shoes) but could also be about y. Once you've made this assertion, a rapid-fire (brainstormed) list might follow in which you keep filling in the blanks (x and y) with different possibilities. Alternatively, you might find that filling in the blanks (x and y) leads to a more sustained exploration of a single point. This is your eventual goal, but doing a little brainstorming first would keep you from shutting down the interpretive process too soon.

Here is one version of a rapid-fire list, any item of which might be expanded:

Seems to be about basketball but is "really" about dance.

Seems to be about selling shoes but is "really" about artistry.

Seems to be about artistry but is "really" about selling shoes.

Seems to be about basketball but is "really" about race.

Seems to be about basketball but is "really" about the greater acceptance of black culture in American media and society.

Seems to be about the greater acceptance of black culture in American media but is "really" about targeting black basketball players as performing seals or freaks.

Seems to be about individual expertise but is "really" about working as a group.

Here is one version of a more sustained exploration of a single seems-to-be-about-x statement.

The Nike Freestyle commercial seems to be about basketball but is really about the greater acceptance of black culture in American media. Of course it is a shoe commercial and so aims to sell a product, but the same could be said about any commercial.

What makes the Nike commercial distinctive is its seeming embrace of African-American culture. The hip-hop sound track, for example, which coincides with the rhythmic dribbling of the basketball, places music and sport on a par, and the dexterity with which the players (actual NBA stars) move with the ball—moonwalking, doing 360s on it, balancing it on their fingers, heads, and backs—is nothing short of dance.

The intrinsic cool of the commercial suggests that Nike is targeting an audience of basketball lovers, not just African-Americans. If I am right, then it is selling blackness to white as well as black audiences. Of course, the idea that blacks are cooler than whites goes back at least as far as the early days of jazz and might be seen as its own strange form of prejudice. . . . In that case, maybe there is something a little disturbing in the commercial, in the way that it relegates the athletes to the status of trained seals. I'll have to think more about this.

Note: Don't be misled by our use of the word *really* in this formula, ("Seems to be about *x*, is really about *y*") into thinking that there should be some single, hidden, right answer. Rather, the aim of the formula is to prompt you to think recursively, to come up, initially, with a range of landing sites for your interpretive leap, rather than just one. The prompt serves to get you beyond the obvious—for example, that the ad appears to be about basketball but is really about selling shoes. Both basketball and shoe sales are the ad's nominal subjects, what it is overtly about. But nominal subjects allow for the expression of other, less immediately obvious ideas and attitudes.

Try this 3.2: Apply the Formula "Seems to Be About *x*, But Could Also Be About *y*"

As we have been saying, this formula is useful for quickly getting past your first responses. An alternative version of this formula is "Initially I thought *x* about the reading, but now I think *y*." Take any reading assignment you have been given for class, and write either formula at the top of a page, fill in the blanks, and then explain the statement in a few paragraphs. You might also try these formulas when you find yourself getting stuck while drafting a paper.

B. EXTENDED EXAMPLE 2: SELECTING AN INTERPRETIVE CONTEXT

This extended example offers in more detail than the previous chapter a writer's decision-making process in choosing an interpretive context and working through the evidence to the conclusions it suggests. A major point of this section is that interpretive contexts are suggested by the material you are studying; they aren't simply imposed. Explaining why you think a subject should be seen through a particular interpretive "lens" is an important part of making interpretations reasonable and plausible. Our discussion will illustrate how, once an interpretive context is selected, a writer goes about analyzing evidence to test as well as support the usefulness of that context.

The example upon which we are focusing is a description of a visual image, a cover from *The New Yorker* magazine. Because we were not able to get permission to reprint the image, you will need to rely on the description, assimilating the details as we list them. Given our emphasis on interpretive context, however, the absence of the actual visual details is not critical. And in any event, producing a close verbal description of anything you are analyzing is one of the best ways to begin.

Description of a *The New Yorker* cover, dated October 9, 2000

The picture contains four women, visible from the waist up, standing in a row in semi-profile, staring out at some audience other than us, since their eyes look off to the side. All four gaze in the same direction. Each woman is dressed in a bathing suit and wears a banner draped over one shoulder in the manner of those worn in the swimsuit competition at beauty pageants. Three of the women are virtually identical. The banners worn by these three women show the letters *gia, rnia,* and *rida,* the remainder of the letters being cut off by the other women's shoulders, so that we have to fill in the missing letters to see which state each woman represents.

The fourth woman, who stands third from the left in line, tucked in among the others who look very much alike, wears a banner reading *york*. This woman's appearance is different in just about every respect from the other three. Whereas they are blonde with long flowing hair, she is dark with her hair up in a tight bun. Whereas their mouths are wide open, revealing a wall of very white teeth, her mouth is closed, lips drawn together. Whereas their eyes are wide open and staring, hers, like her mouth, are nearly closed, under deeply arched eyebrows. The dark woman's lips and eyes and hair are dark. She wears dark eye makeup and has a pronounced dark beauty mark on her cheek. Whereas the other three women's cheeks are high and round, hers are sharply angular. The three blonde women wear one-piece bathing suits in a nondescript gray color. The dark-haired woman, whose skin stands out in stark contrast to her hair, wears a two-piece bathing suit, exposing her midriff. Like her face, the dark-haired woman's breast, sticking out in half profile in her bathing suit, is pointed and angular. The other three women's breasts are round and quietly contained in their high-necked gray bathing suits.

LOOKING FOR PATTERNS OF REPETITION AND CONTRAST: AN EXAMPLE

As we discussed in Chapter 2, looking for repetition is your best means of getting at the essential character of a subject. It will prevent you from generalizing, instead involving you in hands-on engagement with the details of your evidence. Our formula for looking for patterns, the Method, has five steps, which you should try to do one at a time so as not to rush to conclusions. You will find, however, that step 1, looking for things that repeat exactly, tends to suggest items for step 2, repetition of the same or similar kinds of words or details (strands), and that step 2 leads naturally to step 3, looking for binary oppositions and organizing contrasts. And so, in practice, noticing and listing the elements of strands tend to coincide with the discovery of binary oppositions.

Here are our partial lists of exact repetitions and strands and binary oppositions in *The New Yorker* cover:

Some Details that Repeat Exactly

Large, wide open, round eyes (3 pairs)

Long, blonde, face-framing hair (3)

Small, straight eyebrows (3 pairs)

Wide-open (smiling?) mouths with expanses of white teeth (3)

(but individual teeth not indicated)

banners (4) but each with different lettering

round breasts (3)

states that end in a (3)

Some Strands (groups of the same or similar kinds of details)

Lots of loose and flowing blonde hair/large, fully open, round eyes/large, open, rather round (curved) mouths:

Connecting logic = open, round

Skin uniformly shaded on three of the figures/minimal color and shading contrasts/mouths full of teeth but just a mass of white without individual teeth showing:

Connecting logic = homogenous, undifferentiated, indistinct

Binary Oppositions

Blonde hair/black hair

Open mouths/closed mouth

Straight eyebrows/slanted (arched) eyebrows

Round breasts/pointed breast

Covered midriff/uncovered midriff

Notice that we have tried hard to stick with "the facts" here—concrete details in the picture. If we were to try, for example, to name the expression on the three blonde women's faces and the one on the black-haired woman (expressionless versus knowing? vapid versus shrewd? trusting versus suspicious? and so on), we would move from data gathering—direct observation of detail—into interpretation. The longer you delay interpretation in favor of noticing patterns of like and unlike detail, the more thoughtful and better grounded your eventual interpretation will be.

PUSHING OBSERVATIONS TO CONCLUSIONS: SELECTING AN INTERPRETIVE CONTEXT

As we argued in the first extended example of this chapter, the move from observations to conclusions depends on context. You would, for example, come up with different ideas about the significance of particular patterns of detail in *The New Yorker* cover if you were analyzing them in the context of the history of *The New Yorker* cover art than you might if your interpretive context was other art done by the cover's artist. Both of these possibilities suggest themselves, the first by the fact that the title of the magazine, *The New Yorker*, stands above the women's heads, and the second by the fact that the artist's name, Falconer, runs across two of the women.

What other interpretive contexts might one plausibly and fairly choose, based on what the cover itself offers us? Consider the cover's date, for example—October 9, 2000. Some quick research into what was going on in the country in the early fall of 2000 might provide some clues about how to read the cover in a *historical context*. November 2000 was the month of a presidential election. At the time the cover was published, the long round of presidential primaries, with presidential hopefuls courting various key states for their votes, had ended, but the last month of campaigning by the presidential nominees—Al Gore and George W. Bush—was in full swing.

You might wish to consider whether and how the cover speaks to the country's political climate during the Gore/Bush competition for the presidency. The banners and the bathing suits and the fact that the women stand in a line staring out at some implied audience of viewers, perhaps judges, reminds us that the picture's narrative context is a beauty pageant, a competition in which women representing each of the states compete to be chosen the most beautiful of them all. Choosing to consider the cover in the context of the presidential campaign would be reasonable; you would not have to think you were imposing a context on the picture in an arbitrary and ungrounded way.

Clearly there is other information on the cover that might allow you to interpret the picture in some kind of political and or more broadly cultural context. A significant binary opposition is New York versus Georgia, California, and Florida. The three states having names ending in the same letter are represented by look-alike, virtually identical blondes. The anomalous state, New York, is represented by a woman, who, despite standing in line with the others, is about as different from them as a figure could be. *So what* that the woman representing New York looks so unlike the women from the other states? And why those states?

If you continued to pursue this interpretive context, you might want more information. Which presidential candidate won the primary in each of the states pictured? How were each of these states expected to vote in the election in November? When is the Miss America pageant held? Which state won the Miss America title in the time period before the cover was published? Since timing would matter in the case of a topical interpretive context, it would also be interesting to know when the cover art was actually produced and when the magazine accepted it. If possible, you could also try to discover whether other of the cover artist's work was in a similar vein.

MAKING AN INTERPRETATION PLAUSIBLE

As we have been arguing, the picture will "mean" differently, depending on whether we understand it in terms of American presidential politics in the year 2000, or in terms of American identity politics at the same point, specifically attitudes of and about New Yorkers, and *The New Yorker* magazine's place among these attitudes—and influence on them. As we have already observed, analytical thinking involves interpretation, and interpretive conclusions are tentative and open to alternative possibilities. An interpretive conclusion is not a fact, but a theory. Interpretive conclusions stand or fall not so much on whether they can be proved right or wrong (or some combination of the two), but on whether they are demonstrably plausible.

An interpretive conclusion is not a fact, but a theory.

What makes an interpretation plausible? We might choose not to accept your interpretation for a number of reasons. We might, for example, be New Yorkers and, further, inclined to think that New Yorkers are cool and that this is what the picture "says." You might be from one of the states depicted on the cover in terms of look-alike blondes and, further, inclined to think that New Yorkers are full of themselves and forever portraying the rest of the country as shallowly conformist and uncultured.

But none of these personal influences ultimately matters. What matters is that you share your data, show your reasons for believing that it means what you say it means, and do this well enough for a reader to find your interpretation reasonable (whether he or she actually believes it or not). Then you will have passed the plausibility test. Your interpretation will stand until another person offers an analysis with interpretive conclusions that seems more plausible than yours, pointing to more or better evidence, and arguing for the meaning of that evidence more convincingly.

ARRIVING AT AN INTERPRETIVE CONCLUSION: MAKING CHOICES

Let's try on one final interpretive context, and then see which of the various contexts (lenses) through which we have viewed the cover produces the most credible interpretation, the one that seems to best account for the patterns of detail in the evidence. Different interpretations will account better for some details than others—which is why it enriches our view of the world to try on different interpretations. Ultimately, you will have to decide which possible interpretation, as seen through which plausible interpretive context, best accounts for what you think is most important and interesting to notice about your subject.

We will try to push our own interpretive process to a choice by selecting one interpretive context as the most revealing: *The New Yorker* magazine itself. The dark-haired figure wearing the New York banner is, in a sense, the magazine or, at least, a potential reader—a representative New Yorker. What, then, does the cover "say" to and about New Yorkers and to and about the magazine and its readers?

Throughout this book we use the question "So what?" to prompt interpretive leaps. *So what* that the woman representing New York is dark when the other women are light, is closed (narrowed eyes, closed mouth, hair tightly pulled up and back) when the others are open (wide-open eyes and mouths, loosely flowing hair), is pointed and angular when the others are round, sports a bared midriff when the others are covered?

As with our earlier attempt to interpret the cover in the context of the 2000 presidential campaign, interpreting it in the context of other *The New Yorker* covers would require a little research. How do *The New Yorker* covers characteristically represent New Yorkers? What might you discover by looking for patterns of repetition and contrast in a set of *The New Yorker* covers rather than just this one?

We are willing to bet that you would soon discover the magazine's droll awareness of its own heralding of New Yorkers as sophisticated, cultured, and cosmopolitan: it at once embraces and sends up the stereotype. How does the cover read in the context, for example, of various jokes about how New Yorkers think of themselves relative to the rest of the country, such as the cover depicting the United States as two large coastlines, east and west, connected by an almost nonexistent middle?

Armed with the knowledge that the covers are not only characteristically laughing at the rest of the country but also at New Yorkers themselves, you might begin to *make explicit what is implicit* in the cover (one of the analytical moves listed in Chapter 2).

Here are some attempts at making the cover speak. Does the cover "say" that New Yorkers are shrewder, less naïve (less open), warier than other Americans, but largely because they are also more worldly and smarter? Is the cover in some way a "dumb blonde" joke in which the dark woman with the pronounced beauty mark and calculating gaze participates but also sets herself apart from some kind of national "beauty" contest? Are we being invited (intentionally or not) to invert the conventional value hierarchy of dark and light so that the dark woman—the sort that gets represented as the evil stepmother in fairy tales such as "Snow White"—becomes "the fairest of them all," and nobody's fool?

Let's end this sample analysis and interpretation with two possibilities—somewhat opposed to each other, but probably both "true" of what the cover communicates, at least to certain audiences (East and West Coast Americans, and readers of *The New Yorker*). At its most serious, *The New Yorker* cover may speak to American history in which New York has been the point of entry for generations of immigrants, the "dark" (literally and figuratively) in the face of America's blonde northern European legacy.

Within the context of other *The New Yorker* covers, however, we might find ourselves gravitating to a less serious and perhaps equally plausible interpretive conclusion: that the cover is a complex joke. It appears to be saying, yes, America, we do think that we're cooler and more individual and less plastic than the rest of you, but we also know that we shouldn't be so smug about it.

C. EXTENDED EXAMPLE 3: ANALYZING AN ARGUMENT BY REFORMULATING BINARIES AND UNCOVERING ASSUMPTIONS

Our most direct advice on analyzing arguments and thus on learning to write them more effectively can be found in this section. Here you will see how to unearth the essentially binary structure of arguments and how to uncover the unstated assumptions upon which arguments typically rest. The technique of locating, assessing the accuracy of, and recasting binaries is a very effective way of meeting other people's arguments—and revising your own. Arguing with someone else's argument is usually as much a matter of addressing what is left unsaid—the assumptions "underneath" the argument that the arguer takes to be "givens" (obvious truths)—as confronting what gets argued overtly.

THINKING WITH AND ABOUT BINARIES

In human—and computerized—thinking, a binary is a pair of elements, usually in opposition to each other, as in off/on, yes/no, right/wrong, agree/disagree, and so on. Many ideas begin with a writer's noticing some kind of opposition or tension or choice within a subject—capital punishment either does or does not deter crime; a character in a novel is either a courageous rebel or a fool; a new environmental policy is either visionary or blind. A major advantage of looking for and using binaries is that they help you determine what issues are at stake in your subject, because binaries position you among competing choices.

There is an old joke to the effect that there are two kinds of people: those who like binary thinking and those who do not. Part of the humor here seems to lie in the recognition that we cannot help but think in binary terms. As the philosopher Herbert Marcuse says, "We understand that which is in terms of that which is not": light is that which is not dark; masculine is that which is not feminine; civilized is that which is not primitive. Creating opposing categories is fundamental to defining things. But as these examples may suggest, binaries are also dangerous because they can perpetuate what is called reductive thinking, especially if applied uncritically.

If you restrict yourself to thinking in binary terms, you can run into two problems. First, most subjects cannot be adequately considered in terms of only two options—either this or that, with nothing in between. Second, binaries often conceal value judgments: the category "primitive," as opposed to "civilized," is not a neutral description but a devaluation. In sum, it is useful and necessary to construct binaries, but it is dangerous to ignore the gray areas in between and the value judgments that binaries tend to conceal.

> *It is dangerous to ignore the gray areas in between and the value judgments that binaries tend to conceal.*

Often the trouble starts with the ways binaries are phrased. Two of the most common and potentially counterproductive ways of phrasing binaries are *either/or* and *agree/disagree*. In the vast majority of cases, there are more than two alternatives, but the either/or or agree/disagree phrasing prevents you from looking for them. And it does not acknowledge that both alternatives may have some truth to them. A new environmental policy may be both visionary and blind. And there may be more accurate categories than visionary and blind for considering the merits and demerits of the policy.

Framing an issue in either/or terms can be useful for stimulating a chain of thought, but it is usually not a good way to end one. Consider the either/or binary, "Was the Civil War fought over slavery or economics?" You could begin this way, but if you're not careful—conscious of the all-or-nothing force of binary formulations—you could easily get trapped in an overly dichotomized position; in this case, that economics caused the war and that slavery had nothing to do with it, or vice versa.

You can't analyze without binaries, but you need to be wary of putting everything into big, undifferentiated categories, labeled all black or all white, with nothing in between.

A Procedure for Using Binaries Analytically

Strategy 1: Locate a Range of Opposing Categories

The first step in using binaries analytically is to locate and distinguish them carefully. Consider, for example, the binaries contained in the following question: Does the model of management known as Total Quality Management (TQM) that is widely used in Japan work in the American automotive industry? The most obvious binary in this question is work versus not work. But there are also other binaries in the question—Japanese versus American, for example, and TQM versus more traditional and more traditionally American models of management. These binaries imply further binaries. Insofar as TQM is acknowledged to be a team-oriented, collaborative management model, the question requires a writer to consider the accuracy and relative suitability of particular traits commonly ascribed to Japanese versus American workers, such as communal and cooperative versus individualistic and competitive.

Strategy 2: Analyze and Define the Key Terms

Having located the various binaries, you should begin to analyze and define terms. What, for example, does it mean to ask whether TQM *works* in the American automotive industry? Does work mean "make a substantial profit"? Does work mean "produce more cars more quickly"? Does work mean "improving employee morale"? You would probably find yourself drowning in vagueness unless you carefully argued for the appropriateness of your definition of this key term.

Strategy 3: Question the Accuracy of the Binary

Having begun to analyze and define your terms, you would next need to determine how accurately they define the issues raised by your subject. You might consider, for example, the extent to which American management styles actually differ from the Japanese version of TQM. In the process of trying to determine if there are significant differences, you could start to locate particular traits in these management styles and in Japanese versus American culture that might help you formulate your binary more precisely. Think of the binary as a starting point—a kind of deliberate overgeneralization—that allows you to set up positions you can then test in order to refine.

Strategy 4: Substitute "To What Extent?" for "Either/Or"

The best strategy in using binaries productively is usually to locate arguments on both sides of the either/or choice that the binary poses and then choose a position somewhere between the two extremes. Once you have arrived at what you consider the most accurate phrasing of the binary, you can rephrase the original either/or question in the more qualified terms that asking "To what extent?" allows. Making this move does not release you from the responsibility of taking a stand and arguing for it.

So, in answer to a question such as "Was the Civil War fought over slavery or economics?" you would attempt to determine *the extent to which* each side of the binary—slavery and economics—could reasonably be credited as the cause of the war. To do so, you would first rephrase the question thus: To what extent did economics, rather than slavery, cause the Civil War? Rephrasing in this way might also enable you to see problems with the original binary formulation.

By analyzing the terms of the binary, you would come to question them and ultimately arrive at a more complex and qualified position to write about. Admittedly, in reorienting your thinking from the obvious and clear-cut choices that either/or formulations provide to the murkier waters of asking "To what extent?" your decision process will be made more difficult. The gain, however, is that the to-what-extent mind-set, by predisposing you to assess multiple and potentially conflicting points of view, will enable you to address more fairly and accurately the issues raised by your subject.

Applying these steps will usually cause you to do one or more of the following:

1. Discover that you have not adequately named the binary and that another opposition would be more accurate.
2. Weight one side of your binary more heavily than the other, rather than seeing the issue as all or nothing.
3. Discover that the two terms of your binary are not really so separate and opposed after all but are actually parts of one complex phenomenon or issue (collapsing the binary).

Where might you end up if you approached our earlier sample topic (whether or not TQM works in the American automotive industry) by asking *to what extent* one side of the binary better suits available evidence, rather than arguing that one side is clearly the right choice and the other entirely wrong? You would still be arguing that one position on TQM in American industry is more accurate than the other, but you would inevitably arrive at more carefully qualified conclusions than the question might otherwise have led you to. You would most likely take care, for example, to suggest the danger of assuming that all American workers are rugged individualists and all Japanese workers are communal bees.

Try this 3.3: Applying the Strategies for Using Binaries Analytically

Apply the strategies to analyze the assumptions and issues in the statements below, doing with them what we did in our TQM example. This does not mean you must proceed step-by-step through the strategies, but at the least, for each thesis statement or question you should do the following:

• List all the binaries you can find, both implicit and explicit, in each example.
• Isolate the one or two key terms that reveal what is at issue for each writer, and determine what they mean. You should write out the implied definitions.

In number 2, for example, the key binary appears to be "first-world" versus "third-world," but even more important for defining the writer's thinking is arguably what he or she means by "good."

- Even if the original formulation looks okay to you, assume that it is an overgeneralization that needs to be refined and rephrased. On the basis of your list of oppositions and definitions of key terms, rewrite each statement in a more qualified and more accurate form.

In proposing your revised statements, you might try substituting "to what extent" for "either/or" (which will press you to limit the claims that binary formulations are prone to overstate).

1. It is important to understand why leaders act in a leadership role. What is the driving force? Is it an internal drive for the business or group to succeed, or is it an internal drive for the leader to dominate over others?
2. Is nationalism good for emerging third-world countries?
3. The private lives of public figures should not matter in the way they are assessed by the public. What matters is how competently they do their jobs.
4. The Seattle sound of rock 'n' roll known as grunge is not original; it's just a rehash of punk and New Wave elements.

► Try this 3.4: Writing an Analysis from Organizing Contrasts

Locate some organizing contrasts in anything—something you are studying, something you've just written, something you saw on television last night, something on the front page of the newspaper, something going on at your campus or workplace, and so forth. As we've said, binaries are pervasive in the way we think; therefore, you can expect to find them everywhere. Consider, for example, the binaries suggested by current trends in contemporary music or by the representation of women in birthday cards. Having selected the binaries you want to work with, pick one and try out the four steps we suggest for working with binaries.

UNCOVERING ASSUMPTIONS (REASONING BACK TO PREMISES)

All arguments ultimately rest on fundamental assumptions called givens—positions not in need of argument because you assume the reader will "give" them to you as true. Often, however, these assumptions need first to be acknowledged and then argued, or at least tested. You cannot assume that their truth is self-evident. The failure to locate and examine unacknowledged assumptions (premises) is the downfall of many essays. The problem occurs because our categories—the mental boxes we've created over time—have become so fixed, so unquestioned, that we cease to be fully aware of them.

Everything you read has basic assumptions that underlie it. What are assumptions in this context? They are the basic ground of beliefs from which a position springs, its starting points or givens, its basic operating premises. *The Oxford*

English Dictionary defines a premise—from a Latin word meaning "to put before"—as "a previous statement or proposition from which another statement is inferred or follows as a conclusion."

All arguments or articulations of point of view have premises—that is, they are based in a given set of assumptions, which are built upon to arrive at conclusions. A lot of the time, though, the assumptions are not visible; they're implicit (which is why they need to be inferred). They're usually not actively concealed by writers—writers hiding from readers the subterranean bases of their outlooks—which might be considered unethical. Rather, many writers (especially inexperienced ones) remain unaware of the premises that underlie their points of view—probably because they were never taught to be aware of them. Similarly, most readers don't know that they should search out the starting points of what they read, so of course they also don't know how.

Most readers tend to credit what they read as true, or at least relatively neutral, especially if it's in a book. In other words, most people aren't aware that everything they read (and write) comes from given sets of assumptions. It follows that the ability to uncover assumptions is a powerful analytical procedure to learn—it gives you insight into the roots, the basic givens that a piece of writing (or a speaker) has assumed are true.

When you locate assumptions in a text, you understand the text better—where it's coming from and what else it believes that is more fundamental than what it is overtly declaring. You also find things to write about; uncovering assumptions offers one of the best ways of developing and revising your own work. Uncovering assumptions can help you understand why you believe *x*, or may reveal to you that two of your givens are in conflict with each other.

To uncover assumptions, you need to read "backward"—to ask what a reading must also already believe, given that it believes what it overtly claims. In other words, you need to imagine or reinvent the process of thinking by which a writer has arrived at a position.

> *To uncover assumptions, you need to read "backward"—to ask what a reading must also already believe, given that it believes what it overtly claims.*

Say you read a piece that praises a television show for being realistic but faults it for setting a bad example for the kids who watch it. What assumptions might we infer from such a piece?

- Television should attempt to depict life accurately (realistically).
- Television should produce shows that set good examples.
- Kids imitate or at least have their attitudes shaped by what they watch on television.
- Good and bad examples are clear and easily recognizable by everyone.

Note that none of these assumptions is self-evidently true—each would need to be argued for. And some of the assumptions conflict with others—for example, that shows should be both morally uplifting and realistic, given that in "real life" those who do wrong often go unpunished. These are subjects an analytical response to the piece (or a revision of it) could bring out.

Try this 3.5: Uncover Assumptions in Statements

You can practice uncovering assumptions with all kinds of material—newspaper editorials, statements you see on billboards, ideas you are studying in your courses, jokes, and so forth. You could try the kind of fieldwork assignment that we recommend in Chapter 1. Spend a week jotting down in your notebook interesting statements you overhear. Choose the most interesting of these from the standpoint of the implied (but unstated) premises upon which each statement seems to rest. Make a list of the uncovered assumptions.

Uncovering Assumptions (Reasoning Back to Premises): A Brief Example Consider the assertion "Tax laws benefit the wealthy." No matter how you might develop this claim (moving it forward), you would get into trouble if you didn't also move backward to uncover the premises embedded in this thesis about the purpose of tax laws. The wording of this claim seems to conceal an egalitarian premise: the assumption that tax laws should not benefit anyone, or, at least, that they should benefit everyone equally. But what is the purpose of tax laws? Should they redress economic inequities? Should they spur the economy by rewarding those who generate capital? You might go to the U.S. Constitution and/or legal precedents to resolve such questions, but our point here is that you would need to move your thesis back to this point and test the validity of the assumptions upon which it rests.

Regardless of the position you might adopt—attacking tax laws, defending them, showing how they actually benefit everyone, or whatever—you would risk arguing blindly if you failed to question what the purpose of tax law is in the first place. This testing of assumptions would, at the least, cause you to qualify and refine your thesis.

A Step-by-Step Procedure for Uncovering Assumptions How do you actually go about uncovering assumptions? Here's a fairly flexible procedure, which we will apply step-by-step to the claim "Tax laws benefit the wealthy."

1. **Paraphrase the explicit claim.** This activity will get you started interpreting the claim, and it may begin to suggest the claim's underlying assumptions. We might paraphrase the claim as "The rules for paying income tax give rich people monetary advantages" or "The rules for paying income tax help the rich get richer."

2. **List the implicit ideas that the claim seems to assume to be true.** Here are two: "Tax laws shouldn't benefit anybody" and "Tax laws should benefit those who need the benefit, those with the least money."

3. **Determine the various ways that the key terms of the claim might be defined, as well as how the writer of the claim has defined them.** This process of definition will help you see the key concepts upon which

the claim depends. How does the writer intend "benefit"? Does he or she mean that tax laws benefit only the wealthy and presumably harm those who are not wealthy? Where does the line between wealthy and not wealthy get drawn?

4. **Try on an oppositional stance to the claim to see if this unearths more underlying assumptions.** Regardless of your view on the subject, suppose for the sake of argument that the writer is wrong. This step allows you to think comparatively, helping you to see the claim more clearly, to see what it apparently *excludes* from its fundamental beliefs.

Knowing what the underlying assumption leaves out helps us see the narrowness upon which the claim may rest; we understand better its limits. Two positions that the claim appears to exclude are "Tax laws benefit the poor" and "Tax laws do not benefit the wealthy."

A Sample Essay: Analyzing an Argument by Reasoning Back to Premises
Because the following essay originally appeared (in 1993) as a newspaper editorial (in *The New York Times*), it is less expository (explanatory) than much academic analytical writing. We have included it because it so clearly illustrates how a writer reasons forward to conclusions by reasoning backward to premises. The essay also illustrates how the strategies of refocusing binaries and qualifying claims operate in a finished piece of writing. As we noted above, these strategies, which are so useful for recognizing and fixing problems in writing, are equally useful for producing ideas.

As you read this editorial on the controversial rules established at Antioch College to govern sexual conduct among its students, try to focus not only on the content of the argument, but also on its form; that is, how the writer moves from one phase of his thinking to the next. Toward this end, we have added our own summaries of what each paragraph of the editorial accomplishes. At the end of the editorial we sum up the writer's primary developmental strategies in a form you can apply to your own writing.

"Playing by the Antioch Rules"
by Eric Fassin

[1] A good consensus is hard to find, especially on sexual politics. But the infamous rules instituted last year by Antioch College, which require students to obtain explicit verbal consent before so much as a kiss is exchanged, have created just that. They have provoked indignation (this is a serious threat to individual freedom!) as well as ridicule (can this be serious?). Sexual correctness thus proves a worthy successor to political correctness as a target of public debate. [The writer names the issue: the complaint that Antioch's rules threaten individual freedom.]

[2] Yet this consensus against the rules reveals shared assumptions among liberals, conservatives and even radicals about the nature of sex in our culture. [The writer identifies members of an unlikely consensus and focuses on a surprising similarity.]

[3] The new definition of consent at Antioch is based on a "liberal" premise: it assumes that sexual partners are free agents and that they mean what they say—yes means yes, and no means no. But the initiator must now obtain prior consent, step by step, which in practice shifts the burden of clarification from the woman to the man. The question is no longer "Did she say no?" but "Did she say yes?" Silence does not indicate consent, and it becomes his responsibility to dispel any ambiguity. [The writer identifies assumption of freedom underlying the rules.]

[4] The novelty of the rules, however, is not as great as it seems. Antioch will not exert more control over its students; there are no sexual police. In practice, you still do what you want—as long as your partner does not complain . . . the morning after. If this is censorship, it intervenes *ex post facto*, not *a priori*. [The writer questions the premise that rules will actually control individual freedom more than current norms do.]

[5] In fact, the "threat" to individual freedom for most critics is not the invasion of privacy through the imposition of sexual codes, but the very existence of rules. Hence the success of polemicists like Katie Roiphe or Camille Paglia, who argue that feminism in recent years has betrayed its origins by embracing old-style regulations, paradoxically choosing the rigid 1950s over the liberating 1960s. Their advice is simply to let women manage on their own, and individuals devise their own rules. This individualist critique of feminism finds resonance with liberals, but also, strangely, with conservatives, who belatedly discover the perils of regulating sexuality. [The writer locates an antiregulatory (laissez-faire) premise beneath the freedom premise.]

[6] But sexual laissez-faire, with its own implicit set of rules, does not seem to have worked very well recently. Since the collapse of established social codes, people play the same game with different rules. If more women are complaining of sexual violence, while more men are worrying that their words and actions might be misconstrued, who benefits from the absence of regulation? [The writer attacks the laissez-faire premise for ineffectiveness.]

[7] A laissez-faire philosophy toward relationships assumes that sexuality is a game that can (and must) be played without rules, or rather that the invention of rules should be left to individual spontaneity and creativity, despite rising evidence that the rule of one's own often leads to misunderstandings. When acted out, individual fantasy always plays within preordained social rules. These rules conflict with the assumption in this culture that sex is subject to the reign of nature, not artifice, that it is the province of the individual, not of society. [The writer uncovers an assumption beneath the laissez-faire premise: sex is natural and thus outside social rules.]

[8] Those who believe that society's constraints should have nothing to do with sex also agree that sex should not be bound by the social conventions of language. Indeed, this rebellion against the idea of social constraints probably accounts for the controversy over explicit verbal consent—from George Will, deriding "sex amidst semicolons," to Camille Paglia railing, "As if sex occurs in the verbal realm." As if sexuality were incompatible with words. As if the only language of sex were silence. For *The New Yorker*, "the [Antioch] rules don't get rid of the problem of unwanted sex at all; they just shift the advantage from the muscle-bound frat boy to the honey-tongued French major." [The writer develops the linguistic implications of the natural premise and questions the assumption that sex is incompatible with language.]

[9] This is not very different from the radical feminist position, which holds that verbal persuasion is no better than physical coercion. In this view, sexuality cannot be entrusted to rhetoric. The seduction of words is inherently violent, and seduction itself is an object of suspicion. (If this is true, Marvell's invitation "To His Coy Mistress" is indeed a form of sexual harassment, as some campus feminists have claimed.) [The writer develops a further implication: that the attack on rules masks a fear of language's power to seduce—and questions the equation of seduction with harassment.]

[10] What the consensus against the Antioch rules betrays is a common vision of sexuality which crosses the lines dividing conservatives, liberals and radicals. So many of the arguments start from a conventional situation, perceived and presented as natural: a heterosexual encounter with the man as the initiator, and the woman as gatekeeper—hence the focus on consent. [The writer redefines consensus as sharing the unacknowledged premise that conventional sex roles are natural.]

[11] The outcry largely results from the fact that the rules undermine this traditional erotic model. Not so much by proscribing (legally), but by prescribing (socially). The new model, in which language becomes a normal form of erotic communication, underlines the conventional nature of the old one. [The writer reformulates the claim about the antirules consensus: rules undermine attempts to pass off traditional sex roles as natural.]

[12] By encouraging women out of their "natural" reserve, these rules point to a new definition of sexual roles. "Yes" could be more than a way to make explicit the absence of "no"; "yes" can also be a cry of desire. Women may express demands, and not only grant favors. If the legal "yes" opened the ground for an erotic "yes," if the contract gave way to desire and if consent led to demand, we would indeed enter a brave new erotic world. [The writer extends the implication of the claim: rules could make sex more erotic rather than less free.]

[13] New rules are like new shoes: they hurt a little at first, but they may fit tomorrow. The only question about the Antioch rules is not really whether we like them, but whether they improve the situation between men and women. All rules are artificial, but, in the absence of generally agreed-upon social conventions, any new prescription must feel artificial. And isn't regulation needed precisely when there is an absence of cultural consensus? [The writer questions the standard by which we evaluate rules; the writer proposes reformulating the binary from artificial versus natural to whether or not rules will improve gender relations.]

[14] Whether we support or oppose the Antioch rules, at least they force us to acknowledge that the choice is not between regulation and freedom, but between different sets of rules, implicit or explicit. They help dispel the illusion that sexuality is a state of nature individuals must experience outside the social contract, and that eroticism cannot exist within the conventions of language. As Antioch reminds us, there is more in eroticism and sexuality than is dreamt of in this culture. [The writer culminates with his own idea: rules are good because they force us to acknowledge as a harmful illusion the idea that sex operates outside social conventions.]

Despite its brevity, this editorial covers a daunting amount of ground—an examination of "shared assumptions among liberals, conservatives and even radicals about the nature of sex in our culture" (paragraph 2). The writer, given his audience (readers of the Sunday *New York Times*), allows himself more breadth in both his topic and his claims than he would if he were writing an article on the same subject in an academic setting, where he would narrow his focus to supply more analysis of issues and evidence. The aim of editorials like this one is not only to inform or persuade but also to provoke and entertain. Nevertheless, the strategies that direct the thinking in this piece are, with some minor exceptions, the same as they would be in a more extended analytical piece. They are central strategies that you can apply to many sorts of writing situations, such as analyzing arguments and as a means of finding and developing your own ideas.

Strategies for Writing an Argument by Reasoning Back to Premises   The strategies that direct the thinking in this editorial offer a model for uncovering assumptions in the service of arriving at ideas. If you examine what the writer has done—not just what he has said—you might arrive at the following primary moves, which can be phrased as general guidelines.

1. **Paraphrase the explicit claims; search out the meanings of key terms.** The writer does not begin by offering his own conclusion on whether the views he has thus far described are right or wrong. Instead, he slows down the forward momentum toward judgment and begins to analyze what the consensus against the Antioch rules might mean (liberals,

conservatives, and radicals) with respect to the nature of sex in our culture." In fact, the author spends the first three-quarters of the essay trying on various answers to this question of meaning.

Note: A careful reader would recognize by tonal signals such as the exclamation point after "serious threat to individual freedom!" that the opening paragraph has, in fact, begun to announce its position, albeit not overtly, by subtly overstating its opposite. It is not until later in the editorial, however, that we can clearly recognize that the writer is employing a common introductory strategy—defining the position you plan to argue against.

2. **Uncover assumptions to decide what is really at issue.** Rather than proceeding directly to a judgment on whether or not the rules threaten individual freedom, the writer carefully searches out the assumptions— the premises and the givens—underlying the attacks on the rules. He proposes, for example, that underneath the attack by the consensus on the rules and its defense of individual freedom lies a basic assumption about sex and society, that sexuality should not be governed by rules because it is natural rather than cultural: "These rules conflict with the assumption in this culture that sex is subject to the reign of nature, not artifice, that it is the province of the individual, not of society" (paragraph 7).

3. **Attend to organizing contrasts, but be alert to the possibility that they may be false dichotomies, and reformulate them as necessary.** A false dichotomy (sometimes called a false binary) inaccurately divides possible views on a subject into two opposing camps, forcing a choice between black and white when some shade of gray might be fairer and more accurate. It is always a good strategy to question any either/or dichotomy. Consider the extent to which its opposing terms define the issue fairly and accurately before accepting an argument in favor of one side or the other.

   Consider, too, how you might reject *both* choices offered by an either/or opposition to construct an alternative approach that is truer to the issues at hand. This is what the author of the editorial does. He outlines and then rejects as a false dichotomy the assumption he has uncovered that is held by the consensus view—that sexual behavior is either a province of individual freedom or is regulated by society:

   False Dichotomies
   freedom versus regulation
   natural versus artificial
   no rules versus rules

   Reasoning back to premises and reformulating binaries has led the writer to his primary idea. He argues that much of what we perceive to be natural, such as the notion of men as sexual initiators and women as nay-sayers and gatekeepers, is in fact governed by social rules and conventions. He proposes that what is really at stake—the root assumption shared by the anti-rules consensus—is a different dichotomy, a choice between two sets of rules, one implicit and one explicit. If you look for patterns of repetition and contrast in the editorial (see Chapter 2), new organizing contrasts emerge:

> **Reformulated Dichotomies**
> rules versus rules
> implicit versus explicit
> not working versus might work
> based on "no" versus based on "yes"

The editorial concludes that we need to decide questions of sexual behavior—at Antioch and in the culture at large—by recognizing and evaluating the relative merits of the two sets of rules rather than by creating a false dichotomy between rules and no rules, between regulation and freedom: "The choice is not between regulation and freedom, but between different sets of rules" (paragraph 14).

4. **When you write your analysis of the reading, rehearse for your readers the thinking process by which you have uncovered the assumptions—not just the conclusions to which the process has led you.** Notice that virtually the entire editorial has consisted of uncovering assumptions as a way of arriving at new ways of thinking.

Try this 3.6: Uncovering Assumptions in an Argument

In the paragraph below the writer has made her premises quite clear but has not acknowledged the possible validity of competing premises. (It is this same neglect of other possible positions that Fassin makes the substance of his editorial against the detractors of the Antioch Rules—use him as a model). If she could become more self-conscious of reasoning back to premises, she would be more likely to discover these competing claims and either qualify her argument or overtly counter these competing claims.

Field hockey is a sport that can be played by either men or women. All sports should be made available for members of both sexes. As long as women are allowed to participate on male teams in sports such as football and wrestling, men should be allowed to participate on female teams in sports such as field hockey and lacrosse. If females press for and receive equal opportunity in all sports, then it is only fair that men be given the same opportunities. If women object to this type of equal opportunity, then they are promoting reverse discrimination.

First, examine the paragraph and lay out her premises in your own words. That is, find at least two key assumptions that she wishes us to accept. Hint: The writer assumes, for example, that fairness ought to take precedence over other possible values in the selection of athletic teams. More generally, think about how she is defining other key terms she uses.

Then lay out at least two competing premises—the basis upon which a counterargument might be built.

◀ ASSIGNMENT: Analyzing an Editorial or Other Argument by Locating Binaries and Reasoning Back to Premises

Locate the binaries in an editorial or other position piece and explain the extent to which these are adequate and/or inadequate ways of defining the subject. You might want to try the formula "This article/argument/point of view/work appears to be about *x*, but could also be (or is really) about *y*." This formula will impel you to reason back to premises, redefine key terms, and reformulate binaries.

Alternatively, you might write a paper in which you reason back to the premises that underlie some idea or attitude of your own, preferably one that has undergone some kind of change in recent years (for example, your attitude toward the world of work, toward marriage, toward family life, toward community, toward religion, and so on). ▶

◀ ASSIGNMENT: Analyzing a Portrait from Description to Interpretation

Locate any portrait, preferably a good reproduction from an art book or magazine, one that shows detail clearly. Then do a version of what we've done with Whistler in Figure 3.2.

Your goal is to produce an analysis of the portrait with the steps we included in analyzing *Whistler's Mother*. First, summarize the portrait, describing accurately its significant details. Do not go beyond a recounting of what the portrait includes; avoid interpreting what these details suggest.

Then use the various methods offered in this chapter to analyze the data. What repetitions (patterns of same or similar detail) do you see? What organizing contrasts suggest themselves? In light of these patterns of similarity and difference, what anomalies do you then begin to detect? Move from the data to interpretive conclusions by making the implicit explicit (one of the five analytical moves) and by repeatedly asking So what?

This process will produce a set of interpretive leaps, which you should then try to assemble into a more coherent claim of some sort—about what the portrait "says" or reveals within some specified interpretive context. ▶

◀ ASSIGNMENT: Analyzing a Magazine Cover by Researching an Interpretive Context

Choose a magazine that, like *The New Yorker*, has interesting covers. Write an analysis of one such cover by studying other covers from the same magazine. The analysis of *The New Yorker* cover in the middle third of the chapter offers a model for how to do this. You will almost certainly need to do the following:

1. Apply the Method—looking for patterns of repetition and contrast—to the cover itself, so that you arrive at key repetitions, strands, and organizing contrasts and begin to ponder a range of possible interpretive leaps to what they signify.

2. Use these data to suggest plausible interpretive contexts for the cover. Remember that interpretive contexts are not simply imposed from without; they're suggested by the evidence.

3. Then move to the other covers. Perform similar operations on them to arrive at an awareness of common denominators among the covers, and to analyze what those shared traits might reveal or make more evident in the particular cover you are studying. You will be trying to figure out how the magazine conceives of itself and its audience by the way that it characteristically represents its "face." ▶

GUIDELINES FOR PUTTING ANALYSIS TO WORK

1. Look for a range of plausible interpretations rather than assuming that there will be only one right answer. Control the range of possible interpretations by attending carefully to context.

2. Laying out the data is key to any kind of analysis, not simply because it keeps the analysis accurate but because, crucially, it is in the act of carefully describing a subject that analytical writers often have their best ideas. The words you choose to summarize your data will contain the germs of your ideas about what the subject means.

3. All explanations and interpretations occur in a context, which functions like a lens for focusing your subject. An important part of getting an interpretation accepted as plausible is to *argue for the appropriateness of the interpretive context you use*, not just the interpretation it takes you to.

4. It is interesting and sometimes useful to try to determine from something you are analyzing what its makers might have intended. But, by and large, you are best off concentrating on what the thing itself communicates as opposed to what someone might have wanted it to communicate. Besides, intentions can rarely be known with much accuracy.

5. Arguing with someone else's argument is usually as much a matter of addressing what is left unsaid—the assumptions "underneath" the argument that the arguer takes to be "givens" (obvious truths)—as confronting what gets argued overtly.

6. A major advantage of looking for and using binaries is that they help you determine what issues are at stake in your subject; binaries position you among competing choices.

7. Think of the binary as a starting point—a kind of deliberate overgeneralization—that allows you to set up positions you can then test in order to refine. Although framing an issue in either/or terms can be useful for stimulating a chain of thought, it is usually not a good way to end one. Let *either/or* become *the extent to which*.

GUIDELINES FOR PUTTING ANALYSIS TO WORK (CONTINUED)

8. Uncovering assumptions underneath a given position is a powerful analytical tool. To uncover assumptions, you need to read "backward"— to ask *what a reading must also already believe*, given its overt claims. In other words, you need to imagine or reinvent the process of thinking by which a writer has arrived at a position.

CHAPTER 4

Reading: How to Do It and What to Do with It

Quick
Take

This chapter concentrates on how to get better ideas from and about what you read. In a phrase, it endorses "active reading": concrete strategies for questioning and marking and writing about readings more acutely.

These strategies aim to make you more conscious as a reader. For instance, the chapter advocates most strongly the practice of selecting a passage (even a single sentence) from whatever you are reading that you think it is most important to discuss.

What do you do with this passage once you've selected it? If you want to better understand something that you're reading—or revising in your own writing—ask yourself what certain key words mean, even if you think you know what they mean, and start paraphrasing.

The chapter also suggests methods of finding "good" passages, expanding the ways you think about a reading. There's a section of the chapter, for example, on recognizing what a reading *does*, rather than concentrating solely on what it *says*. We talk about how to describe the way a reading behaves—and once you can do that, it is much easier to imitate as a model or apply to another reading.

Other sections discuss how to freewrite about, summarize, compare and contrast, and locate definitions in readings. The latter two are among the original topics of invention in classical rhetoric—the traditional ways of finding and accessing ideas. (They still work.) We approach all these forms from the point of view of both reader and writer, as ways of both accessing readings and exploring primary data in your own writing.

One more thing: many of the skills taught in this chapter are also treated in the first two chapters, so if you are beginning the book here, you might find it beneficial to follow the cross-references to the appropriate sections of those chapters.

A. HOW TO READ: WORDS MATTER

A well-known twentieth-century philosopher, Ludwig Wittgenstein, noted in a famous saying that we cannot make a proposition about the world; we can only make a proposition about another proposition about the world. The statement implies that we live in a world of language. This is not to say that everything is words, that words are the only reality. But to an enormous extent, we understand the world and our relation to it by working through language, by "reading."

As you have probably noticed, this book has been using the word *reading* to mean "interpreting." This usage hearkens back to the idea of the world as a text. The idea wasn't new with Wittgenstein, by the way. The Puritans also envisioned the world as a text in which God read their lives, and so, predictably, they started reading their lives too, reflecting on events that befell them, and querying whether those events were signs of salvation or damnation. (The stakes for being a good reader couldn't have been higher!) In short, reading for them meant gathering evidence and analyzing it to arrive at ideas or conclusions.

We know the world through language; it's the medium in which we dwell.

Considering how central reading is in our lives, it's amazing how little we think about words themselves. We use words all the time, but often unthinkingly. We don't plan out our sentences before we utter them, for example, and the same goes for most of the ones we write. In previous chapters we put forth the notion that there are almost always multiple plausible interpretations. Similarly, all words have multiple meanings; check any dictionary, and you will find more than one definition for virtually every word.

Most of us live, however, as if there were a consensus about what words mean. Often—much more than you suspect—there isn't a consensus. We tend to assume that words (like life itself) have simple and single meanings. Don't believe it. Words are promiscuous; they won't stay put, won't stick to a single meaning. This is often a source of the comic. A posting on the Internet of memorably silly headlines included "Teacher Strikes Idle Kids," "Panda Mating Fails: Veterinarian Takes Over," "New Vaccines May Contain Rabies," "Local High School Drop-outs Cut in Half," and "Include Your Children When Baking Cookies" (or if you prefer, "Kids Make Nutritious Snacks"). Another posting included sentences such as "The bandage was wound around the wound" and "After a number of injections my jaw got number." It's often a nutty language, and we need to remember this whenever we start getting too complacent about the meanings of words being singular and obvious.

BECOMING CONVERSANT VERSUS READING FOR THE GIST

Many readers operate under the dubious impression that they are to "read for the gist"—for the main point that is to be gleaned through a glancing speed-reading. Quite simply, you cannot expect to demonstrate your control of the information without getting closer to it than generalizations allow. One of the most crippling and frustrating things for many students is to expect that if they read through something once and then look away, they should be able either to accurately and productively restate it or to have an idea about it. The vast majority of writing tasks that you will encounter require as a prerequisite your *conversancy* with material that you have read—not inert generalizations about it.

It is a reasonable expectation both in academic courses and in the workplace that you should become *conversant* with the material. To become conversant means that

1. after a significant amount of work with the material, you should be able to talk about it conversationally with other people and answer questions about it without having to look everything up.
2. you should be able to converse with the material—to be in some kind of dialogue with it, to see the questions the material asks, and to pose your own questions about it. (can't believe everything you read)

Few people are able to really understand things they read or see without making the language of that material their own in some way. We can learn, in other words, only by finding ways to actively engage material rather than moving passively through it. This is why working closely with the language that you are reading is essential to becoming conversant with that reading.

> To become conversant with something you have read means that you can talk about it conversationally with other people and answer questions about it without having to look everything up.

Various reading-related writing tasks can enable you to become conversant with a written text. Among them, we have singled out three for particular concentration:

- passage-based focused freewriting
- paraphrasing
- summarizing

Along with note taking and outlining, these are not just empty mechanical tasks, but the mind's means of acquiring material, both the ideas and the language. The first part of this chapter takes up each of these tasks in turn, offering versions of them to use as heuristics (means of finding things out). First, however, we want to pause to introduce a frame for reading critically.

A FRAME FOR READING CRITICALLY: THE PITCH, THE COMPLAINT, AND THE MOMENT

So words matter; they are our primary means of negotiating our relation to the world. But when you actually sit down to read for more than the gist, what can you do to read more actively? What can you look for and make note of? If you set out to choose passages that are "most important," by what criteria can you make such selections?

A useful premise to start from is that information is virtually never neutral. There is, in much of the reading you will do, no such thing as "just information." Rather, most readings—at least those encountered in work and school settings—have the following three components:

- a **pitch**, what the piece wishes you to believe
- a **complaint**, what the piece is reacting to
- a **moment**, the historical context within which the piece is operating

Whether you are paraphrasing, summarizing, selecting a passage for a focused freewriting, or otherwise looking for ways to separate out what is important in a reading, seeking out these three components will always be a boon to reading critically. Here's a bit more on each:

The pitch: A reading is an argument, a presentation of information that makes a case of some sort, even if the argument is not explicitly stated. Look for language that reveals the position or positions the piece seems interested in having you adopt. As we say in the discussion of categorical thinking at the end of Chapter 7, it is not only debate-style argument that makes a case for things. Analysis, for example, argues for understanding a subject in a particular way.

The complaint: A reading is a reaction to some situation, some set of circumstances, that the piece has set out to address. An indispensable means of understanding someone else's writing is to figure out what seems to have caused the person to write the piece in the first place. Writers write, presumably, because they think something needs to be addressed. What? Look for language in the piece that reveals the writer's starting point. If you can find the position or situation he or she is worried about and possibly trying to correct, you will find it much easier to locate the argument, the position the piece asks you to accept.

> If you can find the position a writer is worried about and possibly trying to correct, you will find it much easier to locate the position the piece asks you to accept.

The moment: A reading is a response to the world conditioned by the writer's particular moment in time. In your attempt to figure out not only what a piece says but where it is coming from (the causes of its having been written in the first place and the positions it works to establish), history is significant. When was the piece written? Where? What else was going on at the time that might have shaped the writer's ideas and attitudes? You don't necessarily have to run to a history book for every older text that you encounter, but neither do you want to ignore the extent to which writers are conditioned by their times.

One more thing: the more difficult the reading is to get through, the more this approach will help you. Complex, abstract theoretical pieces will get clearer once you have identified these three components; they can provide invaluable grounding for your reading.

► Try this 4.1: Locating the Pitch and the Complaint

You can read more actively by trying to figure out from the language of the reading what its author is worried about and what he or she is trying to "fix." This is true even of textbooks: informational reading still has a point of view. *Whenever you can, find the position that the reading is trying to resist, revise, or replace.* Take a passage of anything you are reading for work or school, and look for language that reveals the position or positions the piece seems interested in having you adopt. It is easier to find the pitch if you first look for language that reveals the position or situation the writer is trying to correct. Type out the sentences that most fully articulate the pitch and the complaint. Then paraphrase them to enrich your sense of where the writer is coming from and where the piece is trying to take you.

Alternatively, you could tackle the following piece of dyspepsia:

The World Series victory that was earned by the Boston Red Sox *—moment* gratified legions of fans who had suffered for many years. If the media were to be believed, these fans had been mourning their *—moment* unrequited fandom since 1918, when Babe Ruth was sold to the Yankees. But all of the media hoopla surrounding the Sox' victory *pitch* could not obscure the fact that the 2004 World Series will *not* go down in history as one of the better ones. Aside from the first game, there were no close contests. And the usual components that go into making a series memorable—extra-inning games, spectacular *—complaint* rallies, seesaw battles—were sadly absent. Instead, we were left with an overdose of media hype. Because the games were not exciting, and the writers had to write something, we just got more and more and more tired rehearsals of the lifting of "the curse"—itself a media creation of a book written only a decade ago. So maybe the Red Sox lifted the so-called curse, but perhaps, rather than being exorcized, it was merely transferred to baseball fans everywhere.

PASSAGE-BASED FOCUSED FREEWRITING

Passage-based focused freewriting is one of the best analytical exercises you can do to get ideas about what you are reading. It brings together several of the writing strategies discussed earlier in the book, most notably focused freewriting and 10 on 1 (introduced in Chapter 1). Its aim is to prompt in-depth analysis of a representative example, on the assumption that you'll attain a better appreciation of how the whole works after you've explored how a piece works.

In general, freewriting is a method of arriving at ideas by writing continuously about a subject for a specified period (usually ten to twenty minutes) without pausing to edit or correct or bite your pen or stare into space. The rationale behind this activity can be understood through the well-known remark by the novelist E. M. Forster (in regard to the "tyranny" of prearranging everything) we have already quoted, but that bears repeating: "How do I know what I think until I see what I say?" Freewriting gives you the chance to see what you say.

In passage-based focused freewriting, you narrow the scope to a single passage, a brief piece of the reading (at least a sentence, at most a paragraph) to anchor your analysis. You might choose the passage in answer to the following question:

> *What is the one passage in the reading that needs to be discussed, that poses a question or a problem, or that seems (in some way perhaps difficult to pin down) anomalous or even just unclear?*

You can vary this question by selecting the passage that you find most puzzling or most important or most dissonant or whatever. Alternatively, you might apply the strategy of looking for patterns to a piece of the text to help you locate a passage containing a repetition, strand, or organizing contrast you wish to explore further.

One advantage of focused freewriting is that its impromptu nature forces you to articulate what you notice as you notice it, not delaying—or, as is more common, simply avoiding—thinking in a relatively disciplined way about what you are reading. There is no set procedure for such writing, but it usually involves the following:

- It attends to *the context* surrounding the passage, summarizing the larger section of which the passage is a part.
- It selects and *paraphrases key phrases* or terms in the passage, teasing out the possible meanings of these words.
- It relentlessly *asks, So what? about the details*: so what that the passage uses this language, moves in this way, arrives at these points? and so forth.
- It addresses *how the passage is representative of broader issues* in the reading; perhaps it refers to another, similar passage.

Passage-based focused freewriting thus makes use of the other skills that we will discuss in this chapter as well: paraphrasing, summarizing, and narrowing the focus. It is an effective way of preparing for class discussion and of testing possible areas of concentration for a paper.

► Try this 4.2: Doing a Passage-Based Focused Freewrite

Select a passage from any of the material that you are reading and copy it at the top of the page. Then do a twenty-minute focused freewrite on it. Strive by the end of the time allotted to make some kind of interpretive leap, some consolidation of what you have learned about the reading by doing the exercise.

Your primary aim is to generate ideas about the reading. You can do that almost formulaically by following the steps below. You needn't proceed in the numbered order, but you should probably include each of these steps.

1. **Seek to understand before you judge.** Keep your attention on the point of view advanced by the text, not your own agreement/disagreement or like/dislike. Get detached and scientific: focus on what the text is saying and doing and what it is inviting readers to think about various matters.

   Your point of view inevitably suffuses any analysis, since you are the one selecting the evidence and offering the observations about it, but your point of view (POV) should not be foregrounded—at least not as a like/dislike. Insofar as your POV does enter overtly as judgment, that should come after you've analyzed the data and come to a conclusion about what the text thinks or is "saying." In the case of a literary text or a film, your comments should address the work, not a character. Don't offer your POV on Hamlet as if he were a person (he's not); rather, offer your POV on the play's POV of Hamlet.

2. **Choose a limited piece of concrete evidence to focus on.** Select a passage that you find interesting, that you have questions about, probably one that you don't quite understand. That way the writing will have some work to do—to help you understand it by putting your thoughts into some kind of sustained analytical form. Always write out the quote and include the page number. The act of copying it will often induce you to notice more about it.

3. **Contextualize the evidence.** Where does it come from in the text? Who is saying what where to whom when about what? Briefly answering these questions will prevent you from taking things out of context. Identifying the source of the language—the speaker, the POV—is key here, because it always matters who is producing the language you are looking at.

4. **Make observations about the evidence:** stay close to the evidence; dwell with it—most writers leave it far too quickly to launch into generalizations that are often clichés. What words seem interesting and important to you, and why? Try to *paraphrase* parts of the passage; this is one of the best ways of beginning to define and question and get ideas about the evidence. Attend to the possibility of multiple meanings; ask yourself what key words mean; notice the metaphorical use of language as opposed to literal statements, and so forth.

5. **Share your reasoning about what the evidence means as you move from observation to implication.** Remember that evidence can never speak for itself; you need to explain how and why it means what you claim it means.

6. **Culminate your discussion by openly addressing the representativeness of your passage.** That is, move from your analysis of local details to address what, given your analysis, the work is "saying" about this or that issue or question. Even if you are running out of time, you should leap to this move—with a sentence like "I'm out of time, but my big point is . . ."—before you stop.

It is often productive to take the focused freewrite and type it, revising and further freewriting until you have filled the inevitable gaps in your thinking that the time limit has created. Eventually, you can build up, through a process of accretion, the thinking for an entire paper in this way.

▶ **Try this 4.3:** Keeping a Reading Journal

Realistically, there probably isn't time (or at least enough discipline) to do a passage-based focused freewriting at the end of every extended reading session you do. A less labor-intensive alternative is to keep a reading journal, which can supply selections for the focused freewritings and has the added benefit, in an academic setting, of preparing you for class. (This is the standard preparatory assignment for all of our classes: to bring one sentence from the reading that you think it is important for the class to discuss, with some jotted reasons why.)

To keep a reading journal, simply copy key sentences from the reading. How many is up to you—say, at least three—and then briefly make a few informal comments about them: which words you think are key, what the passage leads you to think, how it connects to something else you are reading or thinking about, its anomalous relationship to most of the text, whatever strikes you. The reading journal will not only help make class discussion more substantive—that is, less windy, general, and prone to merely personal likes and dislikes—but more important, you will be compiling your own "book" of the course as you go along—an invaluable resource for writing papers and studying for exams.

In addition, the sheer act of copying (typing is fine) the quotes will sensitize you to the style of the writers you are reading. As chapters 10 and especially 11 discuss, style is essential knowledge, because it is the shape that thinking takes. You will be surprised at what you notice for the first time just in the act of copying.

PARAPHRASE × 3

The exercise we call Paraphrase × 3 offers the quickest means of seeing how a little writing about what you're reading can lead to having ideas about it. Paraphrasing is an activity we introduce in our overture of essential analytical skills in Chapter 1 as a tool for beginning to interpret because it tends to uncover areas of uncertainty and find questions.

Paraphrasing is commonly misunderstood as summary—a way of shrinking an idea you've read about—or perhaps as simply a way to avoid plagiarism by "putting it in your own words." Rather, *the goal of paraphrasing is to open up the possible meanings of the words*; it's a mode of inquiry.

Paraphrasing is particularly helpful in getting you beyond the problem of using secondary sources encountered in your reading as final answers, which can leave you with nothing to say on your own. By paraphrasing you can begin to work your way around a quotation, to see various ways it might be interpreted. (See Chapter 12.) Along the same lines, paraphrasing is essential in making evidence speak—that is, in not leaving it to speak for itself (because it won't do so adequately—see Chapter 5).

When you paraphrase, don't just go for the gist; replace all of the key words. The new words you come up with represent first stabs at interpretation, at having ideas about what you are reading.

If you paraphrase a key passage from a reading several (say, three) times, you will discover that it gets you working with the language. But you need to paraphrase *slavishly*. You can't let yourself just go for the gist; replace all of the key words. The new words you will be forced to come up with represent first stabs at interpretation, at having (small) ideas about what you are reading by unearthing a range of possible meanings embedded in the passage. Then, you will have *something to do* with your writing about the reading beyond simply recording it or agreeing/disagreeing with it.

▶ **Try this 4.4:** Doing Paraphrase × 3

Recast the substantive language of something you are reading into other words that mean as close to the same thing as possible. Try not to make the language more general. Paraphrasing does not condense—that's the job of summary. Regardless of what you paraphrase, remember this key: it is in successive recastings that the meaning grows in depth and variousness.

You might begin with two of our favorite candidates for paraphrase × 3:

- *"I am entitled to my opinion."*
- *"We hold these truths to be self-evident."*

(It is interesting to note that Thomas Jefferson originally wrote the words "sacred and undeniable" in his draft of the Declaration of Independence, instead of "self-evident." So what?)

The productive power of the exercise is more evident when you shift to something more challenging—say, a passage you find central or difficult in any of your assigned reading, the kind of passage most likely to attract yellow highlighter.

SUMMARY

Summary is the standard way that reading—not just facts and figures but also other people's theories and observations—enters your writing. The aim of summarizing is to recount (in effect, to reproduce) someone else's ideas, to achieve sufficient understanding of them to converse productively with what you have been reading.

Summary and analysis go hand in hand. Neither aims to approve or disapprove of its subject; the goal for both is to understand rather than evaluate.

Summary is a necessary early step in analysis because it provides *perspective* on the subject as a whole by explaining the meaning and function of each of that subject's parts. Within larger analyses—papers or reports—summary performs the essential function of *contextualizing* your subject accurately. It creates a fair picture of what's there. If you don't take the time to get your whole subject in perspective, you will be more prone to misrepresenting it in your analysis.

But summarizing isn't simply the unanalytical reporting of information; it's more than just shrinking someone else's words. To write an accurate summary, you have to ask analytical questions, such as the following:

- Which of the ideas in the reading are most significant? Why?
- How do these ideas fit together?
- What do the key passages in the reading mean?

Summarizing is, then, like paraphrasing, a tool of understanding and not just a mechanical task. But a summary stops short of in-depth analysis because summarizing typically makes much smaller interpretive leaps.

> When summaries go wrong, they are just lists. At best, they do very little logical connecting among the parts beyond "next."

STRATEGIES FOR MAKING SUMMARIES MORE ANALYTICAL

What information should be included and what excluded? This is the perennial question that summarizing raises. When summaries go wrong, they are just lists. A list is a simple "this and then this and then this" sequence. Sometimes lists are random, as in a shopping list compiled from the first thing you thought of to the last. Sometimes they are organized: fruit and vegetables here, dried goods there. At best, they do very little logical connecting among the parts beyond "next."

Summaries that are just lists tend to dollop out the information monotonously. They omit the *thinking* that the piece is doing—the ways it is connecting the information, the contexts it establishes, and the implicit slant or point of view. Be aware that the thinking the piece is doing is not necessarily the same as the ideas it may contain. Two articles on European attitudes toward the younger Bush's presidency, for example, may contain essentially the same information but vary widely in how they assemble it, how they connect the dots. Writing analytical summaries can teach you how to read for the connections, the lines that connect the dots. And when you're operating at that level, you are much more likely to have ideas about what you are summarizing. Here are five strategies for seeing and connecting the dots in what you are reading and, by extension, for deciding what to include and exclude in your summaries.

1. **Look for the underlying structure.** Use the strategy of looking for patterns of repetition and contrast. (See Chapter 2.) Even if you apply it to just a few selected paragraphs, it will provide you with the terms that get repeated, and these will almost always suggest strands, which in turn make up the organizing contrasts. This tool, in other words, works to

categorize and then further organize information and, in so doing, to bring out the underlying structure of the reading you are summarizing.

2. **Select the information that you wish to discuss on some principle other than general coverage (usually "and-then" lists) of the material.** Use the Notice-and-focus strategy to *rank* these items in some order of importance. (See Chapter 1.) Let's say that you are writing a paper on major changes in the tax law or on recent developments in U.S. policy toward Eastern Europe. Rather than simply collecting the information, try to arrange it into hierarchies. What are the least or most significant changes or developments, and why? Which are most overlooked or most overrated or most controversial or most practical, and why? All of these terms—*significant, overlooked,* and so forth—have the effect of focusing the summary. In other words, they will guide your decisions about what to include and exclude. As you rank, however, it is important to distinguish between the rankings that are implicit within the piece (for a strict summary) and your own rankings of the material (for beginning to use the summary in a context of your own).

3. **Reduce the scope of what you choose to summarize, and say more about less.** Both the looking-for-pattern and Notice-and-focus strategies inevitably involve some loss of breadth; you won't be able to cover everything. But this is usually a trade-off worth making. Your ability to rank parts of your subject or choose a particularly revealing feature or pattern to focus on will give you surer control of the material than if you just reproduce what is in the text. You can still begin with a brief survey of major points to provide context, before narrowing the focus.

Reducing scope is an especially efficient and productive strategy when you are trying to understand a reading you find difficult or perplexing. It will move you beyond passive summarizing and toward having ideas about the reading. If, for example, you are reading Chaucer's *Canterbury Tales* and start cataloguing what makes it funny, you are likely to end up with unanalyzed plot summary—a list that arranges its elements in no particular order. But narrowing the question to "How does Chaucer's use of religious commentary contribute to the humor of 'The Wife of Bath's Tale'?" reduces the scope to a single tale and the humor to a single aspect of humor. Describe those as accurately as you can, and you will begin to notice things.

4. **Get some detachment: shift your focus from *what?* to *how?* and *why?*** Most readers tend to get too single-minded about absorbing the information. That is, they attend only to the *what:* what the reading is saying or is about. They take it all in passively. But through an act of will, as a tool in your repertoire, you can deliberately shift your focus to *how* it says what it says, and *why*. If, for example, you were asked to discuss the major discoveries that Darwin made on *The Beagle*, you could avoid simply listing his conclusions by redirecting your attention to *how* he proceeds. You could choose to focus, for example, on Darwin's use of the scientific method, examining how he builds and, in some cases, discards hypotheses. Or you might select several passages that illustrate how

Darwin proceeded from evidence to conclusion and then *rank* them in order of importance to the overall theory. Notice that in shifting the emphasis to Darwin's thinking—the *how* and *why*—you would not be excluding the *what* (the information component) from your discussion.

Let's take one more example. If you were studying the reasons the American colonies rebelled against England, so broad a subject would tend to produce passive summary—a list of standard generalizations about the American Revolution. But what if you narrowed the focus to the Boston Tea Party and considered how American and British history textbooks differ in their treatment of this crucial event? Note that this question would still enable you to address, though in much more focused form, the broader question of why the colonies rebelled.

► Try this 4.5: Coverage versus Ranking

Write two summaries of the same article or book chapter. Make the first one consecutive—that is, try to cover the piece by essentially listing the key points as they appear. Limit yourself to a typed page. Then rewrite the summary, doing the following:

- rank the items in order of importance according to some principle that you designate, explaining your rationale;
- eliminate the last few items on the list, or at most, give each a single sentence; and
- use the space you have saved to include more detail about the most important item or two.

The second half of this assignment will probably require closer to two pages.

B. WHAT TO DO WITH THE READING: AVOIDING THE MATCHING EXERCISE

What does it mean "to do something with the reading"? Obviously, you can paraphrase, summarize, or do a focused freewrite with it, but these exercises aim primarily to establish a more accurate, active, and rich understanding of what the reading is doing and saying. That's why they are included under the heading "How to Read: Words Matter." When, by contrast, you *do* something with the reading, you use it for purposes that are different from the aims of the reading itself. This distinction holds for all kinds of reading, not just the academic or literary varieties. In a guide to bike repair, you might paraphrase the directions for replacing the brakes to make sure your understanding of this complex procedure is sufficiently clear. But if you use the knowledge you've gained to fix the brakes on some other machine, adapting what you've learned, you'll be doing something with the reading.

Much of the rest of this book suggests ways of negotiating what you read. In Chapter 12, for example, we concentrate on how to use secondary research. For now, we will discuss four basic approaches to doing things with the reading:

- applying a reading as a lens for examining something else
- comparing one reading with another
- using a reading as a model for writing
- uncovering the assumptions in a reading—where the piece is "coming from"

APPLYING A READING AS A LENS

Problem: A matching exercise, a mere demonstration of applicability.

Solution: Emphasize the shift in context, and then seek out areas of dissonance to analyze.

We apply what we read all the time. It's a standard academic assignment. You read an article on gender and blue jeans and then connect its ideas to something else—how, for example, magazine ads represent jeans-wearing with respect to gender. Or you study Freud's *The Interpretation of Dreams* and then analyze a dream of your own or a friend's as you project what Freud would have done. Or you apply his theory of repression to the behavior of a character in a novel or to some newfound realization about your mother's occasional bouts of frenzied housecleaning or your father's zealous weeding when he's upset. Freud thus becomes a *lens* for seeing the subject.

But what about taking an article on liberation theology as practiced by certain Catholic priests in Latin America and applying it to the rise of Islamic fundamentalism in the Middle East? Or for that matter, what about applying the directions for fixing the brakes on a bicycle to the analogous task on a car? Obviously, the original texts may be somewhat useful, but there are also significant differences between the two religious movements and between the two kinds of brakes.

So what should you do? When using a reading as a lens for better seeing what is going on in something you are studying, assume that the match between the lens and your subject will never be exact. It is often in the area where things don't match up exactly that you will find your best opportunity for having ideas.

> Think about how lens A both fits and *does not fit* subject B: use the differences to develop your analysis.

The big problem with the way most people apply a reading is that they do so too indiscriminately, too generally. They essentially construct a *matching exercise* in which each of a set of ideas drawn from text A is made to equate with a corresponding element (an idea or a fact) from subject B, often in virtual list-like fashion. Matching exercises are more useful in some contexts than in others (great for fixing your bike's brakes, less so for analyzing your parents). At their worst, matching exercises are static, mechanical, and inaccurate. This is because they concentrate on similarities and forget the rest. As a result, the lens screens out what it cannot bring into focus, and the writer applying it distorts what he or she sees. Like an optometrist figuring out the new prescription for your glasses, you need to constantly adjust the lens whenever you bring it to new material. Don't just slap on A: really think about how it both fits *and* doesn't fit B.

Remember that whenever you apply lens A to a new subject B, you are taking A from its original context and using its ideas in at least somewhat different circumstances for at least somewhat different purposes. How does this shift change things, and thus, how may it require you to refocus the lens? Freud's theory of repression wasn't actually talking about your father, after all. The goal is not to dismiss Freud but to adjust his thinking to the particular case. There's always the danger that the reading you're applying will become a club to bludgeon your subject into submission.

Applying a Reading as a Lens: An Example Here is an excerpted version of a student paper that uses the theoretical lens of racial difference to examine Shakespeare's *The Tempest*. The writer considers the way the fatherly power figure and sorcerer Prospero, the ruler of the island where he has been shipwrecked, treats the creature Caliban, whom he finds there and enslaves. We have put inside brackets some commentary on how the writer applies the lens. Brackets and ellipses [. . .] indicate where we have abridged the essay.

> In their *Introduction to Literature, Criticism, and Theory*, Andrew Bennett and Nicholas Royle devote one chapter to the theme of "Racial Difference." They begin this chapter with a reference to Charlotte Bronte's novel *Jane Eyre*, and from this standpoint, they discuss a character in the book named Bertha, a West Indian Creole bound by chains in her white husband's attic. Of a scene in the narrative—told by the white female narrator—wherein Bertha's appearance is described, they write: "No longer a woman, Bertha is the other of humanity, unrecognizable as human, a beast with a purely animal physiognomy. Almost invisible, Bertha cannot be seen. Invisibility, as this suggests [. . .] is the condition of racial otherness" (199). [The writer begins by introducing the theoretical lens.]
>
> It is in such a way that Prospero's narrative portrays Caliban. As *The Tempest* was initially performed in seventeenth-century England, the audience to whom Prospero delivers his epilogue is primarily, if not fully, white—thus, racially homogeneous. And as Bennett and Royle further remind us, "Western humanism necessarily defines itself through racial otherness, by constructing a racial other which then stands in opposition to the humanity of the racially homogeneous" (201). Taking this into account, we begin to see how the construction of Caliban as his nonhuman other, by blatant contrast, could make Prospero seem all the more human to his racially alike audience. [Here the writer applies the theory. Note how he takes care to differentiate the context, suggesting a particularly seventeenth-century reading of the racism.]
>
> The narrative achieves this end by utilizing the speech of several characters in the play to represent Caliban's behavior, nature, and physiognomy as decisively nonhuman. This narratological effect is carried out in several ways,

mostly through appeals to a colonialist audience: by the portrayal of Caliban as verbally belligerent; by asserting that he once tried to rape Prospero's virgin daughter Miranda; by having nearly every character he encounters regard him as a monster on account of his appearance; and by scripting nearly every character, including Caliban himself, to believe that his nature is naturally that of a slave for the colonialist project. [The writer now moves confidently beyond the theoretical reading into his own analysis of Shakespeare's text.]

[. . .] Thus, Caliban's physiognomy in this colony is that of a monster. Such a reference is made numerous times throughout the narrative. In the second scene of the second act, we find several malicious racial slurs referring to Caliban, which in Prospero's narrative are delivered humorously by the drunken butler and jester, Stephano and Trinculo respectively. When Trinculo encounters Caliban lying motionless upon the ground, he observes: "What have we here, a man or a fish? Dead or alive? A fish, he smells like a fish, a very ancient and fishlike smell" (II, ii, 24–26). Soon thereafter, both Trinculo and Stephano refer to Caliban as a "mooncalf" (II, ii, 101, 106); by this they are referring to him as monstrous or as a freak. [As the essay nears its end, the writer has begun to focus on the details for making his case about the play's incorporation of Elizabethan racism.]

This is an effective application of a theoretical lens to open up a text to analysis from a particular interpretive context. The next step the writer might take if he were to extend the discussion would be to ponder the ways that subject B does *not* fit lens A. So what, for example, that Caliban is not "invisible" (199)? And does the play in any way contradict the quote from page 201 by, say, humanizing Caliban despite Prospero's attempts to dehumanize him? Nonetheless, the writer has done very well to recognize and then develop the implications of the different historical context.

▶ Try this 4.6: Using a Quotation as a Lens

Using the preceding paper excerpt as a model, apply the following generalization about talk shows to a talk show of your choice: "These shows obviously offer a distorted vision of America, thrive on feeling rather than thought, and worship the sound-byte rather than the art of conversation" (Stark 243). Alternatively, take any general claim you find in your reading and apply it to some other text or subject. Either way, strive to produce several paragraphs in which you avoid the matching exercise and instead probe both lens A and subject B.

COMPARING AND CONTRASTING ONE READING WITH ANOTHER

Problem: Stopping too soon, with only a list of similarities and differences.

Solution: Look for difference within similarity or for similarity despite difference.

Comparing and contrasting is another traditional assignment done with readings that falls flat when it turns into a mechanical matching exercise. Comparing readings resembles applying a reading as a lens. These activities are not intended as ends in themselves; they almost always contribute to some larger process of understanding.

The rationale for working comparatively is that you can usually discover ideas about a reading much more easily when you are not viewing it in isolation. You can observe it from a different perspective, in relation to something else. When used in this way, the comparison is usually not a 50-50 split; you've moved to a comparison of A with B because you want to better understand A.

In short, a good comparison should open up a reading, not close it down. It does more than demonstrate that you've "done the reading." We're all completely familiar with the formulaic conclusions to the comparisons produced by the matching-exercise mentality: "Thus, we see there are many similarities and differences between A and B." Perfunctory, pointless, and inert lists: that's what you get if you stop the process of comparing and contrasting too soon, before you've focused and explored something interesting that you notice.

A good comparison should open up a reading, not close it down.

How do you avoid the ubiquitous matching-exercise habit? Here are three guidelines for productively comparing A with B:

1. **Focus the comparison to give it a point.** A comparison won't have a point inherently—you need to consciously give it one. It's often useful to assume that what you have originally taken for a point has not yet gone far enough and is still too close to summary. Rather than sticking with a range of broad comparisons, try to focus on a key comparison, one that you find interesting or revealing. (Looking for patterns, Notice and focus, and other tools can help you select your focus.) Although narrowing the focus in this way might seem to eliminate other important areas of consideration, in fact it usually allows you to incorporate at least some of these other areas in a more tightly connected, less list-like fashion.

   If, to return to an earlier example, you were to compare the representations of the Boston Tea Party in British and American history texts, you would *begin but not stop* with identifying similarities and differences. The goal of your reading would be to focus on some particular matches that seem especially revealing—for example, that British and American texts trace the economic background of the incident in different ways. Then, in response to the So what? question, you could attempt to develop some explanation of what these differences reveal and why they are significant. You might, for example, decide that the British texts view the matter from a more global economic perspective, whereas American texts emphasize nationalism.

2. Look for significant difference between A and B, given their similarity.
One of the best ways to arrive at a meaningful and interesting focus is to
follow a principle that we call *looking for difference within similarity*. The
procedure is simple but virtually guaranteed to produce a focused idea.

    a. First, deal with the similarity. Identify what you take to be the essential
similarity and then ask and answer, So what? Why is this similarity
significant?

    b. Then, in this context, identify the differences that you notice.

    c. Choose one difference you find particularly revealing or interesting,
and again ask, So what? What is the significance of this difference?

    You can repeat this procedure with a range of key similarities and
differences. Can you think of ways that the various differences are
connected?

    The phrase *difference within similarity* is to remind you that once you
have started your thinking by locating apparent similarities, you can
usually refine that thinking by pursuing significant, though often less
obvious, distinctions among the similar things. In Irish studies, for
example, scholars characteristically acknowledge the extent to which
contemporary Irish culture is the product of colonization. To this
extent, Irish culture shares certain traits with other former colonies in
Africa, Asia, Latin America, and elsewhere. But instead of simply
demonstrating how Irish culture fits the general pattern of colonialism,
these scholars also isolate the ways that Ireland *does not fit* the model.
They focus, for example, on how its close geographical proximity and
racial similarity to England, its colonizer, have distinguished the kinds of
problems it encounters today from those characteristic of the more generalized model of colonialism. In effect, looking for difference within
similarity has led them to locate and analyze the anomalies. (See the end
of the next chapter for an extended example of looking for difference
within similarity.)

**3. Look for unexpected similarity between A and B, given their
difference.** A corollary of the preceding principle is that you should focus
on *unexpected similarity rather than obvious difference*. The fact that in the
Bush presidency Republicans differ from Democrats on environmental
policy is probably a less promising focal point than their surprising agreement on violating the so-called lockbox policy against tapping Social
Security funds to finance government programs. Most readers would
expect the political parties to differ on the environment, and a comparison
of their positions could lead you to do little more than summarizing. But a
surprising similarity, like an unexpected difference, necessarily raises questions for you to pursue: do the parties' shared positions against the lockbox policy, for example, share the same motives?

Try this 4.7: Looking for Significant Difference or Unexpected Similarity

This exercise is based on those strategies that aim at getting you to rank your comparisons and contrasts by some principle—as the "Try this" on summary invited you to do—as a means of getting beyond a pointless matching exercise.

Choose any item from the list that follows, and practice reading comparatively. After you've done the research necessary to locate material to read and analyze, list as many similarities and differences as you can: go for coverage. Then, review your list, and select the two or three most revealing similarities and the two or three most revealing differences. At this point, you are ready to write a few paragraphs in which you argue for the significance of a key difference or similarity. In so doing, you may find it interesting to focus on an *unexpected* similarity or difference—one that others might not initially notice. (We recommend trying the "unexpected" gambit.)

1. accounts of the same event from two different newspapers or magazines or textbooks
2. two CDs (or even songs) by the same artist or group
3. two ads for the same kind of product
4. graffiti in men's bathrooms versus graffiti in women's bathrooms
5. the political campaigns of two opponents running for the same or similar office
6. courtship behavior as practiced by men and by women
7. two breeds of dog
8. two clothing styles as emblematic of socioeconomic class or a subgroup in your school, town, or workplace

Obviously, these paragraphs could also easily grow into a full-fledged paper.

READING AND WRITING DEFINITIONS

Before leaving comparison/contrast, we would like to pause briefly to consider a common kind of reading-based writing assignment: the definition. Like comparison/contrast, definition can easily fall prey to pointlessness, unless you can give it a point. In other words, definition is meaningful only within some context: you define "rhythm and blues" because it is essential to any further discussion of the evolution of rock 'n' roll music; or because you need that definition to discuss the British Invasion spearheaded by groups such as The Beatles, The Rolling Stones, and The Yardbirds in the late 1960s; or because you cannot classify John Lennon or Mick Jagger or Eric Clapton without it. When you construct a summary of existing definitions with no clear sense of purpose, you tend to list definitions indiscriminately. As a result, you are likely to overlook conflicts among the various definitions and overemphasize their surface similarities.

It is usually effective whenever you need to define a key term to sample a range of definitions. This will enable you to achieve some perspective on the term, to understand its richness of implication. In such cases, you can simply list definitions from a range of sources by exploring competing parts or versions of the definition. The definition of capitalism that you might take from Karl Marx, for example, will differ in its emphases from Adam Smith's. In this case, you would not only isolate the most important of these differences but also try to account for the fact that Marx's villain is Smith's hero. Such an accounting would probably lead you to consider how the definition has been shaped by each of these writers' political philosophies or by the culture in which each theory was composed.

Notice that proceeding in this way also makes use of the strategy called "The Pitch, the Complaint, and the Moment." Many exercises in definition involve attempts to correct or find a problem with the way someone else has defined a term. They exploit difference. Others, it should be noted, look for unexpected similarity among apparently disparate definitions.

▶ **Try this 4.8:** Defining in Depth

This chapter has been suggesting in different contexts that analytical acts require productive tension. The simple application of a lens as a matching exercise too easily becomes mechanical and directionless. A paper on alcoholism, for example, would lose focus if a writer were to use all of the definitions available. If, instead, she could convert the act of definition into a comparison and contrast of competing definitions, her writing would have more analytical edge, and it would more easily achieve a point and purpose for the definition. With an eye to the pitch, the complaint, and the moment, she would also be able to query whether the reading was defining alcoholism as primarily moral or physiological or psychological.

Using this example as a model, write a comparative definition in which you seek out different and potentially competing definitions of the same term or terms. Begin with a dictionary such as the *Oxford English Dictionary* (popularly known as the *OED*, available in most library reference rooms) that contains both historically based definitions that track the term's evolution over time and etymological definitions that identify the linguistic origins of the term—what the words from which it came (in older languages) mean. Locate both the etymology and the historical evolution of the term or terms.

Then look up the term in one, or preferably several, specialized dictionaries. We offer a list of some of these in Chapter 13, "Finding and Citing Sources," but you can also ask your reference librarian for pertinent titles. Summarize key differences and similarities among the ways the dictionaries have defined your term or terms. Then write several paragraphs—or even a comparative essay in which you argue for the significance of a key similarity or difference, or an unexpected one.

Here is the list of words: *hysteria, ecstasy, enthusiasm, witchcraft, leisure, gossip, bachelor, spinster, romantic, instinct, punk, thug, pundit, dream, alcoholism, aristocracy, atom, ego, pornography, conservative, liberal, entropy, election, tariff.* Some of these words are interesting to look at together, such as *ecstasy/enthusiasm* or *liberal/conservative* or *bachelor/spinster.* Feel free to write on a pair instead of a single word.

READING, BINARY THINKING, AND AVOIDING AGREE/DISAGREE

Binary thinking looms large in this chapter's approach to reading critically. As we have seen, binary thinking is a form implicit in our treatment of comparison and contrast. It also informs the solution we offer to energizing writing definitions—to exploit the tension among competing versions of what a word means.

Most important, readings can be mapped in terms of a primary binary of pitch versus complaint. In terms of readings, this binary marks pivotal sites of anxiety or concern, an index of what the reading is grappling with.

Creating opposing categories (binary oppositions) is fundamental to defining things. But binaries are also dangerous because they can invite reductive thinking—oversimplifying a subject by eliminating alternatives between the two extremes. This is the danger posed by the agree/disagree move. Often it is invited by a paper assignment that involves reading comparatively, asking writers to take sides between two positions or to agree or disagree with a given position. This wording is potentially misleading, as you are rarely being asked for as *unqualified* an opinion as agree or disagree. In such cases, beware agreeing or disagreeing 100% with almost any position. The wiser move is usually to locate something you agree with and something you may wish to qualify.

Seek alternatives to agreeing and disagreeing with readings. Look instead for the binaries that inform the reader and observe how the writer qualifies and recasts them.

Your best strategy in dealing with agree/disagree questions is to start not by choosing one side or the other and arguing for it, but with some more expository (explanatory) mode, such as comparison and contrast or definition, that will help you understand what is at stake on each side of the opposition. In most cases, if you take time to analyze the agree/disagree issue, you will come to question its terms and ultimately to arrive at a more complex and qualified position to write about. You should aim, in other words, at using the binary split to organize the issue, but then move beyond the generally oversimplified either/or format to discuss how both sides of the issue are related.

USING A READING AS A MODEL

Most of the critical activities that people do with readings involve assimilating and thinking about the information that is being conveyed to them. But to use a reading as a model is to *focus instead on presentation*. This represents a change in orientation for most readers, and it takes a little practice to learn how to do it. A useful guideline to remember is *look beyond content* (or subject matter).

We are, for the most part, "seduced" by the content of what we read, so we do not see how the piece is "behaving"—how it sets us up, how it repeats certain phrases, how it is patterned. This is the analytical function of focusing on presentation. To focus on presentation is to focus on what a piece of writing *does* rather than on what it *says*. It involves *describing*, as closely as you can, how the piece of writing proceeds—what it does first, then what, then what, and so forth. Consider, for example, what the following sentence does: "Time flies like an arrow; fruit flies like a banana." The first half of the sentence is an old proverb that compares the passage of time to the flight of an arrow. The second half appears to be another comparison presented in exactly the same way. But it's actually a set-up designed to trick readers into misreading, giving us an image of flying fruit rather than of fruit-eating insects. *Flies* is a verb in the first half of the sentence but a noun in the second half. *Like* is a comparative in the first half but a verb in the second half.

Concentrating on presentation—on what the writing is doing—is necessary when you are using a reading as a model. Using a reading as a lens can often come close to adopting it as a model, if we are, say, using the same key terms, the same interpretive context, and perhaps, the same general subject as our model reading. If you were to do an analysis of programs designed to help smokers quit by using an analysis of programs designed to help drinkers quit, the latter might be used as a model for the former. If the drinking cessation piece began with a long anecdote to phrase some central problem in program design, and you then began your piece with an analogous problem serving the same aim for your piece, that would represent a use of a reading as a model.

Consider the following essay opening in regard to presentation. Try to look beyond content to focus on how it behaves, on what it does.

> Why is something comic? Philosophers and social commentators and literary artists have spent millennia trying to answer that question definitively—and failing. At least there still is no consensus, no one theory to which most people subscribe.
>
> The comic is often thought of in opposition to the serious. Consider that often-heard phrase "I was just kidding." When do we hear it uttered? Almost always it's when the kidding has gone too far, and the one thing we know for sure is that the speaker, though he or she may have *also* been kidding, was not *just* kidding. He or she was using humor as a way of speaking the truth.
>
> This suggests at least two ideas about the comic: (1) that it is a way of being serious. And (2) that it is a way of using language that operates under different rules from "normal," non-kidding speech. So the serious/comic opposition is dubious at best, and probably downright false. What lies underneath "I was just

kidding" is the notion that we cannot easily speak what we take to be a truth about another person without pretending not to mean it. What might we conclude from these two ideas? The term we need to oppose to *the comic* is not *serious* but *solemn* or *sober;* for, far from being trivial and unserious, the comic is a rhetoric for voicing matters that are profoundly serious.

How would we describe this piece as a model? Here's one version of how the behavior of the opening paragraph might be described, sentence by sentence:

- It opens by asking a rhetorical question about an abstract subject (the comic).
- It then locates the question in a broad cultural and historical context (it mentions different kinds of thinkers and a long range of time) and concludes anticlimactically—that is, it frustrates the expectation that the question can be answered, but not until the end of the sentence *(failing).*
- It then qualifies this rather bold assertion (of no consensus), shrinking the claim that there is no definitive answer to the question to suggest that there may be a range of answers.

The second paragraph of the example then immediately picks up one approach to defining the comic, offers an example, and begins to analyze it. And so forth.

The larger point that we wish to illustrate here is that a reading can be understood as a series of rhetorical moves—a shift from what something says to what it invites us to think and by what means. (See "The Psychology of Form" in Chapter 9 for more on this.) Moreover, to view a reading in this way is to gain privileged knowledge about it, to understand it more actively and with surer control than is available just from memorizing the information it contains.

When you read try detaching from the pure information-assimilation mode to observe *how* the reading says *what* it says. Where does it make claims? What kind of evidence does it provide? Does the writer overtly reveal his or her premises? How and when does she use metaphors or analogies?

> *Not all reading proceeds in a straight narrative line from A to B to C. Some pieces are organized like quilts, a series of patches or vignettes operating as variations on a theme.*

And what about the overall organization of the piece you are reading? Not all reading proceeds in a straight narrative line from A to B to C. Some pieces are organized like quilts, a series of patches or vignettes operating as variations on a theme. Others favor a radial organization—locating some central issue or example in the center, and then spiraling out to connect it to other matters, then returning to it again and spiraling out again. A 10-on-1 analysis often takes this form, with the writer returning to the 1 for more details to explore.

Inexperienced writers sometimes resist using readings as models because they fear that imitation will suppress their ability to think for themselves. In practice this fear usually proves ungrounded. Learning to see how other writers organize their thinking expands rather than closes down your range as both a reader and a writer.

WAYS TO MARK WHAT A READING DOES (RATHER THAN SAYS)

There is no single way to mark what a reading does. How you describe its behavior will probably depend on the context within which you are studying it. If your goal is to use it as a model for imitation, it would probably make sense to proceed like the essay on comedy, focusing on the writer's rhetorical moves. To some extent that would also entail identifying how the writer uses evidence *(E)*, claim *(C)*, complication *(CL)*, transition *(TR)*, and restatement *(R)*. These initials might be used to mark up any reading to discern what it is doing. And obviously, others could be added (*TOP* for a topic sentence, *M* for a metaphor, *TH* for thesis, and so forth). Transitions are, by the way, particularly useful sites for readers attempting to use a reading as a model. Because transitions typically reach backward to what has already been said before they look forward, they offer us quick reviews and reassessments of the writer's lines of thought.

Even if you do not intend to imitate a reading as a model, there is abundant reason to mark up the readings that you are studying for what that practice can reveal. Close engagement with the text is next to impossible unless you mark it up. If you don't like writing in books, photocopy the relevant pages so that you can free yourself to do the on-the-page sketch work that is essential to careful thinking about the reading. The heuristic Looking for patterns of repetition and contrast (the Method) suggests another vocabulary for marking a reading—less for imitation of its interpretive moves than for analysis of its verbal underpinnings. In this case, you could

- circle repeated words and keep track of how often they repeat
- mark strands—words that repeat as part of a pattern of the same or similar kinds of language—and connect them with lines (aka strands)
- designate in the margins key organizing contrasts, writing the terms next to a +/- sign
- star anomalies

In addition, make use of *marginalia*—brief notes to yourself about what you notice or your response to it. If your reading is marked with these signs and notes, you will inevitably become more conversant with it and better able to find your way around in it. More important, though, the reading will begin to reveal its structure and concerns. Often it will disclose secrets of which it (or its author) may be unaware. See, in this context, the discussion at the end of this chapter on reading with and against the grain.

Try this 4.9: Describing and Marking What a Reading Does

Describe the final two paragraphs of the excerpt from the comedy essay, along the lines that the first paragraph has been described. Where are the claims (C)? Where are the qualifications of the claims (Q)? How does the discussion progress? Then try marking the essay, using either the claim-evidence language or the repetition-strand-contrast language. What do you learn?

UNCOVERING THE ASSUMPTIONS IN A READING

Uncovering assumptions is a primary and powerful move in reading analytically. We have devoted an extended analysis to it at the end of Chapter 3. Since this move—also known as "reasoning back to premises"—is such an important tool in a reader's arsenal, we will briefly revisit the topic here.

An assumption is the basic ground of belief from which a position springs, its starting points or "givens." All arguments or articulations of point of view have underlying assumptions. All readings are built on assumptions. A lot of the time, assumptions are not visible; they are *implicit,* which is why they need to be inferred as a discrete critical act.

Sometimes a text hides its premises (a pro-Nazi website, for example, that is ostensibly concerned with the increasing disorder of society). Sometimes a source just doesn't divulge its premises and perhaps does not know them. In any case, when you locate assumptions in a text, you understand the text better—where it's coming from and what else it believes that is more fundamental than what it is overtly declaring.

Chapter 3 offers a step-by-step procedure for uncovering assumptions. The essential move is to ask, "Given its overt claim, what must this reading also already believe?" To answer this question you need to make inferences from the primary claims to the ideas that underlie them. In effect, you are working backward, reinventing the chain of thinking that led the writer to the position you are analyzing.

► Try this 4.10: What Must the Writer Also Already Believe?

Here's a prime example of a statement that conceals a wealth of assumptions. In the reference application sent to professors for students who are seeking to enter a student-teaching program, the professor is asked to rank the student from one to four (unacceptable to acceptable) on the following criterion: "The student uses his/her sense of humor appropriately."

What must the writers of the recommendation form also already believe? Compile a list of their assumptions. Here are two strategies that can help you do this:

- Do Paraphrase x 3 on the quotation (the explicit claim) to help you see the range of implicit ideas attached to it.
- Articulate what the claim is *not* saying, because understanding that will often bring into relief the underlying positions that it is saying.

For more practice, locate a statement from anything you are reading that you find interesting or challenging. Paraphrase it. Then uncover assumptions, asking what the text must also already believe, given that it believes this. List at least three assumptions. Or uncover the assumptions in the following enigmatic statement: "Telling others about oneself is, then, no simple matter. It depends on what *we* think *they* think we ought to be like—or what selves in general ought to be like" (Jerome Bruner, *Making Stories: Law, Literature, Life* [Cambridge: Harvard UP, 2002, 66]).

Try this 4.11: Uncovering Assumptions in a Reading

Uncover the assumptions in the following brief excerpt from a student paper. You may choose to apply the procedure for uncovering assumptions given in Chapter 3: (1) paraphrase the explicit claim, (2) list the implicit assumptions (the ideas that the claim assumes to be true), (3) define key terms, and (4) try on an oppositional stance to see if this unearths more underlying assumptions. The result of this process should be a list of the premises upon which the writer's argument operates that the paragraph has not made sufficiently clear. At this point, you might write a page about the paragraph, providing the results of your analytical reading.

In all levels of trade, including individual, local, domestic, and international, both buyers and sellers are essentially concerned with their own welfare. This self-interest, however, actually contributes to the health and growth of the economy as a whole. Each country benefits by exporting those goods in which it has an advantage and importing goods in which it does not. Importing and exporting allow countries to focus on producing those goods that they can generate most efficiently. As a result of specializing in certain products and then trading them, self-interest leads to efficient trade, which leads to consumer satisfaction.

READING WITH AND AGAINST THE GRAIN

It is useful to think of both written and visual works as independent entities; independent, that is, of their authors, produced by authors but not ultimately controlled by them. The poet Emily Dickinson expresses this idea in a poem about an author sending his or her words into the world. Dickinson writes, "A word is dead / When it is said, / Some say. / I say it just / Begins to live / That day."

If we allow ourselves to think in this way—that writing, once committed to the page and released into the world by its author, comes to have a life of its own—then we are at liberty to see what is going on in that "life" that may or may not have been part of the author's original intention. If we take this writing-as-a-living-creature analogy a step further, we might reasonably grant that a piece of writing (say, a book), like a person, has an unconscious. In other words, we can ask not only what the book knows, what it seems fully aware of, but also what the book is saying that it seems not to know it is saying.

You might now be saying to yourself, "Doesn't this strategy for thinking about writing take us back to the hidden meaning theory that you debunked in Chapter 2?" Well, not really. Surely you have had the experience of looking back on something really good that you have written and wondering where it came from. You hadn't planned to say it that way ahead of time; it just "came out." This suggests that writers and artists are never fully in control of what they communicate, that words and images always, inescapably, communicate more than we intend. So it does not necessarily follow that writers and artists deliberately hide anything from us.

Instead, their work has revealed meanings that they may not have intended to reveal and that they probably didn't know they were revealing. Any of us who has had what we thought to be a perfectly clear and well-intentioned letter misinterpreted (or so we thought) by its recipient can understand this idea. When we look at the letter again, we usually see what it said that we hadn't realized (at least not consciously) we were saying.

When we ask ourselves what a work (and, by implication, an author) might not be aware of communicating, we are doing what is called reading *against* the grain. When we ask ourselves what a work seems aware of, what its (and, by implication, its author's) conscious intentions are, we are "reading *with* the grain."

Most good reading starts by reading with the grain, with trying to determine what the work and its author intend. This doesn't mean, as we discussed in Chapter 2, that an author's stated intentions get the last word on what his or her work can be taken to mean. But if we appreciate what authors and artists have to offer us, and if we respect them and the creative process, then we owe it to them and to ourselves to try to determine what they wished to say to us.

A philosophy professor at our college communicates this idea in his lectures when he tries to impersonate whatever philosopher the class is reading by responding to questions as he thinks this philosopher might. In this way, he elicits a *sympathetic reading*, which he argues must always come first.

Both reading with the grain and reading against the grain require us to attend to implication (a concept discussed at length in Chapter 2). Sometimes, what readers might reasonably infer fits less easily with what the piece seems to want to tell us. In this case, we are put in the position of reading against the grain—following something other than the dominant pattern in the writer's thinking.

> You can ask not only what the book knows, what it seems fully aware of, but also what the book is saying that it seems not to know it is saying.

For example, in the classic novel *Jane Eyre*, the narrator, Jane, repeatedly remarks on her own plain appearance, with the implication that physical beauty is transient and relatively insignificant. The text is in fact obsessed with her plainness; it is almost obligatory for every new character entering the novel to reflect at some point on Jane's unattractiveness. Not that they don't like Jane—on the contrary, they esteem her greatly even as they acknowledge her lack of physical charms. Are we then to conclude that Jane and the novel believe that physical appearance does not matter? Probably not. Reading against the grain, we'd see the novel's very obsession with plainness as a symptom of how worried it is about the subject, how much it actually believes (but won't admit) that looks matter.

Is reading against the grain—looking for what a work is saying that it might not know it is saying, that it might not mean to say—a hostile and potentially destructive activity? Some authors think so, because writers naturally seek to control the range of meanings their writing communicates. Inquiring into intention can make these writers nervous. They tend to think that the fewer questions asked about their creative process the less likely they will become paralyzed through self-consciousness. Other authors freely admit that writing is a somewhat scary as well as exhilarating process over which they have only tenuous control. Writers in this second camp are more likely to agree that there will be things in their writing—probably things worth finding—that they were not aware of.

In any case, when we seek to uncover assumptions in a reading, we are speculating (making inferences) that may run both with and against the grain. One of the best ways to do this is to use the looking-for-patterns heuristic, which often discovers revealing patterns of repetition of which the author may not be aware.

We can end this discussion of reading with and against the grain by returning to Dickinson's observation that the meaning of words is not fixed when they get put on paper. Her saying that words only begin to live that day is an author's generous acknowledgment that a writer's works belong not just to the writer but also to his or her readers. We cannot make of them what we will (as we argued in opposing the "anything goes" school of interpretation in Chapter 3), but it is part of reading well to uncover ideas and assumptions that are not clearly and obviously evident as part of a writer's stated aims.

► **Try this 4.12:** Appears to Be about X but Is Really about Y

For obvious reasons, this heuristic, introduced in Chapter 3, deserves another try here, in the context of reading with (that is, "about x") and against (that is, "really about y") the grain. You might apply the looking-for-patterns strategy to the passage of your choice to see if it will yield up any implicit, indirect clues to meanings that run counter to the overtly stated ones.

◀ **ASSIGNMENT:** Writing about Reading

These exercises and essay project apply the concepts offered in this chapter. Many of the "Try this" assignments can be expanded into papers as well.

1. Write a summary of a piece of writing using one or more of the following methods:

   a. Paraphrase × 3

   b. Ranking and reducing scope

   c. Finding the underlying structure

   d. Attending to the pitch, the complaint, and the moment

   e. Passage-based focused freewriting

2. Use a reading as a lens for examining a subject. For example, look at a piece of music or a film through the lens of a review that does not discuss the particular piece or film you are writing about. Or you might read about a particular theory of humor and use that as a lens for examining a comic play, film, story, television show, or stand-up routine.

3. Compare and contrast two readings on the same or similar subjects by looking for significant difference, given their similarities, or unexpected similarity, given their differences.

4. Write an essay in which you develop a position by uncovering the assumptions in a reading or set of related readings. You might try this with an editorial or a batch of editorials on the same subject. Reviews are often a good target for this assignment, because they tend to offer judgments. You could also uncover the assumptions of a policy decision at your school or place of work. This will work best if you have not just the policy but some kind of written manifesto on it. (Policies relating to student life are often quite revealing of what the institution actually thinks of its students.) ▶

GUIDELINES FOR READING ANALYTICALLY

1. Get beyond reading for the gist. Always mark a few key passages in whatever you read.

2. Whenever you read critically, look for the pitch and the complaint— what the writer wants to convince you of, and the position that he or she is reacting against. Also be aware of the moment—how the historical context qualifies the way we interpret the reading.

3. Experiment with passage-based focused freewriting. Find out what you think by seeing what you say.

4. Keep a reading journal. The act of copying key sentences from a reading and jotting a few notes will inevitably lead you to remember more and discover more about what you are reading.

5. Paraphrase key passages to open up the language and reveal complexities you may not have noticed. Paraphrasing three times is sure to help get you started interpreting a reading, moving you beyond just repeating pieces of it as answers.

6. Summarize analytically with ranking, not just coverage. Narrow the scope.

7. In applying a reading as a lens, think about how lens A both fits *and* does not fit subject B: use the differences to develop your analysis.

8. Avoid turning comparisons into pointless matching exercises. Set up similarities and differences to discuss the significance of that comparison.

9. Uncover unstated assumptions by asking, Given its overt claim, what must this reading also already believe?

10. A provocative way to open up interpretation is to try reading against the grain of a text. Ask, What does this piece believe that it does not know it believes? Using the method to uncover repetitions will sometimes provide the evidence to formulate against-the-grain claims.

CHAPTER 5

Linking Evidence and Claims:
10 on 1 versus 1 on 10

This chapter is about evidence—what it is, what it is meant to do, and how to recognize when you are using it well. The chapter's overall argument is that you should use evidence to test, refine, and develop your ideas, rather than just to prove that they are correct. The chapter begins by analyzing two common problems—claims without evidence (unsubstantiated claims), and evidence without claims (pointless evidence). It then moves to a discussion of strategies for analyzing evidence in depth. These include the following:

- 10 on 1, a heuristic discussed in Chapter 1 but developed here in the context of organization and evidence
- pan, track, and zoom: organizing a paper like a film
- looking for difference within similarity as a way of developing comparisons beyond matching exercises

The chapter suggests these three heuristics as alternatives to five-paragraph form, a popular organizational model that generally blocks writers from engaging in more sustained, subtle, and revelatory thinking.

By way of definition, a *claim* is an assertion that you make about your evidence—an idea that you believe the evidence supports. The primary claim in a paper is the *thesis*. In analytical writing, the thesis is a theory that explains what some feature or features of a subject mean. The subject itself, the pool of primary material (data) being analyzed, is known as *evidence*.

A. LINKING EVIDENCE AND CLAIMS

THE FUNCTION OF EVIDENCE

A common assumption about evidence is that it is "the stuff that proves I'm right." Although this way of thinking about evidence is not wrong, it is much too limited. Corroboration (proving the validity of a claim) is one of the functions of evidence, but not the only one.

It helps to remember that the word *prove* actually comes from a Latin verb meaning "to test." The noun form of prove, *proof*, has two meanings: (1) evidence sufficient to establish a thing as true or believable, and (2) the act of testing for truth or believability. When you operate on the first definition of proof alone, you are far more likely to seek out evidence that supports only your point of view, ignoring or dismissing other evidence that could lead to a different and possibly better idea. You might also assume that you can't begin writing until you have arrived at an idea you're convinced is right, since only then could you decide which evidence to include. Both of these practices close down your thinking instead of leading you to a more open process of formulating and testing ideas.

Beginning with the goal of establishing an idea as believable and true can interfere with the need to examine the idea. Moreover, this approach can lead to an unnecessarily combative debate style of argument in which the aim is to win the game and defeat one's opponents. In debate style, convincing others that you're right is more important than arriving at a fair and accurate assessment of your subject. By contrast, the advantage to following the second definition of the word proof—in the sense of testing—is that you will be better able to negotiate among competing points of view. In addition, this practice will predispose your readers to consider what you have to say, because you are offering them not only the thoughts a person has had, but also a person in the act of thinking.

THE FALLACY THAT FACTS CAN SPEAK FOR THEMSELVES

Evidence rarely, if ever, can be left to speak for itself. The word *evident* comes from a Latin verb meaning "to see." To say that the truth of a statement is "self-evident" means that it does not need proving because its truth can be plainly seen by all. When a writer leaves evidence to speak for itself, he or she is assuming that it can be interpreted in only one way, and that readers necessarily will think as the writer does.

But the relationship between evidence and claims is rarely self-evident: that relationship virtually *always* needs to be explained. One of the key analytical moves of Chapter 2 was making the implicit explicit. That is also the rule in the domain of evidence. Perhaps the single most important lesson about using evidence that this chapter has to teach is that the thought connections that have occurred to you will not automatically occur to others. Persuasive writing always makes the connections between evidence and claim overt.

> The thought connections that have occurred to you will not automatically occur to others.

Writers who think that evidence speaks for itself often do very little with their evidence except put it next to their claims: "The party was terrible: there was no alcohol"—or, alternatively, "The party was great: there was no alcohol." Just juxtaposing the evidence with the claim leaves out the thinking that connects them, thereby implying that the logic of the connection is obvious. But even for readers prone to agreeing with a given claim, simply pointing to the evidence is not enough.

It should be acknowledged, however, that the types and amounts of evidence necessary for persuading readers and building authority also vary from one discipline to another, as does the manner in which the evidence is presented. Although some disciplines—the natural sciences, for example—require writers to present evidence first and then interpret it, others (the humanities and some social sciences) expect interpretation of the evidence as it is presented. In all disciplines—and virtually any writing situation—it is important to support claims with evidence, to make evidence lead to claims, and especially to be explicit about how you've arrived at the connection between your evidence and your claims (see Figure 5.1).

Of course, before you can attend to the relationship between evidence and claims, you first have to make sure to include both of them. Let's pause to take a look at how to remedy the problems posed by leaving one out: unsubstantiated claims and pointless evidence.

SUPPORTING UNSUBSTANTIATED CLAIMS: PROVIDING EVIDENCE

Problem: Making claims that lack supporting evidence.

Solution: Learn to recognize and support unsubstantiated assertions.

Unsubstantiated claims occur when a writer concentrates only on conclusions, omitting the evidence that led to them. At the opposite extreme, pointless evidence results when a writer offers a mass of detail attached to an overly general claim. Both of these problems can be solved by offering readers the evidence that led to the claim and explaining how the evidence led there. The word *unsubstantiated* means "without substance." An unsubstantiated claim is not necessarily false; it just offers none of the concrete "stuff" upon which the claim is based. When a writer makes an unsubstantiated claim, he or she has assumed that readers will believe it just because the writer put it out there.

Perhaps more important, unsubstantiated claims deprive you of details. As Chapter 1 has argued, without details you're left with nothing concrete to think about. If you lack some actual "stuff" to analyze, you can easily get stuck in a set of abstractions, which tend to overstate your position and leave your readers wondering exactly what you mean. The further away your language gets from the concrete, from references to physical detail—things that you can see, hear, count, taste, smell, and touch—the more abstract it becomes. An aircraft carrier anchored outside a foreign harbor is concrete; the phrase *intervening in the name of democracy* is abstract.

FIGURE 5.1 Linking Evidence and Claims

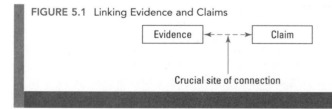

DISTINGUISHING EVIDENCE FROM CLAIMS

To check your drafts for unsubstantiated assertions, you first have to know how to recognize them. A fundamental skill to possess is the ability to *distinguish* evidence from claims. It is sometimes difficult to separate facts from judgments, data from interpretations of the data. Writers who aren't practiced in this skill can believe that they are offering evidence when they are really offering only unsubstantiated claims. In your own reading and writing, pause once in a while to label the sentences of a paragraph as either evidence *(E)* or claims *(C)*. What happens if we try to categorize the sentences of the following paragraph in this way?

> The owners are ruining baseball in America. Although they claim they are losing money, they are really just being greedy. A few years ago, they even fired the commissioner, Fay Vincent, because he took the players' side. Baseball is a sport, not a business, and it is a sad fact that it is being threatened by greedy businessmen.

The first and last sentences of the paragraph are claims. They draw conclusions about as yet unstated evidence that the writer will need to provide. The middle two sentences are harder to classify. If particular owners have said publicly that they are losing money, the existence of the owners' statements is a fact. But the writer moves from evidence to unsubstantiated claims when he suggests that the owners are lying about their financial situation and are doing so because of their greed. Similarly, it is a fact that commissioner Fay Vincent was fired, but only an assertion that he was fired "because he took the players' side." Although many of us might be inclined to accept some version of the writer's claim as true, we should not be asked to accept his opinion as self-evident truth. What is the evidence in support of the claim? What are the reasons for believing that the evidence means what he says it does?

► Try this 5.1: Distinguishing Evidence from Claims

Take an excerpt from your own writing, at least two paragraphs in length—perhaps from a paper you have already written or a draft you are working on—and at the end of every sentence label the sentence as either evidence *(E)* or claim *(C)*. For sentences that appear to offer both, determine which parts of the sentence are evidence and which are claim, and then decide which one, *E* or *C*, predominates. What is the ratio of evidence to claim, especially in particularly effective or weak paragraphs?

As an alternative or a preface to the above exercise, mark the following paragraph with *Cs* and *Es*. We have numbered the sentences for easier isolation and discussion. A few of them—1 and 7, for example—are arguably quite tricky to decide about: which part of the sentence is a claim, and which part evidence? Keep in mind that you are making your decisions on the basis of the writer's use of the sentences, not simply on their content. Is a secondary source's judgment that is

E – prove
C – be proven

imported into an essay as *support* for the writer's point of view ultimately *C* or *E*, for example?

(C) Though many current historians would argue that Andrew Jackson's treatment of the Native Americans was contrary to the ideals and precepts of the American Revolution, one must consider the legal and moral context of both Jackson and the time period in which he lived. (2) Jackson, both as a general and as a president, had no real love for the Native American populations in the southern and western United States. (3) As a military general he had defended the borders of the United States many times against Indian attacks and negotiated treaties with some of the tribes during the term of President James Monroe. (4) However, Jackson was also the archetype of the general American view of the Native Americans. (5) E He described the Indians as barbarians and cruel savages in a letter to a fellow politician (Hollitz 172) and tried to convince President Monroe, during his negotiations with the Creek Indians, that Native Americans "are the subjects of the United States, inhabiting its terri-tory and acknowledging its sovereignty" (Hollitz 174). (6) He subse-quently argued that it was "absurd for the sovereign to negotiate with the subjects" (Hollitz 174). (7) Jackson and many of his contem-poraries also saw the Indians only as a hindrance to America's exploitation of southern and western farmland and that they should be removed to facilitate American expansion. (8) This is clearly seen in a letter Jackson wrote to his wife in which he describes removing the natives of Alabama in terms of the fertile lands and wealth it will bring the United States as well as a secure southern border (Hollitz 173). (9) They were subjects of American sovereignty. (10) In this sense, Jackson's policy of Indian removal was in line with the best wishes of the people that the ideals of the American Revolution were set aside for, the American citizens who wished for more fertile lands and safe borders. (11) Jackson was indeed providing for the citizens that he believed the Declaration of Independence encompassed.

GIVING EVIDENCE A POINT: MAKING DETAILS SPEAK

Problem: Presenting a mass of evidence without explaining how it relates to the claims.

Solution: Make details speak. Explain how evidence confirms and qualifies the claim.

Your thinking emerges in the way that you follow through on the implications of the evidence you have selected. You need to interpret it for your readers. You have to make the details speak, conveying to your readers *why* they mean what you claim they mean.

The following example illustrates what happens when a writer leaves the evidence to speak for itself.

> Baseball is a sport, not a business, and it is a sad fact that it is being threatened by greedy businessmen. For example, Eli Jacobs, the previous owner of the Baltimore Orioles, recently sold the team to Peter Angelos for one hundred million dollars more than he had spent ten years earlier when he purchased it. Also, a new generation of baseball stadiums have been built in the last decade—in Baltimore, Chicago, Arlington (Texas), Cleveland, and most recently, in San Francisco, Milwaukee, Houston, and Philadelphia. These parks are enormously expensive and include elaborate scoreboards and luxury boxes. The average baseball players, meanwhile, now earn more than a million dollars a year, and they all have agents to represent them. Alex Rodriguez, the shortstop for the New York Yankees, is paid more than twenty million dollars a season. Sure, he set a record for most homers in a season by a shortstop, but is any ballplayer worth that much money?

Unlike the previous example, which was virtually all claims, this paragraph, except for the opening claim and the closing question, is all evidence. The paragraph presents what we might call an "evidence sandwich": it encloses a series of facts between two claims. (The opening statement blames "greedy businessmen," presumably owners, and the closing statement appears to indict greedy, or at least overpaid, players.) Readers are left with two problems. First, the mismatch between the opening and concluding claims leaves it not altogether clear what the writer is saying that the evidence suggests. And second, he has not told readers why they should believe that the evidence means what he says it does. Instead, he leaves it to speak for itself.

If readers are to accept the writer's implicit claims—that the spending is too much and that it is ruining baseball—he will have to show *how* and *why* the evidence supports these conclusions. The rule that applies here is that *evidence can almost always be interpreted in more than one way.*

We might, for instance, formulate at least three conclusions from the evidence offered in the baseball paragraph. We might decide that the writer believes baseball will be ruined by going broke or that its spirit will be ruined by becoming too commercial. Worst of all, we might disagree with his claim and conclude that baseball is not really being ruined, since the evidence could be read as signs of health rather than decay. The profitable resale of the Orioles, the expensive new ballparks (which, the writer neglects to mention, have drawn record crowds), and the skyrocketing salaries all could testify to the growing popularity rather than the decline of the sport.

How to Make Details Speak: An Example   The best way to begin making the details speak is to take the time to look at them, asking questions about what they imply.

1. Say explicitly what you take the details to mean.
2. State exactly how the evidence supports your claims.
3. Consider how the evidence complicates (qualifies) your claims.

The writer of the baseball paragraph leaves some of his claims and virtually all of his reasoning about the evidence implicit. What, for example, bothers him about the special luxury seating areas? Attempting to uncover his assumptions, we might speculate that he intends it to demonstrate how economic interests are taking baseball away from its traditional fans because these new seats cost more than the average person can afford. This interpretation could be used to support the writer's governing claim, but *he would need to spell out the connection, to reason back to his own premises.* He might say, for example, that baseball's time-honored role as the all-American sport—democratic and grass-roots—is being displaced by the tendency of baseball as a business to attract higher box office receipts and wealthier fans.

The writer could then make explicit what his whole paragraph implies, that baseball's image as a popular pastime in which all Americans can participate is being tarnished by players and owners alike, whose primary concerns appear to be making money. In making his evidence speak in this way, the writer would be practicing step 3 above—using the evidence to complicate and *refine* his ideas. He would discover which specific aspect of baseball he thinks is being ruined, clarifying that the "greedy businessmen" to whom he refers include both owners and players.

Let's emphasize the final lesson gleaned from this example. When you focus on tightening the links between evidence and claim, the result is almost always a "smaller" claim than the one you set out to prove. This is what evidence characteristically does to a claim: it shrinks and restricts its scope. This process, also known as qualifying a claim, is the means by which a thesis develops (or as we call it in Chapter 6, evolves).

Sometimes it is hard to give up on the large, general assertions that were your first response to your subject. But your sacrifices in scope are exchanged for greater accuracy and validity. The sweeping claims you lose ("Greedy businessmen are ruining baseball") give way to less resounding but also more informed, more incisive, and less judgmental ideas ("Market pressures may not bring the end of baseball, but they are certainly changing the image and nature of the game").

B. DEVELOPING A THESIS IS MORE THAN REPEATING AN IDEA ("1 ON 10")

When the time comes to compose a formal paper with a thesis, it is very common for writers to abandon the wealth of data and ideas they have accumulated in the exploratory writing stage, panic, and revert to old habits: "Now I better have my one idea and be able to prove to everybody that I'm right." Out goes careful attention to detail. Out goes any evidence that doesn't fit. Instead of analysis, they substitute the kind of paper we call a demonstration. That is, they cite evidence to prove that a generalization is generally true. The problem with the demonstration lies with its too limited notions of what a thesis and evidence can do in a piece of analytical thinking.

Demonstrations are the result of two primary mistaken assumptions about what an analytical paper is—that the thesis doesn't change and that evidence exists solely to confirm the general validity of the thesis. For these notions we'd like to substitute the following two:

- A strong thesis *evolves*: it changes as a paper progresses. The changes in the thesis are galvanized by its repeated encounters with evidence.
- Evidence has a second function beyond corroborating claims: to test and develop and evolve the thesis, making the thesis account more accurately for the evidence.

The absence of change is the primary trait of a weak thesis. Like an *inert* (unreactive) material, a weak thesis neither affects nor is affected by the evidence that surrounds it. A paper produced by repeating a single idea generally follows the form we call 1 on 10: the writer makes a single and usually very general claim ("History repeats itself," "Exercise is good for you," and so forth) and then proceeds to affix it to ten examples. (See Figure 5.2 "Doing 1 on 10.") As we discuss in Chapter 1 under "Narrow Your Scope by Doing 10 on 1," a writer who reasserts the same idea about each example is going to produce a list, not a piece of developed thinking. By contrast, in nearly all good writing the thesis evolves by *gaining in complexity* and, thus, in accuracy as the paper progresses.

> The absence of change is the primary trait of a weak thesis. Like an inert (unreactive) material, a weak thesis neither affects nor is affected by the evidence that surrounds it.

Where do writers get the idea in the first place that a thesis should be static? In most cases they learned it early in their writing careers as part of a stubbornly inflexible organizational scheme known as five-paragraph form.

WHAT'S WRONG WITH FIVE-PARAGRAPH FORM?

Perhaps the best introduction to what's wrong with five-paragraph form can be found in Greek mythology. On his way to Athens, the hero Theseus encounters a

FIGURE 5.2

Overly general claim

Example 1 | Example 2 | Example 3 | Example 4 ... Example 10 | Conclusion

Doing 1 on 10. The horizontal pattern of 1 on 10 (in which "10" stands arbitrarily for any number of examples) repeatedly makes the same point about every example. Its analysis of evidence is superficial.

particularly surly host, Procrustes, who offers wayfarers a bed for the night but with a catch. If they do not fit his bed exactly, he either stretches them or lops off their extremities until they do. This story has given us the word "procrustean," which the dictionary defines as "tending to produce conformity by violent or arbitrary means." Five-paragraph form is a procrustean formula that most students learn in high school. Although it has the advantage of providing a mechanical format that will give virtually any subject the appearance of order, it usually lops off a writer's ideas before they have the chance to form or stretches a single idea to the breaking point. In other words, this simplistic scheme blocks writers' abilities to think deeply or logically, restricting rather than encouraging the development of complex ideas.

A complex idea is one that has many sides. To treat such ideas intelligently, writers need a form that will not require them to cut off all of those sides except the one that most easily fits the bed. Most of you will find the basic five-paragraph form familiar:

1. An introduction that announces the writer's main idea, about which he or she will make three points
2. Three paragraphs, each on one of the three points
3. A conclusion beginning "Thus, we see" or "In conclusion" that essentially repeats the introduction.

Here is an example in outline form:

Introduction: The food in the school cafeteria is bad. It lacks variety, it's unhealthy, and it is always overcooked. In this essay I will discuss these three characteristics.

Paragraph 2: The first reason cafeteria food is bad is that there is no variety. (Plus one or two examples—no salad bar, mostly fried food, and so forth)

Paragraph 3: Another reason cafeteria food is bad is that it is not healthy. (Plus a few reasons—high cholesterol, too many hot dogs, too much sugar, and so forth)

Paragraph 4: In addition, the food is always overcooked. (Plus some examples—the vegetables are mushy, the "mystery" meat is tough to recognize, and so forth)

Conclusion: Thus, we see . . . (Plus a restatement of the introductory paragraph)

Most high school students write dozens of themes using this basic formula. They are taught to use five-paragraph form because it seems to provide the greatest good—a certain minimal clarity—for the greatest number of students. But the form does not promote logically tight and intellectually aggressive writing. It is a meat grinder that can turn any content into sausage.

At the root of the problem with five-paragraph form is its most distinctive characteristic—the classic tripartite (three-part) thesis, which generates the organizational format ("The economy of Bolivia is characterized by x, y, z"). The problem with this thesis shape is that it is not really a thesis. It offers a list in place of an idea. It tells the writer that he or she will have to write a paragraph on each of the items in the list, but it doesn't let the reader (or the writer) know why this might be worth doing.

When you are in a pinch, as, for example, when you are trying to write the essay section of the new SAT exam where five-paragraph form *seemingly* still reigns, the form's partitioning aspect can be useful. Partitioning your subject into sections will at least split your thinking tasks into three or more smaller portions. But you need to try to make the thesis and its supporting body paragraphs do more than listing.

As we make clear at various points in the book, a good thesis must have tension in it, the pressure of one possible idea against another. Simply saying that the economy today has three problems, and then listing them, isn't really a thesis. Such a statement might get you by in a standardized essay exam (even though it shouldn't), but in the rest of your writing you want to do more than make lists of broad generalizations. A thesis that says, "There are three reasons for our being bogged down in the war with Iraq today" will direct you to an orderly development of your points, but not to much analysis of them. Good analysis requires narrower scope; its products are more carefully defined idea.

WHAT FIVE-PARAGRAPH FORM LOOKS LIKE

If you have been taught to write in five-paragraph form, you have come to expect your thinking to be tidily packaged. The thesis of a paper in five-paragraph form lists three elements of some kind at the end of the first paragraph: three reasons, three causes, three effects, three characteristics, and so forth. The paper then follows like a paint-by-number picture with a paragraph devoted to each of the three elements in the thesis. Then the paper comes to rest, wearily, with restatement (often exact repetition) of the three-part thesis in the first sentence of the concluding paragraph.

The problem with this orderly scheme is that it doesn't leave much room for thinking. In fact, it actually discourages thinking because it makes writers afraid to look closely at the evidence. If they look too closely, they might find something that doesn't fit. But it is precisely the something that doesn't seem to fit, the thing writers call a *complication*, that triggers good ideas. The tidy packaging of five-paragraph form keeps complications at a safe distance. When complications do force their way onto the scene, five-paragraph form swiftly seeks to dismiss them. It tends to locate them as concessions and refutations—things to be gotten through in an obligatory way so that the writer can return to the main business at hand: reciting his or her idea as if the complication had never been.

> *But it is precisely the something that doesn't seem to fit, the thing writers call a complication, that triggers good ideas. The tidy packaging of five-paragraph form keeps complications at a safe distance.*

The three elements get marched through the paper with no questions asked, and the paper ends the way it began—with a list. This is all quite comforting to some writers, because five-paragraph form papers virtually write themselves. Just come up with a list of three things, preferably things that can be stated in single words, as in "*Dr. Faustus* is a play about lust, greed, and ambition," and then produce an example or two of each in your three body paragraphs. Nothing to it.

The fact that there is almost "nothing to it" is the problem. Ideas that come too easily, that seem to write themselves, are sometimes the worthwhile products of inspiration. More often they are unexamined first responses, exercises in the exposition of the obvious, prefabricated and unreflective recitations of conventional ideas. If one definition of analysis is that it locates significant parts in order to arrive at a better understanding of the whole, then five-paragraph form is a too-mechanical form of analysis.

Here is a short list of the bad mental habits taught by five-paragraph form:

1. that papers need only repeat (rather than develop) their main ideas
2. that an introduction is a conclusion, and thus that nothing need happen to the thesis on the way from the beginning of the paper to the end
3. that a thesis is essentially inert, unaffected by what it passes through
4. that a paper need only provide evidence in support of its thesis, rather than using evidence to test and evolve the main idea; complicating evidence may get acknowledged in the form of concessions and refutations, but such evidence remains too inert to have any effect on the writer's thinking
5. that all body paragraphs are essentially the same—a single claim at the beginning (one of the three elements of the thesis turned into a sentence, as in "We also see that *Dr. Faustus* is a play about greed.") followed by a short list of reasons or examples
6. that a thesis consists of generalities and broadly stated themes, usually ones that no one would be likely to disagree with

Try this 5.2: Identifying Five-Paragraph Form

Take a minute to examine the introductory paragraph below. What evidence do you find there to suggest that it is setting up a five-paragraph form essay?

Throughout the film *The Tempest*, a version of Shakespeare's play *The Tempest*, there were a total of nine characters. These characters were Calibano, Alonso, Antonio, Aretha, Freddy, the doctor, and Dolores. Each character in the film represented a person in Shakespeare's play, but there were four people who were greatly similar to those in Shakespeare, and who played a role in symbolizing aspects of forgiveness, love, and power.

Predict the organization of this essay, paragraph by paragraph. Can you discern any possible openings where the writer might locate and develop an idea? (There are some.)

Here are two *quick checks* to see whether a paper of yours has closed down your thinking through a scheme such as five-paragraph form:

1. *Look at the paragraph openings.* If these read like a list, each beginning with an additive transition such as *another* followed by repetition of your central point ("Once again we see . . . " or "Yet another example is . . ."), you are probably not developing your ideas sufficiently.

2. *Compare the wording in the last statement of the paper's thesis (in the conclusion) with the first statement of it in the introduction.* If the wording at these two locations is virtually the same, you'll know that your thesis has not responded adequately to your evidence.

C. BUILDING A PAPER BY ANALYZING EVIDENCE IN DEPTH: "10 ON 1"

How do you move from making details speak and explaining how evidence confirms and qualifies the claim to actually composing a paper? One way is through the practice we call 10 on 1: a focused analysis of a representative example. (See Figure 5.3.) We first introduced this term near the end of Chapter 1, where it is presented as a heuristic for focusing observation and asking So what? We return to it now in the context of linking evidence and claims in composing an analytical essay.

FIGURE 5.3

Doing 10 on 1. The pattern of 10 on 1 (in which "10" stands arbitrarily for any number of points) successively develops a series of points about a single representative example. Its analysis of evidence is in depth.

To repeat the general rule of 10 on 1, it is better to make ten observations or points about a single representative issue or example than to make the same basic point about ten related issues or examples (as in the static demonstration we call 1 on 10, which repeats the same "answer" ten times). As a guideline, 10 on 1 will lead you to draw out as much meaning as possible from your best examples. It depends upon narrowing the focus and then analyzing in depth.

You can use 10 on 1 to accomplish various ends: (1) to locate the range of possible meanings your evidence suggests, (2) to make you less inclined to cling to your first claim, (3) to open the way for you to discover the complexity of your subject, and (4) to slow down the rush to generalization and thus help to ensure that when you arrive at a working thesis, it will be more specific and better able to account for your evidence.

WHAT THE "1" IS

The "1" is a representative example, what you have narrowed your focus to. How do you select the "1"? One of the best ways is to use the looking-for-patterns heuristic (the Method) to identify a strand or pattern and then to choose the example of it you find most interesting, strange, revealing, and so forth. Here, in effect, you do 1 on 10 as a preliminary step—locating ten examples that share a trait—and then focus on one of these for in-depth analysis.

Proceeding in this way would guarantee that your example was representative, which is essential, because in doing 10 on 1 you are taking one part of the whole, putting it under a microscope, and then generalizing about the whole on the basis of analyzing a single part. In the preceding section we used the baseball example in this way, doing 10 on 1 with the student's paragraph as a way of anchoring our generalizations about giving evidence a point. (See pages 142–143.)

WHAT THE "10" ARE

The "10" comprise both observations and interpretive leaps that you make about the "1," both what you notice about the evidence and what you make of what you notice. To get the "10"—to analyze in depth—use the various tools, prompts, and procedures that have been introduced in this book thus far:

- Look at the example and ask yourself what you notice.
- Use Looking for Patterns of Repetition and Contrast to uncover and organize data.
- Locate anomalies and query them.
- Locate, name, and reformulate binaries.
- Try "seems to be about x but is *also* about y."
- Employ Paraphrase × 3 on key sentences or phrases if your evidence has a verbal component.
- Uncover the assumptions in your example.
- As you try on different interpretations, repeatedly ask, So what? to develop the implications of your thinking.
- As a major claim begins to emerge (and it will), seek out conflicting evidence to enable you to qualify the claim still further.

PAN, TRACK, AND ZOOM: THE FILM ANALOGY

To understand how 10 on 1 can generate the form of a paper, let's turn to an analogy. The language of filmmaking offers a useful way for understanding the different ways that a writer can focus evidence. The writer, like the director of a film, controls the focus through different kinds of shots.

The pan—The camera pivots around a stable axis, giving the viewer the big picture. Using a pan, we see everything from a distance. Pans provide a context, some larger pattern, the "forest" within which the writer can also examine particular "trees." Pans establish the representativeness of the example the writer later examines in more detail, showing that it is not an isolated instance.

The track—The camera no longer stays in one place but follows some sequence of action. For example, whereas a pan might survey a room full of guests at a cocktail party, a track would pick up a particular guest and follow along as she walks across the room, picks up a photograph, proceeds through the door, and throws the photo in a trash can. Analogously, a writer tracks by moving in on selected pieces of the larger picture and following them to make telling connections among them.

The zoom—The camera moves in even closer on a selected piece of the scene, allowing us to notice more of its details. For example, a zoom might focus in on the woman's hand as she crumples the photograph she's about to throw away or on her face as she slams the lid on the trash can. A writer zooms in by giving us more detail on a particular part of his or her evidence and making the details say more. The zoom is the shot that enables you to do 10 on 1.

In a short paper (three to five pages), you might devote as much as 90 percent of your writing to exploring what one example (the "1"—your zoom) reveals about the larger subject. Even in a paper that uses several examples, however, as much as 50 percent might still be devoted to analysis of and generalization from a single case. The remaining portion of the paper would make connections with other examples, testing and applying the ideas you arrived at from your single case. In-depth analysis of your best example thus creates a center from which you can move in two directions: (1) toward generalizations about the larger subject and (2) toward other examples, using your primary example as a tool of exploration.

This same model, applicable across a wide variety of writing situations, can be reduced to a series of steps:

1. Use the Method to find a revealing pattern or tendency in your evidence. (See Chapter 2.)
2. Select a representative example.
3. Do 10 on 1 to produce an in-depth analysis of your example.
4. Test your results in similar cases.

An analysis of the representation of females on television, for example, would fare better if you focused on one show—say, *Buffy, the Vampire Slayer*—narrowed the focus to teenage girls, and tested your results against other shows with teenage girl characters, such as *Felicity*, *Gilmore Girls*, and *Seventh Heaven*. Similarly, a study of the national debt might focus on Social Security, analyzing it in order to arrive at generalizations to be tested and refined in the context of, say, health care or military spending.

A close look at virtually anything will reveal its complexity, and you can bring that complex understanding to other examples for further testing and refining. We call this process of using the "1" as a lens through which to analyze other examples "constellating the evidence." Like the imaginary lines that connect real stars into a recognizable shape, your thinking configures the examples into some larger meaning. This practice often supplies the backbone for longer essays in both exploratory and more polished drafts.

It is, of course, important to let your readers know that you are using the one primary example in this generalizable way. Note how the writer of the following discussion of the people's revolt in China in 1989 sets up his analysis. He first explains how his chosen example—a single photograph (shown in Figure 5.4) from the media coverage of the event—illuminates his larger subject. The image is of a Chinese man in a white shirt who temporarily halted a line of tanks on their way to quell a demonstration in Tiananmen Square in Beijing.

> The tank image provided a miniature, simplified version of a larger, more complex revolution. The conflict between man and tank embodied the same tension found in the conflict between student demonstrators and the Peoples' Army. The man in the white shirt, like the students, displayed courage, defiance, and rebellious individuality in the face of power. Initially, the peaceful revolution succeeded: the state allowed the students to protest; likewise, the tank spared the man's life. Empowered, the students' demands for democracy grew louder. Likewise, the man boldly jumped onto the tank and addressed the soldiers. The state's formerly unshakable dominance appeared weak next to the strength of the individual. However, the state asserted its power: the Peoples' Army marched into the square, and the tanks roared past the man into Beijing.

FIGURE 5.4 Tiananmen Square, Beijing, 1989.

The image appeals to American ideology. The man in the white shirt personifies the strength of the American individual. His rugged courage draws on contemporary heroes such as Rambo. His defiant gestures resemble the demonstrations of Martin Luther King Jr. and his followers. American history predisposes us to identify strongly with the Chinese demonstrators: we have rebelled against the establishment, we have fought for freedom and democracy, and we have defended the rights of the individual. For example, *The New York Times* reported that President George [H. W.] Bush watched the tank incident on television and said, "I'm convinced that the forces of democracy are going to overcome these unfortunate events in Tiananmen Square." Bush represents the popular American perspective of the Chinese rebellion; we support the student demonstrators.

This analysis is a striking example of doing 10 on 1. In the first paragraph, the writer constructs a detailed analogy between the particular image and the larger subject of which it was a part. The analogy allows the writer not just to describe but also to interpret the event. In the second paragraph, he develops his focus on the image as an image, a photographic representation tailor-made to appeal to American viewing audiences. Rather than generalizing about why Americans might find the image appealing, he establishes a number of explicit connections (does 10 on 1) between the details of the image and typical American heroes. By drawing out the implications of particular details, he manages to say more about the significance of the American response to the demonstrations in China than a broader survey of those events would have allowed.

The rule of thumb here is to say more about less (rather than less about more) to allow a carefully analyzed part of your subject to provide perspective on the whole. In the following 10 on 1 draft, what does the writer focus on, and *not* focus on? How does the perspective emerge?

> The rule of thumb here is to say more about less (rather than less about more).

The thing about comic strips is that people always appear to be talking at the same time. Their words hang above them in bubbles—attached loosely to their mouths or the tops of their heads. The words seem to grow from their speakers and then just float there above them—untethered somehow but also fixed—black letters (usually) against a white ground. Another thing about comic strips is that they have a clear end and beginning. They move across the page in a relentless order—one thing following the next. But the beginning remains in full view when we get to the end. We can see how we got to where we end up even though the characters can't—as they are stuck in their individual frames, each a separate moment in time.

I remember the cartoons the artist Andy Warhol used to draw—or paintings, rather, based on cartoons. The faces—usually of a famous person who was already a cartoon of sorts in life (like Marilyn Monroe)—were unusually large and very brightly colored, especially the lips. The texture of the faces was made up of many dots, clearly visible, to remind us that we were looking at a painting of a person rather than, say, a photograph. Perhaps the dots also remind us of how thinly held together we are—not one solid being, but a collection of parts.

Cartoons are flat. When we look at them we imagine the people (or animals) in them to be round, like ourselves. As the reader of a comic strip you are always free to start over when you get to the end—or to start at the end and read back to the beginning. In the second reading, you might find yourself saying to the characters in the first frame, "Wait! You are going to regret saying that!"

Note how the writer has defamiliarized her subject in the opening paragraph, looking at rather than through the conventions of comic strips. As she observes one technical element of the form—the speech bubble—she begins to see other formal elements, such as the printing and the order of the frames. This focus leads her to a digression in the second paragraph, but that is an opportunity rather than a problem, for the Warhol example gets her to think about how stylized human figures are in comics, and by implication, in all representations. She brings this insight back with her in the final paragraph as her gaze returns to the comic strip. Sure, the piece is still in the draft stage, but the writer's use of 10 on 1 has already generated a focus capable of sustaining a paper with a refreshingly offbeat focus on the conventions of its subject.

► Try this 5.3: Doing 10 on 1 with Newspaper Visuals

Search out photographs in the newspaper and do 10 on 1. Or alternatively, spend some time doing 10 on 1 on a comic strip. What perspectives emerge once you have restricted the focus? List details, but also list multiple implications. Remember to ask not just What do I notice? but What else do I notice? And not just What does it imply? but What else might it imply?

DEMONSTRATING THE REPRESENTATIVENESS OF YOUR EXAMPLE

Problem: Generalizing on the basis of too little and unrepresentative evidence.

Solution: Survey the available evidence and argue overtly for the representativeness of the examples on which you focus.

Focusing on your single best example has the advantage of economy, cutting to the heart of the subject, but it runs the risk that the example you select might not in fact be representative. Thus, to be safe, you need to demonstrate its representativeness overtly. This means showing that your example is part of a larger pattern of similar evidence and not just an isolated instance.

In terms of logic, the problem of generalizing from too little and unrepresentative evidence is known as an *unwarranted inductive leap*. The writer leaps from one or two instances to a broad claim about an entire class or category. Just because you see an economics professor and a biology professor wearing corduroy jackets, for example, you would not want to leap to the conclusion that all professors wear corduroy jackets.

The surest way you can guard against this problem is by reviewing the range of possible examples to make certain that the ones you choose to focus on are representative. By looking for patterns of repetition and contrast (the Method) you could identify the strand to which your example belongs, which could then be included as a pan in the introductory paragraph. If you were writing about faith as it is portrayed in the book of Exodus, for example, you might suggest the general trend by briefly panning across instances in which the Israelites have difficulty believing in an unseen God. Then, you could concentrate (zoom in) on the best example.

Most of the time, unwarranted leaps result from making too large a claim and avoiding examples that might contradict it. A good check is *deliberately to seek out the single piece of evidence that might most effectively oppose your point of view and address it.* Doing so will prompt you to test the representativeness of your evidence and often to qualify the claims you have made for it.

▶ Try this 5.4: Doing 10 on 1 with a Reading

Take a piece of reading—a representative example—from something you are studying and do 10 on 1. The key to doing 10 on 1 successfully is to slow down the rush to conclusions so that you can allow yourself to notice more about the evidence and make the details speak. The more observations you assemble about your data *before* settling on your main idea, the better that idea is likely to be. Remember that a single, well-developed paragraph from something you are reading can be enough to practice on, especially because you are working on saying more about less rather than less about more.

10 ON 1 AND DISCIPLINARY CONVENTIONS

In some cases, the conventions of a discipline appear to discourage doing 10 on 1. The social sciences in particular tend to require a larger set of analogous examples to prove a hypothesis. Especially in certain kinds of research, the focus of inquiry rests on discerning broad statistical trends over a wide range of evidence. But some trends deserve more attention than others, and some statistics similarly merit more interpretation than others. The best writers learn to choose examples carefully— each one for a reason—and to concentrate on developing the most revealing ones in depth; the interpretive and statistical models for analyzing evidence are not necessarily opposed to one another.

For instance, proving that tax laws are prejudiced in particularly subtle ways against unmarried people might require a number of analogous cases along with a statistical summary of the evidence. But even with a subject such as this, you could still concentrate on some examples more than others. Rather than moving through each example as a separate case, you could use your analyses of these primary examples as *lenses* for investigating other evidence.

CONVERTING A 1-ON-10 PAPER INTO A 10-ON-1 PAPER: AN EXTENDED EXAMPLE

The following student paper, about the recurrence of flood stories in religious texts and myth, shows what happens when a writer falls into doing 1 on 10. That is, rather than zooming in on representative examples to test and refine his ideas, he attaches the same underdeveloped point to each of his examples. Typical of the 1-on-10 pattern, the flood paper views everything from the same relatively unrevealing distance.

The point is a promising one, however, and the writer has taken some productive steps analytically. As you will see, for example, he locates a pattern of like detail and begins to make the implications of his observations overt. He also offers evidence for his claims rather than leaving them unsupported.

We are using the essay as an extended example because of the way that diagnosing its strengths and weaknesses and contemplating revision strategies allow us to demonstrate several of the analytical moves discussed in this chapter and the previous one:

1. Doing 10 on 1: zooming in more closely on evidence (10 on 1), drawing out more of its possible meanings
2. Using the film analogy: thinking and talking about a piece of writing in regard to the way the writer adjusts the focus and observational distance as the essay progresses
3. Looking for difference within similarity (see Chapter 4): emphasizing contrasts and anomalies, deliberately attending to things that seem not to fit the pattern of like detail
4. Constellating the evidence: organizing the paper by drawing connections among interestingly related examples, each of which is analyzed using 10 on 1

As you may recall from Chapter 4, the phrase *difference within similarity* suggests that once you have started your thinking by locating apparent similarities, you can usually refine that thinking by pursuing significant, though often less obvious distinctions among the similar things. As the revision suggestions for the following paper illustrate, this heuristic is also a way of getting beyond 1 on 10.

In the essay that follows, we have used boldface to track the "one" point—the as-yet-underdeveloped thesis idea—that the writer has attached to each of his examples (1 on 10). Brackets and ellipses [. . .] indicate where we have abridged the essay.

Flood Stories

[1] **The role of people**, as reflected in Genesis, Ovid's *Metamorphoses*, and the *Epic of Gilgamesh*, **is solely to please the gods**. Men, as the gods' subordinates, exist to do right in the gods' eyes **and make them feel more like gods**; for without men, whom could the gods be gods of? [. . .]

[2] In Genesis, for example, God created humans in his own image or likeness, and **when they displeased Him, He destroyed them**. If God

could see wickedness in his creations, perhaps it was like seeing wickedness in himself. Further, the idea of having evidence of God being able to create an imperfect, "wicked" race of humans may have been a point God wasn't willing to deal with. The Lord saw that the wickedness of man was great in the earth, and that every imagination of the thoughts of his heart was only evil continually. And the Lord was sorry that he had made man on the earth and it grieved him to his heart. It seems as though **God had become unhappy with his creations** so they were to be destroyed. Like a toy a child no longer has use for, humankind was to be wasted.

[3] Similarly, in Ovid's *Metamorphoses*, God made humanity and "fashioned it into the image of the all-governing gods." Again here, humans were made in the gods' image to serve as an everlasting monument of their glorification, to honor them and do good by them. In other words, **humans spent less time making the gods happy** and therefore made them unhappy. Some men even questioned the reality of the gods' existence and the strength of their power. Lyacon, for example, had a driving tendency to try to belittle the gods and make them look like fools. **The gods were very displeased** with this trend, and now the entire race had to be destroyed. A flood would be sent to wipe out the race of men. [The writer then summarizes several examples in which the wicked are destroyed and a few upstanding citizens are preserved and arrives at the following conclusion:] Thus, the justification of yet another flood **to appease the gods' egos**.

[4] Further evidence of **humans as being a mere whim of the gods to make them happy** lies in the flood story in the *Epic of Gilgamesh*. It is obvious **the gods weren't concerned with humankind, but rather with their own comfort**. As the story goes, Enlil, the god of earth, wind, and air, couldn't bear the noise humans were making while he tried to sleep, so he gathered all the gods together, and thus they jointly decided to get rid of their grief of having all the humans around by destroying them. Ea [the god of wisdom], however, warned one man (Utnapishtim) of the flood to come. He told him to build a boat for himself and his wife and for the "seeds of all living creatures." [. . .]

[5] Enlil later repented the harshness of his actions, deified Utnapishtim and his wife and then had the two live far away "on the distance of the rivers' mouths." It possibly **could have been belittling** to have Utnapishtim and his wife speaking to the new race of humans in terms of how rash and mindlessly the gods were capable of acting, so he immortalized them and had them live far out of the reach of human ears—"the secret of the gods."

[6] It seems that the **main objective of the gods was to remain gods; for that is what made them happy. And humanity's role, then, was as the gods' stepping-stone to their happiness.** [. . .] Witnessing the fall of humankind, for the gods, was like witnessing imperfection in

themselves, and thus their fall; anything causing these feelings didn't do the gods any good and therefore could be terminated without a second thought. **It was the job of human beings to make the gods happy**, and upon failure at this task, they could be "fired" (death), only to be replaced later—it wasn't a position which the gods could hold vacant for long. Thus were the great flood stories.

An Analysis of the Draft in the Context of the Film Analogy and Looking for Difference within Similarity   The writer of this essay has already accomplished a lot. In terms of the film analogy, he starts with a pan on the "big picture." Panning on all three stories has allowed him to discover similarities among his blocks of evidence and to demonstrate that the examples he has chosen are representative of his generalization—his claim—that in all three flood stories men exist "solely to please the gods." The writer then constructs a series of tracks, summaries of each of the three stories that isolate some interesting parallels for readers to ponder. The problem is that, rather than allowing his tracks to set up zooms, the writer returns again and again to versions of his original pan. The result is a 1-on-10 paper in which the writer sees, in effect, only what he wants to see: opportunities to repeatedly match the evidence to his one governing claim.

What's wrong, one might ask, with showing how the evidence fits the claim? Isn't this what writers are supposed to do? The answer is that writers do want to use evidence to show that their claims have validity, but not in so general and redundant a way. As the final sentence of the essay demonstrates ("Thus were the great flood stories"), the writer never really arrives at a conclusion. To develop his central claim, the writer needs to devote much less space to repeating that claim, and (much) more to actually looking at key pieces of evidence, zooming in on significant variations within the general pattern.

In his second paragraph, for example, the writer makes a claim about the God of Genesis that overlooks significant evidence. The claim is as follows:

> God had become unhappy with his creations so they were to be destroyed. Like a toy a child no longer has use for, humankind was to be wasted.

It is here that the writer allows the 1-on-10 pattern to rush his thinking and distract him from his evidence. The depiction of God as one who treats humans like toys may accurately describe Enlil, the god in Gilgamesh who, as we are later told, decides to get rid of humans because they make too much noise. But it does not so easily fit the God of Genesis, about whom the writer has just told us that "the wickedness of man . . . grieved him to his heart." Doesn't the grief that this evidence mentions suggest that God's decision to flood the earth was possibly ethical rather than childishly selfish and rash? And the statement from Genesis that "every imagination of the thoughts of [man's] heart was only evil continually" would seem to indicate that humans were not simply victims of divine prerogative, but rather that they deserved punishment.

The writer doesn't consider these other possible interpretations because his reliance on pans—the general pattern—has predisposed him to see his evidence only as another sign of the gods' egotism, their desire to remain "happy" at any cost. Pressed by the desire to "match" examples to his one governing idea, the writer is not allowing himself to really examine his evidence. Instead, he has attempted to squeeze that evidence into a pattern he has apparently superimposed from Gilgamesh, thereby neglecting potentially significant differences among his examples. Thus, he is not prepared to deal with potentially significant differences among his examples.

Ways to Revise the Draft Using 10 on 1 and Looking for Difference within Similarity How might the writer make better use of the evidence he has collected, using the principle of looking for difference within similarity?

Revision Strategy 1:
Assume that the essay's "answer"—its conclusion about the evidence—does not yet go far enough. Rather than having to throw out his thinking, the writer should consider, as is almost always the case in revision, that he hasn't refined his initial idea enough. As an interpretation of the evidence, it leaves too much unaccounted for.

Revision Strategy 2:
Find a "1" to use with 10 on 1—a piece of the evidence sufficiently revealing to be analyzed in more detail; then zoom in on it. In the case of the writer of "Flood Stories," that 1 might be a single story, which he could examine in more detail. He could then test his claims about this story through comparison and contrast with the other stories. In the existing draft, the writer has not used comparison and contrast to refine his conclusion; he has just imposed the same conclusion on the other stories. Alternatively, the 1 might be the single most interesting feature that the three stories share.

Revision Strategy 3:
To find the most revealing piece or feature of the evidence, keep asking, What can be said with some certainty about the evidence? This question will induce a writer to rehearse the facts to keep them fresh, so that his or her first impressions don't "contaminate" or distort consideration of subsequent evidence.

   If the writer of the flood paper were to apply these strategies, he might have a conversation with himself that sounded something like this:

   "What can I say with some certainty about my evidence?"

   "In all three of these stories, a first civilization created by a god is destroyed by the same means—a flood."

Notice that this is a factual *description* of the evidence rather than a speculation about it. You are always better off to report the facts in your evidence carefully and fully before moving to conclusions. (This is harder to do than you might think.)

   "What else is certain about the evidence?"

"In each case the gods leave a surviving pair to rebuild the civilization rather than just wiping everybody out and inventing a new kind of being. Interestingly, the gods begin again by choosing from the same stock that failed the first time around."

Mulling over the evidence in this way, taking care to lay out the facts and distinguish them from speculation, can help you decide what evidence to zoom in on. One of the chief advantages of zooms is that they get you in close enough to your evidence to see the questions its details imply.

Revision Strategy 4:

Examine the evidence closely enough to see what questions the details imply and what other patterns they reveal. So far, the writer of the flood paper has worked mostly from two quite general questions: Why did the gods decide to wipe out their creations? And why do the gods need human beings? But there are other questions his evidence might prompt him to ask. In each story, for example, the gods are disappointed by humankind, yet they don't invent submissive robots who will dedicate their lives to making the deities feel good about themselves. Why not? This question might cause the writer to uncover a shared feature of his examples (a pattern) that he has thus far not considered—the surviving pairs.

Revision Strategy 5:

Use zooms to uncover implications that can develop your interpretation further. Having selected the surviving pairs for more detailed examination, what might the writer conclude about them? One interesting fact that the surviving pairs reveal is that the flood stories are not only descriptions of the end of a world but also creation accounts, because they also tell us how a new civilization, the existing one, got started.

At this point, the writer might apply the principle of looking for difference within similarity to the survival pairs. Given the recurrence of the survival pairs in the three stories, where might the writer locate a significant difference? One potentially significant difference involves the survival pair in the story of Gilgamesh, who are segregated from the new world and granted immortality. Perhaps this separation suggests that the new civilization will not be haunted by the painful memory of a higher power's intervention, leaving humans less fearful of what might happen in the future. This distinction could focus the argument in the essay; it does not distract from the writer's overall generalization but rather develops it.

Notice how the hypothetical revision we've been producing has made use of looking for difference within similarity to constellate the zooms on a limited set of details. Instead of repeatedly concluding that the gods destroy humans when humans fail to make them happy, the writer might be on his way to a thesis about the relative optimism or skepticism of the way the flood stories represent change. Such a thesis might posit, for example, that the flood stories propose the view that real change is necessarily apocalyptic rather than evolutionary. Or, the thesis might be that the flood stories present qualified optimism about the possibility of new starts. And so forth.

► **Try this 5.5:** Describing Evidence

Have a conversation with yourself (on paper) about some piece of evidence you are studying. Start with the question we proposed for the student writer of the flood stories essay: What can be said with some certainty about this evidence? What, in other words, is clearly true of the data? What can be reported about it as fact without going on to interpretation of the facts?

This distinction between fact and interpretation can be a tricky one, but it is also essential, because, if you can't keep your data separate from what you've begun to think about them, you risk losing sight of the data altogether. Press yourself to keep answering the same question—What can be said with some certainty about this evidence? or a variant of the question, such as What's clearly true of this evidence is. . . .

You may find it helpful to do this exercise with a partner or in a small group. If you work in a small group, have one member record the results as these emerge. You might also try this exercise as a freewrite and then share your results with others by reading aloud your list of facts or putting them on a blackboard along with other people's results. Once you've assembled a list of what can fairly be stated as fact about your evidence, you are ready to start on some version of the question, What do these facts suggest? or What features of these data seem most to invite/require interpretation?

A TEMPLATE FOR ORGANIZING PAPERS USING 10 ON 1

Here is a template for writing papers to be used with doing 10 on 1. It brings together much of the key terminology introduced in this chapter. Think of it not as a rigid format but as an outline for moving from one phase of your paper to the next.

1. In your introduction, start by noting (panning on) an interesting pattern or tendency you have found in your evidence. Explain what attracted you to it—why you find it potentially significant and worth looking at. This paragraph would end with a tentative theory (working thesis) about what this pattern or tendency might reveal or accomplish.

2. Zoom in on your representative example, some smaller part of the larger pattern.

3. Argue for the example's representativeness and usefulness in coming to a better understanding of your subject.

4. Do 10 on 1—analyze your representative example—sharing with your readers your observations (what you notice) and your tentative conclusions (answers to the So what? question). Then use complicating evidence to refine your claims.

5. In a short paper you might at this point move to your conclusion, with its qualified, refined version of your thesis and brief commentary on what

you've accomplished—that is, the ways in which your analysis has illuminated the larger subject.

6. In a longer paper you would begin constellating—organizing the essay by exploring and elaborating the connections among your representative examples analyzed via 10 on 1. In the language of the film analogy, you would move from your initial zoom to another zoom on a similar case, to see the extent to which the thesis you evolved with your representative example needed further adjusting to better reflect the nature of your subject as a whole. This last move is a primary topic of our next chapter.

❮ **ASSIGNMENT**: Writing a Paper Using 10 on 1

Write a paper in which you do 10 on 1 with a single, representative example of something you are trying to think more carefully about. This could be a representative passage from a story or a representative story from a volume of stories by a single author. It could be a representative poem from a short volume of poetry or a representative passage from a nonfiction book or article. It could be a passage from a favorite columnist or a single representative song from a CD. It could be a single scene or moment or character from a film or play or other performance. It could be one picture or work of art that is representative of a larger exhibit.

Brainstorm your "1" on the page, making observations and asking, So what? Draw out as much meaning as possible from your representative example. Go for depth. Then use this example as a lens for viewing similar examples. Use the template in the previous section as a model for organizing the paper. ❯

GUIDELINES FOR ANALYZING EVIDENCE

1. Learn to recognize unsubstantiated assertions, rather than treating claims as self-evident truths. Whenever you make a claim, offer your readers the evidence that led you to it.

2. Make details speak. Explain how evidence confirms or qualifies your claim, and offer your reasons for believing the evidence means what you say it does.

3. Say more about less rather than less about more, allowing a carefully analyzed part of your subject to provide perspective on the whole.

4. It is generally better to make ten points on a representative issue or example than to make the same basic point about ten related issues or examples; this axiom we call 10 on 1.

5. Argue overtly that the evidence on which you choose to focus is representative. Be careful not to generalize on the basis of too little or unrepresentative evidence.

GUIDELINES FOR ANALYZING EVIDENCE (CONTINUED)

6. Use your best example as a lens through which to examine other evidence. Analyze subsequent examples to test and develop your conclusions, rather than just confirming that you are right.

7. Look for difference within similarity as a way of doing 10 on 1. Rather than repeating the same overly general claim (i.e., doing 1 on 10), use significant variation within the general pattern to better develop your claim.

8. To find the most revealing piece or feature of the evidence, keep asking yourself, What can I say with some certainty about the evidence? If you continually rehearse the facts, you are less likely to let an early idea blind you to subsequent evidence.

9. Whatever kind of evidence you're using, the emphasis rests on how you use what you have: on articulating what the evidence means, and carefully linking it to your claims.

CHAPTER 6

Making a Thesis Evolve

Quick
Take

In a good piece of writing, the thesis—the primary claim—operates as a powerful tool of discovery. Its function is to examine and question your subject to arrive at some point about its meaning that would not have been immediately obvious to your readers. The paper itself records the refining of the thesis, its central idea.

This view of the thesis as fluid and dynamic, growing and changing as it encounters evidence, goes against the way most textbooks present the thesis. They see the thesis as the finished product of an act of thinking: an inert assertion to be marched through a paper from beginning to end. But if you actually study how a thesis behaves in a piece of writing—if you track its recurrences through an essay—you'll see that a strong thesis *evolves*; it is not static.

This chapter will show you ways of querying your own thesis formulations and using evidence to make your thesis evolve. The payoff is that your claims will become more specific, more qualified, more true. But you'll need to get past the idea that what we call complicating evidence—data for which your thesis does not completely account—is a problem that needs to be avoided in favor of a new and simpler claim. Here's the mantra: *the complications you encounter are an opportunity to make your thesis evolve*, not a problem. Formulating a claim, seeking out conflicting evidence, and then using these conflicts to revise the claim is a primary movement of mind in analytical writing. The savvy writer will take advantage of opportunities to make apparent complications overt in order to make his or her claim respond more fully to the evidence.

The chapter contains one heuristic, Six Steps for Making a Thesis Evolve through Successive Complications, which offers a skeletal version of this process.

Before we go further, here's a quick look at the difference between good and bad thesis statements. It summarizes where we've been and points to where we're headed.

WHAT A GOOD WORKING THESIS DOES

Promotes thinking: leads you to greater precision about what things mean

Reduces scope: separates useful evidence from the welter of details

Provides direction: helps you decide what to talk about and what to talk about next

Contains tension: balances *this* against *that* in a form such as "although x, nevertheless y . . ."

WHAT A BAD THESIS DOES

Addicts you too early to a too-large idea, so that you stop actually seeing the evidence in its real-life complexity or thinking about the idea itself

Produces a demonstration rather than discovery of new ideas by making the same overly general point again and again about a range of evidence

Includes too much possible data without helping you see what's most important to talk about

WHAT'S WRONG WITH A STATIC THESIS?

Basically, a static thesis is imprecise, overly general, and redundant. It asserts a meaning that is applied again and again as an answer, using different but similar pieces of evidence. Usually this answer is simple and single. It needs to be, because it is being asked to explain a lot, to contain so much evidence. The truth, though, is rarely either simple or single.

The static thesis—a broad label slapped on a bunch of examples—tends to produce *demonstrations*. Demonstrations point at something—"See?"—and then they're done with it. They're not interested in seeing *into* things, only looking at them from a distance to confirm a point so broad, such as "Exercise is good for you," that it was probably not worth offering as a thesis in the first place.

The staple of the demonstration form of paper writing is the five-paragraph form, which we critiqued earlier. The form predisposes the writer to begin with a BIG claim, such as "Environmentalism prevents economic growth," and then offer a paragraph on three examples (say, statutes that protect endangered wildlife, inhibit drilling for oil, and levy excessive fines on violators). Then the big claim simply gets repeated again, after a "Thus, we see . . ."

At the least, such a thesis is inaccurate. It's too easy to find exceptions to the claim and also to question what its key words actually mean. Mightn't environmentalism also promote economic growth by, say, promoting tourism? And is the meaning of economic growth self-evident? Couldn't a short-term economic boon be a long-term disaster, as might be the case for oil exploration in the polar regions?

In sum, most of what typically goes wrong in using a thesis is the result of a writer leaping too quickly to a generalization that would do as a thesis, and then treating evidence *only* as something to be mustered in support of that idea. Simply repeating the same big idea keeps things too superficial. In papers that contain a static thesis, nothing happens to the claim itself: it doesn't grow, add to our knowledge, or generate new ideas.

> Most of what typically goes wrong in using a thesis is the result of a writer leaping too quickly to a generalization that would do as a thesis, and then treating evidence **only** as something to be mustered in support of that idea.

A. EVOLVING A THESIS

THE RECIPROCAL RELATIONSHIP BETWEEN WORKING THESIS AND EVIDENCE: THE THESIS AS A CAMERA LENS

It's useful to think of the thesis as a camera lens that affects how we see the subject, what evidence we select, and what questions we ask about that evidence. But it's essential to understand that the subject being viewed also affects the lens. In good analytical writing, the analysis of evidence should also focus and refocus (bring about revision of) the thesis. Even in a final draft, writers are usually fine-tuning their governing idea in response to their analysis of evidence. The relationship between thesis and subject is thus *reciprocal* (see Figure 6.1).

In the terms of this analogy, very broad thesis statements, made up of impre-cise (fuzzy) terms, make bad camera lenses. If your lens is insufficiently sharp, you are not likely to see much in your evidence. If you say, for example, that "the economic situation today is bad," you will at least have some sense of direction, but the imprecise terms *bad* and *economic situation* don't provide you with a focus

FIGURE 6.1 The Reciprocal Relationship Between Thesis and Evidence.

Like a lens, the thesis affects the way a writer sees evidence. Evidence should also require the writer to readjust the lens.

clear enough to distinguish significant detail in your evidence. Without significant detail to analyze, you can't develop your thesis, either by showing readers what the thesis is good for (what it allows us to understand and explain) or by clarifying its terms.

Let's take one more brief example of a fuzzy-lens thesis and lay out a few basic moves for evolving it. Say that you're looking for a trend (or strand) in contemporary films you've seen and, as a working thesis, you claim that "Women in contemporary films are represented as being more sensitive than men." To avoid a mere demonstration and instead make this thesis evolve, you would need to

- query its key terms, asking yourself what these actually mean, and
- search for data that not only matched your claim but also didn't match it.

You'd more or less be assuming that you had overstated things, and you'd be looking for ways to press yourself to make further distinctions in your initial formulation, to make it less fuzzy.

Having claimed that the films show women as more sensitive than men, ask yourself what *sensitive* means, and by what criteria you are assessing its presence and absence. Is the overt expression of tender feelings the only acceptable evidence for being sensitive? Couldn't men have less demonstrative ways of being sensitive? What is the best piece or two of evidence that men do show something like sensitivity in the films you're considering?

And surely you could also complicate that claim by locating it within a richer *context*. It's not enough to assert that women are represented as sensitive in the films. What are these films inviting us to think about their sensitivity? Are the women punished for it in the plots? Are they rewarded with being liked (approved of) by the films, even if this trait causes them problems?

Such considerations as these would require significant *reformulation* of the thesis. This procedure will normally be repeated several times, with each new discussion of significant evidence. For this reason you may find it useful to think of the claim-making aspect of a piece of writing not simply as a thesis, which implies that it is a settled thing, but rather as *a working thesis*, which suggests that the claim is in process, metamorphosing through a series of contexts within the paper.

The term working thesis suggests that the claim is in process, not static.

By the end of the paper, the claim that "women are more sensitive than men" should have evolved into a more carefully defined and qualified statement that reflects the thinking you have done in your analysis of evidence. This is what good concluding paragraphs do; they reflect back on and reformulate your paper's initial position in light of the thinking you have done about it (see Figure 6.2).

You might ask, Isn't this reformulating of the thesis something a writer does *before* he or she writes the essay? Certainly some of it is accomplished in your exploratory drafting and note taking, and your revision process should weed out

FIGURE 6.2 Evolving thesis diagram

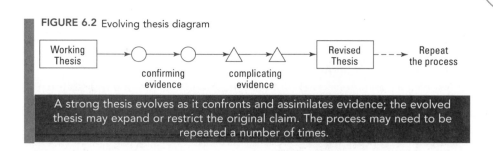

A strong thesis evolves as it confronts and assimilates evidence; the evolved thesis may expand or restrict the original claim. The process may need to be repeated a number of times.

various false starts and dead ends. But your finished paper should include the evolutions of your thesis. To an extent, all good writing re-creates the chains of thought that lead writers to their conclusions. If you just listed your conclusions, your readers might rightly question how you arrived at them. The main routes of your movement from a tentative idea to a refined and substantiated theory should remain visible for readers to follow. (See "The Evolving Thesis in a Final Draft" later in this chapter for further discussion of how much thesis evolution to include in your final draft.)

A FIRST NOTE ON THE SHAPE OF THESIS STATEMENTS

Before we move on to concentrated applications of the procedure for making a thesis evolve, take a look back at the shape of the imprecise thesis statements used as examples in this chapter:

> Environmentalism prevents economic growth.
>
> The economic situation today is bad.
>
> Women in contemporary films are represented as being more sensitive than men.

All three are simple, declarative sentences that offer very abstract assertions. That is, they are both grammatically and conceptually simple. More than that, they're *slack*—especially the first two, which stand alone, not in relation to anything else.

The very *shape* of these weak thesis statements is a warning sign. Most effective working theses, though they may begin more simply, achieve both grammatical and conceptual complexity as they evolve. Such theses contain tension, the balance of this against that; this degree, with that qualification. Often they begin with *although* or incorporate *however* or use an *appears to be about* x *but is actually about* y kind of formulation. Here, by contrast to the weak theses above, are three possible evolutions of the "sensitivity" thesis:

> Although women cry more readily in contemporary films, the men, by not crying, seem to win the audience's favor.

> The complications that fuel the plots in today's romantic comedies arise because women and men express their sensitivity so differently; the resolutions, however, rarely require the men to capitulate.

> A spate of recent films has witnessed the emergence of the new "womanly" man as hero, and not surprisingly, his tender qualities seem to be the reason he attracts the female love interest.

► **Try this 6.1:** Qualifying Overstated Claims

Using as a model of inquiry the treatment of the example thesis "Women in contemporary films are represented as being more sensitive than men," seek out complications in one of the overstated claims in the following list. These complications might include conflicting evidence (which you should specify) and questions about the meaning or appropriateness of key terms (again, which you should exemplify). Illustrate a few of these complications, and then reformulate the claim in language that is more carefully qualified and accurate.

Welfare encourages recipients not to work.
Midwives are more caring than gynecologists.
Religious people are more moral than those who are not religious.
School gets in the way of education.
Herbal remedies are better than pharmaceutical ones.
The book is always better than the film.

PROCEDURE FOR MAKING THE THESIS EVOLVE THROUGH SUCCESSIVE COMPLICATIONS: THE EXAMPLE OF *EDUCATING RITA*

This section of the chapter presents an extended example that illustrates how the initial formulation of a thesis might evolve—through a series of complications—over the course of a draft. It closely follows in organization the "Six Steps for Making a Thesis Evolve."

Let's consider the stages you might go through within a more finished draft to evolve a thesis about a film. In *Educating Rita*, a working-class English hairdresser (Rita) wants to change her life by taking courses from a professor (Frank) at the local university, even though this move threatens her relationship with her husband (Denny), who burns her books and pressures her to quit school and get pregnant. Frank, she discovers, has his own problems: he's a divorced alcoholic who is bored with his life, bored with his privileged and complacent

SIX STEPS FOR MAKING A THESIS EVOLVE

1. Formulate an idea about your subject—a working thesis.
2. See how far you can make this thesis go in accounting for (confirming) evidence.
3. Locate complicating evidence that is not adequately accounted for by the thesis.
4. Make explicit the apparent mismatch between the thesis and selected evidence, asking and answering So what?
5. Reshape your claim to accommodate the evidence that hasn't fit.
6. Repeat steps 2, 3, 4, and 5 several times.

students, and bent on self-destruction. The film follows the growth of Frank and Rita's friendship and the changes it brings about in their lives. By the end of the film, each has left a limiting way of life behind and has set off in a seemingly more promising direction. She leaves her constricting marriage, passes her university examinations with honors, and begins to view her life in terms of choices; he stops drinking and sets off, determined but sad, to make a new start as a teacher in Australia.

Formulate an idea about your subject, a working thesis (step 1).

> **Working thesis:** *Educating Rita* celebrates the liberating potential of education.

The film's relatively happy ending and the presence of the word *educating* in the film's title make this thesis a reasonable opening claim.

See how far you can make this thesis go in accounting for evidence (step 2). The working thesis seems compatible, for example, with Rita's achievement of greater self-awareness and independence. You would go on to locate similar data that would support the idea that education is potentially liberating. She becomes more articulate, which allows her to free herself from otherwise disabling situations. She starts to think about other kinds of work she might do, rather than assuming that she must continue in the one job she has always done. She travels, first elsewhere in England and then to the Continent. So, the thesis checks out as viable: there is enough of a match with evidence to make it worth pursuing.

Locate evidence that is not adequately accounted for by the thesis and ask So what? about the apparent mismatch between the thesis and selected evidence (steps 3 and 4). Other evidence troubles the adequacy of the working thesis, however: Rita's education causes her to become alienated from her husband, her parents, and her social class; at the end of the film she is alone and unsure about her direction in life. In Frank's case, the thesis runs into even more problems. His boredom, drinking, and alienation seem to have been caused, at least in part, by his education rather than by his lack of it. He sees his book-lined study as a prison. Moreover, his profound knowledge of literature has not helped him control his life: he comes to class drunk, fails to notice or care that his girlfriend is having an affair with one of his colleagues, and asks his classes whether it is worth gaining all of literature if it means losing one's soul.

Reshape your claim to accommodate the evidence that hasn't fit (step 5). *Question: What are you to do?* You cannot convincingly argue that the film celebrates the liberating potential of education, because that thesis ignores such a significant amount of the evidence. Nor can you "switch sides" and argue that the film attacks education as life-denying and disabling, because this thesis is also only partially true.

What not to do. Faced with evidence that complicates your thesis, you should not assume that it is worthless and that you need to start over from scratch. View the "problem" you have discovered as an opportunity to modify your thesis rather than abandon it. After all, the thesis still fits a lot of significant evidence. Rita is arguably better off at the end of the film than at the beginning: we are not left to believe that she should have remained resistant to education, like her husband, Denny, whose world doesn't extend much beyond the corner pub.

What to do. Make apparent complications explicit—the film's seemingly contradictory attitudes about education—and then modify the wording of your thesis in a way that might resolve or explain these contradictions. You might, for example, be able to resolve an apparent contradiction between your initial thesis (the film celebrates the liberating potential of education) and the evidence by proposing that there is more than one version of education depicted in the film. You would, in short, start qualifying and clarifying the meaning of key terms in your thesis.

In this case, you could divide education as represented by the film into two kinds: enabling and stultifying. The next step in the development of your thesis would be to elaborate on how the film seeks to distinguish true and enabling forms of education from false and debilitating ones (as represented by the self-satisfied and status-conscious behavior of the supposedly educated people at Frank's university).

> **Revised thesis:** *Educating Rita* celebrates the liberating potential of enabling—in contrast to stultifying—education.

Repeat steps 2, 3, 4, and 5 (step 6). Having refined your thesis in this way, you would then repeat the step of seeing what the new wording allows you to account for in your evidence. The revised thesis might, for example, explain Frank's problems as being less a product of his education than of the cynical and pretentious versions of education that surround him in his university life. You could posit further that, with Rita as inspiration, Frank rediscovers at least some of his idealism about education.

What about Frank's emigration to Australia? If we can take Australia to stand for a newer world, one where education would be less likely to become the stale and exclusive property of a self-satisfied elite, then the refined version of the thesis would seem to be working well. In fact, given the possible thematic connection between Rita's working-class identity and Australia (associated, as a former frontier and English penal colony, with lower-class vitality as opposed to the complacency bred of class privilege), the thesis about the film's celebration of the contrast between enabling and stultifying forms of education could be sharpened further. You might propose, for example, that the film presents institutional education as desperately in need of frequent doses of "real life" (as represented by Rita and Australia)—infusions of working-class pragmatism, energy, and optimism—if it is to remain healthy and open, as opposed to becoming the oppressive property of a privileged social class. This is to say that the film arguably exploits stereotypical assumptions about social class.

> **Revised thesis:** *Educating Rita* celebrates the liberating potential of enabling education, defined as that which remains open to healthy doses of working-class, real-world infusions.

Similarly, you can make your supporting ideas (those on which your thesis depends) more accurate and less susceptible to oversimplification by seeking evidence that might challenge their key terms. Sharpening the language of your supporting assertions will help you develop your thesis.

Consider, for example, the wording of the supporting idea that *Educating Rita* has a happy ending. Some qualification of this idea through consideration of possibly conflicting evidence could produce an adjustment in the first part of the working thesis, that the film celebrates education and presents it as liberating. At the end of the film, Frank and Rita walk off in opposite directions down long, empty airport corridors. Though promising to remain friends, the two do not become a couple. This closing emphasis on Frank's and Rita's alienation from their respective cultures, and the film's apparent insistence on the necessity of each going on alone, significantly qualifies the happiness of the "happy ending."

Once you have complicated your interpretation of the ending, you will again need to modify your thesis in accord with your new observations. Does the film simply celebrate education if it also presents it as being, to some degree, incompatible with conventional forms of happiness? By emphasizing the necessity of having Frank and Rita each go on alone, the film may be suggesting that to be truly liberating, education—as opposed to its less honest and more comfortable substitutes—inevitably produces and even requires a certain amount of loneliness and alienation. Shown in Figure 6.3 are the successive revisions of the thesis.

Final version of thesis: *Educating Rita* celebrates the liberating potential of enabling education (kept open to real-world, working-class energy) but also acknowledges its potential costs in loneliness and alienation.

➤ Try this 6.2: Tracking a Thesis

As should be clear now, various versions of the thesis recur throughout a piece of writing, usually with increasing specificity, complication, and grammatical complexity. The four thesis statements on *Educating Rita* illustrate this pattern of recurrence clearly. One of the best ways to teach yourself how and where to locate statements of the thesis in your own writing is to track the thesis in a piece of reading. Ideally you should choose an essay or article used in one of your courses, because this exercise will also powerfully increase your understanding of the reading. Use a highlighter to mark the evolutions. Where in the essay do you find the thesis? How has it changed in each recurrence? In response to what complication?

B. USING THE EVOLVING THESIS TO ORGANIZE THE FINAL DRAFT

Having achieved a final version of a thesis, *what next?* Why wouldn't a writer just offer the last and fullest statement of the thesis in his or her first paragraph and then prove it?

Usually it's neither possible nor desirable to encapsulate in the opening sentences what it will actually take the whole paper to explain. The position articulated in the fully evolved thesis is typically too complex to be stated intelligibly and concisely in the introduction. But more, if you think of an essay as an

FIGURE 6.3 Successive Revisions of a Thesis.

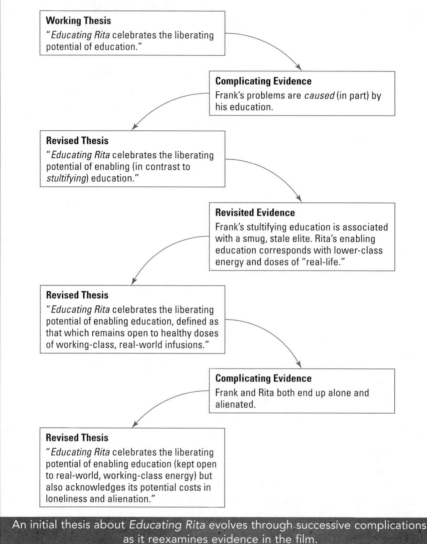

Working Thesis
"*Educating Rita* celebrates the liberating potential of education."

Complicating Evidence
Frank's problems are *caused* (in part) by his education.

Revised Thesis
"*Educating Rita* celebrates the liberating potential of enabling (in contrast to *stultifying*) education."

Revisited Evidence
Frank's stultifying education is associated with a smug, stale elite. Rita's enabling education corresponds with lower-class energy and doses of "real-life."

Revised Thesis
"*Educating Rita* celebrates the liberating potential of enabling education, defined as that which remains open to healthy doses of working-class, real-world infusions."

Complicating Evidence
Frank and Rita both end up alone and alienated.

Revised Thesis
"*Educating Rita* celebrates the liberating potential of enabling education (kept open to real-world, working-class energy) but also acknowledges its potential costs in loneliness and alienation."

An initial thesis about *Educating Rita* evolves through successive complications as it reexamines evidence in the film.

act of thinking, then the evolutions of the thesis record the history of your various changes in thinking as you confronted evidence. If your readers get to see these, they are far more likely to go along with you, literally to follow your trains of thought.

Before treating these matters in more detail, however, let us nail down a general answer to the question of thesis locations.

- The first articulation of the working thesis almost always occurs late in the opening paragraph or early in the second paragraph of a piece, after the writer has presented the problem or question that establishes the tension the thesis aims to resolve, and given some kind of context for it.

■ Subsequent articulations of the thesis usually occur at points of transition, typically at paragraph openings following the analysis of complicating evidence. These thesis evolutions are often overtly marked as such—the writer tells readers that on the basis of this analysis, it is necessary to amend the governing claim. This kind of explicit updating has the added benefit of providing unity to the essay, using the thesis as a kind of spine.

■ The final statement of the thesis occurs in the concluding paragraph, or perhaps the penultimate one. It is usually offered in clear relationship to the terms offered in the introduction, so the reader is offered a last vision of where the essay has traveled.

If you think of an essay as an act of thinking, then the evolutions of the thesis record the history of your various changes in thinking as you confronted evidence.

A more complete answer to the questions of where and how to locate versions of the thesis in a final draft involves two related issues: (1) the location of the thesis statement in relation to the conventional shapes of argument—induction and deduction—and (2) the customary location of the thesis according to the protocols (ways of proceeding) of different disciplines. We will treat each of these in its turn.

THE EVOLVING THESIS AND COMMON THOUGHT PATTERNS: DEDUCTION AND INDUCTION

Put simply, in a deductive paper a fairly full-fledged version of the thesis appears at the beginning; in an inductive paper, it appears at the end (see Figure 6.4, A and B).

As a thought process, deduction reasons from a general principle (assumed to be true) to the particular case. It introduces this principle up front and then uses it to select and interpret evidence. For example, a deductive paper might state in its first paragraph that attitudes toward and rules governing sexuality in a given culture can be seen, at least in part, to have economic causes. The paper might then apply this principle, already assumed to be true, to the codes governing sexual behavior in several cultures or several kinds of sexual behavior in a single culture.

A good deductive argument is, however, more than a mechanical application or matching exercise of general claim and specific details that are explained by it. Deductive reasoning uses the evidence to draw out the implications—what logicians term *inferring the consequences*—of the claim. The general principle explains selected features of particular cases, and *reciprocally*, the evidence brings out implications in the principle.

Thus, the general principle stated at the beginning of the paper and the idea stated as the paper's conclusion are not the same. Rather, the conclusion presents the (evolved) idea that the writer has arrived at through the application of the principle.

FIGURE 6.4 Deduction and Induction.

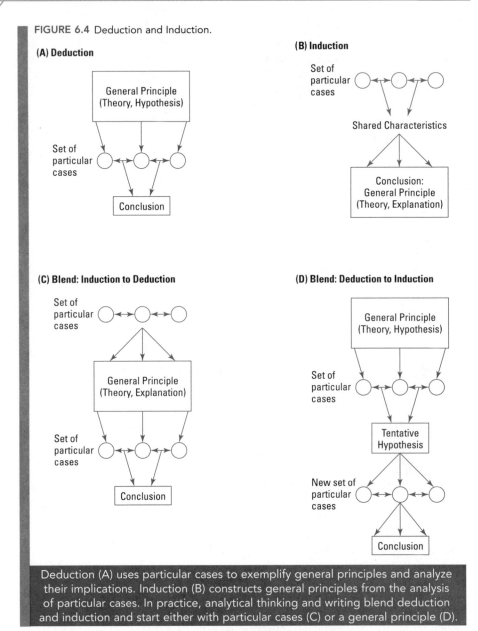

Deduction (A) uses particular cases to exemplify general principles and analyze their implications. Induction (B) constructs general principles from the analysis of particular cases. In practice, analytical thinking and writing blend deduction and induction and start either with particular cases (C) or a general principle (D).

An inductively organized paper typically begins not with a principle already accepted as true but with particular data for which it seeks to generate some explanatory principle.

Whereas deduction moves by applying a generalization to particular cases, induction moves from the observation of individual cases to the formation of a general principle. Because all possible cases can obviously never be examined—every left-handed person, for example, if one wishes to theorize that left-handed people are better at spatial thinking than right-handers—the principle (or thesis) arrived at through inductive reasoning always remains open to doubt.

Nevertheless, the thesis of an inductive paper is generally deemed acceptable if a writer can demonstrate that the theory is based on a reasonably sized sampling of representative instances. (This matter of representativeness was taken up in our earlier discussion of 10 on 1.) Suffice it to say that a child who arrives at the thesis that all orange food tastes bad on the basis of squash and carrots has not based that theory on an adequate sampling of available evidence.

What we hope this discussion makes clear is that whether your analysis is primarily inductive or deductive, the thesis will undergo evolution as it confronts evidence. What still needs to be understood, though, is that in most cases induction and deduction operate in tandem (see Figure 6.4, C and D). It's true that in some disciplines (philosophy, for example) the deductive pattern of argument prevails, but not exclusively: the analysis of evidence, though clearly designed to reflect a general principle, will also lead to new formulations that will modify the general principle in various ways.

It is in the nature of analysis to move between the particular and the general, regardless of which comes first. Whether the overall shape of the analysis—its mode of progression—is primarily inductive or deductive, it will still *gain in complexity* from beginning to end. The statement with which you begin is not also the end (see Figure 6.4).

► Try this 6.3: Formulating an Inductive Principle

Study a group of like things inductively. You might, for example, use greeting cards aimed at women versus greeting cards aimed at men, a group of poems by one author, or ads for one kind of product (jeans) or aimed at one target group (teenage girls).

Make use of the looking-for-patterns heuristic (see the Method in Chapter 2) to compile and organize a set of significant details about the data, and then leap to a general claim about the group that you think is interesting and reasonably accurate. This generalization is your inductive principle. Then use the principle to examine deductively more data of the same kind, exploring its implications as you evolve it more accurately.

THE EVOLVING THESIS AS HYPOTHESIS AND CONCLUSION IN THE NATURAL AND SOCIAL SCIENCES

A thesis functions differently depending on the academic discipline—whether it must be stated in full at the outset, for example, and what happens to it between the beginning of the paper and the end. The differences appear largest as you move back and forth between courses in the humanities and courses in the natural and certain of the social sciences.

VOICES FROM ACROSS THE CURRICULUM

The Hypothesis in the Sciences

It should go without saying that if the empirical evidence doesn't confirm your hypothesis, you rethink your hypothesis, but it's a complex issue. Researchers whose hypotheses are not confirmed in fact often question their *method* ("if I had more subjects," or "a better manipulation of the experimental group," or "a better test of intelligence," etc.) as much as their hypothesis. And that's often legitimate. Part of the challenge of psychological research is its reliance on a long array of assumptions. Failure to confirm a hypothesis could mean a problem in any of that long array of assumptions. So failure to confirm your hypothesis is often difficult to interpret.

—Alan Tjeltveit, Professor of Psychology

The thesis in Experimental Psychology papers is the statement of the hypothesis. It is always carefully and explicitly stated in the last few sentences of the introduction. The hypothesis is usually a deductive statement such as, If color does influence mood, then an ambiguous picture printed on different colors of paper should be interpreted differently, depending on the color of the paper. Specifically, based on the results of Jones (1997), the pink paper should cause participants to perceive the picture as a more calm and restful image, and the green paper should cause the picture to be interpreted as a more anxious image.

—Laura Snodgrass, Professor of Psychology

The thesis is usually presented in the abstract and then again at the end of the introduction. Probably the most frequent writing error is not providing a thesis at all. Sometimes this is because the student doesn't *have* a thesis; other times it is because the student wants to maintain a sense of mystery about the paper, as if driving toward a dramatic conclusion. This actually makes it harder to read. The best papers are clear and up front about what their point is, then use evidence and argument to support and evaluate the thesis. I encourage students to have a sentence immediately after their discussion of the background on the subject that can be as explicit as "In this paper I will argue that although research on toxic effects of methyl bromide provides troubling evidence for severe physiological effects, conclusive proof of a significant environmental hazard is lacking at this time."

I try to avoid the use of the term *hypothesis*. I think it gives the false sense that scientists always start with an idea about how something works. Frequently, that is not the case. Some of the best science has actually come from observation. Darwin's work on finches is a classic example. His ideas about adaptation probably derived *from* observation.

—Bruce Wightman, Professor of Biology

> Economists do make pretense to follow scientific methodology. Thus we are careful not to mix hypothesis and conclusion. I think it's important to distinguish between what is conjectured, the working hypothesis, and what ultimately emerges as a result of an examination of the evidence. Conclusions come only after some test has been passed.
>
> —James Marshall, Professor of Economics

Broadly speaking, papers in the humanities are inclined to begin inductively, and papers in the natural and social sciences deductively. The natural and social sciences generally use a pair of terms, *hypothesis* and *conclusion*, for the single term *thesis*. Because writing in the sciences is patterned according to the scientific method, writers in disciplines such as biology and psychology must report how the original thesis (hypothesis) was tested against empirical evidence and then conclude on this basis whether or not the hypothesis was confirmed.

The gap between this way of thinking about the thesis and the concept of an evolving thesis is not as large as it may seem. The scientific method is in sync with one of the chapter's main points, that something must happen to the thesis between the introduction and the conclusion, so that the conclusion does more than just reassert what was already asserted in the beginning.

Analogously, in a scientific paper, the hypothesis is tested against evidence, the results of which allow the writer to draw conclusions about the hypothesis's validity. Although the hypothesis does not change (or evolve), the testing of it and subsequent interpretation of those results produce commentary on and, often, qualifications of the paper's central claim.

In the natural and social sciences, successive reformulations of the thesis are less likely to be recorded and may not even be expressly articulated. But, as in all disciplines, the primary analytical activity in the sciences is to repeatedly reconsider the assumptions upon which a conclusion is based.

THE EVOLVING THESIS AND INTRODUCTORY AND CONCLUDING PARAGRAPHS

If you are not using the hypothesis/conclusion format, your final drafts could often begin by predicting the evolution of their theses. Thus, the *Educating Rita* paper might open by using a version of the seems-to-be-about-*x* gambit, claiming that at first glance the film seems to celebrate the liberating potential of education. You could then lay out the evidence for this view and proceed to complicate it in the ways we've discussed.

What typically happens is that you lead (usually at the end of the first paragraph or at the beginning of the second) with the best version of your thesis that you can come up with that will be understandable to your readers without a lengthy preamble. If you find yourself writing a page-long introductory paragraph to get to your initial statement of thesis, try settling for a simpler articulation of your central idea in its first appearance. As you move through the paper, substantiate, elaborate on, test, and qualify your paper's opening gambit.

VOICES FROM ACROSS THE CURRICULUM

Recognizing Your Thesis

For an analytical or interpretive historical essay, *thesis* is a conventional term and one of much value. The thesis usually is that point of departure from the surfaces of evidence to the underlying significance, or problems, a given set of sources reveal to the reader and writer. In most cases, the thesis is best positioned up front, so that the writer's audience has a sense of what lies ahead and why it is worth reading on. I say *usually* and *in most cases* because the hard and fast rule should not take precedence over the inspirational manner in which a thesis can be presented. But the inspiration is not to be sought after at the price of the thesis itself. It is my experience, in fact, that if inspiration strikes, one realizes it only after the fact.

Recognizing a thesis can be extremely difficult. It can often be a lot easier to talk "about" what one is writing than to say succinctly what the thrust of one's discussion is. I sometimes ask students to draw a line at the end of a paper after they have finished it, and then write one, at most two sentences, saying what they most want to tell their readers. My comment on that postscript frequently is "Great statement of your thesis. Just move it up to your first paragraph."

—Ellen Poteet, Professor of History

The most important thing to do in the introductory paragraph of an analytical paper is to lay out a genuine issue, which is to say, something that seems to be at stake in whatever you are studying. Ideally, you should select a complex issue—one not easily resolved, seeming to have some truth on both sides—and not an overly general one. Otherwise you run the risk of writing a paper that proves the obvious or radically oversimplifies.

Set up this issue as quickly and concretely as you can, avoiding generic (fits anything) comments, throat clearing, and review-style evaluations. As a general rule, you should assume that readers of your essay will need to know on page 1— preferably by the end of your first paragraph—what your paper is attempting to resolve or negotiate.

The first paragraph does not need to—and usually can't—offer your conclusion; it will take the body of your paper to accomplish that. It should, however, provide a quick look at particular details that set up the issue. Use these details to generate a theory, a *working hypothesis*, about whatever it is you think is at stake in the material. The rest of the paper will test and develop this theory.

Your concluding paragraph will offer the more carefully qualified and evolved version of your thesis that the body of your paper has allowed you to arrive at. Rather than just summarize and restate what you said in your introduction, the concluding paragraph should leave readers with what you take to be your single best insight, and it should put what you have had to say into some kind of perspective. See Chapter 8 for a more extended discussion of introductions and conclusions.

C. EVOLVING A THESIS IN AN EXPLORATORY DRAFT: *LAS MENINAS*

Now let's look at another extended example, this time using it to bring together the strategies that we have suggested so far for writing an analytical paper. The example is a student writer's exploratory draft on a painting called *Las Meninas* (Spanish for "the ladies-in-waiting") by the seventeenth-century painter Diego Velázquez. We have, by the way, selected a paper on a painting because all of the student's data (the painting) is on one page where you can keep referring back to it, trying to share in the writer's thought process.

Look at the painting in Figure 6.5, and then read the student's draft. As you read, you will notice that much of the essay is still unfocused with listlike description, but as we noted in Chapter 1, careful description is a necessary stage in moving toward interpretations of evidence, especially in an exploratory draft where the writer is not yet committed to any single position. Notice how the writer's word choice in her descriptions prompts various kinds of interpretive leaps. We have added in brackets our observations about how the writer is proceeding.

FIGURE 6.5 *Las Meninas* by Diego Velázquez, 1656.

Approximately 10'5" x 9'. Museo del Prado, Madrid.

Velázquez's Intentions in *Las Meninas*

[1] Velázquez has been noted as being one of the best Spanish artists of all time. It seems that as Velázquez got older, his paintings became better. Toward the end of his life, he painted his masterpiece, *Las Meninas*. Out of all his works, *Las Meninas* is the only known self-portrait of Velázquez. There is much to be said about *Las Meninas*. <u>The painting is very complex, but some of the intentions that Velázquez had in painting *Las Meninas* are very clear</u>. [The writer opens with background information and a broad working thesis (underlined).]

[2] First, we must look at the painting as a whole. The question that must be answered is, Who is in the painting? The people are all members of the Royal Court of the Spanish monarch Philip IV. In the center is the king's daughter, who eventually became Empress of Spain. Around her are her *meninas* or ladies-in-waiting. These *meninas* are all daughters of influential men. To the right of the *meninas* are dwarfs who are servants, and the family dog who looks fierce but is easily tamed by the foot of the little dwarf. The more unique people in the painting are Velázquez himself, who stands to the left in front of a large canvas; the king and queen, whose faces are captured in the obscure mirror; the man in the doorway; and the nun and man behind the *meninas*. To analyze this painting further, the relationship between characters must be understood. [The writer describes the evidence and arrives at an operating assumption—focusing on the relationship between characters.]

[3] Where is this scene occurring? Most likely it is in the palace. But why is there no visible furniture? Is it because Velázquez didn't want the viewers to become distracted from his true intentions? I believe it is to show that this is not just a painting of an actual event. This is an event out of his imagination. [The writer begins pushing observations to tentative conclusions by asking, So what?]

[4] Now, let us become better acquainted with the characters. The child in the center is the most visible. All the light is shining on her. <u>Maybe Velázquez is suggesting that she is the next light for Spain</u> and that even God has approved her by shining all the available light on her. Back in those days there was a belief in the divine right of kings, so this just might be what Velázquez is saying. [The writer starts ranking evidence for importance and continues to ask, So what?; she arrives at a possible interpretation of the painter's intention.]

[5] The next people of interest are the ones behind the *meninas*. The woman in the habit might be a nun and the man a priest.

[6] The king and queen are the next group of interesting people. They are in the mirror, which is to suggest they are present, but they are not as visible as they might be. Velázquez suggests that they are not always at the center where everyone would expect them to be. [The writer continues using Notice and focus plus asking So what?; the

writer has begun tackling evidence that might conflict with her first interpretation.]

[7] The last person and the most interesting is Velázquez. He dominates the painting along with the little girl. He takes up the whole left side along with his gigantic easel. But what is he painting? As I previously said, he might be painting the king and queen. But I also think he could be pretending to paint us, the viewers. The easel really gives this portrait an air of mystery because Velázquez knows that we, the viewers, want to know what he is painting. [The writer starts doing 10 on 1 with her selection of the most significant detail.]

[8] The appearance of Velázquez is also interesting. His eyes are focused outward here. They are not focused on what is going on around him. It is a steady stare. Also interesting is his confident stance. He was confident enough to place himself in the painting of the royal court. <u>I think that Velázquez wants the king to give him the recognition he deserves by including him in the "family."</u> And the symbol on his vest is the symbol given to a painter by the king to <u>show that his status and brilliance have been appreciated by the monarch</u>. It is unknown how it got there. It is unlikely that Velázquez put it there himself. That would be too outright, and Velázquez was the type to give his messages subtly. Some say that after Velázquez's death, King Philip IV himself painted it to finally <u>give Velázquez the credit he deserved for being a loyal friend and servant</u>. [The writer continues doing 10 on 1 and asking, So what?; she arrives at three tentative theses (underlined).]

[9] I believe that Velázquez was very ingenious by putting his thoughts and feelings into a painting. He didn't want to offend the king who had done so much for him. It paid off for Velázquez because he did finally get what he wanted, even if it was after he died. [The writer concludes and is now ready to redraft to tighten links between evidence and claims, formulate a better working thesis, and make this thesis evolve.]

DESCRIPTION TO ANALYSIS: THE EXPLORATORY DRAFT

There are a number of good things about this draft. The writer has, for example, used the *interesting* prompt to press herself to notice and emphasize particular details in her evidence. The purpose of the exploratory draft is to use writing as a means of arriving at a working thesis that your next draft can more fully evolve. Most writers find that potential theses emerge near the end of the exploratory draft—which is the case in the student draft (see the three claims that are underlined in paragraph 8).

As you see, the writer has not wasted time trying for a polished introductory paragraph. She has instead crafted an opening that allows her to get started and to start fast—no rambling prefatory material. This introduction, with its overly broad working thesis, does its job. It provides enough direction to guide the writer in her initial examination of evidence, using the artist's intention as her *interpretive context*.

INTERPRETIVE LEAPS AND COMPLICATING EVIDENCE

Notice that as early as paragraphs 3 and 4, the writer has begun to push herself to tentative conclusions (interpretive leaps) about the meaning of selected features of her evidence. What is especially good about the draft is that it reveals the writer's willingness to push on from her first idea (reading the painting as an endorsement of the divine right of kings, expressed by the light shining on the princess) by seeking out *complicating evidence.*

The writer could have settled for the divine-right-of-kings idea, and then simply foregrounded details in the picture that would corroborate it, such as the deferential bowing of the *meninas* arranged in a circle with the princess at the center. But this potential thesis would not have accounted for enough of the evidence, especially evidence that clearly doesn't fit, such as the small size and decentering of the king and queen, and the large size and foregrounding of the painter himself.

Rather than ignoring these potentially troublesome details, the writer instead zooms in on them, making the painter's representation of himself and of his employers the 1 for doing 10 on 1 (making a number of observations about a single representative piece of evidence and analyzing it in depth). This analytical move produces a burst of interpretive thinking in the form of three related claims (underlined in paragraph 8 in the student's draft), all of which have thesis potential.

REVISING THE EXPLORATORY DRAFT

Now what? The writer is ready to rewrite the paper to more carefully formulate and evolve her thesis. What could she do better as she reviews her evidence in preparation for starting this next draft?

First, she could make more use of looking for **patterns of repetition and contrast** (see Chapter 2).

Examples of exact or nearly exact **repetitions**:

the pictures in the background
the fact that both the dwarf and the painter, each on his own side of the painting, stare confidently and directly at the viewer

Examples of **strands** (repetition of a similar kind of detail):

details having to do with family
servants (dwarf, *meninas*, dog? painter?)
details having to do with art and the making of art

Examples of **organizing contrasts**—binaries:

royalty/commoners
employers/servants
large/small
foreground/background
central (prominent)/marginalized (less prominent)

The writer also might make more productive use of the **So what?** question, asking it repeatedly about pieces of evidence and about her own claims. In this way she might press herself to arrive at a range of possible answers until she finds the one that seems to best fit the evidence.

So what that the king and queen are small, but the painter, princess, and dwarf are all large and fairly equal in size and prominence? So what that there are size differences in the painting? What might large or small size mean?

Here are some possible answers to these So what? questions:

- Perhaps the king and queen have been reduced so that Velázquez can show-case their daughter, the princess.
- Perhaps the size and physical prominence of the king and queen are relatively unimportant. In that case, what matters is that they are a presence, always overseeing events (an idea implied but not developed in paragraph 6).
- Perhaps the relative size and/or prominence of figures in the painting can be read as indicators of what the painter wants to say about their importance.
- Perhaps the painter is demonstrating his ability to make the king and queen any size—any level of importance—he chooses. Although the writer does not overtly say so, the king and queen are among the smallest and the least visible figures.

TESTING THE ADEQUACY OF THE THESIS

The evidence that the writer included in paragraphs 6 and 7 (the decentering of the king and queen and the prominence and confident stare of the painter) caused her to drop her initial thinking—that the primary intention was to endorse the divine right of kings. The direction that her thinking takes next is not, however, an entirely new idea. The shift she is apparently making (but not yet overtly articulating) is from the painting as showcase of royal power to the painting as showcase of the painter's own power.

Given the answers posed above to the So what? question about the relative size and importance of the king and queen versus the painter—parallel to if not greater in prominence than the princess herself—the writer should probably choose the second of the two potential theses arrived at in paragraph 8. That idea—that the painting is a bid for recognition of the painter's status and brilliance—explains more of the evidence than anything else she has come up with so far. It explains, for example, the painter's prominence and the relative insignificance of the monarchs; the painter, in effect, creates their stature (size, power) in the world through his paintings. Framed in a mirror and appearing to hang on the wall, the king and queen are, arguably, suspended among the painter's paintings, mere reflections of themselves—or, rather, the painter's reflection of them.

HOW THE NEXT DRAFT MIGHT GO

Let's see how well the status-and-brilliance idea accounts for details in the painting. This thesis seems useful in accounting for the presence of the large dwarf in the right-hand foreground. Positioned in a way that links him with the painter, the dwarf arguably furthers the painting's message and does so, like much else in the painting, in the form of a loaded joke: the small ("dwarfed" by the power of others) are brought forward and made big.

What other features of the painting might the thesis account for? How about the various ways that the painting seems to deny viewers' expectations? Both by decentering the monarchs and concealing what is on the easel, the painter again emphasizes his power, in this case, over the viewers (among whom might be the king and queen if their images on the back wall are mirrored reflections of them standing, like us, in front of the painting). He is not bound by anyone's expectations and in fact appears to take a certain pleasure in using viewers' expectations to manipulate them: he can make them wish to see something he has the power to withhold.

Does this mean that the status-and-brilliance thesis is adequately evolved? If (as the writer has said) the painter is demonstrating that he can make the members of the royal family any size he wants, then the painting is not only a bid for recognition but also a playful, though not so subtle, threat: be aware of my power and treat me well, or suffer the consequences. As artist, the painter decides how the royal family will be seen. The king and queen depend on the painter, as they do in a different way on the princess, with whom Velázquez makes himself equal in prominence, to extend and perpetuate their power.

Before leaving this example we want to emphasize that the version of the thesis that we have just proposed is not necessarily the "right" answer. Looked at in a different context, the painting might have been explained primarily as a demonstration of the painter's mastery of the tools of his trade—light, for example, and perspective. But our proposed revision of the thesis for the *Las Meninas* paper meets two important criteria for evaluating the adequacy of a thesis statement.

1. It unifies the observations the writer has made.
2. It is capable of accounting for a wide range of evidence.

Remember that the thesis develops through successive complications. Allowing your thesis to run up against potentially conflicting evidence ("But what about this?") enables you to build upon your initial idea, extending the range of evidence it can accurately account for by clarifying and qualifying its key terms. Although throwing out the old thesis and starting over may be what is needed, you should first try to use evidence that is not accounted for by your current thesis as a means of evolving the thesis further.

D. THE EVOLVING THESIS IN A FINAL DRAFT

It seems fitting, after the examples of papers in the planning *(Rita)* and drafting *(Meninas)* stages, that we conclude this chapter with an example of an evolving thesis in a final draft. Here is a piece analyzing a recent German film about an East German family around the time of the fall of the Berlin Wall in 1989. (Note: there is also a freewrite on this film at the end of Chapter 1.) Certainly there is more that could be done with this essay, but it is on balance a strong piece that illustrates a number of the features of effective analysis that we have been discussing. In addition, we have included within brackets brief descriptions of how the essay evolves and underlined versions of its thesis.

Good Bye Lenin! Before and After the Fall

[1] The recent German film *Good Bye Lenin!* directed by Wolfgang Becker is a comedy that <u>appears to celebrate the freedom that comes with the tearing down of the Berlin Wall</u> and the reunification of Germany in 1989. It follows the life of Alex Schäfer, who also provides voice-over narration interpreting events from before until after the wall falls. Before, he grows up dreaming of becoming a cosmonaut, but he ends up working in a TV repair shop in East Berlin. Afterward, he peddles satellite TV dishes as part of a joint East–West German venture and visits postmodern nightclubs with his Russian nurse girlfriend, Lara. But amidst the celebratory fireworks and the influx of Mercedes and Burger Kings, there is a bittersweet tone, for the film also <u>appears to mourn the loss of a socialist version of what Alex calls "idealism"</u>—a term that refers to his mother's utopian socialist ideals of social equality, innocent goodwill, and boundless possibility. [The writer establishes a working thesis evident in the tension between the two uses of *appears*, suggesting that the essay will negotiate the tension between celebration and mourning.]

[2] Clearly the film is interested in comparing life before unification with what comes afterward, because the central event of the plot presses Alex to restore the before. His ardent Communist mother, Kathrin, suffers a stroke and falls into a coma as she glimpses her son protesting the regime. When she suddenly awakens eight months later, Alex and his sister Ariane are told that any shocks, any changes in her environment, will threaten her life, and so Alex strives to conceal from her the fact that Germany has reunified while she has been asleep, and that the East has rapidly begun to become Westernized. <u>By superimposing a faux view of the Communist past onto the capitalist present, director Becker is using *Good Bye Lenin!* to assess the change, to explore the profit and loss of both the before and the after</u>. [The terms profit and loss keep this paragraph in touch with the celebrate/mourn binary of its working thesis. But the writer has come to recognize that the director complicates both the celebration of the fall of the wall and the mourning of the lost socialist "utopia."]

[3] Most of the action in the film concerns Alex's attempts to restore the appearance of the past and to preserve the illusion that the past is still present. We repeatedly see him filling old East German–labeled jars with new international products; it is an act of devotion, a sign of his love for his afflicted mother. Of course, complications arise—cracks in the façade that occur when his mother glimpses evidence of the change.

[4] As a repeated strategy—and a major source of the film's comedy—Alex and his coworker Denis conceive and make videotaped bogus television news accounts that explain these cracks. For example, when the mother sees a banner advertising Coca-Cola, the videotape announces the discovery that Coke is actually an East German formula stolen by the West and now returned to its rightful home. Here Alec and his friend have become comic versions of the old socialist state, reinterpreting the facts—and covering up the truth—in order to preserve old loyalties and the status quo. <u>The friends' attempts to reassure the mother by protecting her socialist dreams are comic but also poignant, and so the element of mourning remains</u>. [In this and the preceding paragraph the writer negotiates the tension between the comedy and the sense of mourning for the lost past. Does the mourning get cancelled, he wonders? No, he decides.]

[5] This comic pattern gets repeated several times throughout the film and culminates in the comic climax: one of the final faux news reports interprets footage of the wall being torn down as an act of disgruntled West Germans seeking solace from capitalist greed and competition in the peace and tranquility of the East. This is funny because it inverts the truth. The film actually shows us the East German youth becoming entranced by the outlandish décor (lamp shades of purple fur), rock music, cars, and money that invade from the West. Similarly, Alex's sister Ariane has given up her studies and gone to work at a Burger King managed by her eventual husband. The film focuses in this way on capitalist culture as seen from the socialist point of view.

[6] From this perspective, <u>there is little to celebrate</u>, as the invading western culture seems frivolous, fixated on material goods and inclined to sacrifice the long term good in favor of short term gain. We see Burger King uniforms everywhere; Becker is making it clear that in place of uniformity in the service of the state, there is now uniformity in the service of international fast food corporations. [The writer confronts evidence that causes him to qualify his claim that the film celebrates the fall of the wall.]

[7] The comedy feels good—there are many laugh-out-loud moments—but *Good Bye Lenin!* is not all good times, liberation, and rock 'n' roll. In a film in which videotapes are shown to be calculated deceptions, designed to pacify those too frail to accommodate change, we dare not accept the film itself as offering some uncomplicated vision of things.

[8] Interestingly, the comedy tends to drop out at disruptive moments. For example, we are shown the desperate emptiness of the lives of the older generation of East Germans who feel lost because of the changes, roaming around the apartment house, grumbling amidst the piles of

furniture and other detritus of the previous regime now abandoned to the street. We see the skirmishes between Alex and Ariane about the lengths to which they are going to preserve the illusion for their mother. [The writer notes a deepening of the mourning element called attention to in places in the film where the comedy drops out.]

[9] Surely one of the most important of such moments occurs near the end, when Alex's girlfriend, Lara, who has nursed his mother since she first fell ill, betrays the dream script that he has created for his mother, a script of the past as unchanged in the present, an East Germany intact and self-professedly superior to the West.

[10] It is a very brief scene, lasting only a few seconds, spliced into a longer narrative episode. The mother has suffered a relapse, and in response to her dying request, her son Alex has traveled to the West to retrieve his father, who had fled the Communist regime perhaps fifteen years before. As Alex is returning to the hospital with his father, the scene shifts to Lara telling Kathrin that the wall fell some months ago and that Alex has staged the unchanged present she has been inhabiting since awaking from her coma. Kathrin shakes her head in disbelief. The camera then cuts away and never returns to this conversation.

[11] The scene is, at the same time, a moment of truth-telling to the mother and betrayal of the son. It is not, strictly speaking, required by the plot: shortly thereafter the mother will die, and the film will end amidst fireworks celebrating the official reunification of Germany. So why does the film make the decision to include this moment? [The writer concludes the analysis by formulating a conclusion that follows the pattern of bringing together opposites—truth-telling and betrayal—and then asks So what?]

[12] Without this scene, Alex succeeds in his scheme—the hero achieves his goal. And his goal is humanitarian, surely, in preserving his mother's illusions. But from the outset Ariane opposes the scheme, and later Lara too confronts Alex about the extremity and impractical-ity of his position. We begin to see it as *his obsession*, and somehow, his need or desire to preserve the past, which his mother's infirmity conveniently enables. The scheme of re-creating the past increasingly comes to appear to be an opportunity to create an idealized version of the past that never existed but has been associated with his mother almost from the beginning. Alex admits as much in one of his voice-overs later in the film, speaking of the world his and his friend's video-tapes have created as "an ideal socialism" like the one that he and his mother wished to believe in. [The writer uses evidence to shift his thinking on what it is that the film mourns—not the actual socialist state that is gone, but his and his mother's illusions and powerful desire to idealize the past.]

[13] And so ultimately *Good Bye Lenin!* is a film that is anxious about resisting change and accepting delusions, even beautiful illusions. It seems to insist that if we retain them, we must do so with the knowledge that they are false. Interestingly, the women are in solidarity here: Lara does not allow Kathrin to die deluded. Alex, on the other hand, apparently exits the film oblivious to the fact that his mother has been undeceived—but that is another matter. [The first two sentences of this paragraph represent a late evolution of the thesis as the writer continues to develop the implications of his conclusion. He then introduces a new complication, as he considers how the treatment of gender might bear on the film's critique of socialism.]

[14] The film is also anxious about simply acceding to change—specifically, the capitalism it represents as dominating the West, which the videotaped news report comically represents as a hell worth fleeing. Surely the film recognizes the greater liberties that the West makes possible; it does not confuse the "ideal socialism" in which Alex and Kathrin wish to believe with the somber political realities of East Germany. We learn, for instance, that Kathrin was removed from her beloved teaching job because of her too ardent idealism, and that her husband fled the country to escape the prejudice that was directed against him because he was not a member of the Communist Party. [The writer returns to his earlier claim about the film both celebrating and mourning the changes brought about the fall of the Berlin wall. The writer has discovered that the film is not really about capitalism and socialism so much as it is about the stories we tell ourselves and the ideals we have tried to live by.]

[15] In the end, it seems, *Good Bye Lenin!* wants to value the dream, the utopian vision of ideal socialism, especially because with the advent of Western capitalism into East Germany, one source of that dream has been desiccated. But the film takes great pains to qualify that dream—to distinguish it from East German Communist practice, and crucially, to insist that we recognize that it is only a dream and not the real thing. That is why Lara tells Kathrin the truth. In the spiraling success story of a newly reunited Germany, Wolfgang Becker has made a film that reminds us that the stories we tell others fill psychic needs not just for others but for ourselves, and that we need to be reminded that all stories, however necessary, in one way or another are false. [The writer concludes by returning to his essay's opening binary formulation and offering a more evolved version of his thesis as it pertains to the film's point of view, but that also beckons beyond it, to the constructed and inevitably partisan nature of all accounts of the world. The writer acknowledges the film's anxiety about embracing change but then presents further evidence for what has emerged as his major claim, that the film recognizes that ideal socialism never existed and that the East German version of real socialism may not warrant much mourning.]

RECAP OF THE EVOLVING THESIS IN *GOOD BYE LENIN!* BEFORE AND AFTER THE FALL

As we hope you can see, this essay's thesis evolution does not evolve in a straight line or into a single claim. There is a logic to the thesis development, but it is not a clear and predictable evolution. Rather, we can see that the basic terms of the thesis—celebrating the future versus mourning the past, the individual versus the collective, the dominant and accepted historical script versus the comic inversion of the script—get taken to different places, and impel different kinds of discoveries as the writer raises and revisits them.

The celebration/mourning binary in the essay begins a chain of analysis that allows the writer to discover what is for him a more important binary—between betrayal and truth-telling, evident in the moment Lara talks to Kathrin—that does not erase or replace the original contrast so much as grow out of it.

In the concluding phase of the essay, the writer becomes increasingly concerned with the problematic truth value of all motives and all representations of the past. This emphasis leads him to recognize the distinction the film makes between delusions and necessary but recognized illusions, and by the final paragraph he has arrived at the conclusion that the film impels us to see all representations as necessarily partisan.

And so finally, what might we conclude? Perhaps that the evolving thesis as a principle of development does not necessarily move toward greater truth, only toward new or additional truths, discoveries different from those with which it began. In this context, then, the thesis becomes a necessary constituent of analytical writing because it defines a field of play and allows a writer to go places. That is more than enough for writers who want to increase their understanding, and for their readers.

Try this 6.4: Tracking a Thesis in a Student Draft

Track the evolutions of the thesis in the draft printed below. It is a fairly early draft; the writer has not yet been expected to attend to organization, style, and so forth. In fact, one purpose of such idea-gathering drafts is to invite you to conduct an open-minded survey of the data, which with any luck will culminate in the discovery of one or more possible working theses.

Instructions: Locate significant repetition and contrast; then work with the relationship between thesis and evidence.

1. Circle or underline the paper's key words, its patterns of repetition, and organizing contrasts.
2. Briefly list the details you find most interesting in the draft, and in a sentence explain why.
3. Identify versions of the writer's thesis.
4. Go back through the paper and mark evidence that seems not to fit this thesis.
5. Play around with ranking and renaming the paper's various strands and organizing contrasts. What other possible theses or qualified version of the existing one might these data suggest?

Mall Cuisine Goes International

[1] At the outer reaches of a fantastic enclosed shopping mall near downtown Boston's Copley Square there is a truly unique restaurant named Bon Marche. The mall is huge, connecting several high-rise hotels, and it offers literally hundreds of upscale shops.

[2] My friend and I entered Bon Marche just to look around; we were hungry for some breakfast, and it looked interesting. Almost immediately a Latino guy about twenty wearing a green beret stopped us to give us a check. He told us that there was one for takeout and one for eating there, and then he explained how the restaurant worked. There were a number of different stations serving food, and you were supposed to give them your ticket to be stamped when they served you your food. The ticket, by the way, which was designed to look like a passport, included a comical warning that if you lost it, you would be required to wash dishes there for two days.

[3] The stations were scattered all over this enormous room, and each one offered a different kind of food. (We later learned that they had a market downstairs too, where they sold the food uncooked.) A lot of the foods were international in flavor. There was lots of seafood, especially shellfish of various kinds. Other stations offered omelettes, sushi, wood-oven-cooked pizza, fresh-squeezed juices (including carrot!), soups such as chowders and bouillabaisse, crepes, Oriental stir-fries, and various kinds of bread and pastries. I did notice, though, that there was no lox, though plenty of fresh salmon they would cook for you.

[4] I noticed that at a number of these stations, you could basically design your food choice. For example, you would choose what "innards" you wanted in your omelette from a variety of ingredients in silver bowls at the front of the station. The same went for the stir-fry station and the pizza station, where you chose among toppings. And most of the stations also offered vegetarian options.

[5] We decided to have breakfast, and that's when we discovered one drawback to this station idea. We had to wait in line for about fifteen minutes before we were able to order our omelettes. They looked and smelled great, and they came with hash browns, but when we asked for some bacon, the Latina girl who was cooking told us that we had to go to another station where they cook breakfast meats. That would mean waiting in line again, while our food was getting cold. And then we'd have to wait in line again if we wanted juice, which was at another station.

[6] Just as there is a great variety of exotic foods, there are a lot of diverse seating areas at Bon Marche. One area was glassed in, like a French bistro, with small white tables that had multicolored umbrellas in them. Another seemed Indonesian—rattan furniture and hay bales. We chose an area by the windows looking out over downtown Boston. It was decorated with lattices like a grape arbor at an Italian villa.

[7] Once we noticed the international character of Bon Marche's food and settings, we began to see it in other aspects of the place. First of all, there's the French name of the place. And virtually all of the staff were members of ethnic minorities—especially Latinos, African-Americans, and Asians. Plus the place was awash in the upbeat rhythms of Latino music—a kind of nouveau sound. Although most of the staff were young, the sushi counter proved an exception. That station featured two middle-aged Asian women, bent over their sushi mats, making mostly Boston rolls and California rolls, one after another after another. It was a pretty sad sight, and we were struck with how boring the job must be. How many omelettes was that woman cooking an hour, with the line getting longer every minute?

[8] Still, the food was tasty (and inexpensive!), and the atmosphere was really interesting. I had the overall impression that Bon Marche was all about youth and choice and feeling optimistic. Considering its great location and how busy it was, the staff must make pretty good money, and so they are getting to participate in the American dream of opportunity and freedom as well.

[9] That's when I realized that maybe what makes Bon Marche so great is that it embodies democracy. It has everything for everybody, and the individual gets to choose what he or she wants, down to the last detail. And the whole place was just bursting with food—there seemed to be abundance for all. It makes available to everyone the experience of international cuisines at affordable prices, whereas in the past you would have had to travel abroad or at least to expensive restaurants all over the city, to get this diversity. Mall culture offers the world in one convenient location, as Bon Marche exemplifies.

[10] As we were leaving, we saw more evidence for this democracy idea in the uniforms that the staff were wearing. They all had full-length aprons matching the color of their berets—the men all wore green berets and the women wore red ones. This uniform was bright and happy, and the berets seemed to symbolize that everyone was equal. Also the berets seem to go with the

restaurant's French name, except that the berets themselves had these fitted leather bases that made them seem stiffer than traditional French berets.

[11] The cashier was located at the front of the restaurant, and when she gave us our receipts, we also received what they called "exit visas" that we then had to hand to a guy standing about four feet away, just at the interface of the restaurant and the rest of the mall. It was as if were leaving this fantasy world behind.

[12] Maybe that's why we noticed the contrast in the store next door to Bon Marche. It was a bank—a large, glassed-in open space. There were about fifteen desks equipped with computer workstations, each with a swivel chair and file cabinets. We could see the workers from behind as they went about their business. I'm not sure exactly how this fits with my ideas about Bon Marche, but it was interesting. The bank was not a fantasy space, but it did convey a sense of openness just like the restaurant did. Maybe this openness is related to the democracy idea.

REVISION CHECKLIST FOR ORGANIZING AN ESSAY WITH AN EVOLVING THESIS

The following is a handout that our colleague Professor Barri Gold adapted largely from this chapter to distribute to her students.

I'm pretty sure I have a good idea, but I'm still not sure how to organize a paper . . .

The format of your paper should reflect a willingness to test your own thesis and to advance your thinking. A paper that begins and ends on the same idea, a paper that goes nowhere, suggests that you have closed yourself off to possibilities that don't fit neatly into your preconceived ideas.

The following is a useful though very general outline for structuring the bulk of your paper (does not include introductions and conclusions):

1. Clear statement of **working thesis**.
2. Confirming evidence—that is, evidence that supports your thesis. To a large extent, this is the most familiar part of your paper . . . the part in which you argue your case.

3. **Complicating evidence**—that is, evidence that does not readily support your thesis.

   Many people have trouble with this concept, so, more elaborately:

   Complicating evidence may (but need not) be contradictory (something that actually disproves or undermines your thesis). Such evidence is often quite useful for forcing you to rethink and advance your thesis.

   Complicating evidence may be something for which your thesis does not account. It may seem outside the scope of your thesis.

   As such, it may be used to test the limits of your thesis. It could force you to specify your thesis/categories.

   Complicating evidence may also add another element to your thinking. It may lead you to consider the significance of another theme, etc., on your current working thesis.

4. **Rethink/revise your thesis** in such a way that it incorporates this new, complicating evidence.

5. **Go to step 1.**

Yes. This structure is reiterative. You may go through this several times during the course of a paper. Your judgment should determine which iterations are interesting enough to be incorporated into your final draft. Begin with a working thesis that is neither too obvious nor too far-fetched to convince your reader(s) and work step-by-step through increasingly subtle, difficult, or complex ideas.

Some advice on **microstructure:**

- **Depth** is more useful than breadth. It is better to spend your time really exploring your best representative example than to accumulate many superficially treated examples intended to make the same point.

- **What you need to make your point:** At each moment, you should make it clear to your reader (1) what point you are making, (2) what evidence you are using to support that point, (3) how you read the evidence, (4) how it actually does support your local point, and (5) how it connects to your overall point or current working thesis.

A special note on item 3 above: Remember, different readers will understand any given quote differently. If you do not explain your reading/interpretation, you may lose your reader. If you think your quote does not need explanation, you are probably making a point that is too obvious and you should rethink your point, your working thesis, and/or your paper overall.

◀ **ASSIGNMENT:** Evolving a Thesis on a Film or Painting

The chapter has already modeled this process with these forms. Alternatively, you might use an episode of a television show or an advertisement.

First, begin by formulating a variety of possible statements about the film or painting that could serve as a working thesis. These might be in answer to the question What is the film/painting about? or What does it "say"? Or you might begin with looking for patterns of repetition and contrast and formulate a thesis to explain a pattern of repetition or contrast you have observed. In any case, you shouldn't worry that these initial attempts will inevitably be overstated and thus only partially true—you have to start somewhere. At this point you will have completed step 1.

Next, follow the remainder of the procedure for making the thesis evolve, listed again here for convenience:

1. Formulate an idea about your subject, a working thesis.
2. See how far you can make this thesis go in accounting for confirming evidence.
3. Locate evidence that is not adequately accounted for by the thesis.
4. Make explicit the apparent mismatch between the thesis and selected evidence, asking and answering So what?
5. Reshape your claim to accommodate the evidence that hasn't fit.
6. Repeat steps 2, 3, 4, and 5 several times. ▶

GUIDELINES FOR FINDING AND DEVELOPING A THESIS

1. A thesis is an idea that you formulate and reformulate about your subject. It should offer a theory about the meaning of evidence that would not have been immediately obvious to your readers.

2. Look for a thesis by focusing on an area of your subject that is open to opposing viewpoints or multiple interpretations. Rather than trying to locate a single right answer, search for something that raises questions.

3. Treat your thesis as a hypothesis to be tested rather than an obvious truth.

4. Most effective theses contain tension, the balance of this against that, this degree with that qualification. They are conceptually complex, and that is reflected in their grammatical shape—often they begin with *although* or incorporate *however.*

5. The body of your paper should serve not only to substantiate the thesis by demonstrating its value in selecting and explaining evidence, but also to bring the opening version of the thesis into better focus.

6. Evolve your thesis—move it forward—by seeing the questions that each new formulation of it prompts you to ask.

GUIDELINES FOR FINDING AND DEVELOPING A THESIS (CONTINUED)

7. Develop the implications of your evidence and of your observations as fully as you can by repeatedly asking, So what?

8. When you encounter potentially conflicting evidence (or interpretations of that evidence), don't simply abandon your thesis. Take advantage of the complications to expand, qualify, and refine your thesis until you arrive at the most accurate explanation of the evidence that you can manage.

9. Arrive at the final version of your thesis by returning to your initial formulation—the position you set out to explore—and restating it in the more carefully qualified way you have arrived at through the body of your paper.

10. To check that your thesis has evolved, locate and compare the various versions of it throughout the draft. Have you done more than demonstrate the general validity of an unqualified claim?

CHAPTER 7

Recognizing and Fixing Weak Thesis Statements

This chapter will teach you how to recognize the difference between good thesis statements—statements that make claims that need proving—and weak thesis statements. Weak thesis statements have in common the fact that they don't give the writer enough to do in his or her essay. Typically a weak thesis is an unproductive claim because it doesn't actually require further thinking or proof, as, for example, in the case of "The jeans industry targets its advertisements to appeal to young adults" (probably a statement of fact that doesn't need proving) or "An important part of one's college education is learning to better understand others' points of view" (a piece of conventional wisdom that most people would already accept as true, and thus not in need of arguing).

Solutions? Be suspicious of your first responses to a subject. Privilege live questions over inert answers. Find ways to bring out the complexity of your subject. Look again at "What It Means to Have an Idea" in Chapter 1, which tells you to start with something puzzling that you want to figure out rather than with something you already believe to be clearly and obviously true. When in doubt, do more exploratory writing to trigger better ideas.

A. FIVE KINDS OF WEAK THESES AND HOW TO FIX THEM

A *strong thesis* makes a claim that (1) requires analysis to support and evolve it and (2) offers some point about the significance of your evidence that would not have been immediately obvious to your readers. By contrast, a *weak thesis* either makes no claim or makes a claim that does not need proving. As a quick flash-forward, here are the five kinds of weak thesis statements—ones that

1. make no claim ("This paper will examine the pros and cons of . . .");
2. are obviously true or are a statement of fact ("Exercise is good for you");
3. restate conventional wisdom ("Love conquers all");
4. offer personal conviction as the basis for the claim ("Shopping malls are wonderful places"); and
5. make an overly broad claim ("Individualism is good").

WEAK THESIS TYPE 1: THE THESIS MAKES NO CLAIM

The following statements are not productive theses because they do not advance an idea about the topics the papers will explore.

Problem Examples

I'm going to write about Darwin's concerns with evolution in *The Origin of Species*.

This paper will address the characteristics of a good corporate manager.

Both problem examples name a subject and link it to the intention to write about it, but they don't make any claim about the subject. As a result, they direct neither the writer nor the reader toward some position or plan of attack. The second problem example begins to move toward a point of view through the use of the value judgment *good*, but this term is too broad to guide the analysis. The statement-of-intention thesis invites a list: one paragraph for each quality the writer chooses to call good. Even if the thesis were rephrased as "This paper will address why a good corporate manager needs to learn to delegate responsibility," the thesis would not adequately suggest why such a claim would need to be argued or defended. *There is, in short, nothing at stake, no issue to be resolved.* A writer who produces a thesis of this type is probably unduly controlled by a relatively passive, information in/information out approach to learning.

Solution   Raise specific issues for the essay to explore.

Solution Examples

Darwin's concern with survival of the fittest in *The Origin of Species* initially leads him to neglect a potentially conflicting aspect of his theory of evolution—survival as a matter of interdependence.

The very trait that makes for an effective corporate manager—the drive to succeed—can also make the leader domineering and therefore ineffective.

Some disciplines expect writers to offer statements of method and/or intention in their papers' openings. Generally, however, these openings also make a claim: for example, "In this paper I will examine how congressional Republicans undermined the attempts of the Democratic administration to legislate a fiscally responsible health care policy for the elderly," *not* "In this paper I will discuss America's treatment of the elderly." (See Chapter 8, "Introductions and Conclusions," for further discussion of using overt statements of intention.)

WEAK THESIS TYPE 2: THE THESIS IS OBVIOUSLY TRUE OR IS A STATEMENT OF FACT

The following statements are not productive theses because they do not require proof. A thesis needs to be an assertion with which it would be possible for readers to disagree.

Problem Examples

The jeans industry targets its advertisements to appeal to young adults.

> The flight from teaching to research and publishing in higher education is a controversial issue in the academic world. I will show different views and aspects concerning this problem.

If few people would disagree with the claim that a thesis makes, there is no point in writing an analytical paper on it. Though one might deliver an inspirational speech on a position that virtually everyone would support (such as the value of tolerance), endorsements and appreciations don't usually lead to analysis; they merely invite people to feel good about their convictions.

In the second problem example, few readers would disagree with the fact that the issue is "controversial." In the second sentence of that example, the writer has begun to identify a point of view—that the flight from teaching is a "problem"—but her next declaration, that she will "show different views and aspects," is a statement of fact, not an idea. The phrasing of the claim is noncommittal and so broad that it prevents the writer from formulating a workable thesis. If you find yourself writing theses of this type, review the discussion of the problems with generalizing in Chapter 1.

Solution Find some avenue of *inquiry*—a question about the facts or an issue raised by them. Make an assertion with which it would be possible for readers to disagree.

Solution Examples

> By inventing new terms, such as *loose fit* and *relaxed fit,* the jeans industry has attempted to normalize, even glorify, its product for an older and fatter generation.

> The "flight from teaching" to research and publishing in higher education is a controversial issue in the academic world. As I will attempt to show, the controversy is based to a significant degree on a false assumption, that doing research necessarily leads teachers away from the classroom.

WEAK THESIS TYPE 3: THE THESIS RESTATES CONVENTIONAL WISDOM

Restatement of one of the many clichés that constitute a culture's conventional wisdom is not a productive thesis unless you have something to say about it that hasn't been said many times before.

Problem Examples

> An important part of one's college education is learning to better understand others' points of view.

> From cartoons in the morning to adventure shows at night, there is too much violence on television.

> "*I* was supposed to bring the coolers; *you* were supposed to bring the chips!" exclaimed ex-Beatle Ringo Starr, who appeared on TV commercials for Sun Country Wine Coolers a few years ago. By using rock music to sell a wide range of products, the advertising agencies, in league with corporate giants such as Pepsi, Michelob, and Ford, have corrupted the spirit of rock 'n' roll.

All of these examples say nothing worth proving because they are clichés. (Conventional wisdom is a polite term for cliché.) Most clichés were fresh ideas once, but over time they have become trite, prefabricated forms of nonthinking. Faced with a phenomenon that requires a response, many inexperienced writers rely on a knee-jerk reaction: they resort to a small set of culturally approved "answers." In this sense, clichés resemble statements of fact. So commonly accepted that most people nod to them without thinking, statements of conventional wisdom make people feel a comfortable sense of agreement with one another. The problem with this kind of packaged solution is that because conventional wisdom is so general and so conventional, it doesn't teach anybody—including the writer—anything. Worse, because the cliché appears to be an idea, it prevents the writer from engaging in a fresh, open-minded exploration of his or her subject.

There is some truth in all of the problem examples above, but none of them *complicates* its position. A thoughtful reader could, for example, respond to the claim that advertising has corrupted the spirit of rock 'n' roll by suggesting that rock 'n' roll was highly commercial long before it colonized the airwaves. The conventional wisdom that rock 'n' roll is somehow pure and honest whereas advertising is phony and exploitative invites the savvy writer to formulate a thesis that overturns these clichés. As our solution example demonstrates, one could argue that rock actually has improved advertising, not that ads have ruined rock—or, alternatively, that rock has shrewdly marketed idealism to a gullible populace. At the least, a writer deeply committed to the original thesis would do better to examine what Ringo was selling—what he stands for in this particular case—than to discuss rock and advertising in such general terms.

Solution Seek to complicate—see more than one point of view on—your subject. Avoid conventional wisdom unless you can qualify it or introduce a fresh perspective on it.

Solution Examples

Although an important part of one's college education is learning to better understand others' points of view, a persistent danger is that students will simply be required to substitute their teachers' answers for the ones they grew up believing uncritically.

Although some might argue that the presence of rock 'n' roll sound tracks in TV commercials has corrupted rock's spirit, this point of view not only falsifies the history of rock but also blinds us to the ways that the music has improved the quality of television advertising.

➤ Try this 7.1: Revising Weak Thesis Statements

You can learn a lot about writing strong thesis statements by analyzing and rewriting weak ones. Rewrite the three weak theses that follow. As in the case of our solution examples, revising will require you to add information and thinking to the weak theses. Try, in other words, to come up with some interesting claims that most readers would not already have thought of to develop the subject of television violence. (The third thesis you will recognize as a problem example for which we offered no solution.)

1. In this paper I will discuss police procedures in recent domestic violence cases.
2. The way that the media portrayed the events of April 30, 1975, when Saigon fell, greatly influenced the final perspectives of the American people toward the end result of the Vietnam War.
3. From cartoons in the morning to adventure shows at night, there is too much violence on television.

WEAK THESIS TYPE 4: THE THESIS OFFERS PERSONAL CONVICTION AS THE BASIS FOR THE CLAIM

A statement of one's personal convictions or one's likes or dislikes does not alone supply sufficient grounds for a productive thesis.

Problem Examples

The songs of the punk rock group Minor Threat relate to the feelings of individuals who dare to be different. Their songs are just composed of pure emotion. Pure emotion is very important in music, because it serves as a vehicle to convey the important message of individuality. Minor Threat's songs are meaningful to me because I can identify with them.

Sir Thomas More's *Utopia* proposes an unworkable set of solutions to society's problems because, like communist Russia, it suppresses individualism.

Although I agree with Jeane Kirkpatrick's argument that environmentalists and business should work together to ensure the ecological future of the world, and that this cooperation is beneficial for both sides, the indisputable fact is that environmental considerations should always be a part of any decision that is made. Any individual, if he looks deeply enough into his soul, knows what is right and what is wrong. The environment should be protected because it is the right thing to do, not because someone is forcing you to do it.

Like conventional wisdom, personal likes and dislikes can lead inexperienced writers into knee-jerk reactions of approval or disapproval, often expressed in a moralistic tone. The writers of the problem examples above assume that their primary job is to judge their subjects or testify to their worth, not to evaluate them analytically. As a result, such writers lack critical detachment not only from their topics but, crucially, from their own assumptions and biases. They have *taken personal opinions for self-evident truths.* You can test a thesis for this problem by asking if the writer's response to questions about the thesis would be "because I think so."

The most blatant version of this tendency occurs in the third problem example, which asserts, "Any individual, if he looks deeply enough into his soul, knows what is right and what is wrong. The environment should be protected because it is the right thing to do." Translation (only slightly exaggerated): "Any individual who thinks about the subject will obviously agree with me because my feelings and convictions feel right to me, and therefore they must be universally and self-evidently true." The problem is that this writer is not distinguishing between his own likes and dislikes (or private convictions) and what he takes to be right, real, or true for everyone else. Testing an idea against your own feelings and experience is not an adequate means of establishing whether something is accurate or true.

Solution   Try on other points of view honestly and dispassionately; treat your ideas as hypotheses to be tested rather than obvious truths. In the following solution examples, we have replaced opinions (in the form of self-evident truths) with ideas—theories about the meaning and significance of the subjects that could be supported and qualified with evidence.

Treat your ideas as hypotheses to be tested rather than obvious truths.

Solution Examples

Sir Thomas More's *Utopia* treats individualism as a serious but remediable social problem. His radical treatment of what we might now call "socialization" attempts to redefine the meaning and origin of individual identity.

Although I agree with Jeane Kirkpatrick's argument that environmentalists and business should work together to ensure the ecological future of the world, her argument undervalues the necessity of pressuring businesses to attend to environmental concerns that may not benefit them in the short run.

It is fine, of course, to write about what you believe and to consult your feelings as you formulate an idea. But the risk you run by arguing from your unexamined feelings and convictions is that you will prematurely dismiss from consideration anything that is unfamiliar or does not immediately conform to what you already believe. The less willing you are to test these established and habitual convictions, the less chance you will have to refine or expand the ways in which you think. You will continue to play the same small set of tunes in response to everything you hear. And without the ability to think from multiple perspectives, you will be less able to defend your convictions against the ideas that challenge them, because you won't really have examined the logic of your own beliefs—you just believe them.

At the root of this problem lurks an anti-analytical bias that predisposes many writers to see any challenge to their habitual ways of thinking as the enemy and to view those who would raise this challenge as cynics who don't believe in anything. Such writers often feel personally attacked, when in fact the conviction they are defending is not really so personal after all. Consider, for example, the first two problem examples above, in which both writers take individualism to be an incontestable value. Where does this conviction come from? Neither of the writers arrived at the thesis independent of the particular culture in which they were raised, permeated as it is by the "rugged individualism" of John Wayne and Sylvester Stallone movies.

In other words, *individualism* as an undefined blanket term verges on *cultural cliché*. That it is always good or positive is a piece of conventional wisdom. But part of becoming educated is to take a look at such global and undefined ideas that one has uncritically assimilated. Clearly, the needs and rights of the individual in contemporary American culture are consistently being weighed and balanced against the rights of other individuals and the necessity of cooperation in groups. Look at the recent nationwide concerns with health maintenance organizations (HMOs), which control health costs but constrain the individual prerogative of the physician, or with the rights of crime victims who are banding together to seek support from a government they believe is protecting the individual rights of the criminal at the expense of the individual rights of the victim.

In light of these considerations, the writers of the first two problem examples would have to question *to what extent* they should attack a book or support a rock band merely on the basis of whether or not each honors individualism. If the author of the second problem example had been willing to explore how Thomas More conceives of and critiques individualism, he or she might have been able to arrive at a revealing analysis of the tension between the individual and the collective rather than merely dismissing the entire book.

This is not to say that the first requirement of analytical writing is that you abandon all conviction or argue for a position you do not believe. But we are suggesting that the risk of remaining trapped within a limited set of culturally inherited opinions is greater than the risk that you will run by submerging your personal likes or dislikes and instead honestly and dispassionately trying on different points of view. The energy of analytical writing comes not from rehearsing your convictions but from treating them as hypotheses to be tested, as scientists do—from finding the boundaries of your ideas, reshaping parts of them, and seeing connections you have not seen before.

When a writing assignment asks for your ideas about a subject, it is usually not asking for your opinion, what you think *of* the subject, but for your reasoning on what the subject means. As we discussed in the first chapter, *an idea is not the same thing as an opinion.* The two are closely related, because both, in theory, are based on reasoning. Opinions, however, often take the form of judgments, the reflections of our personal attitudes and beliefs. Although having ideas necessarily involves your attitudes and beliefs, it is a more disinterested process than opinion making. The formulation of ideas, which is one of the primary aims of analysis, involves questioning. By contrast, opinions are often habitual responses, mental reflexes that kick in automatically when an answer seems to be called for. (The discussions of personalizing, judging, and opinions in Chapter 1 explain more fully how placing too much emphasis on yourself can interfere with your thinking.)

VOICES FROM ACROSS THE CURRICULUM

Ideas Versus Opinions

Writers need to be aware of the distinction between an argument that seeks support from evidence, and mere opinions and assertions. Many students taking political science courses often come with the assumption that in politics one opinion is as good as another. (Tocqueville thought this was a peculiarly democratic disease.) From this perspective any position a political science professor may take on controversial issues is simply his or her opinion to be accepted or rejected by students according to their own beliefs/prejudices. The key task, therefore, is not so much the substitution of knowledge for opinions, but substituting well-constructed arguments for unexamined opinions.

What is an argument and how might it be distinguished from opinions? Several things need to be stressed: (1) The thesis should be linked to evidence drawn from relevant sources: polling data, interviews, historical material, and so forth. (2) The thesis should make as explicit as possible its own ideological assumptions. (3) A thesis, in contrast to mere statement of opinion, is committed to making an argument, which means that it presupposes a willingness to engage with others. To the extent that writers operate on the assumption that everything is in the end an opinion, they have no reason to construct arguments; they are locked into an opinion.

—*Jack Gambino, Professor of Political Science*

WEAK THESIS TYPE 5: THE THESIS MAKES AN OVERLY BROAD CLAIM

An overly general claim is not a productive thesis because it oversimplifies and is too broad to direct development. Such statements usually lead either to say-nothing theses or to reductive either/or thinking. (See "Working with Categorical Thinking" later in the chapter.)

Problem Examples

Violent revolutions have had both positive and negative results for man.

There are many similarities and differences between the Carolingian and the Burgundian Renaissances.

Othello is a play about love and jealousy.

It is important to understand why leaders act in a leadership role. What is the driving force? Is it an internal drive for the business or group to succeed, or is it an internal drive for the leader to dominate others?

Overly generalized theses avoid complexity. (See the discussion of generalizing in Chapter 1.) At their worst, as in our first three examples, they settle for assertions broad enough to fit almost any subject and thus say nothing in particular about the subject at hand. A writer in the early stages of his or her drafting process might begin working from a general idea, such as what is positive and negative about violent revolutions or how two historical periods are like and unlike, but these formulations are not specific enough to guide the development of a paper. Such broad categories are likely to generate listing, not thinking. We can, for example, predict that the third thesis will prompt the writer to produce a couple of paragraphs demonstrating that *Othello* is about love and then a couple of paragraphs demonstrating that *Othello* is about jealousy, without analyzing what the play says about either.

Our fourth problem example, inquiring into the motivation of leaders in business, demonstrates how the desire to generalize can drive writers into logical errors. Because this thesis overtly offers readers two possible answers to its central question, it appears to avoid the problem of oversimplifying a complex subject. But this appearance of complexity is deceptive, because the writer has reduced the possibilities to only two answers—an either/or choice: is "the driving force" of leadership a desire for group success or a desire to dominate others? Readers can only be frustrated by being asked to choose between two such options when the more logical answer probably lies somewhere in between or somewhere else altogether. (See the discussion of binaries in Chapters 2 and 3.)

The best way to avoid the problem evident in the first three examples is to sensitize yourself to the characteristic phrasing of such theses: "both positive and negative," "many similarities and differences," or "both pros and cons." Virtually everything from meat loaf to taxes can be both positive and negative.

Solution   Convert broad categories and generic (fits anything) claims to more specific, more qualified assertions; find ways to bring out the complexity of your subject.

Solution Examples

Although violent revolutions begin to redress long-standing social inequities, they often do so at the cost of long-term economic dysfunction and the suffering that attends it.

The differences between the Carolingian and Burgundian Renaissances outweigh the similarities.

Although *Othello* appears to attack jealousy, it also supports the skepticism of the jealous characters over the naïveté of the lovers.

B. HOW TO REPHRASE THESIS STATEMENTS: SPECIFY AND SUBORDINATE

Clear symptoms of an overly generalized thesis can be found by looking at its grammar. Each of the first three problem examples for Weak Thesis Type 5, for example, relies mostly on nouns rather than verbs; the nouns announce a broad heading, but the verbs don't do anything with or to the nouns. In grammatical terms, these thesis statements don't *predicate* (affirm or assert something about the subject of a proposition). Instead, they rely on anemic verbs such as *is* or *are*, which function as equal signs that link general nouns with general adjectives rather than specify more complex relationships.

By replacing the equal sign with a more active verb, you can force yourself to advance some sort of claim, as in one of our solutions; for example, "The differences between the Carolingian and Burgundian Renaissances *outweigh* the similarities." Although this reformulation remains quite general, it at least begins to direct the writer along a more particular line of argument. Replacing the *is* or *are* equal signs with stronger verbs will usually impel you to rank ideas in some order of importance and to assert some conceptual relation among them.

In other words, the best way to remedy the problem of overgeneralization is to move toward specificity in word choice, in sentence structure, and in idea. If you find yourself writing "The economic situation is bad," consider revising it to "The tax policies of the current administration threaten to reduce the tax burden on the middle class by sacrificing education and health-care programs for everyone."

Here's the problem/solution in schematic form:

Broad Noun	+ Weak Verb	+ Vague, Evaluative Modifier
The economic situation	is	bad

Specific Noun	+ Active Verb	+ Specific Modifier
(The) tax policies (of the current administration)	threaten to reduce (the tax burden on the middle class)	by sacrificing education and health-care programs for everyone

By eliminating the weak thesis formula—broad noun plus *is* plus vague evaluative adjective—a writer is compelled to qualify, or define carefully, each of the terms in the original proposition, arriving at a more particular and conceptually rich assertion.

A second way to rephrase overly broad thesis statements, in tandem with adding specificity, is to subordinate one part of the statement to another. The both-positive-and-negative and both-similarity-and-difference formulas are recipes for say-nothing theses because they encourage pointless comparisons. Given that it is worthwhile to notice both strengths and weaknesses—that your subject is not all one way or all another—what can you do to convert the thesis from a say-nothing to a say-something claim? Generally, there are two strategies for this purpose that operate together. The first we have already discussed.

1. *Specify*—Replace the overly abstract terms—terms such as *positive* and *negative* (or *similar* and *different*)—with something specific; *name* something that is positive and something that is negative instead.
2. *Subordinate*—Rank one of the two items in the pairing underneath the other. When you subordinate, you put the most important, pressing, or revealing side of the comparison in what is known as the main clause and the less important side in what is known as the subordinate clause, introducing it with a word such as *although*. (See Chapter 11 for the definitions of main and subordinate clauses.)

In short, specify to focus the claim, and subordinate to qualify (further focus) the claim still more. This strategy produces the remedies to both the *Othello* and the violent revolution examples in "Weak Thesis Type 5: The Thesis Makes an Overly Broad Claim." As evidence of the refocusing work that fairly simple rephrasing accomplishes, consider the following version of the violent revolution example, in which we merely invert the ranking of the two items in the pair.

Although violent revolutions often cause long-term economic dysfunction and the suffering that attends it, such revolutions at least begin to redress long-standing social inequities.

Also see the section titled "A First Note on the Shape of Thesis Statements" in Chapter 6.

VOICES FROM ACROSS THE CURRICULUM

Making the Thesis Specific

Good thesis: "Although Graham and Wigman seem different, their ideas on inner expression (specifically subjectivism versus objectivism) and the incorporation of their respective countries' surge of nationalism bring them much closer than they appear."

Not-so-good thesis/question: "What were Humphrey's and Weidman's reasons behind the setting of *With My Red Fires*, and of what importance were the set and costume design to the piece as a whole?"

What I like about the good thesis is that it moves beyond the standard "they are different, but alike" (which can be said about anything) to actually tell the reader what specific areas the paper will explore. I can also tell that the subject is narrow enough for a fairly thorough examination of one small slice of these two major choreographers' work rather than some overgeneralized treatment of these two historic figures. I would probably encourage the writer of the not-so-good thesis to search for a better thesis with the question, How does the costume design of *With My Red Fires* support this story of young lovers and their revolt against the family matriarch?

—*Karen Dearborn, Professor of Dance*

ANOTHER NOTE ON THE PHRASING OF THESIS STATEMENTS: QUESTIONS

The following question is frequently asked about thesis statements: is it okay to phrase a thesis as a question? The answer is both yes and no. Phrasing a thesis as a question makes it more difficult for both the writer and the reader to be sure of the direction the paper will take, because a question doesn't make an overt claim. Questions, however, can clearly imply claims. And many writers, especially in the early, exploratory stages of drafting, begin with a question. As we note in the discussion "What It Means to Have an Idea" in Chapter 1, an idea answers a question; it explains something that needs to be explained. Also, an idea may result from the discovery of a question where there seemed not to be one. Ideas start with something you want to figure out rather than with something that you and possibly most of your readers already understand.

As a general rule, use thesis questions cautiously, especially in final drafts. Although a thesis question often functions well to spark a writer's thinking, it can too often muddy the thinking by leaving the area of consideration too broad. Just make sure you do not let the thesis-question approach allow you to evade the responsibility of making some kind of claim.

Try this 7.2: Determining What the Thesis Requires
You to Do Next

Learning to diagnose the strengths and weaknesses of thesis statements is a skill that comes in handy as you read the claims of others
and revise your own. A good question for diagnosing a thesis is,
What does the thesis require the writer to do next? This question
should help you figure out what the thesis actually wants to claim,
which can then direct you to possible rephrasings that would better
direct your thinking. Using this question as a prompt, list the strengths
and weaknesses of the two thesis statements below, and then rewrite
them. In the first statement, rewrite just the last sentence (the other
sentences have been included to provide context).

1. Many economists and politicians agree that, along with the Environmental
   Protection Agency's newest regulations, a global-warming treaty could
   damage the American economy. Because of the great expense that such
   environmental standards require, domestic industries would financially suffer. Others argue, however, that severe regulatory steps must be taken to
   prevent global warming, regardless of cost. Despite both legitimate claims,
   the issue of protecting the environment while still securing our global competitiveness remains critical.
2. Regarding the promotion of women into executive positions, they are continually losing the race because of a corporate view that women are too
   compassionate to keep up with the competitiveness of a powerful firm.

C. WORKING WITH CATEGORICAL THINKING

Categorical thinking is an unavoidable and distinctive feature of how all human
beings go about analyzing a subject. It is also extremely useful: to generalize from
particular experiences, we try to put them into meaningful categories. When we
contract an illness, doctors diagnose it by type. When we study personality theory,
different behaviors are grouped by personality type. Subject areas in school are
categorized into divisions: the natural sciences, the social sciences, the humanities.
Analytical thought is quite unthinkable without categories.

But categorical thinking can also be dangerous. It can mislead us into oversimplification when the categories are too broad or too simply connected. This is
especially the case with the either/or choices to which categorical thinking is
prone: approve/disapprove, real/unreal, accurate/inaccurate, believable/unbeliev-
able. Such either/or thinking often provokes thinkers into a premature and overly
narrow decision either to support the subject or to denounce it. This rush to value
judgment can so dominate a writer's attention that he or she fails to examine not
only the values upon which the judgment is based, but also the subject itself.

If you look back over the examples in "Five Kinds of Weak Theses," you will
notice that a number of them engage in the dangerous side of categorical thinking.
That is, they are overly global—inclined to all-or-nothing claims. The writer who

evaluates leadership in terms of its selflessness/selfishness, for example, needs to pause to consider why we should evaluate leadership in those terms in the first place.

Many weak theses are the result of oversimplified categorical thinking. The writer puts everything into big, undifferentiated categories, labeled all black or all white, with nothing in between. The trick is to use categorical thinking in a way that allows you to make careful distinctions.

TWO WAYS TO IMPROVE THE LOGIC OF YOUR THESIS STATEMENTS

We will refer to the following two examples to illustrate two key ways to strengthen the logic of your thesis statements: (1) by qualifying your claims and (2) by checking for the unstated assumptions upon which your claims depend.

> **Example I:** I think there are many things shown on TV that are damaging for people to see. But there is no need for censorship. No network is going to show violence without the approval of the public, obviously for financial reasons. What must be remembered is that the public majority will see what it wants to see in our mass society.

> **Example II:** Some members of our society feel that [the televised cartoon series] *The Simpsons* promotes wrong morals and values for our society. Other members find it funny and entertaining. I feel that *The Simpsons* has a more positive effect than a negative one. In relation to a real-life marriage, Marge and Homer's marriage is pretty accurate. The problems they deal with are not very large or intense. As for the family relationships, the Simpsons are very close and love each other.

Qualifying Overextended Claims   The main problem with Example I is the writer's failure to qualify his ideas, a problem that causes him to generalize to the point of oversimplification. Note the writer's habit of stating his claims absolutely (we have italicized the words that make these claims unqualified):

"there is *no* need for censorship"

"*no* network is going to show violence without"

"*obviously* for financial reasons"

"what *must* be remembered"

"the majority *will* see"

Broad, pronouncement-like claims are difficult to support fairly. The solution is for the writer to limit his claims more carefully, especially his key premise about public approval. The assertion that a commercial television industry will, for financial reasons, give the public "what it wants" is true *to an extent*. But, as with the "extent to which" strategy for refocusing binaries (see Chapter 3), the solution here is to modify this claim as well as consider other possibilities.

Couldn't it also be argued, for example, that given the power of television to shape people's tastes and opinions, the public sees not just what it wants but what it has been taught to want? This necessary complication of the writer's argument about public approval seriously undermines the credibility of his global assertion that "there is no need for censorship." The remedy lies with qualifying his thesis. Simply reversing it to "there is a need for censorship" would not solve the problem, because the need for defining and limiting the writer's position will be just as great on the other side of the issue.

Example II appears to be more qualified than Example I (because it acknowledges the possibility of at least two points of view). The writer opens by attempting to acknowledge the existence of more than one point of view on the show, and rather than broadly asserting that the show is positive and accurate, she tempers these claims (as italics show): "I *feel* that *The Simpsons* has a *more* positive effect *than* a negative one"; Marge and Homer's marriage is *pretty* accurate." These qualifications, however, are superficial. The writer does not explore what *accurate* means. Instead, she assumes the standard of accuracy (that an accurate show is a good show) as a given.

Checking for Unstated Assumptions   Before she could persuade us to approve of *The Simpsons* for its accuracy in depicting marriage, the writer of Example II would have to convince us that accuracy is a reasonable criterion for evaluating TV shows (especially cartoons) rather than simply accepting it as an unstated assumption. Would an accurate depiction of the life of a serial killer, for example, necessarily make for a "positive" show? Similarly, if a fantasy show has no interest in accuracy, is it necessarily "negative" and without moral value?

When writers present a debatable premise as if it were self-evidently true, the conclusions built upon it cannot stand. At the least, the writer of Example II needs to recognize her debatable premise, articulate it, and make an argument in support of it. She might also precede her judgment about the show with more analysis. Before deciding that the show is "more positive than negative" and thus does not promote "wrong morals and values for our society," she could convey what the show has to say about marriage, how it goes about making this statement, and why (in response to what).

> *When writers present a debatable premise as if it were self-evidently true, the conclusions built upon it cannot stand.*

Likewise, if the writer of Example I had looked at his own claims rather than rushing to argue an absolute position on censorship, he would have noticed how much of the thinking that underlies them remains unarticulated and thus unexamined. His argument that "there is no need for censorship," for example, depends on the validity of another of his assertions, that "no network is going to show violence without the approval of the public, obviously for financial reasons." The writer's argument depends on readers' accepting a position that he asserts ("obviously") as though it were too clearly true to need defending.

Spelling out the issue of the networks' financial dependence on public approval would help this writer clarify and qualify his thesis. It would also allow him to sort out the logical contradiction with his opening claim that "there are many things shown on TV that are damaging for people to see." If television networks will broadcast only what the public approves of, then apparently the public must approve of being damaged or fail to notice that it is being damaged. If the public either fails to notice it is being damaged or approves of it, aren't these credible arguments for, rather than against, censorship?

CLOSE READING VERSUS DEBATE-STYLE ARGUMENT

To formulate a revealing and insightful idea—an effective thesis—you may have to alter some of your conceptions of what writing is supposed to do. The agree/disagree mode of writing and thinking that you will often see in editorials, hear in the media, and even practice sometimes in school may incline you to focus all your energy on the bottom line—aggressively advancing a claim either for or against some view—without first engaging in the exploratory interpretation of evidence that is so necessary to arriving at thoughtful arguments.

Writing, especially as it is used in school, is often divided into kinds. And clearly, the kind of writing this book addresses—analysis—differs in both method and aim from, say, descriptive writing or narration. Those of you who have been taught to write arguments may find that some of the prescriptions we offer on analytical writing seem to run counter to what you've learned. Our aim in this section is to break down unnecessary divisions between argument and analysis, proposing that the interpretive skill called close reading is essential to both.

A close reading explicates (unfolds) an interpretation by making selected features of your subject explicit that otherwise might not be readily recognized or understood. A close reading moves beyond the obvious, but it does not leap to some hidden meaning that is unconnected to the evidence. Rather, it follows logically from the evidence; the meaning is implicit in the details, waiting to be brought out by the writer who is careful enough to look closely and questioningly.

It is, we believe, a common misconception that interpretation (close reading) goes on only in art or literature courses, whereas science, social science, and philosophy courses require a different kind of writing called argument. Many of you will have been introduced to writing arguments through the debate-model—writing pro or con on a given position, with the aim of defeating an imagined opponent and convincing your readers of the rightness of your position. But as the *American College Dictionary* says, "to argue implies reasoning or trying to understand; it does not necessarily imply opposition." It is this more exploratory, tentative, and dispassionate mode of argument that this book encourages you to practice.

Adhering to the more restrictive, debate-style definition of argument can create a number of problems for careful analytical writers:

1. By requiring writers to be oppositional, it inclines them to discount or dismiss problems in the side or position they have chosen; they cling to the same static position rather than testing it as a way of allowing it to evolve.
2. It inclines writers to either/or thinking rather than encouraging them to formulate more qualified positions that integrate apparently opposing viewpoints.
3. It overvalues convincing someone else at the expense of developing understanding.

Too often interpretation and argument are treated as essentially different kinds of writing, each with a particular purpose. In practice, interpretation and argument are inseparable. As our examples in Chapter 6 show, even the most tentative and cautiously evolving interpretation is ultimately an argument; it asks readers to accept a particular interpretation of a set of data. And like argument, interpretation carefully connects evidence with claims; it does not, as it is sometimes misconceived, incline the writer toward undirected and purposeless impressionism.

Similarly, even the most passionately committed argument is an interpretation; its credibility rests on the plausibility of its reading of evidence. You cannot argue from evidence unless you are first sure that you know what that evidence means. Most illogical argument occurs when writers assume that the meaning of their data is self-evident. In other words, you need to analyze your subject dispassionately before you can fairly argue a position about it.

Analysis is an important corrective to narrow and needlessly oppositional thinking. A writer who is skeptical of global generalizations and of unexamined value judgments may sound timid and even confused compared with the insistent pronouncements of daytime talk shows and televised political debates. But the effort you put into carefully formulating your ideas by qualifying them, checking for unstated assumptions, and acknowledging rather than ignoring problems in your position will make you a stronger writer and thinker. For more discussion of debate-style argument see the "Counterproductive Habits of Mind" section in Chapter 1.

D. COMMON LOGICAL ERRORS IN CONSTRUCTING A THESIS

In further service to our project of giving you ways of avoiding weak thesis statements, this section will move briefly to the field of logic, which has given us terms that are shorthand for certain common thinking errors. We will treat six errors, all of which involve the root problem of oversimplification in the way the thesis explains the meaning of evidence.

1. **Simple cause–complex effect**—One of the most common problems of thinking, the fallacy of simple cause–complex effect, involves assigning a simple cause to a complex phenomenon that cannot be so easily explained. A widespread version of this fallacy is seen in arguments that blame individual figures for broad historical events. For example, "Eisenhower caused America to be involved in the Vietnam War." This claim ignores the cold war ethos, the long history of colonialism in Southeast Asia, and a multitude of other factors. When you reduce a complex sequence of events to a simple and single cause—or assign a simple effect to a complex cause—you will virtually always be wrong.

2. **False cause**—Another common cause/effect thinking error, false cause, is produced by assuming that two events are causally connected when such a connection does not necessarily exist. One of the most common forms of this fallacy—known as *post hoc, ergo propter hoc* (Latin for "after this, therefore because of this")—assumes that because *A* precedes *B*, *A* causes *B*. For example, it was once thought that the sun shining on a pile of garbage caused the garbage to conceive flies.

   This error is the stuff that superstition is made of. "I walked under a ladder, and then I got hit by a car" becomes "Because I walked under a ladder, I got hit by a car." Because one action precedes a second one, the first action is assumed to be the cause of the second. A more dangerous form of this error goes like this:

Evidence: A new neighbor moved in downstairs on Saturday. My television disappeared on Sunday.
Conclusion: The new neighbor stole my TV.

As the examples illustrate, *typically in false cause some significant alternative has not been considered,* such as the presence of flies' eggs in the garbage. Similarly, it does not follow that if a person watches television and then commits a crime, television watching necessarily causes crime; there are other causes to be considered.

Try this 7.3: Identifying Logical Errors and Formulating Alternative Explanations

Predictably, instances of simple cause/complex effect and false cause are harder to spot when we encounter them in published settings.

Identify possible sites of simple cause/complex effect and false cause in the following real-life example. Then formulate a few alternative explanations that one might offer to the theory that television watching is the primary cause of the increased risk of starting drinking. What cause-and-effect explanations might there be for the decreased risk of drinking that corresponds with adolescents watching movies on a VCR?

A newspaper article on a study conducted at Stanford University about the connection between adolescents' television-viewing habits and drinking reports that high school students who watch a lot of television and music videos are more likely to start drinking than are other students. In the study of 1,553 ninth graders, with each increase of one hour per day of watching music videos there was a 31 percent greater risk of starting to drink. Each hour increase of watching other kinds of television corresponded with a 9 percent greater risk. Each hour spent watching movies in a video cassette recorder corresponded to an 11 percent *decreased* risk of starting to drink alcohol. Computer and video games had no effect either way, and among those who already drank, watching television and videos made no difference. Because these data were reported in the newspaper in very abbreviated form, there was little interpretation of the evidence except for the observations that alcohol is the most common beverage shown on television and that drinking on television is done by attractive people, often in association with sexually suggestive content.

3. **Analogy and false analogy**—An analogy is a device for understanding something that is relatively foreign in terms of something that is more familiar. When you argue by analogy, you are saying that what is true for one thing is also true for something else that it in some way resembles. The famous poetic line "my love is like a red, red rose" is actually an argument by analogy. At first glance, this clichéd comparison seems too far-fetched to be reasonable. But is it a false analogy, or a potentially

enabling one? Past users of this analogy have thought the thorns, the early fading, the beauty, and so forth sufficient to argue from the comparison. Similarly, glance back to the first paragraph of the Tiananmen Square essay on page 151 in Chapter 5 in which the writer's deft use of an extended analogy opens up his subject analytically. Analogies, in short, are not bad or illogical in themselves. In fact, they can be incredibly useful, depending on how you handle them.

The danger that arguing analogically can pose is that an *inaccurate* comparison (usually one that oversimplifies) prevents you from looking at the evidence. Flying to the moon is like flying a kite? Well, it's a little like that, but this kind of oversimplification is essentially falsifying. In most ways that matter, sending a rocket to the moon does not resemble sending a kite into the air.

Another way that an analogy can become false is when it becomes overextended: there is a point of resemblance at one juncture, but the writer then goes on to assume that the two items being compared necessarily resemble each other in most other respects. To what extent is balancing your checkbook really like juggling? On the other hand, an analogy that first appears overextended may not be. How far, for example, could you reasonably go in comparing a presidential election to a sales campaign or an enclosed shopping mall to a village main street?

Let's examine one more false analogy, from a recent ad campaign: "You choose the president; why not choose your cable company?" What's wrong with this comparison? For one thing, each of us is not entitled to our choice of president. If we were, there would be a lot of presidents. And, second, the rules and circumstances covering what is best in the nation's communication network are not necessarily the same as the rules and circumstances guiding the structure of our federal government. So the analogy doesn't work very well. What is true for one side of the comparison is not necessarily true for the other side; the differences are greater than the similarities.

When you find yourself reasoning by analogy, ask yourself two questions: (1) are the basic similarities greater and more significant than the obvious differences? and (2) am I overrelying on surface similarities and ignoring more essential differences?

▶ Try this 7.4: Observing Analogies

We observed at the beginning of this book that one of the best ways of improving your thinking is to become more aware of yourself doing it. To put this observation into practice, here's something you might try. Keep a record during the course of a single day of the number of times you or others around you (in conversation, in the newspaper, on the radio, at work, in the classroom, and so forth) make use of analogy. In some cases a single word will reveal that a common phrase, such as *nuclear family* is actually an analogy. At the end of the day, look over your list and isolate the most appropriate and insightful analogy as well as the most distorting one. If possible, share them with someone else (or a small group) who has been doing the same thing.

You might profitably spend another day doing this same exercise looking for examples of simple cause/complex effect and *post hoc ergo propter hoc*. (If you don't find an astonishing number of these, listen harder!)

4. **Equivocation**—Equivocation is the first of three logical errors that deal with matters of phrasing. As Chapter 6 and this chapter show, finding and developing a thesis emphasizes the importance of word choice—of carefully casting and recasting the language with which you categorize and name your ideas.

   Equivocation—slipping between two meanings for a single word or phrase—confuses an argument. An example would be "Only man is capable of religious faith. No woman is a man. Therefore, no woman is capable of religious faith." Here the first use of *man* is generic, intended to be gender neutral, whereas the second use is decidedly masculine. One specialized form of equivocation results from what are sometimes called *weasel words*. A weasel word is one that has been used so loosely that it ceases to have much (or any) meaning. (The term derives from the weasel's reputed practice of sucking the contents from an egg without destroying the shell.) The word *natural*, for example, can mean "good, pure, and unsullied," but it can also refer to the ways of nature (flora and fauna). Such terms (*love*, *reality*, and *experience* are others) invite equivocation because they mean so many different things to different people.

5. **Begging the question**—To beg the question is to argue in a circle by asking readers to accept without argument a point that is actually at stake. This kind of fallacious argument hides its conclusion among its assumptions. For example, "*Huckleberry Finn* should be banned from school libraries as obscene because it uses obscene language" begs the question by presenting as obviously true issues that are actually in question: the definition of obscenity and the assumption that the obscene should be banned because it is obscene.

6. **Overgeneralization**—An overgeneralization is an inadequately qualified claim. It may be true that some heavy drinkers are alcoholics, but it would not be fair to claim that all heavy drinking indicates or leads to alcoholism. As a rule, be wary of "totalizing" or making global pronouncements; the bigger the generalization, the more likely it will admit of exceptions. See for examples the process of qualifying a claim we illustrate in the discussion of *Educating Rita* in Chapter 6 and in the solutions in "Weak Thesis Type 5" in this chapter.

   One particular form of overgeneralization, the *sweeping generalization*, occurs when a writer overextends the reach of the claim. The claim itself may be adequately qualified, but the problem comes in an overly broad application of that generalization, suggesting that it applies in every case, whereas it applies only in some.

When you move prematurely from too little evidence to a broad conclusion, you have fallen into *hasty generalization*. Much of this book addresses ways of avoiding this problem, also known as an unwarranted inductive leap. See "Demonstrating the Representativeness of Your Example" in Chapter 5.

There are, of course, other common logical errors that can undermine the construction of valid claims. For one more example, see the section called "Strategy 3: Put Your Sources into Conversation with One Another" in Chapter 12 for a discussion of the problem in an argument called *straw man*, in which a writer builds his or her case on a misrepresentation of an opponent's argument.

◀ **ASSIGNMENT:** "Love Is the Answer"—Analyzing Clichés

It's not necessarily that clichés are untrue, just that they are not worth saying (even if you're John Lennon, who offered this sodden truism in one of his more forgettable tunes).

One of the best ways to inoculate yourself against habitually resorting to clichés to provide easy and safe answers to all the problems of the planet—easy because they fit so many situations generically, and safe because, being so common, they *must* be true—is to go out and collect them, and then use this data gathering to generate a thesis. Spend a day doing this, listening and looking for clichés—from overheard conversations (or your own), from reading matter, from anywhere (talk radio and TV are exceptionally rich resources) that is part of your daily round.

Compile a list, making sure to write down not only each cliché but the context in which it is used. From this data, and applying what you have learned from the two thesis chapters, formulate a thesis and write a paper about one or more of the clichés that infect some aspect of your daily life. You might find it useful to use the reading-for-pattern heuristic to identify key shared traits among the clichés and/or among the contexts in which you have discovered them. And you might apply the advice provided under "Weak Thesis Type 3" to work out alternative formulations to certain clichés to discover what that might teach us about the ways clichés function in given situations—how, for example, they do and don't fit the facts of the situation. If you can find a copy of Paul Muldoon's short poem "Symposium," that might anchor an analysis—what is that poem telling us about cliché?—or provide a lens for uncovering aspects of your data. ▶

GUIDELINES FOR RECOGNIZING AND FIXING WEAK THESIS STATEMENTS

1. Your thesis should make a claim with which it would be possible for readers to disagree. In other words, move beyond defending statements that your readers would accept as obviously true.

2. Be skeptical of your first (often semiautomatic) response to a subject: it will often be a cliché (however unintentional). Avoid conventional wisdom unless you introduce a fresh perspective on it.

3. Convert broad categories and generic (fits anything) claims to more specific assertions. Find ways to bring out the complexity of your subject.

4. Submit the wording of your thesis to this grammatical test: if it follows the "abstract noun + is + evaluative adjective" formula ("The economic situation is bad"), substitute a more specific noun and an active verb that will force you to predicate something about a focused subject ("Tax laws benefit the rich").

5. Routinely examine and question your own key terms and categories rather than simply accepting them. Assume that they mean more than you first thought.

6. Always work to uncover and make explicit the unstated assumptions (premises) underlying your thesis. Don't treat debatable premises as givens.

7. As a rule, be suspicious of thesis statements that depend on words such as *real*, *accurate*, *believable*, *right*, and *good*. These words usually signal that you are offering personal opinions—what "feels" right to you—as self-evident truths for everybody.

8. One way to assess the adequacy of a thesis statement is to ask yourself where the writer would need to go next to develop his or her idea. If you can't answer that question, the thesis is still too weak.

9. Qualify your claims; you will avoid the global pronouncements—typical of the dangers of overly categorical thinking—that are too broad to be of much use (or true).

CHAPTER 8

Introductions and Conclusions

T his chapter addresses two perennial trouble-spots in all kinds of writing: introductions and conclusions. Because disciplinary formats often control the final form of beginnings and endings, more than a third of this chapter consists of "Voices from Across the Curriculum" boxes. Nonetheless, the chapter emphasizes the common elements that characterize introductions and conclusions across the curriculum.

The chapter gives special attention to strategies for solving two particular problems: trying to do too much in the introduction and not doing enough in the conclusion.

As with other aspects of writing analytically, there are no absolute rules for writing introductions and conclusions, but there does seem to be a consensus across the disciplines that introductions should raise issues rather than settle them, and conclusions should go beyond merely restating what has already been said. Or, in mantra form, insofar as disciplinary conventions permit, *In introductions, play an ace but not your whole hand; and in conclusions, don't just summarize—culminate.*

Play an ace, establishing your authority with your readers, without having to play your whole hand. Raise the issue; don't settle it.

A. INTRODUCTIONS AND CONCLUSIONS AS SOCIAL SITES

When you read, you enter a world created with written language—a textual world—and to varying degrees, you leave the world "out there." Even if other people are around, we all read in relative isolation; our attention is diverted from the social and physical world upon which the full range of our senses normally operates.

In this context, place yourself in the position of the writer, rather than a reader, and consider the functions that the introduction and conclusion provide for a piece of writing. Your introduction takes the reader from a sensory world and submerges him or her into a textual one. And your conclusion returns the reader to his or her nonwritten reality. Introductions and conclusions *mediate*— they carry the reader from one way of being to another. They function as the most social parts of any written communication, the passageways in which you need to be most keenly aware of your reader.

At both sites, there is a lot at stake. The introduction gives the reader his or her first impression, and we all know how indelible that can be. The conclusion leaves the reader with a last—and potentially lasting—impression of the written world you have constructed.

B. THE FUNCTION OF INTRODUCTIONS

As the Latin roots of the word suggest—*intro*, meaning "within," and *ducere*, meaning "to lead or bring"—an introduction brings the reader into a subject. Its length varies, depending on the scope of the writing project. An introduction may take a paragraph, a few paragraphs, a few pages, a chapter, or even a book. In most academic writing that you will do, one or two paragraphs is a standard length. In that space you should try to accomplish some or all of the following objectives:

- Define your topic—the issue, question, or problem—and say why it matters.
- Indicate your method of approach to the topic.
- Provide necessary background or context.
- Offer the working thesis (hypothesis) that your paper will develop.

An objective missing from this list that you might expect to find there is the admonition to engage the reader. Clearly, all introductions need to engage the reader, but this admonition is too often misinterpreted as a directive to be entertaining or cute. In academic writing, you don't need a gimmick to engage your readers; you can assume they care about the subject. You will engage them if you can articulate why your topic matters, doing so in terms of existing thinking in the field. Especially in a first draft, the objectives just listed are not so easily achieved, which is why many writers defer writing the polished version of the introduction until they have completed at least one draft of the paper. At that point, you will usually have a clearer notion of why your subject matters and which aspect of your thesis to place first. Often the conclusion of a first draft becomes the introduction to the second draft.

Other writers find that they can't proceed on a draft until they have arrived at an introduction that clearly defines the question or problem they plan to write about and its significance. For these writers, crafting an approach to the topic in the introduction is a key part of the planning phase, even though they also expect to revise the introduction based on what happens in the initial draft.

In any case, the standard shape of an introduction is a *funnel*. It starts wide, providing background and generalization, and then narrows the subject to a particular issue or topic. Here is a typical example from a student paper.

> People have a way of making the most important obligations perfunctory, even trivial, by the steps they take to observe them. For many people traditions and rituals become actuality; the form overshadows the substance. They lose sight of the underlying truths and what these should mean in their lives, and they tend to believe that observing the formalities fulfills their obligation. This is true of professional ethics as they relate to the practice of examining and reporting on financial data—the primary role of the auditor.

The paragraph begins with a generalization in the first sentence (about making even important obligations perfunctory) and funnels down in the last sentence to a working thesis (about the ethics of an auditor's report on financial data).

PUTTING AN ISSUE OR QUESTION IN CONTEXT

In the accompanying "Voices from Across the Curriculum" boxes, notice that implicit in all of the professors' accounts is some concept of the funnel. Rather than leaping immediately to the paper's issue, question, or problem, most effective introductions provide some broader context to indicate why the issue matters.

Although the various models we offer here differ in small ways from discipline to discipline, the essential characteristics that they share suggest that most professors across the curriculum want the same things in an introduction: *the locating of a problem or question within a context that provides background and rationale, culminating in a working thesis.*

USING PROCEDURAL OPENINGS

In the interests of clear organization, some professors require students to include in the introduction an explanation of how the paper will proceed. Such a general statement of method and/or intention is known as *procedural openings*. Among the disciplines in which you are most likely to find this format are philosophy, political science, and sociology.

The procedural opening is particularly useful in longer papers, where it can provide a condensed version of what's to come as a guide for readers. Also note that he advises placing it early in the essay but not in the first paragraph, which he reserves for "presenting anomalies." In other words, he seems to value the introduction primarily as a site for the writer's idea, for "stating the specific point of departure," and, that taken care of, only secondarily as a place for forecasting the plan of the paper. These priorities bear mentioning because they imply *a potential danger in relying too heavily on procedural openings—that the writer will avoid making a claim at all.*

The statement of a paper's plan is not the same thing as its thesis. As Chapter 7 discussed, one kind of weak thesis offers a general plan *in place of* supplying an idea about the topic that the paper will explore and defend. Consider the deficiencies of the following procedural opening.

> In this paper I will first discuss the strong points and weak points in America's treatment of the elderly. Then I will compare this treatment with that in other industrial nations in the West. Finally, I will evaluate the various proposals for reform that have been advanced here and abroad.

This paragraph does not fare well in fulfilling the four functional objectives of an introduction listed at the beginning of this chapter. It identifies the subject, but it neither addresses why the subject matters nor suggests the writer's approach. Nor does it provide background to the topic or suggest a hypothesis that the paper will pursue. Even though a procedural opening is built into the conventions of report writing, these conventions also stipulate that the writer include some clear statement of the hypothesis, which counteracts the danger that the writer won't make any claim at all.

VOICES FROM ACROSS THE CURRICULUM
Providing an Introductory Context

Although some expression of the main idea should find its way into the opening paragraph, that paragraph is also an opportunity to draw the reader in, to convince the reader to read on. What's the point of your paper? Why is the issue important? Is it a theoretical issue? A policy issue? What's the historical context? Is this a question that represents a part of a larger question?

—James Marshall, Professor of Economics

I think it is important to understand that an introduction is not simply the statement of a thesis but also the place where the student needs to set a context, a framework that makes such a thesis statement interesting, timely, or in some other way important. It is common to see papers in political science begin by pointing out a discrepancy between conventional wisdom (what the pundits say) and recent political developments, between popular opinion and empirical evidence, or between theoretical frameworks and particular test cases. Papers, in other words, often begin by presenting *anomalies*.

I encourage students to write opening paragraphs that attempt to elucidate such anomalies by:

1. Stating the specific point of departure: are they taking issue with a bit of conventional wisdom? Popular opinions? A theoretical perspective? This provides the context in which a student is able to "frame" a particular problem, issue, and so forth. Students then need to indicate:

2. Why the wisdom/opinion/theory has become problematic or controversial by focusing on a particular issue, event, test case, or empirical evidence. (Here the students' choice of topic becomes important, because topics must be both relevant to the specific point of departure as well as to some degree controversial.) I would also expect the following in the opening paragraph(s):

3. A brief statement of the tentative thesis/position to be pursued in the paper. This can take several forms, including the revising of conventional wisdom/theory/opinion, discarding it in favor of alternative conceptions, or calling for redefinition of an issue and question. In papers directed toward current political practices (for instance, an analysis of a particular environmental policy or of a proposal to reform political parties), the thesis statement may be stated by indicating (a) hidden or flawed assumptions in current practices or (b) alternative reforms and/or policy proposals.

—Jack Gambino, Professor of Political Science

VOICES FROM ACROSS THE CURRICULUM

Procedural Openings

I encourage students to provide a "road map" paragraph early in the paper, perhaps the second or third paragraph. (This is a common practice in the professional journals.) The "road map" tells the reader the basic outline of the argument. Something like the following: "In the first part of my paper I will present a brief history of the issue. . . . This will be followed by an account of the current controversy. . . . Part III will spell out my alternative account and evidence. . . . I then conclude. . . . " I think such a paragraph becomes more necessary with longer papers.

–Jack Gambino, Professor of Political Science

I address the issue of an opening paragraph by having the students conceive of an opening section (or introduction) that tells the uninformed reader what's about to happen. I'll say, "Assume I know next to nothing about what lies ahead; so let me, the reader, know. 'My paper's about boom. In it, I'll do boom, boom. I chose this topic for the following reasons: boom, boom, boom.' Then get on with it."

–Frederick Norling, Professor of Business

C. HOW MUCH TO INTRODUCE UP FRONT

Introductions need to do a lot in a limited space. To specify a thesis and locate it within a larger context, to suggest the plan or outline of the entire paper, and to negotiate first relations with a reader—that's plenty to pack into a paragraph or two. In deciding how much to introduce up front, you must make a series of difficult choices. We list some of these choices next, phrased as questions you can ask yourself:

- How much can I assume my readers know about my subject?
- Which parts of the research and/or the background are sufficiently pertinent to warrant inclusion?
- How much of my thesis do I include, and which particular part or parts should I begin with?
- What is the proper balance between background and foreground?
- Which are the essential parts of my plan or road map to include?

TYPICAL PROBLEMS THAT ARE SYMPTOMS OF DOING TOO MUCH

If you ponder the preceding questions, you can avoid writing introductions that try to turn an introduction into a miniature essay. Consider the three problems discussed next as symptoms of *overcompression*, telltale signs that you need to reconceive, and probably reduce, your introduction.

Digression *Digression* results when you try to include too much background. If, for example, you plan to write about a recent innovation in video technology, you'll need to monitor the amount and kind of technical information you include in your opening paragraphs. You'll also want to avoid starting at a point that is too far away from your immediate concerns, as in "From the beginning of time humans have needed to communicate."

The standardized formats that govern procedural openings in some disciplines can help you to avoid digressing endlessly. There is a given sequence of steps to follow for a psychology report of an empirical study, for instance. Nonetheless, these disciplinary conventions leave plenty of room for you to lose your focus. You still need to be selective about which contexts are sufficiently relevant to be included up front.

In disciplines that do not stipulate a specific format for contextualizing, the number of choices is greater, and so is the danger that you will get sidetracked into paragraphs of background that bury your thesis and frustrate your readers. One reason that many writers fall into this kind of digression in introductions is that they misjudge how much their audience needs to know. As a general rule in academic writing, *don't assume that your readers know little or nothing about the subject.* Instead, use the social potential of the introduction to negotiate your audience, setting up your relationship with your readers and making clear what you are assuming they do and do not know.

Incoherence *Incoherence* results when you try to preview too much of your paper's conclusion. Incoherent introductions move in too many directions at once, usually because the writer is trying to conclude before going through the discussion that will make the conclusion comprehensible. The language you are compelled to use in such cases tends to be too dense, and the connections between the sentences tend to get left out, because there isn't enough room to include them. After having read the entire paper, your readers may be able to make sense of the introduction, but in that case, the introduction has not done its job.

The following introductory paragraph is incoherent, primarily because it tries to include too much. It neither adequately connects its ideas nor defines its terms.

> Twinship is a symbol in many religious traditions. The significance of twinship will be discussed and explored in the Native American, Japanese Shinto, and Christian religions. Twinship can be either in opposing or common forces in the form of deities or mortals. There are several forms of twinship that show duality of order versus chaos, good versus evil, and creation versus destruction. The significance of twinship is to set moral codes for society and to explain the inexplicable.

Prejudgment *Prejudgment* results when you appear to have already settled the question to be pursued in the rest of the paper. The problem here is logical. In the effort to preview your paper's conclusion at the outset, you risk appearing to assume something as true that your paper will in fact need to test. In most papers in the humanities and social sciences, where the thesis evolves in specificity and complexity between the introduction and conclusion, writers and readers can find such assumptions prejudicial. Opening in this way, at any event, can make the rest of the paper seem redundant. Even in the sciences, where a concise statement of objectives, plan of attack, and hypothesis are usually required up front, a separate "Results" section is reserved for the conclusion.

The following introductory paragraph *prejudges*: it offers a series of conclusions already assumed to be true without introducing the necessary background issues and questions that would allow the writer to adequately explore these conclusions.

> Field hockey is a sport that can be played by either men or women. All sports should be made available for members of both sexes. As long as women are allowed to participate on male teams in sports such as football and wrestling, men should be allowed to participate on female teams in sports such as field hockey and lacrosse. If women press for and receive equal opportunity in all sports, then it is only fair that men be given the same opportunity. If women object to this type of equal opportunity, then they are promoting reverse discrimination.

This paragraph also exemplifies the type of weak thesis that can result when its assumptions are left unstated (and so earlier in the book we invited you to ferret out unstated assumptions in this passage). Prejudgment is in fact a case of assuming too much up front. Read what an economics professor says on the same subject.

VOICES FROM ACROSS THE CURRICULUM

Avoiding Strong Claims in the Introduction

I might be careful about how tentative conclusions should play in the opening paragraph, because this can easily slide into a prejudging of the question at hand. I would be more comfortable with a clear statement of the prevailing views held by others. For example, a student could write on the question, "Was Franklin Delano Roosevelt a Keynesian?" What purpose would it serve in an opening paragraph to reveal without any supporting discussion that FDR was or was not a Keynesian?

What might be better would be to say that in the public mind FDR is regarded as the original big spender, that some people commonly associate New Deal policies with general conceptions of Keynesianism, but that there may be some surprises in store as that common notion is examined.

In sum, I would discourage students from making strong claims at or near the beginning of a paper. Let's see the evidence first. We should all have respect for the evidence. Strong assertions, bordering on conclusions, too early on are inappropriate.

—James Marshall, Professor of Economics

> **▶ Try this 8.1:** Introductions and Audience
>
> Compare and contrast introductory paragraphs from a popular magazine with those from an academic journal aimed at a more specialized audience. Select one of each and analyze them to determine what each author assumes the audience knows. Where in each paragraph are these assumptions most evident? If you write out your analysis, it should probably take about a page, but this exercise can also be done productively with others in a small group.

D. OPENING GAMBITS: FIVE GOOD WAYS TO BEGIN

The primary challenge in writing introductions, it should now be evident, lies in occupying the middle ground between overassertive prejudgment and avoidance of taking a position. There are a number of fairly common opening gambits that can help you to stake out an effective middle ground. An opening gambit in games such as chess is the initial move—not an announcement of the entire game plan.

GAMBIT 1: CHALLENGE A COMMONLY HELD VIEW

One of the best opening gambits is to challenge a commonly held view. This is what the economics professor advises when he suggests that rather than announcing up front the answer to the question at which the paper arrives, you convey that "there may be some surprises in store as that common notion is examined." This move has several advantages. Most important, it provides you with a framework *against* which to respond; it allows you to begin by reacting. Moreover, because you are responding to a known position, you have a ready way of integrating context into your paper. As the economics professor notes of the FDR example, until we understand why it matters whether or not FDR was a Keynesian, it is pointless to answer the question.

GAMBIT 2: BEGIN WITH A DEFINITION

In the case of the FDR example, a writer would probably include another common introductory gambit, *defining* "Keynesianism." Beginning with a definition is a reliable way to introduce a topic, so long as that definition has some significance for the discussion to follow. If the definition doesn't do any conceptual work in the introduction, the definition gambit becomes a pointless cliché.

You are most likely to avoid a cliché if you cite a source other than a standard dictionary for your definition. The reference collection of any academic library contains a range of discipline-specific lexicons that provide more precise and authoritative definitions than Webster ever could. A useful alternative is to quote a particular author's definition of a key term (such as Keynesianism) because you want to make a point about his or her particular definition: for example, "Although the *Dictionary of Economics* defines Keynesianism as *XYZ*, Smith treats only *X* and *Y* (or substitutes *A* for *Z*, and so forth)."

GAMBIT 3: OFFER A WORKING HYPOTHESIS

But, you may be wondering, where is the thesis in the FDR example? As the economics professor proposes, you are often better off introducing a working hypothesis—an opening claim that stimulates the analytical process—instead of offering some full declaration of the conclusion. The introduction he envisions, for example, would first suggest that the question of FDR's Keynesianism is not as simple as is commonly thought and then imply further that the common association of "New Deal policies with general conceptions of Keynesianism" is, to some extent, false.

GAMBIT 4: LEAD WITH YOUR SECOND-BEST EXAMPLE

Another versatile opening gambit, where disciplinary conventions allow, is to use your *second-best example* to set up the issue or question that you later develop in depth with your best example. This gambit is especially useful in papers that proceed inductively on the strength of representative examples. As you are assembling evidence in the outlining and prewriting stage, in many cases you will accumulate a number of examples that illustrate the same basic point. For example, several battles might illustrate a particular general's military strategy; several primaries might exemplify how a particular candidate tailors his or her speeches to appeal to the religious right; several scenes might show how a particular playwright romanticizes the working class; and so on.

Save the best example to receive the most analytical attention in your paper. If you were to present this example in the introduction, you would risk making the rest of the essay vaguely repetitive. A quick close-up of another example will strengthen your argument or interpretation. By using a different example to raise the issues, you suggest that the phenomenon exemplified is not an isolated case and that the major example you will eventually concentrate upon is indeed representative.

What kind of example should you choose? By calling it second best, we mean to suggest only that it should be another resonant instance of whatever issue or question you have chosen to focus upon. Given its location up front and its function to introduce the larger issues to which it points, you should handle it more simply than subsequent examples. That way your readers can get their bearings before you take them into a more in-depth analysis of your best example in the body of your paper.

GAMBIT 5: EXEMPLIFY THE TOPIC WITH A NARRATIVE

A common gambit in the humanities and social sciences, the narrative opening introduces a short, pertinent, and vivid story or anecdote that exemplifies a key aspect of a topic. Although generally not permissible in the formal reports assigned in the natural and social sciences, narrative openings turn up in virtually all other kinds of writing across the curriculum. Here is an example from a student paper in psychology.

> In the past fifteen years, issues surrounding AIDS have incited many people to examine their thoughts and feelings about homosexuality. As a result, instances of prejudice and discrimination toward gays, lesbians, and bisexuals

have risen recently (Herek 1989). Although some instances are sufficiently damaging to warrant criminal charges, other less serious instances of prejudice occur every day. Nonetheless, they demonstrate a problem with our society that needs to be addressed. I witnessed one of these subtle demonstrations of prejudice in a social psychology class. The topic of the class was love and relationships, how they develop, endure, and deteriorate. Although the professor had not specifically stated it previously, the information being presented was relevant to homosexual relationships as well as heterosexual ones. At one point during her lecture, the professor was presenting an example using a hypothetical sorority member. The professor, in passing, referred to the sorority member's love relationship partner as a "she." This reference to a homosexual relationship did not seem intentional on the professor's part. However, many in the class noticed and reacted with silence at first, then glances at neighbors, which led finally to nervous laughter. After this disruption ended, a student explained to the professor what had been said that caused the disruption. And in response the professor promptly explained that the theories for love and relationships also apply to homosexual relationships.

In that moment of nervous laughter, many in the class displayed prejudice against homosexual relationships. In particular, they were displaying a commonly held belief that homosexual relationships are not founded on the same emotions, thoughts, and feelings that heterosexual relationships are. The main causes of prejudice displayed in class against homosexuality include social categorization and social learning.

As this introduction funnels to its thesis, the readers receive a graphic sense of the issue that the writer will now develop nonnarratively. Such nonnarrative treatment is usually necessary because by itself anecdotal evidence can be seen as merely personal. Storytelling is suggestive but usually does not constitute sufficient proof; it needs to be corroborated. In the preceding paragraph the writer has strengthened his credibility by focusing not on his personal responses but rather on the lesson to be drawn from his experience—a lesson that other people might also draw from it.

Like challenging a commonly held view or using a second-best example, a narrative opening will also help to safeguard you from trying to do too much up front. All three of these gambits enable you to play an ace, establishing your authority with your readers, without having to play your whole hand. They offer a starting position rather than a miniaturized version of the entire paper. As a general rule (disciplinary conventions permitting), use your introduction to pose one problem and offer one enigmatic example—seeking in some way to engage readers in the thought process that you are beginning to unfold. Raise the issue; don't settle it.

▶ Try this 8.2: Analyzing Introduction

One of the best ways to learn about introductions is to gather some sample introductory paragraphs and, working on your own or in a small group, figure out how each one works, what it accomplishes.

Here are some particular questions you might pose:

- Why does the writer start in this way—what is accomplished?
- What kind of relationship does this opening establish with the audience and to what ends?
- How does the writer let readers know why the writing they are about to read is called for, useful, and necessary?
- Where and by what logic does the introduction funnel?

E. THE FUNCTION OF CONCLUSIONS

Like the introduction, the conclusion has a key social function: it escorts the readers out of the paper, just as the introduction has escorted them in. What do readers want as they leave the textual world you have taken them through? Although the form and length of the conclusion depend on the purpose and disciplinary conventions of the particular paper, it is possible to generalize a set of shared expectations for the conclusion across the curriculum. In some combination most readers want three things: a judgment, a culmination, and a send-off.

Judgment—The conclusion is the site for final judgment on whatever question or issue or problem the paper has focused upon. In most cases, this judgment occurs in overt connection with the introduction, often repeating some of its key terms. The conclusion normally reconsiders the question raised by the opening hypothesis and, however tentatively, rules yea or nay. It also explicitly revisits the introductory claim for why the topic matters.

Culmination—More than simply summarizing what has preceded or reasserting your main point, the conclusion needs to culminate. The word "culminate" is derived from the Latin *"columen,"* meaning "top or summit." To culminate is to reach the highest point, and it implies a mountain (in this case, of information and analysis) that you have scaled. When you culminate a paper in a conclusion, you bring things together and ascend to one final statement of your thinking.

When you culminate a paper in a conclusion, you bring things together and ascend to one final statement of your thinking.

Send-Off—The climactic effects of judgment and culmination provide the basis for the send-off. The send-off is both social and conceptual, a final opening outward of the topic that leads the reader out of the paper with something further to think about. As is suggested by most of the professors in the accompanying "Voices from Across the Curriculum" boxes, the conclusion needs to move beyond the close analysis of data that has occupied the body of the paper into a kind of speculation that the writer has earned the right to formulate.

Here is an example of a conclusion that contains a final judgment, a culmination, and a send-off. The paper, a student's account of what she learned about science from doing research in biology, opens by claiming that, to the apprentice, "science assumes an impressive air of complete reliability, especially to its distant human acquaintances." Having been attracted to science by the popular view that it proceeds infallibly, she arrives at quite a different final assessment:

> All I truly know from my research is that the infinite number of factors that can cause an experiment to go wrong make tinkering a lab skill just as necessary as reading a buret. A scientist can eventually figure out a way to collect the data she wants if she has the patience to repeatedly recombine her materials and tools in slightly different ways. A researcher's success, then, often depends largely on her being lucky enough to locate, among all the possibilities, the one procedure that works.
>
> Aided more by persistence and fortune than by formal training, I evolved a method that produced credible results. But, like the tests from which it derived, the success of that method is probably also highly specific to a certain experimental environment and so is valid only for research involving borosilicate melts treated with hydrofluoric and boric acids. I've discovered a principle, but it's hardly a universal one: reality is too complex to allow much scientific generalization. Science may appear to sit firmly on all-encompassing truths, but the bulk of its weight actually rests on countless little rules tailored for particular situations.

This writer deftly interweaves the original claim from her introduction—that "science assumes an impressive air of complete reliability"—into a final *judgment* of her topic, delivered in the last sentence. This judgment is also a *culmination*, as it moves from her account of doing borosilicate melts to the small but acute generalization that "little rules tailored for particular situations" rather than "all-encompassing truths" provide the mainstay of scientific research. Notice that *a culmination does not need to make a grand claim in order to be effective*. In fact, the relative smallness of the final claim, especially in contrast to the sweeping introductory position about scientific infallibility, ultimately provides a *send-off* made effective by its unexpected understatement.

VOICES FROM ACROSS THE CURRICULUM

Expanding Possibilities in the Conclusion

I tell my students that too many papers "just end," as if the last page or so were missing. I tell them the importance of ending a work. One could summarize main points, but I tell them this is not heavy lifting. They could raise issues not addressed (but hinted at) in the main body: "given this, one could consider that." I tell them that a good place for reflection might be a concluding section in which they take the ball and run: react, critique, agree, disagree, recommend, suggest, or predict.

I help them by asking, "Where does the paper seem to go *after* it ends on paper?" That is, I want the paper to live on even though the five pages are filled. I don't want to suddenly stop thinking or reacting just because I've read the last word on the bottom of page 5. I want an experience, as if the paper is still with me.

I believe the ending should be an expansion on or explosion of possibilities, sort of like an introduction to some much larger "mental" paper out there. I sometimes encourage students to see the concluding section as an option to introduce ideas that can't be dealt with now. Sort of a "Having done this, I would want to explore boom, boom, boom if I were to continue further." Here the students can critique and recommend ("Having seen 'this,' one wonders 'that'").

–Frederick Norling, Professor of Business

There must be a summation. What part did the stock market crash of 1929 play in the onset of the Great Depression? Let's hear that conclusion one more time. Again, but now in an abbreviated form, what's the evidence? What are the main ambiguities that remain? Has your paper raised any new questions for future research? Are there any other broader ramifications following in the wake of your paper?

–James Marshall, Professor of Economics

VOICES FROM ACROSS THE CURRICULUM

Limiting Claims in the Conclusion

In the professional journals, conclusions typically appear as a refined version of a paper's thesis—that is, as a more qualified statement of the main claim. An author might take pains to point out how this claim is limited or problematic, given the adequacy of available evidence (particularly in the case of papers dependent on current empirical research, opinion polls, etc.). The conclusion also may indicate the implications of current or new evidence on conventional wisdom/theory—how the theory needs to be revised, discarded, and so forth. Conclusions of papers that deal with contemporary issues or trends usually consider the practical consequences or the expectations for the future.

The conclusion does not appear simply as a restatement of a thesis, but rather as an attempt to draw out its implications and significance (the "So what?"). This is what I usually try to impress upon students. For instance, if a student is writing on a particular proposal for party reform, I would expect the concluding paragraph to consider both the significance of the reform and its practicality.

I should note that professional papers often indicate the tentativeness of their conclusions by stressing the need for future research and indicating what these research needs might be. Although I haven't tried this, maybe it would be useful to have students conclude papers with a section entitled "For Further Consideration" in which they would indicate those things that they would have liked to have known but couldn't, given their time constraints, the availability of information, and lack of methodological sophistication. This would serve as a reminder of the tentativeness of conclusions and the need to revisit and revise arguments in the future (which, after all, is a good scholarly habit).

–Jack Gambino, Professor of Political Science

WAYS OF CONCLUDING

The three professors quoted on pages 230–232 all advise some version of the judgment/ culmination/send-off combination. The first professor stresses the send-off.

Although it is true that the conclusion is the place for "broader ramifications," this phrase should not be understood as a call for a global generalization. As the professor in the "Voices from Across the Curriculum" box suggests, often the culmination represents a final limiting of a paper's original claim.

THREE STRATEGIES FOR WRITING EFFECTIVE CONCLUSIONS

There is striking overlap in the advice offered in the cross-disciplinary "voices." All caution that the conclusion should provide more than a restatement of what you've already said. All suggest that the conclusion should, in effect, serve as the introduction to some "larger 'mental' paper out there" (as one professor puts it) beyond the confines of your own paper. By consensus, the professors make three recommendations for conclusions:

1. *Pursue implications.* Reason inductively from your particular study to consider broader issues, such as the study's practical consequences or applications, or future-oriented issues, such as avenues for further research. To unfold implications in this way is to broaden the view from the here and now of your paper by looking outward to the wider world and forward to the future.
2. *Come full circle.* Unify your paper by interpreting the results of your analysis in light of the context you established in your introduction.
3. *Identify limitations.* Acknowledge restrictions of method or focus in your analysis, and qualify your conclusion (and its implications) accordingly.

Try this 8.3: Analyzing a Sample Conclusion

Consider the following example, which supplies the concluding paragraphs to the paper whose introduction we analyzed earlier as an example of a narrative opening on pages 227–228. That opening anecdote, you may recall, introduced the problems of social categorization and social learning as causes of homophobia in the academic environment.

First reread the writer's introduction (under Gambit 5). Then determine how his conclusion has implemented the three strategies for concluding effectively—unfolding implications, coming full circle, and limiting claims. Jot answers to the following questions: What does he repeat of the claims made in the introduction? How does he change the context in which these claims are now to be viewed? What words does he use to qualify both the final summary of evidence and his concluding claim?

> There are many other instances of prejudice, stereotyping, and discrimination against homosexuals. These range from beliefs that homosexual partners cannot be adequate parents, to exclusion from the military, to bias (hate) crimes resulting in murder. But in recent decades, attempts have been made to help end these discriminations. One of the first occurred in 1973 when the American Psychological Association changed its policy so that homosexuals were no longer regarded as mentally ill (Melton, 1989). Thus the stigma that homosexuals are not able to fully contribute to society was partially lifted.

> Other ways that have been suggested to reduce prejudice regarding homosexuals include increasing intergroup contact. In this way, each group may come to recognize similarities and encounter counterstereotypical information. Herek (1989) also suggests that education in elementary through high schools about diversity and tolerance of it—for students as well as teachers—may help prevent stereotypes, prejudice, and hate crimes. And if people are made aware of their schemas and stereotypes, they may consider information they would have ignored based on their schemas. We may never be able to eliminate the process of social categorization, but perhaps we may be able to teach that all out-groups are not necessarily "bad."

F. SOLVING TYPICAL PROBLEMS IN CONCLUSIONS

The primary challenge in writing conclusions, it should now be evident, lies in finding a way to culminate your analysis without claiming either too little or too much. There are a number of fairly common problems to guard against if you are to avoid either of these two extremes.

REDUNDANCY

In Chapter 5 we lampooned an exaggerated example of the five-paragraph form for constructing its conclusion by stating "Thus, we see" and then repeating the introduction verbatim. The result is *redundancy*. As you've seen, it's a good idea to refer back to the opening, but it's a bad idea just to reinsert it mechanically. Instead, reevaluate what you said there in light of where you've ended up, repeating only key words or phrases from the introduction. This kind of *selective repetition* is a desirable way of achieving unity and will keep you from making one of two opposite mistakes— either repeating too much or bringing up a totally new point in the conclusion.

RAISING A TOTALLY NEW POINT

Raising a totally new point can distract or bewilder a reader. This problem often arises out of a writer's praiseworthy desire to avoid repetition. As a rule, you can guard against the problem by making sure that you have clearly expressed the conceptual link between your central conclusion and any implications you may draw. *An implication is not a totally new point but rather one that follows from the position you have been analyzing.*

Similarly, although a capping judgment or send-off may appear for the first time in your concluding paragraph, it should have been *anticipated* by the body of your paper. Conclusions often indicate where you think you (or an interested reader) may need to go next, but you don't actually go there. In a paper on the economist Milton Friedman, for example, if you think that another economist offers a useful way of critiquing him, you probably should not introduce this person for the first time in your conclusion.

OVERSTATEMENT

Many writers are confused over how much they should claim in the conclusion. Out of the understandable (but mistaken) desire for a grand (rather than a modest and qualified) culmination, writers sometimes *overstate* the case. That is, they assert more than their evidence has proven or even suggested. Must a conclusion arrive at some comprehensive and final answer to the question that your paper has analyzed? Depending on the question and the disciplinary conventions, you may need to come down exclusively on one side or another. In a great many cases, however, the answers with which you conclude can be more moderate. Especially in the humanities, good analytical writing seeks to unfold successive layers of implication, so it's not even reasonable for you to expect neat closure. In such cases, you are usually better off qualifying your final judgments, drawing the line at points of relative stability.

> *Must a conclusion arrive at some final answer? You are usually better off qualifying your final judgments, drawing the line at points of relative stability.*

ANTICLIMAX

It makes a difference precisely where in the final paragraph(s) you qualify your concluding claim. The end of the conclusion is a "charged" site, because it gives the reader a last impression of your paper. As the next chapter on formats will discuss in more detail, if you end with a concession—an acknowledgement of a rival position at odds with your thesis—you risk leaving the reader unsettled and possibly confused. The term for this kind of letdown from the significant to the inconsequential is "anticlimax." In most cases, you will flub the send-off if you depart the paper on an anticlimax.

There are many forms of anticlimax besides ending with a concession. If your conclusion peters out in a random list or an apparent afterthought or a last-minute qualification of your claims, the effect is anticlimactic. And for many readers, *if your final answer comes from quoting an authority in place of establishing your own, that, too, is an anticlimax.*

At the beginning of this section we suggested that a useful rule for the introduction is to play an ace but not your whole hand. In the context of this card-game analogy, it is similarly effective to *save an ace for the conclusion.* In most cases, this high card will provide an answer to some culminating "So what?" question—a last view of the implications or consequences of your analysis.

> Save an ace for the conclusion—a high card that answers some culminating "So what?" question or offers a last view of the implications or consequences of your analysis.

G. SCIENTIFIC FORMAT: INTRODUCTIONS AND CONCLUSIONS

Formats control fairly strictly the form of standard writing projects in the natural sciences and psychology.

INTRODUCTIONS OF REPORTS IN THE SCIENCES

The professors quoted in the "Voices from Across the Curriculum" boxes in the remainder of this chapter emphasize the importance of isolating a specific question or issue and locating it within a wider context. Notice, as you read these voices, how *little* the model for an introduction changes in moving from a social science (psychology) to the natural sciences of biology and physics.

In the sciences, the introduction is an especially important and also somewhat challenging section of the report to compose because it requires a writer *not merely to assemble but also to assimilate* the background of information and ideas that frame his or her hypothesis.

VOICES FROM ACROSS THE CURRICULUM

Introductions in the Sciences

A paper usually starts by making some general observation or a description of known phenomena and by providing the reader with some background information. The first paragraphs should illustrate an understanding of the issues at hand and should present an argument for why the research should be done. In other words, a context or framework is established for the entire paper. This background information must lead to a clear statement of the objectives of the paper and the hypothesis that will be experimentally tested. This movement from broad ideas and observations to a specific question or test starts the deductive scientific process.

–*Richard Niesenbaum, Professor of Biology*

VOICES FROM ACROSS THE CURRICULUM
Assimilating Prior Research

The introduction is one of the hardest sections to write. In the introduction, students must summarize, analyze, and integrate the work of numerous other authors and use that to build their own argument.

Students frequently have trouble writing the introduction. They tend to just list the conclusions of previous authors. So-and-So said this, and So-and-So said this, and on and on in a list format. Usually, they *quote* the concluding statements from an article. But the task is really to read the article and *summarize* it in your own words. The key is to analyze rather than just repeat material from the articles so as to make clear the connections among them. (It is important to note that experimental psychologists almost never use direct quotes in their writing. Many of my students have been trained to use direct quotation for their other classes, and so I have to spend time explaining how to summarize without directly quoting or plagiarizing the work that they have read.)

Finally, in the introduction the students must show explicitly how the articles they have summarized lead to the hypothesis they have devised. Many times the students see the connection as implicitly obvious, but I require that they explicitly state the relationships between what they read and what they plan to do.

–Laura Snodgrass, Professor of Psychology

One distinctive feature of scientific papers is that a separate prefatory section called the *abstract* precedes the introduction. Authors also produce abstracts for papers in many other disciplines, but these are usually published separately—for example, in a bibliography, in a journal's table of contents, and so forth. (See the end of Chapter 13 for further discussion of abstracts.)

VOICES FROM ACROSS THE CURRICULUM
Writing Abstracts

The publishable paper in physics begins with an abstract, which briefly describes the experiment, gives the conclusion, and the significance of the work, all in three or four sentences. In the opening paragraph of the main body of the paper, the writer tries to put the work to be described into some larger context. This context usually includes reference to the following:

- similar experiments, which may, or may not, have shown similar results; and
- theoretical work suggesting the importance of the experiment, the scientific or technological significance of the work.

–Robert Milligan, Professor of Physics

VOICES FROM ACROSS THE CURRICULUM

Writing Conclusions in the Sciences

The conclusion occurs in a section labeled "Discussion" and, as quoted from the *Publication Manual of the American Psychological Association* (4th ed., Washington, DC, 1994), is guided by the following questions:

- What have I contributed here?
- How has my study helped to resolve the original problem?
- What conclusions and theoretical implications can I draw from my study? (p. 19)

In a broad sense, one particular research report should be seen as but one moment in a broader research tradition that *preceded* the particular study being written about and that will *continue after* this study is published. And so the conclusion should tie this particular study into both previous research considering implications for the theory guiding this study and (when applicable) practical implications of this study. One of the great challenges of writing a research report is thus to place this particular study within that broader research tradition. That's an analytical task.

–Alan Tjeltveit, Professor of Psychology

Papers are concluded with a "Discussion" section in which conclusions are analyzed and qualified and in which ultimately their implications for the "bigger picture" are presented. The conclusion of the paper often represents the move from the deductive to the inductive aspect of science. The specific results first are interpreted (but not restated), and their implications and limitations are then discussed. The original question should be rephrased and discussed in light of the results presented. Conclusions should be qualified, and alternative explanations should be considered. Finally, conservative generalizations and new questions are posed.

–Richard Niesenbaum, Professor of Biology

In the "Discussion" section, students must critically evaluate the extent to which the empirical evidence they have collected supports the hypothesis they put forth in the introduction. If the data does not support their hypothesis, they need to explain why. The reasons typically are either that there was something wrong with the hypothesis or something wrong with the experiment. Interestingly, students usually find it easier to write the "Discussion" section if their hypothesis was not supported than if it was—to guess what went wrong—because it is difficult to integrate new results into existing theory.

–Laura Snodgrass, Professor of Psychology

DISCUSSION SECTIONS OF REPORTS IN THE SCIENCES

As is the case with introductions, the conclusions of reports written in the natural sciences and psychology are regulated by formalized disciplinary formats.

Conclusions, for example, occur in a section entitled "Discussion." As the voices in the "Voices from Across the Curriculum" box on page 237 demonstrate, the organization and contents of discussion sections vary little from discipline to discipline. For that matter, the imperatives that guide discussion sections share essential traits with conclusions across the curriculum. Look for these similarities in the three comments in the box.

◀ **ASSIGNMENT:** Revising the Introduction and Conclusion of a Previous Paper

---

Select one of your previous papers and entirely rewrite the introductory and concluding paragraphs. Your revisions should be guided by the chapter's overarching points: *Introductions should raise issues rather than settle them, and conclusions should culminate, going beyond restating what has already been said.* As you plan your revisions, consciously apply the concrete suggestions contained in the chapter's lists of gambits and discussion of strategies. How might the introduction be rewritten to use one of the opening gambits? Which of the opening gambits would be most appropriate? Experiment with at least two. Then rewrite your conclusion in explicit conversation with your introduction, qualifying your opening claims and pushing to answer one culminating but qualified "So what?" at which the original ending never arrived. ▶

GUIDELINES FOR WRITING INTRODUCTIONS AND CONCLUSIONS

Introductions

1. The introduction seeks to raise the issue, not settle it. Articulate why, in the context of existing thinking on the subject, your topic matters.

2. Don't try to do too much. Offer only the most relevant context, the most essential parts of your road map, and (disciplinary conventions permitting) a first rather than last claim.

3. Always introduce a working (hypo)thesis, frame it with (appropriately cited) background or other context, and specify your method or angle of approach.

4. Especially in longer papers, you can use a procedural opening to forecast the organization clearly, but don't let it distract you from also stating your claim.

5. Experiment with opening gambits: challenge a common view, use your second-best example to set up the issue, or exemplify the problem with a narrative opening.

Conclusions

6. Culminate—don't just summarize. Offer your most fully evolved and qualified statement of the thesis or your final judgment on the question posed in the introduction.

GUIDELINES FOR WRITING INTRODUCTIONS AND CONCLUSIONS (CONTINUED)

7. Come full circle: revisit the introductory hypothesis and context. This strategy will unify your paper and locate it within an ongoing conversation on your topic.

8. Your conclusion should not unqualifiedly claim more than your evidence has established, but it should leave the reader with further implications or speculations to ponder (a send-off).

9. Let your conclusion gradually escort the reader out of the paper. Like the introduction, it is a social site, so try to leave the reader with a positive last impression.

CHAPTER 9

Organization:
Forms and Formats

Quick
Take

This is a chapter about organization, about the forms and formats writers use to give structure to their ideas. The first half of the chapter concentrates on *disciplinary formats*—the rules governing the forms of finished papers in the various disciplines. More specifically, it argues for recognizing the *heuristic value* of these formats—that is, their function as tools of invention, offering writers means for finding things out. The second half of the chapter broadens the focus beyond formats to consider *rhetoric*: how a writer's awareness of an audience's attitudes and needs affects the shape of her or his writing.

What the chapter does not focus on are the various models of overall organization treated earlier in the book as alternatives to five-paragraph form. See the sections titled "Pan, Track, and Zoom: The Film Analogy" in Chapter 5 (on evidence) as well as the "Procedure for Making the Thesis Evolve through Successive Complications" in Chapter 6 (on the evolving thesis). Both of these offer flexible wide-scale models for organization.

This chapter is less concerned with teaching you particular formats than with teaching you ways of thinking about and putting to best use whatever formats you are asked to write in. As you will see, academic disciplines differ in the extent to which they adhere to prescribed organizational schemes. In biology and psychology, for example, formal papers and reports generally follow an explicitly prescribed pattern of presentation. Some other disciplines are less uniform and less explicit about their reliance on formats, but writers in these fields—economics, for example, or political science— usually operate within fairly established forms as well.

The second half of the chapter, titled "The Psychology of Form," raises rhetorical issues as a lead-in to discussion of such topics as how to organize comparisons, how to situate concessions and refutations, how to use thesis shape to determine the shape of a paper, and how to use transitions and paragraphing in the overall organization of an essay.

A. THE TWO FUNCTIONS OF FORMATS: PRODUCT AND PROCESS

Most of the writing (and thinking) we do is generated by some kind of format, even if we are not aware of it. Writers virtually never write in the absence of conventions. Accordingly, you should not regard most of the formats that you encounter simply as *prescriptive* (that is, strictly required) sets of artificial rules. Rather, try to think of them as descriptive accounts of the various *heuristics*—sets of questions and categories—that humans typically use to guide and stimulate their thinking.

The first step in learning to use formats productively is to recognize that they have two related but separate functions: product and process.

- *As sets of rules for organizing a final product,* formats make communication among members of a discipline easier and more efficient. By standardizing the means of displaying thinking in a discipline, the format enables readers to compare more readily one writer's work with that of others in the field, because readers will know where to look for particular kinds of information— the writer's methodology, for example, or his or her hypothesis or conclusions.

- *As guides and stimulants to the writing process,* formats offer writers a means of finding and exploring ideas. The procedures that formats contain seek to guide the writer's thinking process in a disciplined manner, prompting systematic and efficient examination of a subject. The notion of formats functioning as aids to invention—idea generation—goes back at least as far as Aristotle, whose *Rhetoric* defined twenty-eight general "topics" (such as considering causes and effects or dividing a subject into parts) that speakers might pursue to invent arguments.

Perhaps the biggest problem that formats can create for writers is *a premature emphasis on product*—on the form of the finished paper at the expense of process. When this happens, they tend to lose sight of *the logic* that formats provide for dividing the subject into parts, arranged in a particular order. The conventional format of the scientific paper, for example, stipulates the inclusion of a review of prior research to induce writers to arrive at thoughtful connections between their own work and earlier experiments.

USING FORMATS HEURISTICALLY: AN EXAMPLE

To lose sight of the heuristic value of formats is to become preoccupied with formats as disciplinary etiquette. The solution to this problem probably sounds easier than it is: you need to *find the spaces in a format that will allow it to work as a heuristic.* Consider how you might go about using even a highly specified organizational scheme like the following:

1. State the problem.
2. Develop criteria of adequacy for a solution.
3. Explore at least two inadequate solutions.
4. Explicate the proposed solution.
5. Evaluate the proposed solution.
6. Reply to anticipated criticisms.

The best reason not to ignore any of the six steps in this problem/solution format is that the format does have a logic, although it leaves that logic unstated. The purpose of including at least two inadequate solutions (step 3), for example, is to protect the writer against moving to a conclusion too quickly on the basis of too little evidence. The requirements that the writer evaluate the solution and reply to criticisms (steps 5 and 6) press the writer toward complexity, to prevent a one-sided and uncritical answer. In short, heuristic value in the format is there for a writer to use if he or she doesn't allow a premature concern with matters of form to take precedence over thinking. It would be a mistake, in other words, to assume that one must move through the six steps consecutively; the writer would need to arrange his or her thinking in that order only when putting together the final product.

FORMATS IN THE NATURAL AND SOCIAL SCIENCES

In some disciplines, especially in the natural sciences and psychology, the pattern of presentation for formal papers and reports is explicitly prescribed and usually mandatory. As noted in Chapter 13, for example, the American Psychological Association (APA) issues a disciplinary style guide (now in its fifth edition) to which all writers seeking to publish in the field must adhere. In other disciplines, particularly in the humanities and other of the social sciences, the accepted patterns of organization are less rigidly defined. Nonetheless, writers in these fields also operate to a significant extent within established forms, such as those set forth by the Modern Language Association (MLA) handbook.

Because formats offer a means not only of displaying thinking in a discipline but also of shaping it, the format that a discipline tacitly or overtly requires conditions its members to think in particular ways. Learning to use the format that scientists use predisposes you to think like a scientist. Learning the differences among the various disciplines' formats can help you recognize differences in *epistemology* (ways of knowing). As we stress elsewhere in this book, how you say something is always a part of what you say; the two can't be easily separated. Although knowing the required steps of a discipline's writing format won't write your papers for you, not knowing how writers in that discipline characteristically proceed can keep you from being read.

Nonetheless, the various formats across the disciplines, the skeletons that both shape and display thinking in those disciplines, are actually quite similar. They usually contain most of the same elements, although these elements may be called by different names and arranged in slightly different orders. A science paper and a history paper, for example, both advance a hypothesis, provide context for it, specify methodology, and support their claims by carefully weighing the evidence.

The various formats across the disciplines are actually quite similar. A science paper and a history paper both advance a hypothesis, provide context for it, specify methodology, and support their claims by carefully weighing the evidence.

VOICES FROM ACROSS THE CURRICULUM

Using the Scientific Format

There are firm rules in organizing scientific writing. Papers are usually divided into four major sections: (1) Introduction: provides context and states the question asked and the hypothesis tested in the study; (2) Methodology: describes experimental procedure; (3) Results: states the results obtained; and (4) Discussion: analyzes and interprets results with respect to the original hypothesis, and discusses implications of the results. As this organizational model should make clear, scientific papers are largely deductive, with a shift to inductive reasoning in the discussion when the writer usually attempts to generalize or extend conclusions to broader circumstances.

Scientific papers also include an abstract, which is placed on the page after the title page. The abstract summarizes the question being investigated in the paper, the methods used in the experiment, the results, and the conclusions drawn. The reader should be able to determine the major topics in the paper without reading the entire paper. Compose the abstract after the paper is completed.

–Richard Niesenbaum, Professor of Biology

In writing in the social sciences, there is a standard plot with three alternative endings. The Introduction (a standard section of APA style) sets forth the problem, which the Methods section promises to address. The Results section "factually" reports the outcome of the study, with the Discussion section interpreting the results. The data are given the starring role in determining which ending is discussed in the Discussion section: hypothesis confirmed, hypothesis rejected, or hard to say. (I would say "which ending the author chooses" versus "which ending is discussed," but the data are supposed to be determinative, and the role of the author/investigator neutral.) Analytical thinking comes in setting up the problem and making sense of the results in conjunction with existing literature on the subject.

–Alan Tjeltveit, Professor of Psychology

Experimental Psychology uses a very rigid format. I explain to the students the functions of the different sections for the reader. Once students start to read journal articles themselves, the functions of the sections become clear. Readers do not always want to read or reread the whole article. If I want to replicate someone's research, I may read just the Methods section to get the technical details I need. I may read just the Results section to get a sense of the numerical results I might expect. On the other hand, I may not care about the details of how the experiment was run. I might just want to know if it worked, in which case I would read the first few sentences of the Discussion section. The format lets me know exactly where to find whatever I might be looking for, without having to read through the whole article.

–Laura Snodgrass, Professor of Psychology

VOICES FROM ACROSS THE CURRICULUM
Treating the Format Flexibly

Scientific format appears highly formulaic at first glance. Papers are generally broken into four sections: Introduction (What is this all about, What do we already know, Why do we care?), Experimental Procedures (What did you actually do?), Results (What happened in your experiments?), and Discussion (What do you think it means? What are the remaining questions?). This breakdown is useful because it emphasizes the process of argument (introduction and results), providing evidence (results) and analysis (discussion). However, although this may seem different from writing in other disciplines, I think of it as a codification of basic analytical writing that is common in most disciplines.

A common mistake made by beginning and intermediate students is taking this breakdown too literally. To be comprehensible, the rules must be broken periodically. For example, results frequently must be referred to in the Experimental Procedures section to understand *why* the next procedure was performed. Similarly, the Results section frequently must include some discussion, so that the reader understands the immediate significance of the results, if not the broader implications. For example, the following sentences might appear in a Results section: "These data suggest that the p53 protein may function in repressing cell division in potential cancer cells. To test this possibility, we overexpressed p53 protein in a transformed cell line." The first sentence provides an interpretation of the results that is necessary to understand why the next experiment was performed.

–Bruce Wightman, Professor of Biology

You should note that the observations in the preceding "Voices from Across the Curriculum" boxes apply to much, but certainly not all, of the writing that goes on in the sciences. In the last box, a professor of biology concentrates on the logic of the scientific format, but he also stresses its relative *flexibility*. That is, the distinctions among the various parts are not always as clear-cut as some students may think they are.

B. THE PSYCHOLOGY OF FORM

Thus far in this book we have talked about form primarily in relation to the search for meaning. We've demonstrated that some forms of arranging ideas (five-paragraph form, for example) interfere with a writer's ability to have ideas in the first place. Whatever form one uses, we've argued, has to be flexible enough to allow ideas to evolve. The point is that various factors influence a writer's decisions about forms and formats. These include both the demands of the subject itself and those of the discourse community within which the writing seeks to communicate.

We now wish to expand upon the role that a writer's sense of his or her *audience* plays in determining the formal presentation of ideas. We have titled this section "The Psychology of Form" to emphasize the effects that a chosen form has on an audience—on its receptiveness to a writer's ideas, for example.

Since classical times, there have been numerous studies of this subject, known as *rhetoric*. The study of rhetoric is primarily concerned with the various means at a writer's (or speaker's) disposal for influencing the views of an audience. In early rhetorics, Greek and Roman writers divided these means into three large categories: *ethos*, *logos*, and *pathos*. We'll use these categories for organizing what we wish to say about the relationship between formal structures and audience.

1. ***Ethos.*** The category of ethos has to do with the character of the speaker or writer. The basic idea of ethos is that if an audience perceives a speaker to be ethical and rational, it will be inclined to perceive her or his argument as ethical and rational too. Thus, writers attend to the kind of *persona* they become on the page, the personality conveyed by the words and the tone of the words. In classical orations—the grandparent of virtually all speech and essay formats—the first section was always allotted to particular means of establishing an appealing persona, one that an audience would want to listen to and believe.

   Although there are many ways of talking about ethos, throughout this book we implicitly recommend essentially the same kind of writer's persona—one that is primarily interested in understanding a subject and conveying that understanding. Such a persona assumes a relationship of mutual interest with his or her audience and avoids a defensive posture toward the material or the audience.

2. ***Logos.*** This category has to do with the character of the thinking itself, which has been our emphasis throughout this book—the rational component, evident in the presence and development of the ideas.

3. ***Pathos.*** This category includes appeals to the audience's emotions—which writing does all of the time, whether a writer wants it to or not. It is possible to think of the form of a paper in terms of how it might negotiate, for example, the likes and dislikes, the hopes and fears, of its assumed audience. If, for instance, you were to present an argument in favor of a position with which you knew in advance that your audience was predisposed to disagree, you would probably choose to delay making a case for it until you had found various ways of earning that audience's trust. By contrast, when presenting an argument to an audience of like-minded people, you would be much more likely to start out with the position you planned to advance.

In any piece of writing, there are always issues of authority. As a writer you need to concern yourself with using language in a way that will incline readers to credit what you say. We have been advancing as the best source of authority your ability to show others why and how you take the evidence to mean what you say it does. A premise of this book is that rather than spend a lot of time cultivating a set of rhetorical strategies for defeating opponents, writers should find ways to make their thinking about evidence clear and convincing in its clarity. Moreover, we have generally supported a more Rogerian approach to argument, whereby a writer seeks to negotiate among competing possibilities and invite collaboration from readers. (See the discussion of Carl Rogers in Chapter 1.)

HOW TO LOCATE CONCESSIONS AND REFUTATIONS

In the language of argument you *concede* whenever you acknowledge that a position at odds with your own does indeed have merit, even though you continue to believe that your position overall is the more reasonable one. A central idea of Chapter 6, "Making a Thesis Evolve," in fact, is that one option for dealing with views that conflict with your own is to use them to evolve your own position, thereby assimilating them. Another option is to argue against these views so as to *refute* their reasonableness.

There are several guidelines for locating concessions and refutations in an argument. It is a rule of thumb, for example, not to make your readers wait too long before you either concede or refute a view that you can assume will already have occurred to them. If you delay too long, you may inadvertently suggest either that you are unaware of the competing view or that you are afraid to bring it up.

You can often house short and easily managed concessions and refutations within the first several paragraphs and, in this way, clear a space for the position you wish to promote. In the case of more complicated and potentially more threatening alternative arguments, you may need to express your own position clearly and convincingly first. But to avoid the rhetorical problem of appearing to ignore the threat, you will probably need to give it a nod, telling readers that you will return to a full discussion of it later, once you have laid out your own position in some detail.

Here are some more specific guidelines:

- Don't end on a concession. If you do include a concession in your concluding paragraph, be sure to return to your own position in the final sentences.
- If you state an opposing argument in your introduction, you should be sure that it can be accurately presented in the brief form that introductory paragraphs require. The danger here is turning the opposing view into a straw man—an easily knocked-down version of the opposing view. (See Chapter 12 for a discussion of straw man.)
- One way of making sure you don't treat an opposing argument unfairly, but also don't inadvertently convince your readers that this argument is better than your own, is to concede the merits of this opposing view but then argue that, in the particular context you are addressing, your argument is more important, more appropriate, and so forth.
- The placement of arguments has much to do with their relative complexity. Reasonably straightforward and easily explained concessions and refutations can often be grouped in one place, perhaps as early as the second or third paragraph of a paper. The approach to concession and refutation in more complex arguments does not allow for such grouping. For each part of your argument, you will probably need to concede and refute as necessary, before moving to the next part of your argument and repeating the procedure.

To qualify as a concession, a writer needs to represent the competing point of view as genuinely creditable—rather than only seemingly creditable until he or she lays out a means of opposing it. Refutations typically operate not just by revealing poor thinking or inadequate evidence in a competing point of view, but also by proposing the greater value of adopting another position. Refutations often concede an opposing argument's genuine merits but then refute its importance in favor of a position that holds more promise under a given set of circumstances.

▶ Try this 9.1: Locating Concessions and Refutations

The following passage from a student essay on the relation between gender inequality and language makes skillful use of concessions and refutations. The excerpt is part of an introductory paragraph, after the writer has set up the issue: whether or not the elimination of sexism in language (the use of male pronouns and words such as *mankind,* for example, in circumstances applying to both men and women) through the use of generic pronouns (those that do not indicate gender, such as *they* rather than *he*) can help eliminate gender exclusion in the culture. The paragraph names the two sides of the issue and moves from there to a tentative thesis.

Study the paragraph to answer the following questions: (1) What language functions as concession? (2) What language functions as refutation? (3) What part of the competing argument does the refutation still appear willing to concede? (4) How is the refutation that the writer offers different from the position to which he concedes?

Gender Inequality and Linguistic Bias

The more conservative side on this issue questions whether the elimination of generic pronouns can, in fact, change attitudes, and whether intentionally changing language is even possible. The reformist side believes that the elimination of generic pronouns is necessary for women's liberation from oppression and that reshaping the use of male pronouns as generic is both possible and effective. Although the answer to the debate over the direct link between a change in language and a change in society is not certain, it is certain that the attitudes and behaviors of societies are inseparable from language. Language conditions what we feel and think. The act of using *they* to refer to all people rather than the generic *he* will not automatically change collective attitudes toward women. These generic pronouns should be changed, however, because (1) the struggle itself increases awareness and discussion of the sexual inequalities in society, and subsequently, this awareness will transform attitudes and language, and (2) the power of linguistic usage has been mainly controlled by and reserved for men. Solely by participating in linguistic reform, women have begun to appropriate some of the power for themselves.

ORGANIZING COMPARISONS AND CONTRASTS

Chapter 4 discusses reading comparatively as a means of arriving at ideas. Here we address this subject from the perspective of organizing a paper. The first decision a writer has to make when arranging comparisons and contrasts is whether to address the two items being compared and contrasted *sequentially* in blocks or *point by point*. For example, if you are comparing subject A with subject B, you might first make all the points you wish to make about A and then make points about B by explicitly referring to A as you go. The advantage of this format is that it will allow you to use comparing and contrasting to figure out what you wish to say as you are drafting.

The disadvantage of this subject-A-then-subject-B format is that it can easily lose focus. If you don't manage to keep the points you raise about each side of your comparison parallel, you may end up with a paper comprising two loosely connected halves. The solution is to make your comparisons and contrasts in the second half of the paper connect explicitly with what you said in the first half. What you say about subject A, in other words, should set the subtopics and terms for discussion of subject B.

The alternative pattern of organization for comparisons and contrasts is to organize by topic—not A and then B but A1 and B1, A2 and B2, A3 and B3, and so forth. That is, you talk about both A and B under a series of subtopics. If, for example, you were comparing two films, you might organize your work under such headings as directing, script, acting, special effects, and so forth.

The advantage of this format is that it better focuses the comparisons, pressing you to use them to think with. The disadvantage is that organizing in this way is sometimes difficult to manage until you've already done quite a bit of thinking about the two items you're comparing. The solution, particularly in longer papers, is sometimes to use both formats. You begin by looking at each of your subjects separately to make the big links and distinctions apparent and then focus what you've said by further pursuing selected comparisons one topic at a time.

Regardless of which format you adopt, the comparisons and contrasts will not really begin to take shape until you have done enough preliminary drafting to discover what the most significant similarities and differences are and, beyond that, whether the similarities or the differences are most important—whether, that is, your primary goal is to compare or to contrast. At this point, you can begin to operate according to the principle we discuss next: climactic order.

CLIMACTIC ORDER

Climactic order has to do with arranging the elements in a list from least important to most important. The idea is to build to your best points, rather than leading with them and thereby allowing the paper to trail off from your more minor and less interesting observations.

Build to your best points, rather than leading with them and thereby allowing the paper to trail off.

But what are your best points? A frequent mistake that writers commit in arranging their points climactically—and one that has much to do with the psychology of form—is to assume that the best point is the most obvious, the one with the most data attached to it and the one least likely to produce disagreement with readers. Such writers end up giving more space than they should to ideas that really don't need much development because they are already evident to most readers.

A better strategy is to define as your best points those that the Notice-and-focus strategy locates as the *most revealing, most thought-provoking, and often, at first glance, least obvious*. In this case, if you followed the principle of climactic order, you would begin with the most obvious and predictable points—and ones that, psychologically speaking, would get readers assenting—and then build to the more revealing and less obvious ones. For example, if the comparisons between film A and film B are fairly mundane but the contrasts are really provocative, you'd get the comparisons out of the way first and build to the contrasts, exploiting difference within similarity. (See Chapter 4.)

Note that the principle of climactic order works with all kinds of organizational schemes, not just with comparison and contrast. If, for example, there are three important reasons for banning snowmobiling in your town, you might choose to place the most compelling one last. If you were to put it first, you might draw your readers in quickly (a principle used by news stories) but then lose them as your argument seemed to trail off into less interesting rationales. Similarly, if you have four examples for a point you wish to make, you might use a pan to cover the first three to pave the way for a zoom on the one you think is the best and most revealing.

HOW THESIS SHAPES PREDICT THE SHAPE OF THE PAPER

Early in Chapter 6 we noted that a strong thesis usually contains tension, the balance of this against that, this degree with that qualification. This tension is often evident in the actual sentence structure of the thesis statement. Many thesis statements begin with a grammatically subordinate idea that they go on to replace or outweigh with a more pressing claim: "Although x appears to account for z, y accounts for it better." (You will probably recognize this sentence structure as a version of one of the earlier prompts to interpretation: saying something "seems to be about x, but is really or could also be about y.") This formula can also organize a paper, which proceeds by following the pattern predicted by the order of clauses in the thesis statement. The first part of the paper deals with the claims for x and then moves to a fuller embrace of y (usually in overt relation to x). (See Chapter 11 for a discussion of grammatical subordination.)

The advantage of this subordinate construction (and the reason that so many theses are set up this way) is that the subordinate idea helps you define your own position by giving you something to define it against. As should be evident at this point, both the thesis shape containing subordination and the paper that follows from it are versions of climactic order.

In practice, using this shape will often lead you to arrive at some compromise position between the claims of both x and y. What appeared to be a binary opposition—"not *x* but *y*"—emerges as a complex combination of the two. (See Chapter 2 on refocusing binaries.)

Sometimes this combination is already evident in a thesis shape related to the subordination model: *"not only x but also y."* Here the emphasis predicts that you will make *additional* claims, probably less obvious ones *(y)*, after you have discussed *x*.

As is evident in the previous chapter's discussion of introductory paragraphs, one of the most important things to accomplish in an introduction is to locate an issue, question, or problem—something that is at stake—and then place it in an explanatory context. The subordinate clause of a thesis helps you demonstrate that there is in fact an issue involved—that is, more than one possible explanation for the evidence you are considering—and thus a reason to write the paper in the first place.

Another thesis shape that can predict the shape of a paper is the *list*. This shape, in which a writer might offer three points and then devote a section to each, often leads to sloppier thinking than one having a thesis statement containing both subordinate and independent clauses, because the list often does not sufficiently specify the connections among its various components. As a result, it fails to assert a relationship among ideas. The list is in fact the shape used by five-paragraph form—a form that does (we'll concede!) achieve considerable clarity of organization but at the (very high) cost of oversimplifying and derailing analysis.

▶ Try this 9.2: Predicting Thesis Shapes

It is a useful skill, both in reading and writing, to predict paper shapes from thesis shapes. Unlike the multiple parts of the thesis that merely lists, productive thesis statements arrange the parts in some sort of overt relation to each other. For each of the theses below, what shape is predicted? That is, what will probably be discussed first, what second, and why? Which words in the thesis are especially predictive of the shape the paper will take?

1. The reforms in education, created to alleviate the problems of previous reforms, have served only to magnify the very problems they were meant to solve.
2. Joinville paints, though indirectly, a picture of military, social, and political gain having very little to do with religion and more to do with race hatred and the acquisition of material wealth.
3. Although women more readily cry in contemporary films, the men, by not crying, seem to win the audience's favor.
4. The complications that fuel the plots in today's romantic comedies arise because women and men express their sensitivity so differently; the resolutions, however, rarely require the men to capitulate.

THE SHAPING FORCE OF TRANSITIONS

A list, we have said, is a slack form of organization: overly loose, not identifying how *this* is related to *that* with the tension necessary to give a paper tensile strength. The same criticism applies to the *connective tissue* among the parts of an essay. Although transitional wording such as *another example of* or *also* at the beginning of paragraphs does tell readers that a related point or example will follow, it does not specify that relationship beyond piling on another *and*. The organizational model at work in this sort of additive scheme is again the list—the most diffuse and potentially illogical form of organization. (For additional analysis of the shortcomings of listing, see "Strategies for Making Summaries More Analytical" in Chapter 4.)

If you find yourself relying on *another* and *also* at points of transition, force yourself to substitute other transitional wording that indicates *more precisely* the nature of the relationship with what has gone before in the paper. Language such as *similarly* and *by contrast* can sometimes serve this purpose. In many cases, however, some restatement of what has been said and its relation to what will come next is called for. Don't underestimate the amount of productive restating that goes on in papers—it's not necessarily redundant. It can also be a "saying again" in different language for the purpose of advancing the writer's thinking further. *A good transition reaches backward, telling where you've been, as the grounds for making a subsequent move forward.*

The linkage between where you've been and where you're going is usually a point in your writing at which thinking is taking place. Often this kind of transitional thinking will require you to concentrate on articulating *how* what has preceded connects to what will follow—the logical links. This is especially the case in the evolving rather than the static model of thesis development, in which the writer continually updates the thesis as it moves through evidence. It follows that thinking tends to occur at points of transition. If it doesn't, you're far more likely to run into problems in organization.

> *Thinking tends to occur at points of transition.*

The first step toward improving your use of transitions (and thereby, the organization of your writing) is to become *conscious* of them. If you notice that you are beginning successive paragraphs with *Another reason*, for example, you can probably conclude that you are listing rather than developing your ideas.

► Try this 9.3: Tracking Transitions

To see how the transitions work as a skeleton for something you are reading (or have written), search out words that function as *directional indicators*, especially at the beginnings of paragraphs but also within them. *And*, for example, is a plus sign. It indicates that the writer will add something, essentially continuing in the same direction. The words *but, yet, nevertheless*, and *however* are among the many transitional words that alert readers to changes in the direction of the writer's thinking. They might indicate, for example, the introduction of a qualification, a potentially contradictory piece of evidence, an alternative point of view, and so forth. Note as well that some additive transitions do more work than *also* or *another*. The word *moreover* is an additive transition, but it adds emphasis to the added point. The transitional sequence *not only . . . but also* restates and then adds information in a way that clarifies what has gone before.

As an exercise in becoming more conscious of how transitions shape the thinking—the advancing and connecting of ideas—in a piece of writing, track the transitions. Take a few pages of something you are reading (preferably a complete piece, such as a short article) and circle or underline all the directional indicators. Remember to check not only the beginnings of paragraphs but within them. Then, survey your markings. What do you notice now about the shape of the piece? Describe the shape. This exercise is also a splendid way to expand your repertoire of transitional words to use in your own writing.

THE VIRTUES OF PARAGRAPHING

Be sure to paragraph, both for your own and for your readers' benefit. Paragraphing is a kindness to your reader because it divides your thinking into manageable bites. If you find a paragraph growing longer than half a page—particularly if it is your opening or second paragraph—search out a place to make a paragraph break. More frequent paragraphing provides readers with convenient resting points from which to relaunch themselves into your thinking.

Long paragraphs are daunting—rather like mountains are—and they are easy to get lost in, for both readers and writers. When writers try to do too much in a single paragraph, they often lose the focus and lose contact with the larger purpose or point that got them into the paragraph in the first place. Remember that old high school rule about one idea to a paragraph? Well, it's not a bad rule, though it isn't exactly right, because sometimes you need more space than a single paragraph can provide to lay out a complicated phase of your overall argument. In that case, just break wherever it seems reasonable to do so to keep your paragraphs from becoming ungainly.

> *Long paragraphs are daunting—rather like mountains are—and they are easy to get lost in.*

When you draft, start a new paragraph whenever you feel yourself getting stuck—it's the promise of a fresh start. When you revise, use paragraphs as a way of cleaning up your thinking, dividing it into its most logical parts.

> *When you draft, start a new paragraph whenever you feel yourself getting stuck—it's the promise of a fresh start.*

A short paragraph always provides emphasis, for which most readers will thank you.

◀ **ASSIGNMENT:** Inferring the Format of a Published Article

---

Often the format governing the organization of a published piece is not immediately evident. That is, it is not subdivided according to conventional disciplinary categories that all members of a given discourse community obey. Especially if you are studying a discipline in which the writing does not follow an explicitly prescribed format, such as history, literature, or economics, you may find it illuminating to examine representative articles or essays in that discipline, looking for an implicit format. In other words, you can usually discern some underlying pattern of organization: the formal conventions, the rules that are being followed even when these are not highlighted.

The following assignment works well whether you tackle it individually or in a group. It can lead to a paper, an oral report, or both. First, you need to assemble several articles from the same or a similar kind of journal or magazine. *Journal* is the name given to publications aimed at specialized, usually scholarly, audiences, as opposed to general or popular audiences. *Time, Newsweek,* and *The New Yorker* are called magazines rather than journals because they are aimed at a broader general audience. *Shakespeare Quarterly* is a journal; *Psychology Today* is a magazine.

Having found at least three journal or magazine articles, study them to focus on the following question: Insofar as there appears to be a format that articles in this journal or magazine adhere to, what are its parts?

How, for example, does an article in this journal or magazine typically begin and end? Does there seem to be a relatively uniform place in which these articles include opposing arguments? You will, in other words, be analyzing the articles inductively (reasoning from particular details to general principles). Begin with the product and reason backward to the skeleton beneath the skin.

Note that if your professor directs you to work with magazines rather than journals, you should probably further narrow the focus—to a *Time* cover story, to *The New Yorker*'s "Letter from [the name of a city]," or another such recurring feature. Even gossip columns and letters of advice to the lovelorn in teen magazines adhere to certain visible though not explicitly marked formats.

Write up your results. Cite particular language from at least two articles in support of your claims about the implicit format. In presenting your evidence, keep the focus on the underlying form, showing how the different articles proceed in the same or similar ways. Don't let yourself get too distracted by the articles' content, even though there may be similarities here as well. Instead, work toward formulating a rationale for the format—what you take to be its psychology of form. You will need (for example) both to lay out the typical form of the introduction and to account for its taking that typical form. Devote several paragraphs to this rationale, either at the end of your report or integrated within it. ▶

GUIDELINES FOR ORGANIZATION: FORMS AND FORMATS

1. Find the space in a format that will allow it to work as a heuristic, a set of steps designed not just to organize but to stimulate and guide your thinking. Avoid the slot-filler mentality.

2. Look for and expect to find the common denominators among the various formats you learn to use across the curriculum. You can master—and benefit from—virtually any format if you approach it not as a set of arbitrary and rigid rules, but as a formalized guide to having ideas.

3. Don't make your readers wait too long before you concede or refute a view that you can assume will already have occurred to them. Otherwise, they may assume you are unaware of the competing view or afraid to bring it up.

4. Always treat opposing views fairly. A good strategy is to concede their merits but argue that, in the particular context you are addressing, your position is more important or appropriate.

5. Use climactic order to organize your points, building to your best ones. The best ones are usually the most revealing and thought-provoking, not the most obvious or commonly agreed upon.

6. Phrasing your thesis to include a subordinate construction—"although *x* appears to account for *z*, *y* accounts for it better"—will give your paper a ready-made organizational shape, along with giving you something to define your own position against.

7. A good transition reaches backward, telling where you've been, as the grounds for making a subsequent move forward. Opt for *similarly* and *by contrast*, for example, which specify connections for your readers, rather than merely additive transitions such as *another* and *also*.

8. Half a page is a healthy length for most paragraphs, long enough to launch an idea but short enough to give your reader time to rest.

CHAPTER 10

Style:
Choosing Words

S tyle, loosely defined, refers to the choices a writer makes among linguistic options. Each time this book has undergone revision, its two style chapters have been moved farther forward, and pieces of them have been located still earlier. This is because we have become increasingly convinced of the importance of style to *how* a writer thinks and to *what* a writer thinks.

This first chapter on style addresses word choice, also known as **diction**, and its effect on style. As an overarching aim, the chapter seeks to make you more self-conscious about the kinds of words you habitually use, and to expand the range of choices. Chapter 11 attempts to do the same with respect to sentence shapes, also known as **syntax**.

This chapter takes as a premise that most people simply don't pay attention to words. That is, they use words as if their sounds and shapes were invisible and their meanings were single and self-evident. One goal of this chapter is to interest you in words themselves—as *things* with particularized qualities, complex histories, and varied shades of meaning.

The two chapters have three primary lessons to teach, which we have bold-faced as objectives, followed by a little commentary:

1. **Understanding that style is not merely decorative.** It is often mistakenly assumed that style is separate from meaning and in that sense largely decorative. From this perspective, paying close attention to style seems finicky, or worse, cynical—a way of dressing up the content to sell it to readers or listeners. The problem with this perspective is that it subscribes to what linguistic philosophers call *the transparent theory of language*. This is the idea that meaning exists outside of language—that we somehow see *through* words to meaning and can then address that meaning without addressing the words that embody it. In the transparent theory of language, words are merely pointers to get past.

These chapters seek to persuade you to adopt the perspective that words *constitute* meaning; that is, that words are the medium in which we dwell. How something is phrased is an integral part of what it says, not subtractable. If you say something in another way, you are saying something else. (This position, known as *the constitutive theory of language*, has been embraced by virtually all contemporary rhetoricians.) In practical terms, this means that *how things are said profoundly affects what they say*.

2. **Seeing style as a matter of choices.** You may have been taught that you should always avoid the first-person *I* in academic writing, steer clear of jargon, and never start a sentence with *and* or *but*. These are matters of usage, not hard-and-fast rules of grammar. There are occasions when all three rules, and others like them, should be rejected. This chapter seeks to persuade you that all writing is *contextual*, its appropriateness dependent on the rhetorical situation.

3. **Learning that simplicity does not equal clarity.** This chapter targets the unexamined cultural bias in favor of "straight talk." The assumption seems to be that people who use too many words, especially big ones, are needlessly complicating what would otherwise be obvious to anyone's common sense. *Not so.* (The previous sentence intends to illustrate that those imperious arbiters of style, Strunk and White, are sometimes correct—"Never use six words when three will do," they say in *The Elements of Style*—but not always.) Of course, simplicity is sometimes preferable, and Chapter 11 devotes considerable attention to ways of reducing excess verbiage.

A. NOT JUST ICING ON THE CAKE

It is commonly assumed that "getting the style right" is a task that begins at the editing stage of producing a paper, as part of polishing the final draft. This assumption is only partly true. You probably should delay a full-fledged stylistic revision until a late stage of drafting, but that doesn't mean that you should totally ignore stylistic questions as you draft, because the decisions you make about how to phrase your meaning inevitably exert a powerful influence on the meaning you make.

And what is style? Well, it's not just icing on the cake—cosmetic, a matter of polishing the surface. Broadly defined, *style refers to all of a writer's decisions in selecting, arranging, and expressing what he or she has to say*. Many factors affect your style: your aim and sense of audience, the ways you approach and develop a topic, the kinds of evidence you choose, and, particularly, the kinds of syntax and diction you characteristically select.

Getting the style right is not as simple as proofreading for errors in grammar or punctuation. Proofreading occurs in the relatively comfortable linguistic world of simple right and wrong. Stylistic considerations, by contrast, take place in the more exploratory terrain of *making choices* among more and less effective ways of formulating and communicating your meaning.

In this sense, style is personal. The foundations of your style emerge in the dialogue you have with yourself about your topic. When you revise for style, you consciously reorient yourself toward communicating the results of that dialogue to your audience. Stylistic decisions, then, are a mix of the unconscious and conscious, of chance and choice. You don't simply impose style onto your prose; it's not a mask you don or your way of icing the cake. Revising for style is more like sculpting. As a sculptor uses a chisel to "bring out" a shape from a block of walnut or marble, a writer uses style to "bring out" the shape of the conceptual connections in a draft of an essay. As the two style chapters will suggest in various ways, this "bringing out" demands a certain *detachment from your own language*. It requires that you *become aware of your words as words and of your sentences as sentences*.

If stylistic considerations are not merely cosmetic, then it follows that rethinking the way you have said something can lead you to rethink the substance of what you have said. This point is sufficiently important to illustrate here for both syntax and diction, before this chapter narrows its focus to diction alone.

How does the difference in sentence structure affect the meaning of the following two sentences?

Draft: The history of Indochina is marked by colonial exploitation as well as international cooperation.

Revision: The history of Indochina, *although* marked by colonial exploitation, testifies to the possibility of international cooperation.

In the draft, the claim that Indochina has experienced colonial exploitation is equal in weight to the claim that it has also experienced international cooperation. But the revision ranks the two claims. The "although" clause makes the claim of exploitation secondary to the claim of cooperation. The first version of the sentence would probably lead you to a broad survey of foreign intervention in Indochina. The result would likely be a static list in which you judged some interventions to be "beneficial" and others "not beneficial." The revised sentence redirects your thinking, tightens your paper's focus to prioritize evidence of cooperation, and presses you to make decisions, such as whether the positive consequences of cooperation outweigh the negative consequences of colonialism. In short, the revision leads you to examine the dynamic relations between your two initial claims.

Rethinking what you mean is just as likely to occur when you attend to word choice. Notice how the change of a single word in the following sentences could change the entire paper.

Draft: The president's attitude toward military spending is ambiguous.

Revision: The president's attitude toward military spending is ambivalent.

In the draft, the use of the word "ambiguous" (meaning "open to many interpretations") would likely lead to a paper on ways that the president's decisions are unclear. The choice of "ambiguous" might also signal that the writer and not the president is unclear on what the president's actions could be taken to mean. If the president's policies aren't unclear—hard to interpret—but are divided, conflicted over competing ways of thinking, then the writer would want the word "ambivalent." This recognition would lead not only to reorganizing the final draft but also to refocusing the argument, building to the significance of this ambivalence (that the president is torn between adopting one of two stances) rather than to the previous conclusion (that presidential policy is incoherent).

B. TONE

Tone is the *implied attitude* of a piece of language toward its subject and audience. Whenever you revise for style, your choices in syntax and diction will affect the tone. There are no hard and fast rules to govern matters of tone, and your control of it will depend upon your sensitivity to the particular context—your understanding of your own intentions and your readers' expectations.

Let's consider, for example, the tonal implications of the warning signs in the subways of London and New York.

London: Leaning out of the window may cause harm.

New York: Do not lean out of the window.

Initially, you may find the English injunction laughably indirect and verbose in comparison with the shoot-from-the-hip clarity of the American sign. But that is to ignore the very thing we are calling *style*. The American version appeals to authority, commanding readers what not to do without telling them why. The English version, by contrast, appeals to logic; it is more collegial toward its readers and assumes they are rational beings rather than children prone to misbehave.

In revising for tone, you need to ask yourself if the attitude suggested by your language is appropriate to the aim of your message and to your audience. Your goal is to keep the tone *consistent* with your rhetorical intentions. The following paragraph, from a college catalogue, offers a classic mismatch between the overtly stated aim and the tonal implications:

> The student affairs staff believes that the college years provide a growth and development process for students. Students need to learn about themselves and others and to learn how to relate to individuals and groups of individuals with vastly different backgrounds, interests, attitudes and values. Not only is the tolerance of differences expected, but also an appreciation and a celebration of these differences must be an outcome of the student's experience. In addition, the student must progress toward self-reliance and independence tempered by a concern for the social order.

The explicit content of this passage—*what* it says—concerns tolerance. The professed point of view is student-friendly, asserting that the college exists to allow students "to learn about themselves and others" and to support the individual in accord with the "appreciation . . . of . . . differences." But note that the implicit tone—*how* the passage goes about saying *what* it says—is condescending and intolerant. Look at the verbs. An imperious authority lectures students about what they "*need* to learn," that tolerance is "*expected*," that "celebration . . . *must* be an outcome," and that "the student *must* progress" along these lines. Presumably, the paragraph does not intend to adopt this high-handed manner, but its deafness to tone subverts its desired meaning.

Try this 10.1: Analyzing Tone-Deaf Prose

Using the example from the college catalogue as a model, locate and bring to class examples of tonal inconsistency or inappropriateness that you encounter in your daily life. If you have difficulty finding examples, try memos from those in authority at your school or workplace, which often contain excruciating examples of officialese. Type one of your passages, and underneath it compose a paragraph of analysis in which you single out particular words and phrases and explain how the tone is inappropriate. Then rewrite the passage to remedy the problem.

LEVELS OF STYLE: WHO'S WRITING TO WHOM, AND WHY DOES IT MATTER?

How you say something is always a significant part of *what* you say. To look at words as words is to focus on the *how* as well as the *what*. Imagine that you call your friend on the phone, and a voice you don't recognize answers. You ask to speak with your friend, and the voice responds, "With whom have I the pleasure of speaking?" By contrast, what if the voice instead responds, "Who's this?" What information do these two versions of the question convey, beyond the obvious request for your name?

> How something is phrased is an integral part of what it says. If you say something in another way, you are saying something else.

The first response—"With whom have I the pleasure of speaking?"—tells you that the speaker is formal and polite. He is also probably fastidiously well educated: he not only knows the difference between "who" and "whom" but also obeys the etiquette that outlaws ending a sentence with a preposition ("Whom have I the pleasure of speaking *with?*"). The very formality of the utterance, however, might lead you to label the speaker pretentious. His assumption that conversing with you is a "pleasure" suggests empty flattery. On the other hand, the second version—"Who's this?"—while also grammatically correct, is less formal. It is more direct but also terse to a fault; the speaker does not seem particularly interested in treating you politely.

The two hypothetical responses represent two different levels of style. Formal English obeys the basic conventions of standard written prose, and most academic writing is fairly formal. An informal style—one that is conversational and full of slang—can have severe limitations in an academic setting. The syntax and vocabulary of written prose aren't the same as those of speech, and attempts to import the language of speech into academic writing can result in your communicating less meaning with less precision.

Let's take one brief example:

> Internecine quarrels within the corporation destroyed morale and sent the value of the stock plummeting.

The phrase "internecine quarrels" may strike some readers as a pretentious display of formal language, but consider how difficult it is to communicate this concept economically. "Fights that go on between people related to each other" is awkward; "brother against brother" is sexist and a cliché; and "mutually destructive disputes" is acceptable but long-winded.

It is arguably a part of our national culture to value the simple and the direct as more genuine and democratic than the sophisticated, which is supposedly more aristocratic and pretentious. This "plain-speaking" style, however, can hinder your ability to develop and communicate your ideas. In the case of "internecine," the more formal diction choice actually communicates more, and more effectively, than the less formal equivalents.

Our national culture values the simple and the direct as more genuine and democratic than the sophisticated, but the plain-speaking style can hinder your ability to communicate your ideas.

When in doubt about how your readers will respond to the formality or informality of your style, you are usually better off opting for some version of "With whom have I the pleasure of speaking?" rather than "Who's this?" The best solution will usually lie somewhere in between: "May I ask who's calling?" would protect you against the imputation of either priggishness or piggishness.

What generalizations about style do these examples suggest?

- There are many ways of conveying a message.
- The way you phrase a message constitutes a significant part of its meaning.
- Your phrasing gives your reader cues that suggest your attitude and your ways of thinking.
- There are no transparent (absolutely neutral) delivery systems.
- All stylistic decisions depend on your sensitivity to context—who's talking to whom about what subject and with what aims.

The last of these generalizations concerns what is called the *rhetorical situation*. *Rhetoric* is the subject that deals with how writers and speakers behave in given situations and, more specifically, how they can generate language that produces the effects they desire on a particular audience. Obviously, as you make stylistic choices, you need to be aware of the possible consequences of making certain statements to a certain audience in a certain fashion.

> **Try this 10.2:** Analyzing Effective Tone
>
> Find an example of tone that you think is just about perfect for the message and audience. Type it, and underneath discuss why it succeeds. Be as specific as you can about how the passage functions stylistically. Talk about particular phrasings and the match between what is being said and how it is said. Factor into your discussion the relationship between levels of style in the example and its presumed audience.

C. THE PERSON QUESTION

"The person question" concerns which of the three basic forms of the pronoun you should use when you write. Here are the three forms, with brief examples.

First person: I believe Heraclitus is an underrated philosopher.

Second person: You should believe that Heraclitus is an underrated philosopher.

Third person: He or she believes that Heraclitus is an underrated philosopher.

Which person to use is a stylistic concern, since it involves a writer's *choices* as regards to level of formality, the varying expectations of different audiences, and overall tone.

As a general rule, in academic writing you should discuss your subject matter in the third person and avoid the first and second person. There is logic to this rule: most academic analysis focuses on the subject matter rather than on you as you respond to it. If you use the third person, you will keep the attention where it belongs.

THE FIRST-PERSON PRONOUN "I": PRO AND CON

Using the first-person "I" can throw the emphasis on the wrong place. Repeated assertions of "in my opinion" actually distract your readers from what you have to say. Omit them except in the most informal cases. You might, however, consider using the first person in the drafting stage if you are having trouble bringing your own point of view to the forefront. In this situation, the "I" becomes a strategy for loosening up and saying what you really think about a subject rather than adopting conventional and faceless positions. In the final analysis, though, most analytical prose will be more precise and straightforward in the third person. When you cut "I am convinced that" from the beginning of any claim, what you lose in personal conviction, you gain in concision and directness by keeping the focus on the main idea in a main clause.

Are there cases when you should use "I"? Contrary to the general rule, some professors actually prefer the first-person pronoun in particular contexts, as noted in the accompanying "Voices from Across the Curriculum" box.

VOICES FROM ACROSS THE CURRICULUM

Using the First-Person *I* in Academic Writing

Avoid phrases like *"The author* believes (or will discuss) . . ."* Except in the paper's abstract, *"I* believe (or will discuss)" is okay, and often best.

–Alan Tjeltveit, Professor of Psychology

I prefer that personal opinion or voice (for example, "I this," or "I that") appear throughout. I like the first person. No "the author feels" or "this author found that," please! Who is the author? Hey, it's you!

–Frederick Norling, Professor of Business

The biggest stylistic problem is that students tend to be too personal or colloquial in their writing, using phrases such as the following: *"Scientists all agree . . .";* *"I find it amazing that . . .";* *"The thing that I find most interesting . . ."* Students are urged to present data and existing information in their own words, but in an objective way. My preference in writing is to use the active voice in the past tense. I feel this is the most direct and least wordy approach: *I asked this . . . ; I found out that . . . ; These data show. . . .*

–Richard Niesenbaum, Professor of Biology

Note that these are not blanket endorsements; they specify a limited context within which "I" is preferred. The biology professor's cautioning against using an overly personal and colloquial tone is also probably the consensus view.

Although a majority of professors may prefer the first-person "I think" to the more awkward "the writer (or 'one') thinks," we would point out that, in the service of reducing wordiness, you can often avoid both options. For example, in certain contexts and disciplines, the first-person-plural "we" is acceptable usage: "The president's speech assumes that *we* are all dutiful but disgruntled taxpayers." The one case in which the first person is particularly appropriate occurs when you are citing an example from your own experience. Otherwise, if you are in doubt about using "I" or "we," avoid these first-person pronouns.

THE SECOND-PERSON PRONOUN "YOU" AND THE IMPERATIVE MOOD

As for the second person, proceed with caution. Using "you" is a fairly assertive gesture. Many readers will be annoyed, for example, by a paper about advertising that states, "When you read about a sale at the mall, you know it's hard to resist." Most readers resent having a writer airily making assumptions about them or telling them what to do. Some rhetorical situations, however, call for the use of "you." Textbooks, for example, use "you" frequently because it creates a more direct relationship between authors and readers. Yet, even in appropriate situations, directly addressing readers as "you" may alienate them by ascribing to them attitudes and needs they may not have.

The readiest alternative to "you," the imperative mood, requires careful handling for similar reasons. The *imperative mood* of a verb expresses a direct request or command, leaving "you" understood, as in the following instance: "Don't [you] dismiss the European perspective too quickly." Such a sentence, though, runs the same kind of risk as the previous example: readers might resent your assumption that they would dismiss the European perspective or, at any rate, dislike being told so forcefully how to think about it. On the other hand, in certain writing situations the imperative mood is both appropriate and useful: when you are giving a set of step-by-step instructions (*"Take* a right on 12th Street and then turn left at the light onto Vine") or politely soliciting your readers' attention (*"Consider* the plight of Afghan refugees"). In both cases, the imperative engages readers more unobtrusively than would inserting an awkward "you should" or "one should" before the verbs.

The conventional argument for using the first and second person is that "I" and "you" are personal and engage readers. It is not necessarily the case, however, that the third person is therefore impersonal. Just as film directors put their stamps on films by the way they organize the images, move among camera viewpoints, and orchestrate the sound tracks, so writers, even when writing in the third person, have a wide variety of resources at their disposal for making the writing more personal and accessible for their audiences. See, for example, the discussion of the passive voice in the next chapter.

D. SHADES OF MEANING: CHOOSING THE BEST WORD

The nineteenth-century English statesman Benjamin Disraeli once differentiated between "misfortune" and "calamity" by commenting on his political rival William Gladstone: "If Mr. Gladstone fell into the Thames, it would be a misfortune; but if someone dragged him out, it would be a calamity." "Misfortune" and "calamity" might mean the same thing to some people, but in fact the two words allow a careful writer to discriminate fine shades of meaning.

One of the best ways to get yourself to pay attention to words as words is to practice making subtle distinctions among related words. The "right" word contributes accuracy and precision to your meaning. The "wrong" word, it follows, is inaccurate or imprecise. The most reliable guide to choosing the right word and avoiding the wrong word is a dictionary that includes not only concise definitions but also the origin of words (known as their *etymology*). A dicey alternative is a thesaurus (a dictionary of synonyms, now included in most word processing software): it can offer you a host of choices, but you run a fairly high risk of choosing an inappropriate word. If you go the thesaurus route, check the word you select in the dictionary. The best dictionary for the job, by the way, is the *Oxford English Dictionary*, which commonly goes by its initials, *OED*. Available in every library reference collection and usually online at colleges and universities as well, it provides historical examples of how every word has been used over time.

Frankly, many of the most common diction errors are caused by ignorance. The writer has not learned the difference between similar terms that actually have different meanings. If you confuse "then" and "than," or "infer" and "imply," you will not convey the meaning that you intend, and you will probably confuse your readers and invite them to question your control of language. Getting the wrong word is, of course, not limited to pairs of words that are spelled similarly. A *notorious* figure is widely but unfavorably known, whereas a *famous* person is usually recognized for accomplishments that are praiseworthy. Referring to a famous person as notorious—a rather comic error—could be an embarrassing mistake. Take the time to learn the differences among seemingly similar words.

A slightly less severe version of getting the wrong word occurs when a writer uses a word with a shade of meaning that is inappropriate or inaccurate in a particular context. Take, for example, the words "assertive" and "aggressive." Often used interchangeably, they don't really mean the same thing—and the difference matters. Loosely defined, both terms mean "forceful." But "assertive" suggests being "bold and self-confident," whereas "aggressive" suggests being "eager to attack." In most cases, you compliment the person you call assertive but raise doubts about the person you call aggressive (whether you are giving a compliment depends on the situation: "aggressive" is a term of praise on the football field but less so if used to describe an acquaintance's behavior during conversation at the dinner table).

One particularly charged context in which shades of meaning matter to many readers involves the potentially sexist implications of using one term for women and another for men. If, for example, in describing a woman and a man up for the same job, we referred to the woman as *aggressive* but the man as *assertive*, our diction would deservedly be considered sexist. It would reveal that what is perceived as poised and a sign of leadership potential in a man is being construed as unseemly belligerence in a woman. The sexism enters when word choice suggests that what is assertive in a man is aggressive in a woman.

In choosing the right shade of meaning, you will get a sharper sense for the word by knowing its etymological history—the word or words from which it evolved. In the preceding example, "aggressive" derives from the Latin "*aggressus,*" meaning "to go to or approach"; and "*aggressus*" is itself a combination of "*ad,*" a prefix expressing motion, and "*gradus,*" meaning "a step." An aggressive person, then, is "coming at you." "Assertive," on the other hand, comes from the Latin "*asserere,*" combining "*ad*" and "*serere,*" meaning "to join or bind together." An assertive person is "coming to build or put things together"—certainly not to threaten.

► Try this 10.3: Playing with Etymology

One of the best ways to get yourself to pay attention to words as words is to practice making fine distinctions among related words, as we did with "aggressive" and "assertive." The following exercise will not only increase your vocabulary but also acquaint you with that indispensable reference work for etymology, the *Oxford English Dictionary* (OED).

Look up one of the following pairs of words in the *OED*. Write down the etymology of each word in the pair, and then, in a paragraph for each, summarize the words' linguistic histories—how their meanings have evolved across time. (The *OED*'s examples of how the word has been used over time will be helpful here.)

ordinal/ordinary	explicate/implicate
tenacious/stubborn	induce/conducive
enthusiasm/ecstasy	adhere/inhere
monarchy/oligarchy	overt/covert

Alternatively, select a pair of similar words or, for that matter, any key words from your reading for a course, and submit them to this exercise.

WHAT'S BAD ABOUT "GOOD" AND "BAD" (AND OTHER BROAD, JUDGMENTAL TERMS)

Vague evaluative terms such as "good" and "bad" can seduce you into stopping your thinking while it is still too general and ill-defined—a matter discussed at length in Chapter 1 in the section entitled "The Judgment Reflex." If you train yourself to select more precise words whenever you encounter "good" and "bad" in your drafts, not only will your prose become clearer but also the search for new words will probably start you thinking again, sharpening your ideas. If, for example, you find yourself writing a sentence such as "The subcommittee made a *bad* decision," ask yourself *why* you called it a bad decision. A revision to "The subcommittee made a shortsighted decision" indicates what in fact is bad about the decision and sets you up to discuss why the decision was myopic, further developing the idea.

Be aware that often these evaluative terms are disguised as neutrally descriptive ones—"natural," for instance, and "realistic." Realistic according to whom, and defined by what criteria? Something is natural according to a given idea about nature—an assumption—and the same goes for "moral." These are not terms that mean separately from a particular context or ideology (that is, an assumed hierarchy of value). Similarly, in a sentence such as "Society disapproves of interracial marriage," the broad and apparently neutral term "society" can blind you to a host of important distinctions about social class, about a particular culture, and so on.

CONCRETE AND ABSTRACT DICTION

At its best, effective analytical prose uses both concrete and abstract words. Simply defined, *concrete diction* evokes: it brings things to life by offering your readers words that they can use their senses upon. "Telephone," "eggshell," "crystalline," "azure," "striped," "kneel," "flare," and "burp" are examples of concrete diction. In academic writing, there is no substitute for concrete language whenever you are describing what happens or what something looks like—in a laboratory experiment, in a military action, in a painting or film sequence. In short, the language of evidence and of detail usually consists of concrete diction.

Concrete diction evokes: it brings things to life by offering your readers words they can use their senses upon.

By contrast, *abstract diction* refers to words that designate concepts and categories. "Virility," "ideology," "love," "definitive," "desultory," "conscientious," "classify," and "ameliorate" are examples of abstract diction. So are "democracy," "fascism," "benevolence," and "sentimentality." In academic writing, by and large, this is the language of ideas. We cannot do without abstract terms, and yet writing made up only of such words loses contact with experience, with the world that we can apprehend through our senses.

The line between abstract and concrete is not always as clear as these examples may suggest. You may recall the concept of the ladder of abstraction that we discuss in the section entitled "Generalizing" in the first chapter. There we propose that abstract and concrete are not hard-and-fast categories so much as a continuum, a sliding scale. Word A (for example, "machine") may be more abstract than word B ("computer") but more concrete than word C ("technology").

Just as evidence needs to be organized by a thesis and a thesis needs to be developed by evidence, so concrete and abstract diction need each other. Use concrete diction to illustrate and anchor the generalizations that abstract diction expresses. Note the concrete language used to define the abstraction "provinciality" in this example.

> There is no cure for *provinciality* like traveling abroad. In America the waiter who fails to bring the check promptly at the end of the meal we rightly convict for not being watchful. But in England, after waiting interminably for the check and becoming increasingly irate, we learn that only an ill-mannered waiter would bring it without being asked. We have been rude, not he.

In the following example, the abstract terms "causality," "fiction," and "conjunction" are integrated with concrete diction in the second sentence.

> According to the philosopher David Hume, *causality* is a kind of *fiction* that we ascribe to what he called "the constant *conjunction* of observed events." If a person gets hit in the eye and a black semicircle develops underneath it, that does not necessarily mean the blow caused the black eye.

A style that omits concrete language can leave readers lost in a fog of abstraction that only tangible details can illuminate. The concrete language helps readers see what you mean, much in the way that examples help them understand your ideas. Without the shaping power of abstract diction, however, concrete evocation can leave you with a list of graphic but ultimately pointless facts. The best writing integrates concrete and abstract diction.

Try this 10.4: Recasting the Diction

Compose a paragraph using only concrete diction and then one using only abstract diction. Compare results with another person who has done the same task, as this can lead to an interesting discussion of kinds of words, where they reside on the ladder of abstraction, and why.

Try this 10.5: Replacing Abstract Assertions with Concrete Details

Rewrite the sentences listed below, substituting more concrete language and/or more precise abstractions. Support any abstractions you retain with appropriate detail. Just for the challenge, try to rewrite so that your sentences include no abstract claims; that is, use only concrete details to convey the points.

It was a great party; everybody had fun.
It was a lousy party; everybody disliked it.
The book was really boring.
The film was very interesting.
His morals were questionable.
Social Security is not an entitlement.
He became extraordinarily angry.

LATINATE DICTION

One of the best ways to sensitize yourself to the difference between abstract and concrete diction is to understand that many abstract words are examples of what is known as Latinate diction. This term describes words in English that derive from Latin roots, words with such endings as "–tion," "–ive," "–ity," "–ate," and "–ent." (Such words will be designated by an *L* in the etymological section of dictionary definitions.) Taken to an extreme, Latinate diction can leave your meaning vague and your readers confused. Note how impenetrable the Latinate terms make the following example:

The examination of different perspectives on the representations of sociopolitical anarchy in media coverage of revolutions can be revelatory of the invisible biases that afflict television news.

This sentence actually makes sense, but the demands it makes upon readers will surely drive off most of them before they have gotten through it. Reducing the amount of Latinate diction can make it more readable.

Because we tend to believe what we see, the political biases that afflict television news coverage of revolutions are largely invisible. We can begin to see these biases when we focus on how the medium reports events, studying the kinds of footage used, for example, or finding facts from other sources that the news has left out.

Although the preceding revision retains a lot of Latinate words, it provides a ballast of concrete, sensory details that allows readers to follow the idea. Although many textbooks on writing argue against using Latinate terms where shorter, concrete terms (usually of Anglo-Saxon origin) might be used instead, such an argument seems needlessly limiting in comparison with the advantages offered by a thorough mixture of the two levels of diction. It's fine to use Latinate diction; just don't make it the sole staple of your verbal diet.

Try this 10.6: Distinguishing Latinate from Anglo-Saxon Diction

Select a paragraph or two from one of your papers and identify the Latin and Anglo-Saxon diction. Actually mark the draft—with an *L* or an *A*, with a circle around one kind of word and a square around the other. Then find Anglo-Saxon substitutes for Latinate terms and Latinate substitutes for Anglo-Saxon terms if you can (with the help of a dictionary and perhaps a thesaurus). Ideally, you might then do a final revision in which you synthesize the best from both paragraphs to arrive at a consummate revision of your original paragraph.

USING AND AVOIDING JARGON

Many people assume that all jargon—the specialized vocabulary of a particular group—is bad: pretentious language designed to make most readers feel inferior. Many writing textbooks attack jargon in similar terms, calling it either polysyllabic balderdash or a specialized, gatekeeping language designed by an in-group to keep others out.

In many academic contexts, jargon is downright essential. It is conceptual shorthand.

Yet, in many academic contexts, jargon is downright essential. It is conceptual shorthand, a technical vocabulary that allows the members of a group (or a discipline) to converse with one another more clearly and efficiently. Certain words that may seem odd to outsiders in fact function as connective tissue for a way of thought shared by insiders. The following sentence, for example, although full of botanical jargon, is also admirably cogent:

> In angiosperm reproduction, if the number of pollen grains deposited on the stigma exceeds the number of ovules in the ovary, then pollen tubes may compete for access to ovules, which results in fertilization by the fastest growing pollen tubes.

We would label this use of jargon acceptable, because it is written, clearly, *by* insiders *for* fellow insiders. It might not be acceptable language for an article intended for readers who are not botanists, or at least not scientists.

The problem with jargon comes when this insiders' language is ostensibly directed at outsiders as well. The language of contracts offers a prime example of such jargon at work.

> The Author hereby indemnifies and agrees to hold the Publisher, its licensees, and any seller of the Work harmless from any liability, damage, cost, and expense, including reasonable attorney's fees and costs of settlement, for or in connection with any claim, action, or proceeding inconsistent with the Author's warranties or representations herein, or based upon or arising out of any contribution of the Author to the Work.

Run for the lawyer! What does it mean to "hold the Publisher . . . harmless"? To what do "the Author's warranties or representations" refer? What exactly is the author being asked to do here—release the publisher from all possible lawsuits that the author might bring? We might label this use of jargon *obfuscating*; although it may aim at precision, it leaves most readers bewildered. Although average readers are asked to sign them, such documents are really written by lawyers for other lawyers.

As the botanical and legal examples suggest, the line between *acceptable* and *obfuscating* jargon has far more to do with the audience to whom the words are addressed than with the actual content of the language. Because most academic writing is addressed to insiders, students studying a particular area need to learn its jargon. Using the technical language of the discipline is a necessary skill for conversing with others in that discipline. Moreover, by demonstrating that you can "talk the talk," you will validate your authority to pronounce an opinion on matters in the discipline.

Here are two guidelines that can help you in your use of jargon: (1) when addressing *insiders*, use jargon accurately ("talk the talk"); and (2) when addressing *outsiders*—the general public or members of another discipline—either define the jargon carefully or replace it with a more generally known term, preferably one operating at the same level of formality (which is to say that you would not substitute "gut" for "abdominal cavity").

As the anecdote in the accompanying "Voices from Across the Curriculum" box illustrates, questions of jargon—which are also questions of tone—are best resolved by considering the particular contexts for given writing tasks.

VOICES FROM ACROSS THE CURRICULUM

When to Use and Not Use Jargon

I worked for the Feds for many years before seeking the doctorate. My job required immense amounts of writing: reports, directives, correspondence, and so forth. But, on a day-to-day basis for almost seven years I had to write short "write-ups" assessing the qualifications of young people for the Peace Corps and VISTA programs. I'd generate "list-like," "bullet-like" assessments: "Looks good with farm machinery, has wonderful volunteer experience, would be best in a rural setting, speaks French." But I had to conclude each of these assessments with a one-page narrative. Here I tended to reject officious governmentese for a more personal style. I'd write as I spoke. Rather than "Has an inclination for a direction in the facilitation of regulation," I'd write "Would be very good directing people on projects." I'd drop the "-tion" stuff and write in "speak form," not incomplete sentences, but in what I call "candid, personal" style. I carry this with me today.

–Frederick Norling, Professor of Business

THE POLITICS OF LANGUAGE

We cannot leave the domain of style without reflecting on its place in what we might label the culture of inattention and cliché that surrounds us. To make this move is to acknowledge that style has political and ethical implications. A little over a half-century ago, in his famous essay "Politics and the English Language," George Orwell warns of the "invasion of one's mind by ready-made phrases . . . [which] can only be prevented if one is constantly on guard against them." The worst modern writing, he declares, "consists in gumming together long strips of words which have already been set in order by someone else, making the results presentable by sheer humbug."

Insofar as style is an expression of the writer's self, Orwell implies (1) we are under attack from broad cultural clichés and sentimental nostrums that do our thinking for us, and (2) it is thus a matter of personal integrity and civic responsibility to ask ourselves a series of questions about the sentences that we write.

What am I trying to say? What words will express it? What image or idiom will make it clearer? Is this image fresh enough to have an effect? [. . .] Could I put it more shortly? Have I said anything that is avoidably ugly?"

Words matter. They matter in how we name things, in how we phrase meanings—but also in how we are shaped by the words we read and hear in the media. Words don't simply reflect a neutral world that is out there in some objectively hard way that offers self-evident meanings we can universally agree upon. Words don't reflect—they constitute; they call the world into being. They call us into being when we write them.

Earlier in this chapter we noted, for example, that the decision to call a woman "aggressive" as opposed to "assertive" matters. There are examples all around you of language creating rather than merely reflecting reality. Start looking for these on the front page of your newspaper, in political speeches, in advertising, even in everyday conversation. Does it matter, for instance, that there are no equivalents to the words "spinster" or "whore" for men? Does it change things to refer to a bombing mission as a "containment effort" or, by way of contrast, to call an enthusiastic person a "fanatic"?

An article a few years back in the journal *Foreign Affairs* by Peter van Ham (October 2001) offers one last dispatch from the frontier of the culture of inattention and cliché. The article is about the rise of the so-called brand state—about how nations market themselves not only to consumers but to other nations. A brand, defined as "a customer's idea about a product," is a powerful tool to replace what a thing is with what other people, for reasons of their own, would have you think it is. This is the world we inhabit, and style can be its adversary or its accomplice. In the last analysis, that's what's at stake in choosing to care about style.

◖ ASSIGNMENT: Style Analysis

Write a paper that analyzes the style of a particular group or profession (for example, sports, advertising, bureaucracy, show business, or music reviewing). Or as an alternative, adopt the voice of a member of this group, and write a parody that critiques or analyzes the language practices of the group. If you choose (or are assigned) the latter, be aware that there is always a risk in parody of belittling in an unduly negative way a style that is not your own.

Obviously, you will first need to assemble and make observations about a number of samples of the style that you are analyzing or parodying. Use the Method to help you uncover the kinds of words that get repeated, the most common strands, and so forth. Look at the level of formality, the tone, the use of concrete and abstract diction, and the predilection for Latinate as opposed to Anglo-Saxon words. Who's writing to whom about what, and so what that the writing adopts this style?

Also, see the assignments at the end of Chapter 11. ◗

GUIDELINES FOR CHOOSING WORDS

1. Remember that revision is not merely cosmetic: to change the words is to change the meaning.

2. Strive for distance on your own prose as you edit for diction: place yourself in the position of the audience. Is the tone appropriate to the rhetorical context?

3. There are always shades of meaning. Strive to choose the best—the most accurate and appropriate—word for the situation. When in doubt, consult etymology, the history of the word, as the most reliable guide to its usage.

GUIDELINES FOR CHOOSING WORDS (CONTINUED)

4. Avoid *good*, *bad*, *real*, and other broad, judgmental terms that prematurely close off analysis.

5. Blend concrete and abstract diction, which is generally the language of details and the language of abstractions, respectively. In particular, go easy on those Latinate *–tion* words.

6. In given contexts, jargon is useful shorthand, but there is always the danger of getting used by it. Make sure you know what the words mean, and don't overrely on them.

CHAPTER 11

Style: Shaping Sentences
(and Cutting the Fat)

When you write, you build. Writing, after all, is also known as composition—from the Latin *compositio*, meaning "made up of parts." We speak of *constructing* sentences and paragraphs and essays. The fundamental unit of composition is the sentence. Every sentence has a shape, and learning to see that shape is essential to editing for style. Once you can recognize the shape of a sentence, you can recast it to make it more graceful or logical or emphatic.

A sentence is a pathway to having ideas. Recasting sentences is thus not just a stylistic practice, but a thinking practice. The way a sentence is structured reveals a way of thinking. Casting and recasting sentences in different words and in different shapes helps you experiment with the way you arrive at ideas, with the path you characteristically take.

Whether we recognize it or not, most of us have a "go to" sentence—the sentence shape we repeatedly go to as we write and talk. If a person's "go to" sentence takes the form "Although _____, the fact is that _____," we might see that person as inclined to qualify his or her thoughts ("Although") and as someone who is disinclined to immediately impose his or her ideas on others ("the fact that" comes in the second half of the sentence, where it gets a lot of emphasis but is also delayed and qualified by the sentence's opening observation).

When you read something, you should be looking for the writer's "go to" sentence and considering what it might reveal about his or her characteristic ways of thinking. As a regular practice, select one sentence in whatever you are reading that you think is typical of that writer's way of putting sentences together. Then ask yourself why this type of sentence is appropriate to the kind of thinking going on in the reading, how it can be seen as doing what it describes.

Then find your own "go to" sentence. What does it reveal to you about how you think?

A. HOW TO RECOGNIZE THE FOUR BASIC SENTENCE SHAPES

Style, defined in Chapter 10, has to do with choices—the choices a writer makes about how to express something. But these decisions can be realized only if you can recognize and use the basic building blocks of composition. Although many of these building blocks are named in the rest of the chapter, you may encounter some terms you're not sure about. If that happens, consult the "Glossary of Grammatical Terms" at the end of Chapter 14. (In particular, see entries for the following terms: *clause, conjunction, conjunctive adverb, coordination, direct object, phrase, preposition, subject, subordination,* and *verbals.*)

Every sentence is built upon the skeleton of its independent clause(s), the subject and verb combination that can stand alone. Consider the following four sentences:

Consumers shop.

Consumers shop; producers manufacture.

Consumers shop in predictable ways, so producers manufacture with different target groups in mind.

Consumers shop in ways that can be predicted by such determinants as income level, sex, and age; consequently, producers use market research to identify different target groups for their products.

Certainly these four sentences become progressively longer, and the information they contain becomes increasingly detailed, but they also differ in their structure—specifically, in the number of independent and dependent clauses they contain. Given that the sentence is the fundamental unit of composition, you will benefit immensely, both in composing and in revising your sentences, if you can identify and construct the four basic sentence types.

THE SIMPLE SENTENCE

The *simple sentence* consists of a single independent clause. At its simplest, it contains a single subject and verb.

Consumers shop.

Other words and phrases can be added to this sentence, but it will remain simple so long as "Consumers shop" is the only clause.

Most consumers shop unwisely.

Even if the sentence contains more than one grammatical subject or more than one verb, it remains simple in structure.

Most consumers *shop* unwisely and *spend* more than they can afford. [two verbs]

Both female consumers and their husbands shop unwisely. [two subjects]

The sentence structure in the example that uses two verbs ("shop" and "spend") is known as a *compound predicate*. The sentence structure in the example that uses two subjects ("consumers" and "husbands") is known as a *compound subject*. If, however, you were to add both another subject and another verb to the original simple sentence, you would have the next sentence type, a compound sentence.

THE COMPOUND SENTENCE

The *compound sentence* consists of at least two independent clauses and no subordinate clauses. The information conveyed in these clauses should be of roughly equal importance.

Producers manufacture, and consumers shop.

Producers manufacture, marketers sell, and consumers shop.

As with the simple sentence, you can also add qualifying phrases to the compound sentence, and it will remain compound, as long as no dependent clauses are added.

Consumers shop in predictable ways, so producers manufacture with different target groups in mind.

Consumers shop recklessly during holidays; marketers are keenly aware of this fact.

Note that a compound sentence can connect its independent clauses with either a coordinate conjunction or a semicolon. (The primary use of the semicolon is as a substitute for a coordinate conjunction, separating two independent clauses.) If you were to substitute a subordinating conjunction for either of these connectors, however, you would have a sentence with one independent clause and one dependent clause. For example:

Because consumers shop in predictable ways, producers manufacture with different target groups in mind.

This revision changes the compound sentence into the next sentence type, the complex sentence.

THE COMPLEX SENTENCE

The *complex sentence* consists of a single independent clause and one or more dependent clauses. The information conveyed in the dependent clause is subordinated to the more important independent clause (a matter we take up in more detail momentarily under subordination). In the following example, the subject and verb of the main clause are underlined, and the subordinating conjunctions are italicized:

Although mail-order merchandising—*which* generally saves shoppers money—has increased, most <u>consumers</u> still <u>shop</u> unwisely, buying on impulse rather than deliberation.

This sentence contains one independent clause ("consumers shop"). Hanging upon it are two introductory dependent clauses ("although merchandising has increased" and "which saves") and a participial phrase ("buying on impulse"). If you converted either of these dependent clauses into an independent clause, you would have a sentence with two independent clauses (a compound sentence) and a dependent clause. In the following example, the subjects and verbs of the two main clauses are underlined, and the conjunctions are italicized:

Mail-order <u>merchandising</u>—*which* generally saves shoppers money—<u>has increased</u>, *but* <u>consumers</u> still <u>shop</u> unwisely, buying on impulse rather than deliberation.

This revision changes the complex sentence into the next sentence type, the compound-complex sentence.

THE COMPOUND-COMPLEX SENTENCE

The *compound-complex sentence* consists of two or more independent clauses and one or more dependent clauses.

> Consumers shop in ways that can be predicted by such determinants as income level, sex, and age; consequently, producers use market research that aims to identify different target groups for their products.

This sentence contains two independent clauses ("consumers shop" and "producers use") and two dependent clauses ("that can be predicted" and "that aims").

▶ Try this 11.1: Composing the Four Sentence Shapes

As we have done with the consumers-shop example, compose a simple sentence and then a variety of expansions: a compound subject, a compound predicate, a compound sentence, a complex sentence, and a compound-complex sentence.

To prevent this exercise from becoming merely mechanical, keep in mind how different sentence shapes accomplish different ends. In other words, make sure your compound sentence balances two items of information, that your complex sentence emphasizes one thing (in the main clause) over another (in the subordinate clause), and that your compound-complex sentence is capable of handling and organizing complexity.

B. COORDINATION, SUBORDINATION, AND EMPHASIS

A *clause* is a group of words containing a subject and a predicate. The syntax of a sentence can give your readers cues about whether the idea in one clause is equal to (coordinate) or subordinate to the idea in another clause. In this context, grammar operates as a form of implicit logic, defining relationships among the clauses in a sentence according to the choices that you make about coordination, subordination, and the order of clauses. In revising your sentences, think of coordination and subordination as tools of logic and emphasis, helping to rank your meanings.

COORDINATION

Coordination uses grammatically equivalent constructions to link ideas. These ideas should carry roughly equal weight as well. Sentences that use coordination connect clauses with coordinating conjunctions (such as *and*, *but*, and *or*). Here are two examples.

> Historians organize the past, *and* they can never do so with absolute neutrality.

> Homegrown corn is incredibly sweet, *and* it is very difficult to grow.

If you ponder these sentences, you may begin to detect the danger of the word *and*. It does not specify a precise logical relationship between the things it connects but instead simply adds them.

Notice that the sentences get more precise if we substitute *but* for *and*.

Historians organize the past, *but* they can never do so with absolute neutrality.

Homegrown corn is incredibly sweet, *but* it is very difficult to grow.

These sentences are still coordinate in structure; they are still the sentence type known as compound. But they achieve more emphasis than the *and* versions. In both cases, the *but* clause carries more weight, because *but* always introduces information that qualifies or contradicts what precedes it.

REVERSING THE ORDER OF COORDINATE CLAUSES

In both the *and* and *but* examples, the second clause tends to be stressed. The reason is simple: *the end is usually a position of emphasis.*

You can see the effect of clause order more starkly if we reverse the clauses in our examples.

Historians are never absolutely neutral, but they organize the past.

Homegrown corn is very difficult to grow, but it is incredibly sweet.

Note how the meanings have changed in these versions by emphasizing what now comes last. Rather than simply having their objectivity undermined ("Historians are never absolutely neutral"), historians are now credited with at least providing organization ("they organize the past"). Similarly, whereas the previous version of the sentence about corn was likely to dissuade a gardener from trying to grow it ("it is very difficult to grow"), the new sentence is more likely to lure him or her to nurture corn ("it is incredibly sweet").

Nonetheless, all of these sentences are examples of coordination because the clauses are grammatically equal. As you revise, notice when you use coordinate syntax, and think about whether you really intend to give the ideas equal weight. Consider as well whether reversing the order of clauses will more accurately convey your desired emphasis to your readers.

▶ **Try this 11.2:** Rearranging Coordinate Clauses

Rearrange the parts of the following coordinate sentence, which is composed of four sections, separated by commas. Construct at least three versions, and jot down how the meaning changes in each version.

I asked her to marry me, two years ago, in a shop on Tremont Street, late in the fall.

Then subject two sentences of your own, perhaps taken from your papers, to the same treatment. Make sure to describe how the meaning changes in each case, because it will get you accustomed to seeing the effects of the rearrangings.

SUBORDINATION

In sentences that contain *subordination*, there are two "levels" of grammar—the main clause and the subordinate clause—that create two levels of meaning. When you put something in a main clause, you emphasize its significance. When you put something in a subordinate clause, you make it less important than what is in the main clause.

As noted in the discussion of complex sentences, a subordinate clause is linked to a main clause by words known as *subordinating conjunctions*. Here is a list of the most common ones: *after, although, as, as if, as long as, because, before, if, rather than, since, than, that, though, unless, until, when, where, whether,* and *while*. All of these words define something *in relation to* something else:

If you study hard, you will continue to do well.

You will continue to do well, *if* you study hard.

In both of these examples, *if* subordinates "you study hard" to "you will continue to do well," regardless of whether the *if* clause comes first or last in the sentence.

REVERSING MAIN AND SUBORDINATE CLAUSES

Unlike the situation with coordinate clauses, the emphasis in sentences that use subordination virtually always rests on the main clause, regardless of the clause order. Nevertheless, the principle of end-position emphasis still applies, though to a lesser extent than among coordinate clauses. Let's compare two versions of the same sentence.

Although the art of the people was crude, it was original.

The art of the people was original, although it was crude.

Both sentences emphasize the idea in the main clause ("original"). Because the second version locates the "although" clause at the end, however, the subordinated idea ("crude") has more emphasis than it does in the first version.

The end is a site of maximum emphasis in a sentence: if it matters a lot, put it last.

You can experiment with the meaning and style of virtually any sentence you write by reversing the clauses. Here, taken almost at random, is an earlier sentence from this chapter, followed by two such transformations.

When you put something in a subordinate clause, you make it less important than what is in the main clause.

Put information in a subordinate clause if you want to make it less important than what is in the main clause.

If you want to make information less important than what is in the main clause, put it in a subordinate clause.

Try this 11.3: Experimenting with Coordination, Subordination, and the Order of Clauses

Do two rewrites of the following sentence, changing the order of clauses and subordinating or coordinating as you wish. We recommend that you make one of them end with the word *friendly*.

Faculty members came to speak at the forum, and they were friendly, but they were met with hostility, and this hostility was almost paranoid.

How does each of your revisions change the meaning and emphasis?

PARALLEL STRUCTURE

One of the most important and useful devices for shaping sentences is *parallel structure* or, as it is also known, *parallelism*. Parallelism is a form of symmetry: it involves placing sentence elements that correspond in some way into the same (that is, parallel) grammatical form. Consider the following examples, in which the parallel items are underlined or italicized:

The three kinds of partners in a law firm who receive money from a case are popularly known as <u>finders</u>, <u>binders</u>, and <u>grinders</u>.

The Beatles acknowledged their musical debts <u>to</u> American rhythm and blues, <u>to</u> English music hall ballads and ditties, and later <u>to</u> classical Indian ragas.

There was <u>no way that</u> the president <u>could gain</u> the support of party regulars *without alienating* the Congress, and <u>no way that</u> he <u>could appeal</u> to the electorate at large *without alienating* both of these groups.

In the entertainment industry, the money that <u>goes out</u> to hire *film stars* or *sports stars* <u>comes back</u> in increased ticket sales and video or television rights.

As all of these examples illustrate, at the core of parallelism lies repetition—of a word, a phrase, or a grammatical structure. *Parallelism uses repetition to organize and emphasize certain elements in a sentence, so that readers can perceive more clearly the shape of your thought.* In the Beatles example, each of the prepositional phrases beginning with *to* contains a musical debt. In the president example, the repetition of the phrase *no way that* emphasizes his entrapment.

Parallelism has the added advantage of *economy*: each of the musical debts or presidential problems might have had its own sentence, but in that case the prose would have been wordier and the relationships among the parallel items more obscure. Along with this economy come *balance* and *emphasis*. The trio of rhyming words (*finders, binders,* and *grinders*) that concludes the law-firm example gives each item equal weight; in the entertainment-industry example, "comes back" answers "goes out" in a way that accentuates their symmetry.

> **Try this 11.4:** Finding Parallelisms
>
> List all of the parallelisms in the following famous passage from the beginning of the Declaration of Independence:
>
> We hold these truths to be self-evident: that all men are created equal; that they are endowed by their Creator with certain inalienable rights; that, among these, are life, liberty, and the pursuit of happiness.
>
> Remember that parallelism can occur with clauses, phrases, and prepositional phrases. You might find it useful to review the entries for these terms in the glossary in Chapter 14. After you have completed your list, what do you notice about the way that the parallel structures accumulate? And what is the effect of the placement and phrasing of these parallelisms? In other words, try to describe how this famous passage develops stylistically.

One particularly useful form of balance that parallel structure accommodates is known as *antithesis* (from the Greek word for "opposition"), a conjoining of contrasting ideas. Here the pattern sets one thing against another thing, as in the following example:

> Where bravura failed to settle the negotiations, tact and patience succeeded.

"Failed" is balanced antithetically against "succeeded," as "bravura" against "tact and patience." Antithesis commonly takes the form of "if not *x*, at least *y*" or "not *x*, but *y*."

When you employ parallelism in revising for style, there is one grammatical rule you should obey. It is important to avoid what is known as *faulty parallelism*, which occurs when the items that are parallel in content are not placed in the same grammatical form.

> **Faulty:** *To study* hard for four years and then *getting* ignored once they enter the job market is a hard thing for many recent college graduates to accept.

> **Revised:** *To study* hard for four years and then *to get* ignored once they enter the job market is a hard thing for many recent college graduates to accept.

As you revise your draft for style, search for opportunities to place sentence elements in parallel structure. Try this consciously: include and underline three uses of it in a draft of your next writing assignment. Remember that parallelism can occur with *clauses, phrases,* and *prepositional phrases.* Often the parallels will be hidden in the sentences of your draft, but they can be brought out with a minimum of labor. After you've acquired the habit of casting your thinking in parallel structures, they will rapidly become a staple of your stylistic repertoire, making your prose more graceful, clear, and logically connected.

Try this 11.5: Correcting Errors in Parallelism

Rewrite the following examples of faulty parallelism using correct parallel structure. In the last of these sentences you will need to contemplate the thinking behind it as well as its form.

1. The problems with fast food restaurants include the way workers are exploited, eating transfatty acids, and that the food can damage your liver.
2. Venus likes to play tennis and also watching baseball games.
3. In the 1960s the use of drugs and being a hippie was a way for some people to let society know their political views and that they were alienated from the mainstream.

C. PERIODIC AND CUMULATIVE SENTENCES: ADDING SHAPES TO THE MAIN CLAUSE

The shape of a sentence governs the way it delivers information. The order of clauses, especially the placement of the main clause, affects what the sentence means.

There are two common sentence shapes defined by the location of their main clauses; these are known as *periodic* and *cumulative* sentences.

The shape of a sentence governs the way it delivers information.

THE PERIODIC SENTENCE: SNAPPING SHUT

The main clause in a periodic sentence builds to a climax that is not completed until the end. Often, a piece of the main clause (such as the subject) is located early in the sentence, as in the following example.

The *way* that beverage companies market health—"No Preservatives," "No Artificial Colors," "All Natural," "Real Brewed"—*is* often, because the product also contains a high percentage of sugar or fructose, *misleading*.

We have italicized the main clause to clarify how various modifiers interrupt it. The effect is suspenseful: not until the final word does the sentence consummate its fundamental idea. Pieces of the main clause are spread out across the sentence. (The term *periodic* originates in classical rhetoric to refer to the length of such units within a sentence.)

Another version of the periodic sentence locates the entire main clause at the end, after introductory modifiers.

Using labels that market health—such as "No Preservatives," "No Artificial Colors," "All Natural," and "Real Brewed"—while producing drinks that contain a high percentage of sugar or fructose, *beverage companies are misleading*.

As was previously discussed, the end of a sentence normally receives empha-sis. When you use a periodic construction, the pressure on the end intensifies because the sentence needs the end to complete its grammatical sense. In both of the preceding examples, the sentences "snap shut." They string readers along, delaying *grammatical closure*—the point at which the sentences can stand alone independently—until they arrive at climactic ends. (Periodic sentences are also known as *climactic sentences*.)

> **If you are revising and want to underscore some point, try letting the sentence snap shut upon it.**

You should be aware of one risk that accompanies periodic constructions. If the delay lasts too long because there are too many "interrupters" before the main clause gets completed, your readers may forget the subject that is being predicated. To illustrate, let's add more subordinated material to one of the preceding examples.

> The way that beverage companies market health—"No Preservatives," "No Artificial Colors," "All Natural," "Real Brewed"—is often, because the product also contains a high percentage of sugar or fructose, not just what New Agers would probably term "immoral" and "misleading" but what a government agency such as the Food and Drug Administration should find illegal.

Arguably, the additions (the "not just" and "but" clauses after "fructose") push the sentence into incoherence. The main clause has been stretched past the breaking point. If readers don't get lost in such a sentence, they are at least likely to get irritated and wish the writer would finally get to the point.

Nonetheless, with a little care, periodic sentences can be extraordinarily use-ful in giving emphasis. If you are revising and want to underscore some point, try letting the sentence snap shut upon it. Often the periodic *potential* will already be present in the draft, and stylistic editing can bring it out more forcefully. Note how minor the revisions are in the following example:

> **Draft:** The novelist Virginia Woolf suffered from acute anxieties for most of her life. She had several breakdowns and finally committed suicide on the eve of World War II.

> **Revision:** Suffering from acute anxieties for most of her life, the novelist Virginia *Woolf* not only *had* several *breakdowns but,* finally, on the eve of World War II, *committed suicide.*

This revision has made two primary changes. It has combined two short sentences into a longer sentence, and it has made the sentence periodic by stringing out the main clause (italicized). What is the effect of this revision? Stylistically speaking, the revision radiates a greater sense of its writer's authority. The information has been arranged for us. After the opening dependent clause ("Suffering . . ."), the subject of the main clause ("Woolf") is introduced, and the predicate is protracted in a *not only/but* parallelism. The interrupters that follow "had several breakdowns" ("finally, on the eve of World War II") increase the suspense, before the sentence snaps shut with "committed suicide."

In general, when you construct a periodic sentence with care, you can give readers the sense that you are in control of your material. You do not seem to be writing off the top of your head, but rather from a position of greater detachment, rationally composing your meaning.

THE CUMULATIVE SENTENCE: STARTING FAST

The cumulative sentence is in many respects the opposite of the periodic. Rather than delaying the main clause or its final piece, the cumulative sentence begins by presenting the independent clause as a foundation and then *accumulates* a number of modifications and qualifications. As the following examples illustrate, the independent clause provides quick grammatical closure, freeing the rest of the sentence to amplify and develop the main idea.

> *Robert F. Kennedy was assassinated* by Sirhan B. Sirhan, a twenty-four-year-old Palestinian immigrant, prone to occultism and unsophisticated left-wing politics and sociopathically devoted to leaving his mark in history, even if as a notorious figure.

> *There are two piano concerti* composed solely for the left hand, one by Serge Prokofiev and one by Maurice Ravel, and both commissioned by Paul Wittgenstein, a concert pianist (and the brother of the famous philosopher Ludwig Wittgenstein) who had lost his right hand in combat during World War I.

Anchored by the main clause, a cumulative sentence moves serially through one thing and another thing and the next thing, close to the associative manner in which people think. To an extent, then, cumulative sentences can convey more immediacy and a more conversational tone than can other sentence shapes. Look at the following example:

> The film version of *Lady Chatterley's Lover* changed D. H. Lawrence's famous novel a lot, omitting the heroine's adolescent experience in Germany, making her husband much older than she, leaving out her father and sister, including a lot more lovemaking, and virtually eliminating all of the philosophizing about sex and marriage.

Here we get the impression of a mind in the act of thinking. Using the generalization of changes in the film as a base, the sentence then appends a series of parallel participial phrases ("omitting," "making," "leaving," "including," "eliminating") that moves forward associatively, gathering a range of information and laying out possibilities. Cumulative sentences perform this outlining and prospecting function very effectively. On the other hand, if we were to add four or five more changes to the sentence, readers would likely find it tedious, or worse, directionless. As with periodic sentences, overloading the shape can short-circuit its desired effect.

▶ **Try this 11.6:** Writing Periodic and Cumulative Sentences

If you consciously practice using periodic and cumulative constructions, you will be surprised how quickly you can learn to produce their respective effects in your own writing. You will also discover that both of these sentence shapes are already present in your prose in some undiscovered and thus unrefined way. It is often simply a case of bringing out what is already there. Try including at least one of each in the next paper you write.

Toward that end, compose a simple sentence on any subject, preferably one with a direct object. Then construct two variations expanding it, one periodic and one cumulative. Here, as a model, is an example using the core sentence "James Joyce was a gifted singer."

> **Periodic:** Although known primarily as one of the greatest novelists of the twentieth century, James Joyce, the son of a local political functionary who loved to tip a few too many at the pub, was also a gifted—and prizewinning—singer.

> **Cumulative:** James Joyce was a gifted singer, having listened at his father's knee to the ballads sung in pubs, having won an all-Ireland prize in his early teens, and having possessed a miraculous ear for the inflections of common speech that was to serve him throughout the career for which he is justly famous, that of a novelist.

> Can't think of a core sentence? Okay, here are a few:

Why do airlines show such mediocre films?
The Abu Ghraib prison scandal rocked the nation.
Manny Ramirez and friends lifted the curse of the Bambino.
Every senator is a millionaire.

D. CUTTING THE FAT

If you can reduce verbiage, your prose will communicate more directly and effectively.

In cutting the fat, you need to consider both the diction and the syntax. When it comes to diction, the way to eliminate superfluous words is deceptively simple: ask yourself if you need all of the words you've included to say what you want to say. Such revision requires an aggressive attitude. *Expect* to find unnecessary restatements or intensifiers such as "quite" and "very" that add words but not significance.

In terms of syntax, there are a few technical operations that you can perform—particularly on the *verbs* in your sentences—to reduce the number of words. The remainder of the chapter discusses these matters in more depth, but here's a preview.

- Convert sentences from the passive into the active voice. Writing "He read the book" reduces by a third "The book was read by him," and eliminating the prepositional phrase ("by him") clarifies the relationships within the sentence.
- Replace anemic forms of the verb "to be" with vigorous verbs and direct subject–verb–object syntax. Often you will find such verbs lurking in the original sentence, and once you've recognized them, conversion is easy: "The Watergate *scandal* was an event whose effects were felt across the nation" becomes "Watergate *scandalized* people across the nation."

■ Avoid unnecessary subordination. It is illogical to write, *"It is true that* more government services mean higher taxes." If "it is true," then just write, "More government services mean higher taxes"—don't muffle your meaning in a subordinate "that" clause.

> Writing "He read the book" reduces by a third "The book was read by him."

Beyond these technical operations, perhaps the most useful way to cut the fat is to have confidence in your position on a subject and state it clearly in your paper. A lot of fat in essays consists of "throat clearings," attempts to avoid stating a position. Move quickly to an example that raises the question or issue you wish to analyze.

EXPLETIVE CONSTRUCTIONS

The syntactic pattern for "It is true *that* more government services mean higher taxes" is known as an *expletive* construction. The term *expletive* comes from a Latin word that means "serving to fill out." The most common expletives are *it* and *there*. Consider how the expletives function in the following examples.

There are several prototypes for the artificial heart.

It is obvious that the American West exerted a profound influence on the photography of Ansel Adams.

Compare these with versions that simply eliminate the expletives.

The artificial heart has several prototypes.

The American West exerted a profound influence on the photography of Ansel Adams.

As the revisions demonstrate, most of the time you can streamline your prose by getting rid of expletive constructions. The "It is obvious" opening, for example, causes the grammar of the sentence to subordinate its real emphasis. In some cases, however, an expletive can provide a useful way of emphasizing, as in the following example: "There are three primary reasons that you should avoid litigation." Although this sentence subordinates its real content (avoiding litigation), the expletive provides a useful frame for what is to follow.

STATIC (INTRANSITIVE) VERSUS ACTIVE (TRANSITIVE) VERBS: "TO BE" OR "NOT TO BE"

Verbs energize a sentence. They do the work, connecting the parts of the sentence with each other. In a sentence of the subject–verb–direct object pattern, the verb—known as a *transitive verb*—functions as a kind of engine, driving the subject into the predicate, as in the following examples.

John F. Kennedy effectively *manipulated* his image in the media.

Thomas Jefferson *embraced* the idea of America as a country of yeoman farmers.

Verbs energize a sentence. A transitive verb functions as an engine, driving the subject into the predicate.

By contrast, "is" and other forms of the verb "to be" provide an equal sign between the subject and the predicate but otherwise tell us nothing about the relationship between them. "To be" is an *intransitive* verb; it cannot take a direct object. Compare the two preceding transitive examples with the following versions of the same sentences using forms of the verb "to be."

John F. Kennedy *was* effective at the manipulation of his image in the media.

Thomas Jefferson's idea *was* for America to be a country of yeoman farmers.

Rather than making things happen through an active transitive verb, these sentences let everything just hang around in a state of being. In the first version, Kennedy did something—*manipulated* his image—but in the second he just *is* (or *was*), and the energy of the original verb has been siphoned into an abstract noun, "manipulation." The revised Jefferson example suffers from a similar lack of momentum compared with the original version: the syntax doesn't help the sentence get anywhere.

Certain situations, however, dictate the use of forms of "to be." For definitions in particular, the equal sign that an "is" provides works well. For instance, "Organic gardening *is* a method of growing crops without using synthetic fertilizers or pesticides." As with choosing between active and passive voices, the decision to use "to be" or not should be just that—a conscious decision on your part.

If you can train yourself to eliminate every unnecessary use of "to be" in a draft, you will make your prose more vital and direct. In most cases, you will find

TABLE 11.1 Static and Active Verbs

Action Hidden in Nouns and "to be" Verbs	Action Emphasized in Verbs
The <u>cost</u> of the book *is* ten dollars.	The book *costs* ten dollars.
The <u>acknowledgment</u> of the fact *is* increasingly widespread that television *is* a <u>replacement</u> for reading in American culture.	People increasingly *acknowledge* that television *has replaced* reading in American culture.
A computer *is* ostensibly a labor–<u>saving</u> device—until the hard disk *is* the <u>victim</u> of a <u>crash</u>.	A computer ostensibly *saves labor*—until the hard disk *crashes*.
In the <u>laying</u> of a flagstone patio, the important preliminary steps to remember *are* the <u>excavating</u> and the <u>leveling</u> of the area and then the <u>filling</u> of it with a fine grade of gravel.	To *lay* a flagstone patio, first *excavate* and *level* the area and then *fill* it with a fine grade of gravel.

the verb that you need to substitute for "is" lurking somewhere in the sentence in some other grammatical form. In the preceding sentence about Kennedy, "manipulate" is implicit in "manipulation." In Table 11.1, each of the examples in the left-hand column uses a form of "to be" for its verb (italicized) and contains a potentially strong active verb lurking in the sentence in some other form (underlined). These "lurkers" have been converted into active verbs (italicized) in the revisions in the right-hand column.

If you can eliminate every unnecessary use of "to be" in a draft, you will make your prose more vital and direct.

Clearly, the examples in the left-hand column have problems other than their reliance on forms of "to be"—notably wordiness. "To be" syntax tends to encourage this circumlocution and verbosity.

▶ **Try this 11.7:** Finding the Active Verb

Take a paper you've written and circle the sentences that rely on forms of "to be." Then, examine the other words in these sentences, looking for "lurkers." Rewrite the sentences, converting the lurkers into vigorous verbs. You will probably discover many lurkers, and your revisions will acquire more energy and directness.

ACTIVE AND PASSIVE VOICES: DOING AND BEING DONE TO

In the *active voice*, the grammatical subject acts; in the *passive voice*, the subject is acted upon. Here are two examples.

Active: Adam Smith wrote *The Wealth of Nations* in 1776.

Passive: *The Wealth of Nations* was written by Adam Smith in 1776.

The two sentences convey identical information, but the emphasis differs—the first focuses on the author, the second on the book. As the examples illustrate, using the passive normally results in a longer sentence than using the active. If we consider how to convert the passive into the active, you can see why. In the passive, the verb requires a form of "to be" plus a past participle. (For more on participles, see the "Glossary of Grammatical Terms" in Chapter 14.) In this case, the active verb "wrote" becomes the passive verb "was written," the grammatical subject ("Smith") becomes the object of the preposition "by," and the direct object ("*The Wealth of Nations*") becomes the grammatical subject.

Now consider the activity being described in the two versions of this example: a man wrote a book. That's what happened in life. The grammar of the active version captures that action most clearly: the grammatical subject ("Smith") performs the action, and the direct object (*"The Wealth of Nations"*) receives it, just as in life. By contrast, the passive version alters the close link between the syntax and the event: the object of the action in life (*"The Wealth of Nations"*) has become the grammatical subject, whereas the doer in life ("Smith") has become the grammatical object of a prepositional phrase.

Note, too, that the passive would allow us to omit "Smith" altogether: "*The Wealth of Nations* was written in 1776." A reader who desired to know more and was not aware of the author would not appreciate this sentence. More troubling, the passive can also be used to conceal the doer of an action—not "I made a mistake" (active) but rather "A mistake has been made" (passive).

In sum, there are three reasons for avoiding the passive voice when you can: (1) it's longer, (2) its grammatical relationships often reverse what happened in life, and (3) it can omit the performer responsible for the action.

On the other hand, sometimes there are good reasons for using the passive. If you want to emphasize the object or recipient of the action rather than the performer, the passive will do that for you: "*The Wealth of Nations* was written in 1776 by Adam Smith" places the stress on the book. The passive is also preferable when the doer remains unknown: "The president has been shot!" is probably a better sentence than "Some unknown assailant has shot the president!"

▶ **Try this 11.8:** Identifying Different Verb Forms

Circle and identify every verb in the paragraph below. Use the abbreviations *VA* = active voice, *VP* = passive voice, *VB* = verb of being. This exercise will give you helpful training in identifying the forms of verbs, so that you can see what the different forms do as well as manipulate them more easily.

The 2004 World Series victory that was earned by the Boston Red Sox gratified legions of fans who had suffered for many years. Indeed, if the media were to be believed, these fans had been mourning their unrequited fandom since 1918, when Babe Ruth was sold to the Yankees. But all of the media hoopla about the fact that the Sox had been victorious could not obscure the fact that the series will not go down in history as one of the better ones. Aside from the first game, there were no close contests. And the usual components that go into making a series memorable—extra-inning games, spectacular rallies, seesaw battles— were sadly absent. Instead, we were left with an overdose of media hype. Because the games were lousy, and the writers had to write something, we just got more and more and more tired rehearsals of the lifting of the curse. So maybe the Sox lifted the curse, but perhaps it was laid upon the fans.

Alternatively, you might use a passage from a book you are reading or from one of your own drafts.

Especially in the natural sciences, the use of the passive voice is a standard practice. There are sound reasons for this disciplinary convention: science tends to focus on what happens to something in a given experiment, rather than on the actions of that something. Compare the following sentences.

Passive: Separation of the protein was achieved by using an electrophoretic gel.

Active: The researcher used an electrophoretic gel to separate the protein.

If you opted for the active version, the emphasis would rest, illogically, on the agent of the action (the researcher) rather than on what happened and how (electrophoretic separation of the protein).

More generally, the passive voice can provide a way to avoid using the pronoun "I," whether for reasons of convention, as indicated earlier, or for other reasons. For example, the following passive sentence begins a business memo from a supervisor to the staff in her office.

The Inventory and Reprint departments have recently been restructured and merged.

Like many passive sentences, this one names no actor; we do not know for sure who did the restructuring and merging, though we might imagine that the author of the memo is the responsible party. The supervisor might, then, have written the sentence in the active voice.

I have recently restructured and merged the Inventory and Reprint departments.

But the active version is less satisfactory than the passive one for two reasons: one of practical emphasis and one of sensitivity to the audience (tone). First, the fact of the changes is more important for the memo's readers than is the announcement of who made the changes. The passive sentence appropriately emphasizes the changes; the active sentence inappropriately emphasizes the person who made the changes. Second, the emphasis of the active sentence on "I" (the supervisor) risks alienating the readers by taking an autocratic tone and by seeming to exclude all others from possible credit for the presumably worthwhile reorganization.

On balance, "consider" is the operative term when you choose between passive and active as you revise the syntax of your drafts. Recognize that you do have choices—in emphasis, in relative directness, and in economy. All things being equal and disciplinary conventions permitting, the active is usually the better choice.

▶ Try this 11.9: Converting Passive to Active

Identify all of the sentences that use the passive voice in one of your papers. Then, rewrite these sentences, converting passive into active wherever appropriate. Finally, count the total number of words, the total number of prepositions, and the average sentence length (words per sentence) in each version. What do you discover? Alternatively, you could do this with the World Series example in the previous "Try this" exercise.

For more practice, here's another exercise. Compose a paragraph of at least half a page in which you use only the passive voice and verbs of being, followed by a paragraph in which you use only the active voice. Then, rewrite the first paragraph using only active voice, if possible, and rewrite the second paragraph using only passive voice and verbs of being as much as possible. How do the paragraphs differ in shape, length, and coherence?

EXPERIMENT!

A key idea of this chapter is that there are not necessarily right and wrong choices when it comes to sentence style but instead better and best choices for particular situations. The from-the-hip plain style of a memo or a set of operating instructions for your lawn mower is very likely not the best style choice for a good-bye letter to a best friend, a diplomatic talk on a sensitive political situation, or an analysis of guitar styles in contemporary jazz.

Is style a function of character and personality? Is it, in short, personal, and thus something to be preserved in the face of would-be meddlers carrying style manuals and grammar guides? Well, as you might guess at this point in the book, the answer is yes and no. We all need to find ways of using words that do not succumb to the mind-numbing environment of verbal cliché in which we dwell. It helps then, to become more self-conscious about style and not assume that it is inborn. Staying locked into one way of writing because that is "your style" is as limiting as remaining locked into only one way of thinking.

This chapter has presented some terms and techniques for experimenting with sentence styles. Equipped with these, you might profitably begin to read and listen for style more self-consciously. Find models. When a style appeals to you, figure out what makes it work. Copy sentences you like. Try imitating them. Know, by the way, that imitation will not erase your own style—it will allow you to experiment with new moves, new shapes into which to cast your words.

Try this 11.10: Finding the Representative Sentence in a Reading

As we discussed in the Quick Take for this chapter, the ability to isolate a characteristic stylistic passage in any writing and then analyze it can yield privileged insights into how the writer makes meanings and by extension, what those meanings are. Try this with any writer whose work you are studying. Talk about particular stylistic features of diction and syntax. How is the passage representative? What is the significance of these representative characteristics?

VOICES FROM ACROSS THE CURRICULUM

Reading Attentively to Improve One's Style

Aside from the usual basic writing errors, the stylistic problems I most frequently encounter in students' papers are odd word selection and awkward sentence structure. I think both problems find their genesis in the same broader problem. You learn how to make telling use of the vocabulary you've been forced to memorize only by reading. You fashion an appealing sentence based on what you've read others doing.

—*James Marshall, Professor of Economics*

▶ **Try this 11.11:** Finding Your "Go To" Sentence

Bring it all back home. Examine your own stylistic habits in diction but particularly in syntax. What is the favored shape with which you compose the world when you write? And once you have it, ask and answer, So what?

◀ **ASSIGNMENTS:** Stylistic Analysis

1. Analyze the style—the syntax but also the diction—of two writers doing a similar kind of writing; for example, two sportswriters, two rock music reviewers, or two presidents. Study first the similarities. What style characteristics does this type of writing seem to invite? Then study the differences. How is one writer (Bush, Reagan, or Clinton, for example) recognizable through his or her style?

2. Analyze your own style, past and present. Assemble some pieces you have written, preferably of a similar type, and study them for style. Do you have some favorite stylistic moves? What sentence shapes (simple, compound, complex, compound-complex, highly parallel, periodic, or cumulative) dominate in your writing? What verbs? Do you use forms of "to be" a lot, and so forth?

3. For many people, Lincoln's Gettysburg Address (see p. 52) is one of the best examples of the careful matching of style to situation. Delivered after a long talk by a previous speaker at the dedication of a Civil War battlefield on a rainy day, the speech composed by Abraham Lincoln (some say on the back of an envelope) is a masterpiece of style. Analyze its sentence structure, such as its use of parallelism, antithesis, and other kinds of repetition. Which features of Lincoln's style seem to you to be most important in creating the overall effect of the piece? (Or do this with any popular journalist whom you read regularly and who you

think has an especially effective style. Or look for another inspirational speech and see if such occasional writing has anything in common.)

4. Do a full-fledged stylistic revision of a paper. The best choice might well be an essay you already have revised, resubmitted, and had returned, because in that case, you will be less likely to get distracted by conceptual revision and so can concentrate on stylistic issues. As you revise, try to accomplish each of the following:

   a. Sharpen the diction.

   b. Blend concrete and abstract diction.

   c. Experiment with the order of and relation among subordinate and coordinate clauses.

   d. Choose more knowingly between active and passive voice.

   e. Cut the fat, especially by eliminating unnecessary "to be" constructions.

   f. Vary sentence length and shape.

   g. Use parallelism.

   h. Experiment with periodic and cumulative sentences.

   i. Fine-tune the tone. ▶

GUIDELINES FOR SHAPING SENTENCES

1. Revise sentences to clarify their meaning by revealing the organization of thought. Align like with like, set difference against difference, and in general use form to emphasize what's important and demote what is not.

2. Become aware of your own syntactic habits. What is your "go-to sentence," and how might you build upon it to extend your range and force?

3. Cut the fat. Don't use five words ("due to the fact that") when one will do ("because"). Root out expletives that needlessly subordinate ("It is true that . . ."). Avoid redundancy.

4. Tighten the syntax of your sentences by energizing the verbs. The active voice generally achieves directness and economy; it will promote clarity and cut fat.

5. Look for potentially strong active verbs "lurking" in sentences that use a form of "to be." Beware habitual use of "to be" and passives, since these forms tend to blur or submerge the action, omit its performers, and generally lack momentum.

6. Look at the order and arrangement of clauses. Are ideas of equal importance in coordinate constructions? Have you used subordination to rank ideas? Have your sentences exploited the end as a position of emphasis?

7. Look at the shapes of your sentences. Do they use parallelism to keep your ideas clear? Where do you find opportunities for composing periodic and cumulative sentences that revision can bring out?

CHAPTER 12

Writing the
Researched Paper

Quick Take

This chapter is about how to integrate secondary sources into your writing. That is often a daunting task, because it requires you to negotiate with authorities who generally know more than you do about the subject at hand. Simply ignoring sources is a head-in-the-sand attitude, and besides, you miss out on learning what people interested in your subject are talking about. But what role can you invent for yourself when the experts are talking? Just agreeing with a source is an abdication of your responsibility to present your thinking on the subject, but taking the opposite tack by disagreeing with some professor who has studied your subject and written books about it would also appear to be a fool's game. So what are you to do?

This chapter attempts to answer that question. It lays out the primary trouble spots that arise when writers use secondary materials, and it suggests remedies—for the most part, ways of using sources as points of departure for your own thinking rather than using them as either The Answer or a whipping boy. We call this concept *conversing with sources*.

In demonstrating ways of conversing with sources, the chapter also makes use of specialized applications of the tools introduced in the earlier chapter (4) on reading. That chapter addresses skills such as paraphrasing, summarizing, applying a reading as a lens, comparing readings, and uncovering assumptions in readings. Those same skills can be applied to secondary materials to raise issues and questions rather than just plugging them in as the conventional solution to the clichéd problem—what a colleague of ours calls Plug 'n' Chug.

Here's a short list of the chapter's chief strategies by name:

Strategy 1: Make Your Sources Speak

Strategy 2: Use Your Sources to Ask Questions, Not Just to Provide Answers

Strategy 3: Put Your Sources into Conversation with One Another

Strategy 4: Find Your Own Role in the Conversation

Strategy 5: Supply Ongoing Analysis of Sources (Don't Wait until the End)

Strategy 6: Attend Carefully to the Language of Your Sources by Quoting or Paraphrasing Them

This is, by the way, the first of two chapters on using sources. The next chapter treats such practical matters as finding and evaluating sources in print and electronic media, integrating quotations into one's own prose, and citing sources.

A. WHAT TO DO WITH SECONDARY SOURCES

First, by way of definition, we use the terms *source* and *secondary source* interchangeably to designate ideas and information about your subject that you find in the work of other writers. Secondary sources allow you to gain a richer, more informed, and complex vantage point on your *primary sources*. Here's how primary and secondary sources can be distinguished: if you were writing a paper on the philosopher Nietzsche, his writing would be your primary source, and critical commentaries on his work would be your secondary sources. If, however, you were writing on the poet Yeats, who read and was influenced by Nietzsche, a work of Nietzsche's philosophy would become a secondary source of yours on your primary source, Yeats's poetry.

"SOURCE ANXIETY" AND WHAT TO DO ABOUT IT

Typically, inexperienced writers either use sources as "answers"—they let the sources do too much of their thinking—or ignore them altogether as a way of avoiding "losing their own ideas." Both of these approaches are understandable but inadequate. We will take up the first of these in some detail in a moment, but for now let's concentrate on the second, ignoring sources altogether.

> *Typically, inexperienced writers either use sources as "answers"—they let the sources do too much of their thinking—or ignore them altogether as a way of avoiding "losing their own ideas."*

Confronted with the seasoned views of experts in a discipline, you may well feel that there is nothing left for you to say because it has all been said before or, at least, it has been said by people who greatly outweigh you in reputation and experience. This anxiety explains why so many writers surrender to the role of conduit for the voices of the experts, providing conjunctions between quotations. So why not avoid what other people have said? Won't this avoidance ensure that your ideas will be original and that, at the same time, you will be free from the danger of getting brainwashed by some "expert"?

The answer is "no." If you don't consult what others have said, you run at least two risks: you will waste your time reinventing the wheel, and you will undermine your analysis (or at least leave it incomplete) by not considering information or acknowledging positions that are commonly discussed in the field.

If you don't consult what others have said, you run the risk of reinventing the wheel.

By remaining unaware of existing thinking, you choose, in effect, to stand outside of the conversation that others interested in the subject are having. Standing in this sort of intellectual vacuum sometimes appeals to writers who fear that consulting sources will leave them with nothing to say. But it is possible, as this chapter shows, to find a *middle ground* between developing an idea that is entirely independent of what experts have written on a subject and producing a paper that does nothing but repeat other people's ideas. A little research—even if it's only an hour's browse in the reference collection of the library—will virtually always raise the level of what you have to say above what it would have been if you had consulted only the information and opinions that you carry around in your head.

By remaining unaware of existing thinking, you choose, in effect, to stand outside of the conversation that others interested in the subject are having.

A good rule of thumb for coping with "source anxiety" is to formulate a tentative position on your topic before you consult secondary sources. In other words, give yourself time to do some preliminary thinking. Try writing informally about your topic, analyzing some piece of pertinent information already at your disposal. That way you will have your initial responses written down to weigh in relation to what others have said. Writing of this sort can also help you to select what to look at in the sources you eventually consult.

THE CONVERSATION ANALOGY

Now, let's turn to *the major problem in using sources—a writer leaving the experts he or she cites to speak for themselves.* In this situation, the writer characteristically makes a generalization in his or her own words, juxtaposes it to a quotation or other reference from a secondary source, and assumes that the meaning of the reference will be self-evident. This practice not only leaves the connection between the writer's thinking and his or her source material unstated but also substitutes mere repetition of someone else's viewpoint for a more active interpretation. The source has been allowed to have the final word, with the effect that it stops the discussion and the writer's thinking.

First and foremost, then, you need to do something with the reading. Clarify the meaning of the material you have quoted, paraphrased, or summarized and explain its significance in light of your evolving thesis.

It follows that the first step in using sources effectively is to reject the assumption that sources provide final and complete answers. If they did, there would be no reason for others to continue writing on the subject. As in conversation, we raise ideas for others to respond to. Accepting that no source has the final word does not mean, however, that you should shift from unquestioning approval to the opposite pole and necessarily assume an antagonistic position toward all sources. Indeed, a habitually antagonistic response to others' ideas is just as likely to bring your conversation with your sources to a halt as is the habit of always assuming that the source must have the final word.

Most people would probably agree on the attributes of a really good conversation. There is room for agreement and disagreement, for give and take, among a variety of viewpoints. Generally, people don't deliberately misunderstand each other, but a significant amount of the discussion may go into clarifying one's own as well as others' positions. Such conversations construct a genuinely collaborative *chain* of thinking: Karl builds on what David has said, which induces Jill to respond to Karl's comment, and so forth.

There are, of course, obvious differences between conversing aloud with friends and conversing on paper with sources. As a writer, you need to construct the chain of thinking, orchestrate the exchange of views with and among your sources, and give the conversation direction. A good place to begin in using sources is to recognize that you need not respond to everything another writer says, nor do you need to come up with an entirely original point of view—one that completely revises or refutes the source. You are using sources analytically, for example, when you note that two experiments (or historical accounts, or whatever) are similar but have different priorities or that they ask similar questions in different ways. Building from this kind of observation, you can then analyze what these differences imply.

WAYS TO USE A SOURCE AS A POINT OF DEPARTURE

There are, in any case, many ways of approaching secondary sources, but these ways generally share a common goal: to use the source as a point of departure. Here is a partial list of ways to do that.

- Make as many points as you can about a single representative passage from your source, and then branch out from this center to analyze other passages that "speak" to it in some way. (See "Building a Paper by Analyzing Evidence in Depth: '10 on 1'" in Chapter 5.)
- Use Notice and focus to identify what you find most strange in the source (see Chapter 1); this will help you cultivate your curiosity about the source and find the critical distance necessary to thinking about it.
- Use Looking for Patterns of Repetition and Contrast to identify the most significant organizing contrast in the source (see Chapter 2); this will help you see what the source itself is wrestling with, what is at stake in it.
- Apply an idea in the source to another subject. (See "Applying a Reading as a Lens" in Chapter 4.)
- Uncover the assumptions in the source, and then build upon the source's point of view, extending its implications. (See "Uncovering the Assumptions in a Reading" in Chapter 4.)
- Agree with most of what the source says, but take issue with one small part that you want to modify.
- Identify a contradiction in the source, and explore its implications, without necessarily arriving at a solution.

In using a source as a point of departure you are in effect using it as a stimulus to have an idea. As you may recall from the discussion of what it means to have an idea in Chapter 1, most strong analytical ideas launch you into a process of resolving problems and bringing competing positions into some kind of alignment. They locate you where there is something to negotiate, where you are required not just to list answers but also to ask questions, make choices, and engage in reasoning about the significance of your evidence.

If you quote with the aim of conversing with your sources rather than allowing them to do your thinking for you, you will discover that sources can promote rather than stifle your ability to have ideas. So try to think of sources not as answers but as voices inviting you into a community of interpretation, discussion, and debate. As the discussion of reporting versus analyzing in the "Voices from Across the Curriculum" box demonstrates, this practice is common to different academic disciplines.

Try to think of sources not as answers but as voices inviting you into a community of interpretation, discussion, and debate.

VOICES FROM ACROSS THE CURRICULUM

Reporting Versus Analyzing in Scientific Experiments

There is a big difference between simply reporting on what has been done in a scientific venture and analyzing and evaluating the venture. One of the problems with trying to *read* critical analyses of scientific work is that few scientists want to be in print criticizing their colleagues. That is, for political reasons scientists who write reviews are likely to soften their criticism or even avoid it entirely by reporting the findings of others simply and directly. However, by definition such a review is not critical. That author stakes out no particular point of view and thus does not have to defend anything.

What I want from students in molecular biology is a critical analysis of the work they have researched. This can take several forms.

First, *analyze* what was done. What were the assumptions (hypotheses) going into the experiment? What was the logic of the experimental design? What were the results?

Second, *evaluate* the results and conclusions. Here, it's even appropriate to use the first person. *You* are commenting on the field. Foremost, how well do the results support the conclusions? What alternative interpretations are there? What additional experiments could be done to strengthen or refute the argument? This is hard, no doubt, but it is what you should be doing every time you read anything in science or otherwise.

Third, *synthesize* the results and interpretations of a given experiment in the context of the field. How does this study inform other studies? Even though practicing scientists are hesitant to do this in print, everyone does it informally in journal clubs held usually on a weekly basis in every lab all over the world.

—Bruce Wightman, Professor of Biology

B. SIX STRATEGIES FOR ANALYZING SOURCES

Many people never get beyond like/dislike responses with secondary materials. If they agree with what a source says, they say it's "good," and they cut and paste the part they can use as an answer. If the source somehow disagrees with what they already believe, they say it's "bad," and they attack it or—along with readings they find "hard" or "boring"—discard it. As readers they have been conditioned to develop a point of view on a subject without first figuring out the <u>conversation</u> (the various points of view) that their subject attracts. They assume, in other words, that their subject probably has a single meaning—a gist—disclosed by experts, who mostly agree. The six strategies that follow offer ways to avoid this trap.

STRATEGY 1: MAKE YOUR SOURCES SPEAK

Quote, paraphrase, or summarize *in order to* analyze—not *in place of* analyzing. Don't assume that either the meaning of the source material or your reason for including it is self-evident. Stop yourself from the habit of just stringing together citations for which you provide little more than conjunctions. Instead, explain to your readers what the quotation or paraphrase or summary of the source means. What elements of it do you find interesting or revealing or strange? Emphasize how those affect your evolving thesis.

> *Make your sources speak. Quote, paraphrase, or summarize* in order to analyze—not in place of analyzing. Don't assume that either the meaning of the source material or your reason for including it is self-evident.

In making a source speak, focus on articulating how the source has led to the conclusion you draw from it. Beware of simply putting a generalization and a quotation next to each other (juxtaposing them) without explaining the connection. Instead fill the crucial site between claim and evidence (see Figure 5.1) with your *thinking*. Consider this problem in the following paragraph from a student's paper on political conservatism.

> Edmund Burke's philosophy evolved into contemporary American conservative ideology. There is an important distinction between philosophy and political ideology: philosophy is "the knowledge of general principles that explain facts and existences." Political ideology, on the other hand, is "an overarching conception of society, a stance that is reflected in numerous sectors of social life" (Edwards 22). Therefore, conservatism should be regarded as an ideology rather than a philosophy.

The final sentence offers the writer's conclusion—what the source information has led him to—but how did it get him there? The writer's choice of the word "therefore" indicates to the reader that the idea following it is the result of a process of logical reasoning, but this reasoning has been omitted. Instead, the writer assumes that the reader will be able to connect the quotations with his conclusion. The writer needs to *make the quotation speak* by analyzing its key terms more closely. What is "an overarching conception of society," and how does it differ from "knowledge of general principles"? More important, what is the rationale for categorizing conservatism as either an ideology or a philosophy?

Here, by contrast, is a writer who makes her sources speak. Focus on how she integrates analysis with quotation.

> Stephen Greenblatt uses the phrase "self-fashioning" to refer to an idea he believes developed during the Renaissance—the idea that one's identity is not created or born but rather shaped, both by one's self and by others. The idea of self-fashioning is incorporated into an attitude toward literature that has as its ideal what Greenblatt calls "poetics of culture." A text is examined with three elements in mind: the author's own self, the cultural self-fashioning process that created that self, and the author's reaction to that process. Because our selves, like texts, are "fashioned," an author's life is just as open to interpretation as that of a literary character.

> If this is so, then biography does not provide a repository of unshakeable facts from which to interpret an author's work. Greenblatt criticizes the fact that the methods of literary interpretation are applied just to art and not to life. As he observes, "We wall off literary symbolism from the symbolic structures operative elsewhere, as if art alone were a human creation" (Begley 37). If the line between art and life is indeed blurred, then we need a more complex model for understanding the relationship between the life and work of an author.

In this example, the writer shows us how her thinking has been stimulated by the source. At the end of the first paragraph and the beginning of the second, for example, she not only specifies what she takes to be the meaning of the quotation but also draws a conclusion about its implications (that the facts of an author's life, like his or her art, require interpretation). And this manner of proceeding is habitual: the writer repeats the pattern in the second paragraph, *moving beyond what the quotation says to explore what its logic suggests.*

STRATEGY 2: USE YOUR SOURCES TO ASK QUESTIONS, NOT JUST TO PROVIDE ANSWERS

Use your selections from sources as a means of raising issues and questions. Avoid the temptation to plug in such selections as answers that require no further commentary or elaboration. You will no doubt find viewpoints you believe to be valid, but it is not enough to drop these answers from the source into your own writing at the appropriate spots. You need to *do* something with the reading, even with those sources that seem to have said what you want to say.

As long as you consider only the source in isolation, you may not discover much to say about it. Once you begin considering it in other contexts and with other sources, you may begin to see aspects of your subject that your source does not adequately address. Having recognized that the source does not answer all questions, you should not conclude that the source is "wrong"—only that it is limited in some ways. Discovering such limitations is in fact advantageous, because it can lead you to identify a place from which to launch your own analysis.

It does not necessarily follow that your analysis will culminate in an answer to replace those offered by your sources. Often—in fact, far more often than many writers suspect—it is enough to discover issues or problems and raise them clearly. Phrasing *explicitly* the issues and questions that remain *implicit* in a source is an important part of what analytical writers do, especially with cases in which there is no solution, or at least none that can be presented in a relatively short paper. Here, for example, is how the writer on Stephen Greenblatt's concept of self-fashioning concludes her essay:

> It is not only the author whose role is complicated by New Historicism; the critic also is subject to some of the same qualifications and restrictions. According to Adam Begley, "it is the essence of the new-historicist project to uncover the moments at which works of art absorb and refashion social energy, an endless process of circulation and exchange" (39). In other words, the work is both affected by and affects the culture. But if this is so, how then can we decide which elements of culture (and text) are causes and which are effects? If we add the critic to this picture, the process does indeed appear endless. The New Historicists' relationship with their culture infuses itself into their assessment of the Renaissance, and this assessment may in turn become part of their own self-fashioning process, which will affect their interpretations, and so forth... .

Notice that this writer *incorporates the quotation into her own chain of thinking*. By paraphrasing the quotation ("In other words"), she arrives at a question ("how then") that follows as a logical consequence of accepting its position ("but if this is so"). Note, however, that she does not then label the quotation right or wrong. Instead, she tries to figure out *to what position it might lead* and to what possible problems.

By contrast, the writer of the following excerpt, from a paper comparing two films aimed at teenagers, settles for plugging in sources as answers and consequently does not pursue the questions implicit in her quotations.

> In both films, the adults are one-dimensional caricatures, evil beings whose only goal in life is to make the kids' lives a living hell. In *Risky Business*, director Paul Brickman's solution to all of Joel's problems is to have him hire a prostitute and then turn his house into a whorehouse. Of course, as one critic observes, "the prostitutes who make themselves available to his pimply faced buddies are all centerfold beauties: elegant, svelte, benign and unquestionably healthy (after all, what does V.D. have to do with prostitutes?)" (Gould 41)—not exactly a realistic or legal solution. Allan Moyle, the director of *Pump Up the Volume*, provides an equally unrealistic solution to Mark's problem. According to David Denby, Moyle "offers self-expression as the cure to adolescent funk. Everyone should start his own radio station and talk about his feelings" (59). Like Brickman, Moyle offers solutions that are neither realistic nor legal.

This writer is having a hard time figuring out what to do with sources that offer well-phrased and seemingly accurate answers (such as "self-expression is the cure to adolescent funk"). Her analysis of both quotations leads her to settle for the bland

and undeveloped conclusion that films aimed at teenagers are not "realistic"—an observation that most readers would already recognize as true. But unlike the writer of the previous example, she does not ask herself, "*If this is true, then what follows?*" Had she asked some such version of the So what? question, she might have inquired how the illegality of the solutions is related to their unrealistic quality. So what, for example, that the main characters in both films are not marginalized as criminals and made to suffer for their illegal actions, but rather are celebrated as heroes? What different kinds of illegality do the two films apparently condone, and how might these be related to the different decades in which each film was produced? Rather than use her sources to think with, in order to clarify or complicate the issues, the writer has used them to confirm a fairly obvious generalization.

STRATEGY 3: PUT YOUR SOURCES INTO CONVERSATION WITH ONE ANOTHER

Rather than limiting yourself to agreeing or disagreeing with your sources, aim for conversation with and among them. Although it is not wrong to agree or disagree with your sources, it is wrong to see these as your only possible moves. It is sometimes useful and perhaps even necessary to agree or disagree, but these judgments should (1) always be *qualified* and (2) occur only *in certain contexts*.

Rather than limiting yourself to agreeing or disagreeing with your sources, aim for conversation with and among them.

Selective analytical summarizing of a position with which you essentially agree or disagree, especially if located early in a final draft (after you've figured out what to think in your previous drafts), can be extraordinarily helpful in orienting your readers for the discussion to follow. This practice of *framing the discussion* typically locates you either for or against some well-known point of view or frame of reference; it's a way of sharing your assumptions with the reader. You introduce the source, in other words, to succinctly summarize a position that you plan to develop or challenge in a qualified way. This latter strategy—sometimes known as **straw man**, because you construct a "dummy" position specifically in order to knock it down—can stimulate you to formulate a point of view, especially if you are not accustomed to responding critically to sources.

As this boxing analogy suggests, however, setting up a straw man can be a dangerous game. If you do not fairly represent and put into context the straw man's argument, you risk encouraging readers to dismiss your counterargument as a cheap shot and to dismiss you for being *reductive*. On the other hand, if you spend a great deal of time detailing the straw man's position, you risk losing momentum in developing your own point of view.

In any case, if you are citing a source in order to frame the discussion, the more reasonable move is both to agree *and* disagree with it. First, identify shared premises; give the source some credit. Then distinguish the part of what you have cited that you intend to develop or complicate or dispute. This method of proceeding is obviously less combative than the typically blunt straw man approach; it verges on conversation.

In the following passage from a student's paper on Darwin's theory of evolution, the student clearly recognizes that he needs to do more than summarize what Darwin says, but he seems not to know any way of conversing with his source other than indicating his agreement and disagreement with it.

> The struggle for existence also includes the dependence of one being on another being to survive. Darwin also believes that all organic beings tend to increase. I do not fully agree with Darwin's belief here. I cannot conceive of the fact of all beings increasing in number. Darwin goes on to explain that food, competition, climate, and the location of a certain species contribute to its survival and existence in nature. I believe that this statement is very valid and that it could be very easily understood through experimentation in nature.

This writer's use of the word "here" in his third sentence is revealing. He is tagging summaries of Darwin with what he seems to feel is an obligatory response—a polite shake or nod of the head: "I can't fully agree with you there, Darwin, but here I think you might have a point." The writer's tentative language lets us see how uncomfortable, even embarrassed, he feels about venturing these judgments on a subject that is too complex for this kind of response. It's as though the writer moves along, talking about Darwin's theory for a while, and then says to himself, "Time for a response," and lets a particular summary sentence trigger a yes/no switch. Having pressed that switch, which he does periodically, the writer resumes his summary, having registered but not analyzed his own interjections. There is no reasoning in a chain from his own observations, just random insertions of unanalyzed agree/disagree responses.

Here, by contrast, is the introduction of an essay that uses summary to frame the conversation that the writer is preparing to have with her source.

> In *Renaissance Thought: The Classic, Scholastic and Humanist Strains*, Paul Kristeller responds to two problems that he perceives in Renaissance scholarship. The first is the haze of cultural meaning surrounding the word "humanism": he seeks to clarify the word and its origins, as well as to explain the apparent lack of religious concern in humanism. Kristeller also reacts to the notion of humanism as an improvement upon medieval Aristotelian scholasticism.

Rather than leading with her own beliefs about the source, the writer emphasizes the issues and problems she believes are central in it. Although the writer's position on her source is apparently neutral, she is not summarizing passively. In addition to making choices about what is especially significant in the source, she has also located it within the conversation that its author, Kristeller, was having with his own sources—the works of other scholars whose view of humanism he wants to revise ("Kristeller responds to two problems").

As an alternative to formulating your opinion of the sources, try constructing the conversation that you think the author of one of your sources might have with the author of another. *How might they recast each other's ideas, as opposed to merely agreeing or disagreeing with those ideas?* Notice how, farther on in the paper, the writer uses this strategy to achieve a clearer picture of Kristeller's point of view:

> Unlike Kristeller, Tillyard [in *The Elizabethan World Picture*] also tries to place the seeds of individualism in the minds of the medievals. "Those who

know most about the Middle Ages," he claims, "now assure us that humanism and a belief in the present life were powerful by the 12th century" (30). Kristeller would undoubtedly reply that it was scholasticism, lacking the humanist emphasis on individualism that was powerful in the Middle Ages. True humanism was not evident in the Middle Ages.

In Kristeller's view, Tillyard's attempts to assign humanism to medievals are not only unwarranted, but also counterproductive. Kristeller ends his chapter on "Humanism and Scholasticism" with an exhortation to "develop a kind of historical pluralism. It is easy to praise everything in the past that appears to resemble certain favorable ideas of our own time, or to ridicule and minimize everything that disagrees with them. This method is neither fair nor helpful" (174). Tillyard, in trying to locate humanism within the medieval world, allows the value of humanism to supersede the worth of medieval scholarship. Kristeller argues that there is inherent worth in every intellectual movement, not simply in the ones that we find most agreeable.

Kristeller's work is valuable to us primarily for its forthright definition of humanism. Tillyard has cleverly avoided this undertaking: he provides many textual references, usually with the companion comment that "this is an example of Renaissance humanism," but he never overtly and fully formulates the definition in the way that Kristeller does.

As this excerpt makes evident, the writer has found something to say about her source by putting it into conversation with another source with which she believes her source, Kristeller, would disagree ("Kristeller would undoubtedly reply"). Although it seems obvious that the writer prefers Kristeller to Tillyard, her agreement with him is not the main point of her analysis. She focuses instead on foregrounding the problem that Kristeller is trying to solve and on relating that problem to different attitudes toward history. In so doing, she is deftly orchestrating the conversation between her sources. Her next step would be to distinguish her position from Kristeller's. Having used Kristeller to get perspective on Tillyard, she now needs somehow to get perspective on Kristeller. The next strategy addresses this issue.

▶ **Try this 12.1:** Making One Source Speak to Another

This exercise requires you to filter one source through another, speculating (imagining) how each source would respond to the other's position. Choose two articles or book chapters by different authors or by the same author at different points in his or her career. The overriding aim of the exercise is to give you practice in getting beyond merely reacting and generalizing, and instead, participating in your sources' thinking.

As a kind of model for this exercise, you might look again at the preceding example in which the student writer compares and contrasts two historical scholars on the nature of Renaissance humanism. This example demonstrates the difference between having an idea about someone else's idea and simply reacting to someone else's idea.

> Keep in mind that your aim in this exercise is not to arrive at your opinion of the sources, but to construct the conversation that you think the author of one of your sources might have with the author of another. How might they recast each other's ideas, as opposed to merely agreeing or disagreeing with those ideas? It's useful to confine yourself to thinking as impartially as you can about the ideas found in your two sources.

STRATEGY 4: FIND YOUR OWN ROLE IN THE CONVERSATION

Even in cases in which you find a source's position entirely congenial, it is not enough simply to agree with it. In order to converse with a source, you need to find some way of having a distinct voice in that conversation. This does not mean that you should feel compelled to attack the source but rather that you need to find something of your own to say about it.

In general, you have two options when you find yourself strongly in agreement with a source. You can (1) apply it in another context to qualify or expand its implications. Or you can (2) seek out other perspectives on the source in order to break the spell it has cast upon you. "To break the spell" means that you will necessarily become somewhat disillusioned but not that you will then need to dismiss everything you previously believed.

How, in the first option, do you take a source somewhere else? Rather than focusing solely on what you believe your source finds most important, *locate a lesser point, not emphasized by the reading, that you find especially interesting and develop it further.* This strategy will lead you to uncover new implications that depend upon your source but lie outside its own governing preoccupations. In the preceding humanism example, the writer might apply Kristeller's principles to new geographic (rather than theoretical) areas, such as Germany instead of Italy.

The second option, researching new perspectives on the source, can also lead to uncovering new implications. Your aim need not be simply to find a source that disagrees with the one that has convinced you and then switch your allegiance, because this move would perpetuate the problem from which you are trying to escape. Instead, you would use additional perspectives to gain some critical distance from your source. An ideal way of sampling possible critical approaches to a source is to consult book reviews on it found in scholarly journals. Once the original source is taken down from the pedestal through additional reading, there is a greater likelihood that you will see how to distinguish your views from those it offers.

You may think, for example, that another source's critique of your original source is partly valid and that both sources miss things that you could point out; in effect, you *referee* the conversation between them. The writer on Kristeller might play this role by asking herself: "So what that subsequent historians have viewed his objective—a disinterested historical pluralism—as not necessarily desirable and in any case impossible? How might Kristeller respond to this charge, and how has he responded already in ways that his critics have failed to notice?" Using additional research in this way can lead you to *situate* your source more fully and fairly, acknowledging its limits as well as its strengths.

VOICES FROM ACROSS THE CURRICULUM
Bringing Sources Together

Avoid serial citation summaries; that is, rather than discussing what Author A found, then what Author B found, then what Author C found, and so forth, *integrate* material from all of your sources. For instance, if writing about the cause and treatment of a disorder, discuss what all authors say about cause, then what all authors say about treatment, and so forth, addressing any contradictions or tensions among authors.

—Alan Tjeltveit, Professor of Psychology

In other words, this writer, in using Kristeller to critique Tillyard, has arrived less at a conclusion than at her next point of departure. A good rule to follow, especially when you find a source entirely persuasive, is that if you can't find a perspective on your source, you haven't done enough research.

STRATEGY 5: SUPPLY ONGOING ANALYSIS OF SOURCES (DON'T WAIT UNTIL THE END)

Unless disciplinary conventions dictate otherwise, analyze *as* you quote or paraphrase a source, rather than summarizing everything first and leaving your analysis for the end. A good conversation does not consist of long monologues alternating among the speakers. Participants exchange views, query, and modify what other speakers have said. Similarly, when you orchestrate conversations with and among your sources, you need to *integrate your analysis into your presentation* of them.

In supplying ongoing analysis, you are much more likely to explain how the information in the sources fits into your unfolding presentation, and your readers will be more likely to follow your train of thought and grasp the logic of your organization. You will also prevent yourself from using the sources simply as an answer. A good rule of thumb in this regard is to *force yourself to ask and answer "So what?" at the ends of paragraphs*. In laying out your analysis, however, take special care to distinguish your voice from the sources'. (For further discussion of integrating analysis into your presentation of sources, see the commentary on the research paper later in this chapter.)

STRATEGY 6: ATTEND CAREFULLY TO THE LANGUAGE OF YOUR SOURCES BY QUOTING OR PARAPHRASING THEM

Rather than generalizing broadly about ideas in your sources, you should spell out what you think is significant about their key words. In those disciplines in which it is permissible, *quote sources if the actual language that they use is important to your point*. This practice will help you to represent the view of your source fairly and accurately. In situations where quoting is not allowed—such as in the report format in psychology—you still need to attend carefully to the meaning of key words in order to arrive at a paraphrase that is not overly general. As we have suggested repeatedly, paraphrasing provides an ideal way to begin interpreting, since the act of careful rephrasing usually illuminates attitudes and assumptions implicit in a text. It is almost impossible not to have ideas and not to see the questions when you start paraphrasing.

Another reason that quoting and paraphrasing are important is that your analysis of a source will nearly always benefit from attention to the way the source represents its position (not just from dwelling on the position itself). Although focusing on the manner of presentation matters more with some sources than with others—more with a poem or scholarly article in political science than with a paper in the natural sciences—the information is never wholly separable from how it is expressed. If you are going to quote *Newsweek* on Pakistan, for example, you will be encountering not "the truth" about American involvement in this Asian nation but rather one particular representation of the situation—in this case, one crafted to meet or shape the expectations of mainstream popular culture. Similarly, if you quote President Bush on terrorism, what probably matters most is that the president chose particular words to represent—and promote—the government's position. *It is not neutral information.* The person speaking and the kind of source in which his or her words appear usually acquire added significance when you make note of these words rather than just summarizing them.

Try this 12.2: Using Passage-Based Freewriting to Converse with Sources

Select a passage from a secondary source that appears important to your evolving thinking about a subject you are studying, and try doing a passage-based focused freewrite on it. You might choose the passage in answer to the question "What is the one passage in the source that I need to discuss, that poses a question or a problem or that seems, in some way perhaps difficult to pin down, anomalous or even just unclear?" Copy the passage at the top of the page, and go for 20 minutes. As noted in the discussion of freewriting in Chapter 4, try to isolate and paraphrase key terms as you relentlessly ask "So what?" about the details. Also, remember to consider how the passage is representative of broader issues in the source; you may wish to refer to a similar passage for this purpose.

Try this 12.3: Freewriting by Applying a Secondary Source to a Primary Source

As a variation on the preceding exercise, *apply a brief passage from a secondary source to a brief passage from a primary source.* Choose the secondary source passage first—one that you find particularly interesting, revealing, or problematic. Then locate a corresponding passage from the primary source to which the sentence from the first passage can be connected in some way. Copy both passages at the top of the page, and then write for 20 minutes. You should probably include paraphrases of key phrases in both—not just the primary text—but your primary goal is to think about the two together, to allow them to interact.

C. MAKING THE RESEARCH PAPER MORE ANALYTICAL: A SAMPLE ESSAY

The following is an example of a typical college research paper. We offer a brief analysis of each paragraph with an eye to diagnosing what typically goes wrong in writing a research paper and how applying a version of the six strategies for analyzing sources can be used to remedy the problems.

The Flight from Teaching

[1] The "flight from teaching" (Smith 6) in higher education is a controversial issue of the academic world. The amount of importance placed on research and publishing is the major cause of this flight. I will show different views and aspects concerning the problem plaguing our colleges and universities, through the authors whom I have consulted. [The introductory paragraph needs to be revised to eliminate prejudgment. Calling the issue "controversial" implies that there are different points of view on the subject. The writer, however, offers only one and words it in a way that suggests she has already leaped to a premature and oversimplified conclusion. Instead, she needs to better frame the issue and then replace the procedural opening (see Chapter 8) with a more hypothetical working thesis that will enable her to explore the subject.]

[2] Page Smith takes an in-depth look at the "flight from teaching" in *Killing the Spirit*. Smith's views on this subject are interesting, because he is a professor with tenure at UCLA. Throughout the book, Smith stresses the sentiment of the student being the enemy, as expressed by many of his colleagues. Some professors resent the fact that the students take up their precious time—time that could be better used for research. Smith goes on about how much some of his colleagues go out of their way to avoid their students. They go as far as making strange office hours to avoid contact. Smith disagrees with the hands-off approach being taken by the professors: "There is no decent, adequate, respectable education, in the proper sense of that much-abused word, without personal involvement by a teacher with the needs and concerns, academic and personal, of his/her students. All the rest is 'instruction' or 'information transferal,' 'communication technique,' or some other impersonal and antiseptic phrase, but it is not teaching and the student is not truly learning" (7). [The writer summarizes and quotes one of her sources but does not analyze or offer any perspective on it.]

[3] Page Smith devotes a chapter to the ideal of "publish or perish," "since teaching is shunned in the name of research." Smith refutes the idea that "research enhances teaching" and that there is a "direct relationship between research and teaching" (178). In actuality, research inhibits teaching. The research that is being done, in most cases, is too specialized for the student. As with teaching and research, Smith believes there is not necessarily a relationship between research and publication. Unfortunately those professors who are devoted to teaching find themselves without a job and/or tenure unless they conform to the requirements of publishing. Smith asks, "Is not the atmosphere hopelessly polluted when professors are forced to do research in order to validate themselves, in order to make a living, in order to avoid being humiliated (and terminated)?" (197). Not only are the students and the professors suffering, but also as a whole, "Under the publish-or-perish standard, the university is perishing" (180). [The writer continues her summary of her source, using language that implies but does not make explicit her apparent agreement with it. She appears to use the source to speak for her but has not clearly distinguished her voice from that of her source. See, for example, the third sentence and the last sentence of the paragraph. Is the writer only reporting what Smith says or appropriating his view as her own?]

[4] Charles J. Sykes looks at the "flight from teaching" in *Profscam: Professors and the Demise of Higher Education*. Sykes cites statistics to show the results of the reduction of professors' teaching loads enabling them time for more research. The call to research is the cause of many problems. The reduced number of professors actually teaching increases both the size of classes and the likelihood that students will find at registration that their courses are closed. Students will also find they do not have to write papers, and often exams are multiple choice, because of the large classes. Consequently, the effects of the "flight from teaching" have "had dramatic ramifications for the way undergraduates are taught" (40). [The writer summarizes another of her sources without analysis of its reasoning and again blurs the distinction between the source's position and her own.]

[5] E. Peter Volpe, in his chapter "Teaching, Research, and Service: Union or Coexistence?" in the book *Whose Goals for American Higher Education?*, disagrees strongly that there is an overemphasis on research. Volpe believes that only the research scholar can provide the best form of teaching because "Teaching and research are as inseparable as the two faces of the same coin" (80). The whole idea of education is to increase the student's curiosity. When the enthusiasm of the professor, because of his or her research, is brought into the classroom, it intensifies that curiosity and therefore provides "the deepest kind of intellectual enjoyment" (80). Volpe provides suggestions for

solving the rift between students and professors, such as "replacing formal discourse by informal seminars and independent study programs" (81). He feels that this will get students to think for themselves and professors to learn to communicate with students again. Another suggestion is that the government provide funding for "research programs that are related to the education function" (82). This would allow students the opportunity to share in the research. In conclusion, Volpe states his thesis to be, "A professor in any discipline stays alive when he carries his enthusiasm for discovery into the classroom. The professor is academically dead when the spark of inquiry is extinguished within him. It is then that he betrays his student. The student becomes merely an acquirer of knowledge rather than an inquirer into knowledge" (80). [Here the writer summarizes a source that offers an opposing point of view. It is good that she has begun to represent multiple perspectives, but as with the preceding summaries, there is not yet enough analysis. If she could put Volpe's argument into active conversation with those of Sykes and Smith, she might be able to articulate more clearly the assumptions her sources share and to distinguish their key differences. How, for example, do the three sources differ in their definitions of research and of teaching?]

[6] The "flight from teaching" is certainly a problem in colleges and universities. When beginning to research this topic, I had some very definite opinions. I believed that research and publication should not play any role in teaching. Through the authors utilized in this paper and other sources, I have determined that there is a need for some "research" but not to the extent that teaching is pushed aside. College and universities exist to provide an education; therefore, their first responsibility is to the student. [Here the writer begins to offer her opinion of the material, which she does, in effect, by choosing sides. She appears to be compromising—"there is a need for some 'research' but not to the extent that teaching is pushed aside"—but as her last sentence shows, she has in fact dismissed the way that Volpe complicates the relationship between teaching and research.]

[7] I agree with Smith that research, such as reading in the professor's field, is beneficial to his or her teaching. But requiring research to the extent of publication in order to secure a tenured position is actually denying education to both the professors and their students. I understand that some of the pressure stems from the fact that it is easier to decide tenure by the "tangible" evidence of research and publication. The emphasis on "publish or perish" should revert to "teach or perish" (Smith 6). If more of an effort is required to base tenure upon teaching, then that effort should be made. After all, it is the education of the people of our nation that is at risk. [The writer continues to align herself with one side of the issue, which she continues to summarize but not to raise questions about.]

[8] In conclusion, I believe that the problem of the "flight from teaching" can and must be addressed. The continuation of the problem will lead to greater damage in the academic community. The leaders of our colleges and universities will need to take the first steps toward a solution. [The writer concludes with a more strongly worded version of her endorsement of the position of Smith and Sykes on the threat of research to teaching. Notice that the paper has not really evolved from the unanalyzed position it articulated in paragraph 2.]

D. STRATEGIES FOR WRITING AND REVISING RESEARCH PAPERS

Here we offer some general strategies gleaned from and keyed to our analysis of a typical paper, "The Flight from Teaching," that can be applied to any research project.

1. **Be sure to make clear who is talking.** When, for example, the writer refers to the professors' concern for their "precious time" in paragraph 2 or when she writes that "In actuality, research inhibits teaching" in paragraph 3, is she simply summarizing Smith or endorsing his position? You can easily clarify who's saying what by inserting attributive tag phrases such as "in Smith's view" or "in response to Smith, one might argue that." Remember that your role is to provide explanation of and perspective on the ideas in your source—not, especially early on, to cheerlead for it or attack it.

2. **Analyze as you go along rather than saving analysis for the end (disciplinary conventions permitting).** It is no coincidence that a research paper that summarizes its sources and delays discussing them, as "The Flight from Teaching" does, should have difficulty constructing a logically coherent and analytically revealing point of view. The *organization* of this research paper interferes with the writer's ability to have ideas about her material because the gap is too wide between the presentation and analysis of her sources. As a result, readers are left unsure how to interpret the positions she initially summarizes, and her analysis, by the time she finally gets to it, is too general.

3. **Quote *in order to* analyze: make your sources speak.** Even if the language you quote or paraphrase seems clear in what it means to you, the aim of your analysis is to put what you have quoted or paraphrased into some kind of frame or perspective. Quoting is a powerful form of evidence, but recognize that you can quote *very* selectively—a sentence or even a phrase will often suffice. After you quote, you will usually need to paraphrase in order to discover and articulate the implications of the quotation's key terms. *As a general rule, you should not end a discussion with a quotation but rather with some point you want to make about the quotation.*

    The following sentence from the second paragraph of "The Flight from Teaching" demonstrates the missed opportunities for analysis that occur when a quotation is allowed to speak for itself.

> Smith disagrees with the hands-off approach being taken by the pro-
> fessors: "There is no decent, adequate, respectable education, in the
> proper sense of that much-abused word, without personal involvement
> by a teacher with the needs and concerns, academic and personal, of
> his/her students" (7).

This sentence is offered as part of a neutral summary of Smith's position, which, the writer informs us "disagrees with the hands-off approach." But notice how Smith's word choices convey additional information about his point of view. The repetition of "personal" and the quarrelsome tone of "much-abused" suggest that Smith is writing a polemic—that he is so pre-occupied with the personal that he wishes to restrict the definition of education to it. The writer may agree with Smith's extreme position, but the point is that if she attends to his actual language, she will be able to charac-terize that position much more accurately.

By contrast, notice how the writer in the following example quotes *in order to* analyze the implications of the source's language:

> If allegations that top levels of U.S. and British governments acted
> covertly to shape foreign policy are truthful, then this scandal, according
> to Friedman, poses serious questions concerning American democracy.
> Friedman explains, "The government's lack of accountability, either to
> Congress or to the public, was so egregious as to pose a silent threat to
> the principles of American democracy" (286). The word "principles" is
> especially important. In Friedman's view, without fundamental ideals such
> as a democracy based on rule by elected representatives *and* the people,
> where does the average citizen stand? What will happen to faith in the
> government, Friedman seems to be asking, if elected representatives
> such as the president sully that respected office?

By emphasizing Friedman's word choice ("principles"), this writer uses quotation not only to convey information but also to frame it, making a point about the source's point of view.

4. **Try converting key assertions in the source into questions.** When you are under the spell of a source, its claims sound more final and unquestionably true than they actually are. So, a useful habit of mind is to experiment with rewording selected assertions as questions. Consider, for example, what the writer of "The Flight from Teaching" might have dis-covered had she tried converting the following conclusions (in paragraph 4) drawn from one of her sources into questions.

> The call to research is the cause of many problems. The reduced number
> of professors actually teaching increases both the size of classes and the
> likelihood that students will find at registration that their courses are closed.
> Students will also find they do not have to write papers, and often exams
> are multiple choice, because of the large classes.

Some questions: Is it only professors' desire to be off doing their own research that explains closed courses, large class sizes, and multiple-choice tests? What about other causes for these problems, such as the cost of hiring additional professors or the pressure universities put on professors to publish in order to increase the status of the institution? We are not suggesting that the writer should have detected these particular problems in the passage but rather that she needs, somewhere in the paper, to *raise questions about the reasoning implicit in her sources*.

By *querying how your sources are defining, implicitly and explicitly, their key terms*, you can gain perspective on the sources, uncovering their assumptions. Consider in this context the writer's own fullest statement of her thesis.

> Through the authors utilized in this paper and other sources, I have determined that there is a need for some 'research' but not to the extent that teaching is pushed aside. Colleges and universities exist to provide an education; therefore, their first responsibility is to the student (paragraph 6).

More questions: What do she and her sources mean by "research" and what do they mean by "teaching"? To what extent can the writer fairly assume that the primary purpose of universities is and should be "to provide an education"? Can't an education include being mentored in the skills that university teachers practice in their own research? And isn't teaching only one of a variety of contributions that universities make to the cultures they serve?

5. **Get your sources to converse with one another, and actively referee the conflicts among them.** By doing so, you will often find the means to reorganize your paper around issues rather than leave readers to locate these issues for themselves as you move from source to source. Both looking for difference within similarity and looking for similarity despite difference are useful for this purpose. (See Chapter 4.)

The organizing contrast that drives "The Flight from Teaching" is obviously that between teaching and research, but what if the writer actively sought out an unexpected similarity that spanned this binary? For example, Smith asserts that "research inhibits teaching" (paragraph 3), whereas Volpe contends that "only the research scholar can provide the best form of teaching because 'teaching and research are as inseparable as the two faces of the same coin'" (paragraph 5). But both sides *agree* that educating students is the "first responsibility" of colleges and universities, despite differing radically on how this responsibility is best fulfilled. Given this unexpected similarity, the writer could then explore the significance of the difference—that Smith believes professors' research gets in the way of excellent teaching, whereas Volpe believes research is essential to it. If the writer had brought these sources into dialogue, she could have discovered that the assertion she offers as her conclusion is, in fact, inaccurate, even an evasion.

By way of conclusion, we would like to emphasize that these five strategies share a common aim: to get you off the hot seat of judging the experts when you are not an expert. Most of us are more comfortable in situations in which we can converse amicably rather than judge and be judged. Think of that as you embark on research projects, and you will be far more likely to learn and to have a good time doing it.

AN ANALYTICAL RESEARCH PAPER: A GOOD EXAMPLE

What does an effective analytical research paper look like? Look at the following piece, which demonstrates the analytical skills we discuss in this chapter. We include brief commentary at the ends of selected paragraphs, but for the most part, you should notice how the writer uses her sources to focus questions, analyzing as she goes along. Also, note her habitual use of complicating evidence to evolve the conversation she is having with her sources.

Horizontal & Vertical Mergers Within the Healthcare Industry

[1] The United States healthcare industry is constantly changing, as new ideas and strategies are developed to make healthcare more accessible and affordable for a greater number of people. Mergers within the industry are one of the new influential methods of altering the relationship between buyers and sellers of healthcare. Mergers distort the traditional roles of physicians, hospitals, and patients, but do so with an emphasis on cost-cutting, more efficient management, and better quality of care. Whether these mergers actually succeed in their outward goals is debatable; many studies have shown that these acquisitions seldom fully meet their objectives. Mergers are business deals, occurring in every market. But the healthcare market is unique in that its product, a necessity, often becomes an economic luxury—not everyone can afford the costs of medical coverage or care. [The introduction opens with a clear premise—constant change—and rapidly limits the focus to mergers as one cause of change. The writer raises but does not prematurely resolve the question of mergers' successes and ends the paragraph by distinguishing what is at stake in her topic.]

[2] The first distinct type of acquisition is known as a horizontal merger. It describes the joining of two hospital systems into one. Some simple examples of horizontal mergers include the transaction between Memorial Health System and Adventist Health System, both located in Florida: the four-hospital Memorial purchased the thirty-two-hospital Adventist in late August, 2000. Another example is the purchase of St. Mary Medical Hospital by Trinity Health, in separate parts of Michigan, completed in July 2000. In this case, the new hospital system was renamed St. Mary Mercy Hospital.[1] There are advantages and disadvantages to horizontal mergers, which will be explored, but a hospital system's main objectives in merging include reducing managerial costs, combining marketing efforts, pooling capital, and reducing excess equipment. [Having used a panning shot to establish context in the first paragraph, the writer now tracks one kind of merger and suggests that further debate is to come.]

---

[1] "Mergers & Acquisitions," *Business Watch*: July 2000, p. 63.

[3] A vertical merger, however, is one in which a company is bought by another company within the same "supply chain" – that is, a firm might purchase its merchandise supplier.[2] In healthcare economies, this applies to suppliers and buyers of healthcare services, such as hospitals and HMO's, or hospitals and physicians. There are several complications to vertical mergers, especially apparent when the level of competition between the two merging entities is explored. Esther Gal-Or's article, "The Profitability of Vertical Mergers Between Hospitals and Physician Practices," will be used to illustrate these complications. [The writer begins to foreground a complication that she will develop into an organizing contrast in the next paragraph, that between private profit and public good.]

[4] The selling point for all horizontal and vertical mergers is the expected increase in efficiency under the new system. But mergers benefit the merging parties immensely; are their public goals of efficiency and, in turn, lowered costs, really being achieved? In their article, "Are Multihospital Systems More Efficient?" economists Dranove, Durkac, and Shanley write that although "the conventional wisdom is that [horizontal mergers] will generate efficiencies in the production of services, surprisingly little systematic evidence exists to support this view."[3] By studying local Californian hospital systems in the 1980's and 1990's, the three researchers found that "the benefits of horizontal integration stem from greater efficiencies in marketing hospital systems . . . than from efficiencies in the production of services." [The writer uses sources to frame questions. She then cites sources offering slightly different answers to the question of efficiency.]

[5] Using data from the California Office of Statewide Health Planning and Development, the researchers selected eleven hospital systems that met their requirements for inclusion in the study. After investigating costs per admission, administrative costs, price/cost margins, and limitations, the research "[challenged the idea] that horizontally integrated hospitals generate production efficiencies." More specifically, the study showed that the multihospital systems did not consistently reduce high-tech services, or have lower patient costs. In fact, the study concluded that "integrated hospital systems are more likely than their nonintegrated hospital counterparts to have unusually high administrative costs" and that they had "unusually high price/cost margins and operating profits."[4] These findings raise questions as to why hospitals merge if a merger does not provide a substantial increase in the method of operation's efficiency. If it actually results in higher costs for consumers in certain instances, what benefit does a

---

[2] Ibid, 1.
[3] Dranove, Durkac, Shanley. "Are Multihospital Systems More Efficient?" *Health Affairs*: Volume 15, 1996.
[4] Ibid, 102.

merger bring? [The writer again uses her sources to focus relevant questions. Notice how she moves beyond what one of her sources says to query what it suggests.]

[6] The instance is similar with vertical mergers. Many times, the joining of a hospital and HMO plan or hospital and physician practice does not result in the expected lowered costs and higher quality care for consumers. In her article "The Profitability of Vertical Mergers Between Hospitals and Physician Practices," Esther Gal-Or outlines her complex and thorough study of vertical mergers. Gal-Or details several different facets of the vertical merger: there are possible restrictions that these new systems face, all of which jeopardize their original intent for efficiency. She also notes the importance of the competition between the two, writing

> When the degree of competitiveness [between the hospital and physician practice] is comparable, a vertical merger enhances the bargaining position of both merging parties vis-à-vis insurers. In contrast, when one provider's market is much more competitive than the other a vertical merger may reduce the joint profits of the merged entity.[5]

Therefore, the success of a vertical merger depends upon the relationship between the two merging parties. [Here the writer leads with similarity despite difference to get her to her next source, which she briefly summarizes before zooming on a selected piece. Her final sentence draws a conclusion from the quotation, though more analysis of it might have enriched the conversation.]

[7] Two examples noted in Gal-Or's study show the types of vertical mergers that are changing U.S. healthcare today. One of these is Allina Health System, a Minnesota-based system that covers over 25% of the state's residents through its HMO and PPO plans. A 1994 merger between a hospital chain and a health plan, Allina is continuing to acquire more hospitals and physician practices. Blue Cross of Western Pennsylvania, another example in the article, has also been purchasing physician practices.[6] Gal-Or's study eventually finds that when "two providers' markets are characterized by comparable degrees of competitiveness . . . both the merging hospital and the merging physician can negotiate higher rates with insurers . . . . Consumers are obviously worse off, as a result, since the higher rates translate to higher premia charged by insurers."[7] This offers a major criticism of vertical mergers because consumers are surely not looking to raise the cost of their premiums. These mergers, especially with the

---

[5] Gal-Or, Esther. "The Profitability of Vertical Mergers Between Hospitals and Physician Practices. *Journal of Health Economics*: October 1999, p.623.
[6] Ibid, 624.
[7] Ibid, 625.

evidence provided in this article, seem to benefit the suppliers of healthcare but only at the financial expense of the patients. [Using representative examples from her source, the writer interprets significant detail to draw a conclusion.]

[8] By contrast, in a study entitled "What Types of Hospital Mergers Save Consumers Money," four researchers studied 3,500 United States hospitals from 1986–1994, including 122 horizontal mergers. Their study found that the mergers saved consumers by approximately 7%, which may show that vertical mergers (which also accounted for a large section of the systems studied) do reduce costs to consumers.[8] [The paper pauses here to introduce complicating evidence, which leads to a brief concession (see Chapter 9). Note how the writer qualifies it with her choice of the word "may."]

[9] Mergers, especially between hospitals, also provoke an interesting ethical dilemma. Special interest groups like Planned Parenthood and the American Civil Liberties Union (ACLU) have recently argued that these mergers are being treated as business contracts between two "sellers" and that the emphasis on providing better coverage for all has been disregarded. They argue that mergers aim not to help consumers, but to reduce internal costs and therefore raise profits for the hospitals. There are two aspects of hospital mergers that most concern these groups: first, the acquisition between religious and non-religious health facilities, resulting in religiously restrictive hospital systems, and, second, the possibility of a system becoming the only option for patients in rural communities. The ACLU recently released the following:

> Many nonsectarian hospitals have recently been merging with religiously controlled hospitals. As a condition of the merger . . . these hospitals observe religious prohibitions against providing certain health services. The most publicized and significant prohibitions are found in the *Ethical and Religious Directives for Catholic Health Care Services*. . . . The *Directives* bar Catholic health care facilities from providing tubal ligation, vasectomy, abortion, in vitro fertilization, contraception, and emergency contraception in the case of rape.[9]

[Notice the evolving conversation, as the writer shifts from economic issues to the ethics these issues entail. Also note her habitual focus on complication, citing the "aspects that most concern."]

[10] In many instances, even when a Catholic hospital is acquired by a non-religious facility, the terms of the agreement include the system's

---

[8] "Which Types of Hospital Mergers Save Consumers Money?" *Health Affairs:* Volume 16, p. 62–74.
[9] "Hospital Mergers: The Threat to Reproductive Health Services." www.aclu.org.

adherence to these Catholic provisions. A statement from Planned Parenthood notes, "a Catholic hospital, or an HMO contracted with a Catholic hospital, is a community's only provider—leaving women with little or no access to reproductive health services."[10] For some, the decision to choose a hospital is religiously motivated; for others, especially women, they believe it is a personal right to have access to these reproductive health services. The ACLU and Planned Parenthood, however, feel strongly that it is a patient's right to choose whether or not to use these specific services. They also feel that mergers between hospitals jeopardize that right by creating a system in which certain services may not be available, regardless of patient preference. [The conversation continues to evolve as the writer introduces new complicating evidence ("the second ethical issue") and analyzes its implications. Notice as well the diverse range of sources she has brought to bear.]

[11] This argument is closely related to the second ethical issue against horizontal hospital mergers. In more rural communities, where there may be few options from which medical care consumers can choose, mergers create a monopolistic environment. The ACLU states that "low-income women and women in rural areas with few choices in medical care are the most vulnerable . . . Women who live in rural communities frequently have little choice . . . ."[11] This is detrimental to consumer choice because mergers in rural communities most likely create only one hospital system. A dissatisfied consumer in this situation does not have the power to switch medical suppliers; the power is taken away from the consumer and the seller has the ultimate control over the cost, type, and quality of care. Mergers in rural communities greatly resemble a monopolistic market force, and for this reason, are often the targets of antitrust cases against the new hospital system.

[12] The issue of antitrust violations frequently arises regarding mergers in the healthcare industry. This, too, is a criticism of the acquisitions. The majority of the antitrust cases in the United States involve horizontal mergers because, often, they produce one hospital system that borders closely on the definition of a monopoly. But there have also been antitrust questions raised regarding vertical mergers. The Marshfield Clinic case, from 1996, shows some of the questions. The Marshfield Clinic was a physician-owned clinic in Wisconsin that had vertically integrated with its HMO. But in the merger, the clinic had also excluded Blue Cross/Blue Shield HMO coverage from its services. Eventually, the courts found in favor of the Marshfield Clinic because its HMO obviously did not have the power to eliminate Blue Cross/Blue Shield from the healthcare market. [As has been the case

---

[10] "Opposing Dangerous Hospital Mergers." www.plannedparenthood.org.
[11] "Hospital Mergers: The Threat to Reproductive Health Services." www.aclu.org.

throughout the paper, the writer continues to focus on the important questions raised by her representative examples.]

[13] The most recent development in the antitrust cases of hospital mergers is the influential lobby groups, petitioning state governments on behalf of the hospital systems to exempt mergers within the medical industry from antitrust laws. The state of Maine lately encountered such a request. The 565-bed Maine Medical Center, in an effort to merge with two other hospitals, successfully lobbied the state government in 1996 to pass legislation exempting hospitals from state antitrust laws. Since the enactment of the Maine law, nearly twelve other states have also passed laws to free multihospital systems from antitrust regulations.[12] These laws have significant implications for the future of horizontal hospital mergers. They create a safer environment for mergers to occur: without antitrust laws, hospitals can freely merge and even assume a monopolistic form that jeopardizes the market of healthcare. [As the paper approaches its end, the writer cites the "most recent" developments and opens out the conversation to "significant implications for the future."]

[14] The advantages for horizontal and vertical mergers seem clear – by combining efforts, and creating one system, a multihospital facility should manage its administrative duties more efficiently, provide a higher level of care, and lower costs for its patients. Mergers should make the healthcare industry more successfully directed. The ultimate aim of any improvement or change in the industry should be to make better healthcare more accessible to a broader number of Americans. It appears as though horizontal and vertical mergers have the opposite effect on the industry. Their failure to provide a more efficient means of business and the way multihospital systems capitalize on reduced costs by simply earning a larger profit show that these mergers serve the providers, not the consumers. Additionally, multihospital systems jeopardize choices in care for those patients who would want specific services (which might not be available from a large system, religiously controlled). They also create a monopoly for consumers geographically distant from other choices. The horizontal and vertical mergers within the medical care market have not met expectations; instead, they reduce medical choices for consumers, do not guarantee increased efficiency, and create additional profits for the hospitals, physicians, and insurance companies involved. [The paper concludes by coming full circle—back to change—and focusing on an unexpected similarity between horizontal and vertical mergers that leads her to take a stand in the debate that the paper's sources have been staging.]

---

[12] "Smaller Hospitals Quicker to Use Maine Merger Law." *Modern Healthcare*: October 7, 1996.

◖ ASSIGNMENTS: Exercises in Researched Writing

At the end of the next chapter, we place a research sequence that makes use of the skills discussed in both chapters.

1. Here are a series of exercises organized in ascending order of complexity that go into writing a researched paper. You can practice these one at a time, and then learn to put them together.

   a. Compose an analytical summary of a single source (try ranking).

   b. Write about a primary source using a single secondary source as a lens.

   c. Compose a comparative analytical summary of two sources (try difference within similarity or similarity despite difference).

   d. Write a synthesis that brings together three or more sources, using them to raise questions and allowing each to help you complicate positions in the others (as the paper on mergers in healthcare does).

2. Here are a set of writing assignments, each using a strategy discussed in the chapter. The skills called for in the following sequence are also discussed in Chapter 4, "Reading: How to Do It and What to Do with It."

   a. Practice making quotations speak by using paraphrase as a means of uncovering assumptions and bringing out implications. Use this method to zoom in on how sources define key terms.

   b. Practice putting two or more sources in conversation with each other: figure out how each source might see and recast the other's ideas. Construct and referee a conversation among your sources.

   c. Practice finding your voice in the conversation: take a source and apply it to another context, or locate a point it makes but does not dwell on and develop it further.

   d. Repeatedly do the two "Try this" exercises on passage-based focused freewriting contained in this chapter (12.2 and 12.3). Make these into regular exercises—habits of mind. Also apply the heuristic "Looking for Patterns of Repetition and Contrast" (see Chapter 2) as a means of developing a more detailed and in-depth knowledge of your source and what is at stake in it. ▮

GUIDELINES FOR WRITING THE RESEARCHED PAPER

1. Avoid the temptation to plug in sources as answers. Aim for a *conversation* with them. Think of sources as voices inviting you into a community of interpretation, discussion, and debate.

2. Quote, paraphrase, or summarize *in order to* analyze. Explain what you take the source to mean, showing the reasoning that has led to the conclusion you draw from it.

GUIDELINES FOR WRITING THE RESEARCHED PAPER (CONTINUED)

3. Quote sparingly. You are usually better off centering your analysis on a few quotations, analyzing their key terms, and branching out to aspects of your subject that the quotations illuminate.

4. Don't underestimate the value of close paraphrasing. You will almost invariably begin to interpret a source once you start paraphrasing its key language.

5. Locate and highlight what is at stake in your source. Which of its points does the source find most important? What positions does it want to modify or refute, and why?

6. Look for ways to develop, modify, or apply what a source has said, rather than simply agreeing or disagreeing with it.

7. If you challenge a position found in a source, be sure to represent it fairly. First, give the source some credit by identifying assumptions you share with it. Then, isolate the part that you intend to complicate or dispute.

8. Look for sources that address your subject from different perspectives. Avoid relying too heavily on any one source.

9. When your sources disagree, consider playing mediator. Instead of immediately agreeing with one or the other, clarify areas of agreement and disagreement among them.

This chapter shifts attention to more technical matters associated with writing the researched paper, including finding and citing sources. Although doing conventional library research has obviously changed a lot since the advent of computers, many of the basic strategies remain the same. More than just mechanically gathering information, research continues to be a primary means of discovering the ongoing conflicts about a subject and having ideas about it. Engaging the information sparks thinking, not just arranging.

The core of this chapter is a discussion of research methodologies written by a reference librarian. It offers a wealth of insider's tips for making more productive use of your research time, especially online and with databases. Among the featured topics are the following:

- **How to assess a web page, including how to find out more about its author's credentials**
- **How to search databases by subject heading in addition to keyword**
- **Where to find full-text databases in different disciplines**
- **The best subject-specific databases by discipline**
- **A "Fool-Proof Recipe for Great Research—Every Time"**
- **Where to find citation guides on the web**

The chapter also offers sections on the following topics:

- How to cite secondary sources in MLA and APA style
- How to integrate source material smoothly into your own prose while clearly distinguishing it from your comments about it
- What plagiarism is and isn't, and how to avoid it
- How to compose abstracts of sources

A. GETTING STARTED

The problem with doing research in the Information Age is that there is so much information available. How do you know which information is considered respectable in a particular discipline and which isn't? How can you avoid wasting time with source materials that have been effectively refuted and replaced by subsequent thinking? A short answer to these questions is that you should start not in the stacks but in the reference room of your library or with its electronic equivalent.

If you start with specialized dictionaries, abstracts, and bibliographies, you can rapidly gain both a broad perspective on your subject and a summary of what particular sources contain. This is the purpose of the reference room: it offers sources that review and summarize material for you in shorthand forms. In any case, you should take care not to get bogged down in one author's book-length argument until you've achieved a wider view of how other sources treat your subject.

You should be aware that reference sources use agreed-upon keywords for different subjects. Thus, don't be surprised if the subject headings you enter initially yield nothing. Always check first at the reference desk for the *Library of Congress Subject Headings* to see what headings might be appropriate for your subject. It will tell you, for example, that fraternities and sororities are listed not under "fraternities and sororities" but rather under "Greek letter organizations."

Ask your reference librarian to direct you to the printed and online *indexes, bibliographies, specialized dictionaries,* and compilations of *abstracts* that are pertinent to your subject or discipline. An index offers a list of titles directing you to scholarly journals; often this list is sufficient to give you a clearer idea of the kinds of topics about which writers in the field are conversing. Here are a few index titles, indicating the range of what's available: *Applied Science and Technology Index, Art Index, Biography Index, Business Periodicals Index, Education Index, General Science Index, Humanities Index, Literary Criticism Index, New York Times Index, Philosopher's Index, Religion Index, Reader's Guide to Periodical Literature,* and *Social Sciences Index.*

> *A half-hour spent with a reference librarian can save you a half a day wandering randomly though the stacks.*

Compilations of abstracts and annotated bibliographies provide more information—anywhere from a few sentences to a few pages that summarize each source. (See the section on abstracts and how to write them at the end of this chapter.) Here are a few commonly used titles: *Abstracts of English Studies, Chemical Abstracts, Communication Abstracts, Dissertation Abstracts, Historical Abstracts, MLA (Modern Language Association) International Bibliography, Psychological Abstracts, Monthly Catalog of United States Government Publications, Sociological Abstracts.*

Specialized dictionaries and encyclopedias are sometimes extraordinarily useful in sketching the general terrain for a subject, and they often include bibliographical leads as well. Here are some titles, ranging from the expected to the eccentric: *Dictionary of the History of Ideas, Dictionary of Literary Biography, Encyclopedia of American History, Encyclopedia of Bioethics, Encyclopedia of Crime and Justice, Encyclopedia of Economics, Encyclopedia of Native American Religions, Encyclopedia of Philosophy, Encyclopedia of Psychology, Encyclopedia of Unbelief, Encyclopedia of World Art, Encyclopedic Dictionary of Mathematics, Macmillan Encyclopedia of Computers, Encyclopedia of Medical History, McGraw Hill Encyclopedia of Science and Technology, New Grove Dictionary of Music and Musicians, Oxford English Dictionary.*

Most of the indexes just listed also include book reviews. The *Reader's Guide to Periodical Literature* will locate reviews as well as articles in popular—general audience—publications such as *Time* and *Newsweek*. For a broader range of titles, you might also consult *Book Review Index*, *Book Review Digest*, and *Subject Guide to Books in Print*. Indexes organized by discipline are more likely to take you to sources reviewed in academic journals; consult with your reference librarian for the indexes most pertinent to your subject.

Periodicals and journals offer an effective next step in finding sources once you've surveyed your topic in digest form. These are generally more up to date than either reference materials or books. Most library reference rooms have either a booklet that lists all of the periodicals and journals to which the library subscribes or a means of accessing a list of such holdings through the electronic catalogue. There are thousands of specialized journals available. If an index or bibliography refers you to a journal that your library does not hold, the library can usually get it for you (sometimes for a small fee) through a service known as interlibrary loan. Now, many articles and reviews can be downloaded electronically; see the next section entitled "Electronic Research: Finding Quality on the Web."

A FEW RULES OF THUMB FOR GETTING STARTED

We might generalize a rule voiced by the psychology professor on the next page: Start in the present and work backward. Usually the most current materials will include bibliographical citations that can help you identify the most important sources in the past. Along the same lines, you are usually better off starting with journal articles rather than books, because they are more current.

> *Start in the present and work backward. The most current materials include citations that identify the most important sources in the past.*

As a second rule of thumb, the reliability of the source is always an issue, but what's most important is knowing its slant. For example, *Newsweek* can be a useful source if you want evidence about popular understanding of a subject or issue, but in this case, the fact that the material comes from *Newsweek* and thus represents a position aimed at a mainstream, nonacademic audience provides the central reason for citing it. The evidence is *always* qualified by the frame.

> *The reliability of the source is always an issue, but what's most important is knowing its slant. There is no such thing as neutral information; it's always framed, and so it always has, at least implicity, a point of view.*

The matter of deciding what kinds of sources are best suited to your topic and how to discern their point of view is the subject of the following section, written by a reference librarian, on using and evaluating sources via the computer. And let us say here that as a final rule of thumb for doing research economically, a half-hour spent with a reference librarian in the reference collection before you go randomly through the stacks collecting books is always time well spent.

VOICES FROM ACROSS THE CURRICULUM

Tips for Starting Your Research

A useful research technique is to begin with indexes that will take you to specialized periodicals rather than beginning with books. Most scholarly journals have an index in the last issue for each year. Listed alphabetically by author, subject, or title are articles for a given year. Also, you may want to use any number of indexes. Here you look up a key word or phrase (of your choosing), and the index tells you when, what, where, and so forth for the word/phrase. Some of the key indexes are: *Social Science Index, Wall Street Journal Index* (for *WSJ* stories), *New York Times Index* (for *NYT* stories), and the *Public Affairs Information Service.*

A critical part of the bibliographic effort is to find a topic on which there are materials. Most topics can be researched. The key is to choose a flexible keyword/phrase and then try out different versions of it. For example, a bibliography on "women in management" might lead you to look up *women, females, business* (women in), *business* (females in), *gender in the workplace, sexism and the workplace, careers* (of men, of women, in business), *women and CEOs, women in management, affirmative action and women, women in corporations, female accountants,* and so forth. Be imaginative and flexible. A little bit of time with some of the indexes, listed earlier, will provide you with a wealth of sources.

—Frederick Norling, Professor of Business

Use quality psychological references. That is, use references that professional psychologists use and regard highly. *Psychology Today* is not a good reference; *Newsweek* and *Reader's Digest* are worse. And don't even think about the *National Enquirer.* APA journals, such as the *Journal of Abnormal Psychology,* on the other hand, are excellent.

In looking for reference material, be sure to search under several headings. For example, look under *depression, affective disorders,* and *mood disorders.*

Books (e.g., *The Handbook of Affective Disorders*) are often very helpful, especially for giving a general overview of a topic. Books addressing a professional audience are generally preferable to those addressing a general, popular audience.

Finally, references should be reasonably current. In general, the newer, the better. For example, with rare exceptions (classic articles), articles from before 1970 are outdated and so should not be used.

—Alan Tjeltveit, Professor of Psychology

B. ELECTRONIC RESEARCH: FINDING QUALITY ON THE WEB

By Kelly Cannon, Reference Librarian

The Internet has dramatically altered public access to information. But the quality of information has also changed; it is almost as easy to publish on the web as it is to surf it. A general caveat might well be Reader Beware.

Take as an example *Martinlutherking.org* (http://www.martinlutherking.org). This site appears prominently in any web search for information about Martin Luther King, Jr. The website is visually appealing, claiming to include "essays, speeches, sermons, and more." But who created the site? As it turns out, after a little digging (see Tips #1 and #2 later in the chapter), the site is sponsored by Stormfront, Inc. (http://stormfront.org/), an organization out of West Palm Beach, Florida, serving "those courageous men and women fighting to preserve their White Western culture, ideals and freedom of speech." This author is concealed behind the work, a ghost writer of sorts. While the site is at one's fingertips, identifying the author is a challenge, more so than in the world of print publications, where author and publisher are located on the same pages as the title. For those websites with no visible author, no publishing house, no recognized journal title, no peer-review process, and no library selection process (the touchstones of scholarship in the print world), seemingly easy Internet research is now more problematic: the user must discern for him- or herself what is and is not authoritative information.

UNDERSTANDING DOMAIN NAMES

But how is the user to begin evaluating a web document? Fortunately, there are several clues to assist you through the Internet labyrinth. One clue is in the web address itself. For example, the *Internet Movie Database* has http://imdb.com as its web address (also known as URL, or uniform resource locator). One clue lies at the very end of the URL, in what is known as the domain name, in this case the abbreviation ".com." Websites ending in ".com" are commercial, often with the purpose of marketing a product. Sites ending in ".org" generally signal nonprofits, but many have a veiled agenda, whether it is marketing or politics. Like the ".coms," ".org" addresses are sold first-come first-served. (The organization that oversees the many vendors of ".com" and ".org" domain names is The Internet Corporation for Assigned Names and Numbers, or ICANN [http://www.icann.org/].)

On the other hand, ".edu" and ".gov" sites may indicate less bias, as they are ostensibly limited exclusively to educational and government institutions, and they are often the producers of bonafide research. In particular, ".gov" sites contain some of the best information on the Internet. This is in part because the U.S. government is required by an act of Congress to disseminate to the general public a large portion of its research. The U.S. government, floated as it is by tax dollars, provides the high-quality, free websites reminiscent of the precommercial Internet era. This means that government sites offer high-quality data, particularly of a statistical nature. Scholars in the areas of business, law, and the social sciences can benefit tremendously, without subscription fees, from a variety of government databases. Prime examples are the legislative site known as *Thomas* (http://thomas.loc.gov) and data gathered at the website of the Census Bureau (http://www.census.gov).

PRINT COROLLARIES

But a domain name can be misleading; it is simply one clue in the process of evaluation. Another clue, perhaps more significant, is the correlation between a website and the print world. Many websites offer print corollaries, and some have print equivalents. For example, Johns Hopkins University Press now publishes all its journals, known and respected for years by scholars, in both print and electronic formats. Many college and university libraries subscribe to these Johns Hopkins journals electronically, collectively known as *Project Muse* (http://muse.jhu.edu/). In this case, the scholar can assume that the electronic form of the journal undergoes the same editorial rigor as the print publication, because they are identical in content.

WEB CLASSICS

Building a reputation of high quality takes time. But the Internet has been around long enough now that some publications with no pre-web history have caught the attention of scholars who turn to these sites regularly for reliable commentary on a variety of subject areas.

These high-quality sites can best be found by tapping into scholarly web directories such as the *Librarians' Index to the Internet* (http://lii.org/), which work like mini search engines but are managed by humans who sift through the chaff, including in these directories only what they deem to be gems.

The student looking specifically for free, peer-reviewed journals original to the web can visit a highly specific directory called the *Directory of Open Access Journals* (http://www.doaj.org/), listing nothing more or less than several hundred journals in a variety of subject areas. Many libraries have begun to link to these journals to promote their use by students and faculty.

Then there are gems that compare better to highbrow magazines or newspapers such as *The New Yorker*. Two celebrated examples are *Salon.com* (http://salon.com), and *Slate* (http://slate.com), both online literary reviews. Once tapped into, these sites do a good job of recommending other high-quality websites. Scholars are beginning to cite from these web-based publications just as they would from any print publication of long-standing reputation.

ASKING THE RIGHT QUESTIONS

In the end, it is up to the individual user to evaluate each website independently. Here are some critical questions to consider:

Question: Who is the author?

Response: Check the website's home page, probably near the bottom of the page.

Question: Is the author affiliated with any institution?

Response: Check the URL to see who sponsors the page.

Question: What are the author's credentials?

Response: Check an online database like *Academic Search* (http://www.epnet.com) or LexisNexis Academic (http://www.lexis-nexis.com) to see if this person is published in journals or books.

Question: Has the information been reviewed or peer-edited before posting?

Response: Probably not, unless the posting is part of a larger publication; if so, the submission process for publication can be verified at the publication home page.

Question: Is the page part of a larger publication?

Response: Try the various links on the page to see if there is an access point to the home page of the publication. Or try the "backspacing" technique mentioned later in the chapter.

Question: Is the information documented properly?

Response: Check for footnotes or methodology.

Question: Is the information current?

Response: Check the "last update," usually printed at the bottom of the page.

Question: What is the purpose of the page?

Response: Examine content and marginalia.

Question: Does the website suit your purposes?

Response: Review what the purpose of your project is. Review your information needs: primary vs. secondary, academic vs. popular. And always consult with your instructor.

FOR SUBSCRIBERS ONLY

An organized and indexed collection of discreet pieces of information is called a *database*. Two examples of databases are a library's card catalogue and online catalogue. The World Wide web is full of databases, though they are often restricted to subscribers. Subscription fees can be prohibitive, but fortunately for the average researcher, most college and university libraries foot the bill. The names of these databases are now well known, and arguably contain the most thoroughly reviewed (i.e., scholarly) full text available on the web: *Academic Search* from Ebsco (http://www.epnet.com), *Expanded Academic* from Thomson Gale (http://www.galegroup.com/), *Proquest Direct* from ProQuest (http://www.proquest.com), and *Omnifile* from Wilson (http://www.hwwilson.com). Inquire at your library to see if you have access to these databases.

Each of these databases contains its own proprietary search engine, allowing refinement of searches to a degree unmatched by search engines on the Internet at large. Why? For one, these databases are exclusive rather than inclusive, as the Internet is. More is not better in an information age. The fact that information is at your fingertips, and sometimes "in your face," can be a problem. Well-organized databases are shaped and limited by human hands and minds, covering only certain media types or subject areas.

More is not better in an information age.

Secondly, *databases allow searching by subject heading, in addition to keyword searching*. This means that a human has defined the main subject areas of each entry, consequently allowing the user much greater manipulation of the search. For example, if I enter the words "New York City" in a simple keyword search, I will retrieve everything that simply mentions New York City even once; the relevance will vary tremendously. On the other hand, if subject headings have been assigned, I can do a subject search on New York City and find only records that are devoted to my subject. This may sound trivial, but in the age of information overload, precision searching is a precious commodity.

> *In the age of information overload, precision searching is a precision commodity.*

While there is no foolproof way to a perfect database search, here is a point that will save you hours of frustration: consult with the most frequent users of research databases—reference librarians. Ask them (a) which databases they would use for your research topic and (b) how they would construct a search.

BIBLIOGRAPHIC RESEARCH

Up until now, we've only addressed electronic information that is full text. There may come a time when most secondary information needed for research is available online and as full text, but because of copyright and other restrictions, much scholarly information is still available only in print. This almost always implies a slight delay in retrieving the information: where full-text databases and the Internet promise instant gratification, more traditional modes of research necessitate either document delivery (fax or mail) or a visit to the library or other holding institution where a copy of the item can be retrieved. As individual journals begin to publish online (bypassing print altogether), the access to scholarly material may improve, but for now print copies remain the norm.

What has improved tremendously—with few exceptions—is the *indexing* of scholarly journals. Even if the journals themselves are not readily available in an electronic format, the indexing is available electronically. These electronic indexes provide basic bibliographic information and sometimes an abstract (summary) of the article or book chapter. When professors refer to bibliographic research, they probably mean research done with indexes. These indexes are available in any of three formats—print, CD-ROM, or online—depending on the academic institution. Inquire at your library about index availability.

Many academic institutions now subscribe to the following indexes online: *MLA* (literary criticism), *ERIC* (education), *PsycInfo* (psychology), *Historical Abstracts* (non-U.S. history), *Sociological Abstracts* (sociology), *Biological Abstracts* (biology), and a host of others. Note that these indexes are specific to particular subject areas. Their coverage is not broad, but deep and scholarly. *These are the indexes to watch for when seeking the most scholarly information in your area of study.* If a professor asks students to support their papers with scholarly secondary research, these indexes provide that kind of information. While the full text is often not included, the indexing will provide information sufficient to track down the complete article, whether it is in the library or available through interlibrary loan or other document delivery service.

These indexes are a great aid in evaluating the scholarly merit of a publication, as they usually eliminate any reference that isn't considered scholarly by the academy. For example, *MLA* only indexes literary criticism that appears in peer-reviewed journals and academically affiliated books. So, consider the publications that appear in these indexes to have the academic "Good Housekeeping" seal of approval.

TUNING IN TO YOUR ENVIRONMENT

Every university and college is different, each with its own points of access to information. Below are some exercises to help you familiarize yourself with your own scholarly environment.

Exercise #1: Go to your library's reference desk and get a list of all the scholarly journal indexes that are available electronically at your school. Then get a list of all online, full-text databases that are available to you.

Exercise #2: Go to your library's reference desk and get a list of all the journals that the library subscribes to electronically. Then get a list of all journals that are available at your library either in print or electronically in your major area of study.

Exercise #3: Ask the reference librarian about web access in general for your major area of study. What tips can the library give you about doing electronic research at your academic institution? Are there any special databases, web search engines/directories, or indexes that you should consult in your research?

Exercise #4: Try out some or all of the full-text databases available on your campus. Now try the same searches in a scholarly index. What differences do you see in the quality/scope of the information?

Search Tips

Tip #1: Backspacing
"Backspacing" a URL can be an effective way to evaluate a website. It may reveal authorship or institutional affiliation. To do this, place the cursor at the end of the URL and then backspace to the last slash and press Enter. Continue backspacing to each preceding slash, examining each level as you go.

Tip #2: Using WHOIS
WHOIS (http://www.networksolutions.com/en_US/whois/) is an Internet service that allows anyone to find out who's behind a website.

Tip #3: Beware of the ~ in a Web Address
Many educational institutions allow the creation of personal home pages by students and faculty. While the domain name remains ".edu" in these cases, the fact that they are personal means that pretty much anything can be posted, and so cannot assure academic quality.

Tip #4: Phrase Searching
Not finding relevant information? Trying using quotation marks around key phrases in your search string. For example, search in *Google* for this phrase, enclosed in quotation marks: "whose woods these are I think I know."

Tip #5: Title Searching
Still finding irrelevant information? Limit your search to the titles of web documents. A title search is an option in several search engines, among them *Altavista*

(advanced search) (http://www.altavista.com) and *Google* (advanced search) (http://www.google.com).

Tip #6: Full Text

The widest selection of previously published full text (newspapers, magazines, journals, book chapters) is available in subscription databases via the web. Inquire at your library to see if you have access to *LexisNexis Academic* (http://www.lexis-nexis.com), *Omnifile* (http://www.hwwilson.com), *Academic Search* (http://www.epnet.com), *ProQuest Direct* (http://www.proquest.com), *Expanded Academic* (http://www.galegroup.com), or other full-text databases.

The leading *free* full-text site is *LookSmart's FindArticles* (http://www.findarticles.com). This database of "hundreds of thousands of articles from more than 300 magazines and journals, dating back to 1998" can be searched by all magazines, magazines within categories, or specific magazine.

For the full text of books, try the *IPL Online Texts* directory (http://www.ipl.org/div/subject/browse/hum60.60.00/), pointing to the major digital text archives.

For more of the best full-text sites on the web, search on the term "full-text" in the *Librarians' Index to the Internet* (http://lii.org).

Tip #7: Archives of Older Published Materials

Full text for newspapers, magazines, and journals published prior to 1990 is difficult to find on the Internet. One subscription site that your library may offer is *JSTOR* (http://www.jstor.org), an archive of scholarly full-text journal articles dating back in some cases into the late 1800s. *LexisNexis Academic* (http://www.lexis-nexis.com), also a subscription service, includes the full text of popular periodicals such as the *New York Times* as far back as 1980.

Two free sites offer the full text of eighteenth- and nineteenth-century periodicals from Great Britain and the U.S. respectively: *Internet Library of Early Journals* (http://www.bodley.ox.ac.uk/ilej/) and *Nineteenth Century in Print* (http://memory.loc.gov/ammem/ndlpcoop/moahtml/snchome.html).

Use interlibrary loan or another document delivery service like *Ingenta* (http://www.ingenta.com) to have a copy of the print version of older titles sent to you. Electronic indexing (no full text) for older materials is readily available, back as early as 1900, sometimes earlier. Inquire at your library.

Tip #8: Best Sites, Free or Subscription, for Quantity and Quality of Scholarly Information Across the Disciplines

Below are a few of the sites most relied upon by academic librarians. For the subscription databases, you will need to inquire at your library for local availability.

A FOOLPROOF RECIPE FOR GREAT RESEARCH—EVERY TIME

First, search at least one of these multidisciplinary subscription databases; check your library's website for availability.

- *Academic Search Elite/Premier* (EBSCOhost) for journals
- *Expanded Academic* (Thomson Gale) for journals
- *Omnifile* (WilsonWeb) for journals
- *Proquest* for journals
- *WorldCat* (OCLC FirstSearch) for books

Second, search subject-specific databases. These too are mostly subscription databases; check your library's website for availability.

- Anthropology: *Anthropological Abstracts*
- Art: *Art Abstracts*
- Biology: *Biological Abstracts, Biosis*
- Business: *ABI Inform, Business Source Elite/Premier, Business & Company Resource Center, Dow Jones, LexisNexis*
- Chemistry: *SciFinder Scholar, Science Citation Index Expanded (ISI)*
- Communication: *Communication and Mass Media, Communication Abstracts*
- Computer Science: *INSPEC*
- Economics: *EconLit*
- Education: *ERIC* (free)
- Film Studies: *MLA*
- Geography/Geology: *GeoBase*
- History: *America History and Life, Historical Abstracts*
- Language, Literature: *MLA, LION (Literature Online)*
- Law: *LexisNexis, WestLaw*
- Mathematics: *MathSciNet*
- Medicine: *PubMed* (free)
- Music: *RILM*
- Philosophy: *Philosopher's Index*
- Physics: *INSPEC*
- Political Science: *PAIS*
- Psychology: *PsycInfo*
- Religion: *ATLA Religion*
- Sociology: *Sociological Abstracts*

Third, visit these not-to-be-missed free websites and meta-sites:

- Anthropology: *Anthropological Index Online* http://aio.anthropology.org.uk/cgi-bin/uncgi/search_bib_ai/anthind, *Anthropology Resources on the Internet* http://www.archeodroit.net/anthro/
- Art: *ArtCyclopedia* http://www.artcyclopedia.com/
- Biology: *Biology Browser* http://www.biologybrowser.org/, *Agricola* http://agricola.nal.usda.gov/
- Business: *EDGAR* http://www.sec.gov/edgar.shtml, *Hoover's Online* http://hoovers.com/free
- Chemistry: *Chemdex.org* http://www.chemdex.org/, *World of Chemistry* http://scienceworld.wolfram.com/chemistry/
- Communication: *ACA Communication Studies Center* http://www.americancomm.org/
- Computer Science: *CompInfo* http://www.compinfo-center.com/
- Economics: *Social Science Information Gateway (SOSIG)* http://sosig.esrc.bris.ac.uk/
- Education: *Educator's Reference Desk* http://eduref.org/
- Film Studies: *Film Studies Resources* http://www.lib.berkeley.edu/MRC/filmstudies/index.html
- Geography/Geology: *GeoSource* http://www.library.uu.nl/geosource/
- History: *American Memory* http://memory.loc.gov/ammem/amhome.html

- Language, Literature: *Online Literary Criticism Collection* http://www.ipl.org/div/litcrit/
- Law: *FindLaw* http://www.findlaw.com/
- Mathematics: Mathworld http://www.mathworld.wolfram.com/, *MathSearch* http://www.maths.usyd.edu.au:8000/MathSearch.html
- Medicine: *BioMed Central* http://www.biomedcentral.com/
- Music: *Internet Resources for Music Scholars* http://hcl.harvard.edu/loebmusic/online-ir-intro.html
- Philosophy: *Stanford Encyclopedia of Philosophy* http://plato.stanford.edu/contents.html
- Physics: *World of Physics* http://scienceworld.wolfram.com/physics/
- Political Science: *Social Science Information Gateway (SOSIG)* http://sosig.esrc.bris.ac.uk/, THOMAS http://thomas.loc.gov/
- Psychology: *Social Science Information Gateway (SOSIG)* http://sosig.esrc.bris.ac.uk/
- Religion: *Religion Online* http://www.religion-online.org/, *Hartford Institute for Religion Research* http://www.hartfordinstitute.org/
- Sociology: *Social Science Information Gateway (SOSIG)* http://sosig.esrc.bris.ac.uk/

CITATION GUIDES ON THE WEB

The two most common styles of documentation are those established by the Modern Language Association (MLA) and the American Psychological Association (APA). These associations each provide examples of basic citations of electronic and print resources at their websites; you will find the MLA at http://www.mla.org/publications/style and APA at http://www.apastyle.org.

Also, many writing centers have made available citation guides at their websites. One recommended site is by the writing center of Purdue University (http://owl.english.purdue.edu/handouts/research/index.html).

For citation examples not given at these websites, it is advisable to consult the associations' printed manuals—*Publication Manual of the American Psychological Association* or the *MLA Handbook for Writers of Research Papers*—in their most recent editions.

A LIBRARIAN'S GUIDELINES TO SUCCESSFUL RESEARCH

1. Consult with your professor to determine what types of resources will be most appropriate for the project at hand.
2. Consider whether you need scholarly or popular sources or a mixture of both.
3. Consider whether you need primary or secondary works or a mixture of both.
4. With the assistance of a reference librarian, find which search tools will direct you to the most relevant resources.
5. Range widely. Try a new search tool with each new research project.
6. Begin early, in case interlibrary loan is needed to obtain research owned only by other libraries.
7. Examine bibliographies at the end of the articles and books you've already found. Remember that one quality source can, in its bibliography, point to many other resources.

C. PLAGIARISM AND THE LOGIC OF CITATION

It is impossible to discuss the rationale for citing sources without reference to plagiarism, even though the primary reason for including citations is not to prove that you haven't cheated. It's essential that you give credit where it's due as a courtesy to your readers. Along with educating readers about who has said what, citations enable them to find out more about a given position and to pursue other discussions on the subject. Nonetheless, plagiarism is an important issue: academic integrity matters. And because the stakes are very high if you are caught plagiarizing, we think it necessary to pause in order to discuss how to avoid it.

In recent years there has been a significant rise in the number of plagiarism cases nationally. Many commentators blame the Internet, with its easily accessible, easy to cut-and-paste information, for increasing the likelihood of plagiarism. Others cite a lack of clarity about what plagiarism is and why it is a serious problem. So, let's start by clarifying.

Most people have some idea of what plagiarism is. You already know that it's against the rules to buy a paper from an Internet "paper mill" or to download others' words verbatim and hand them in as your own thinking. And you probably know that even if you change a few words and rearrange the sentence structure, you still need to acknowledge the source. By way of formal definition, plagiarism (as one handbook puts it) gives "the impression that you have written or thought something that you have in fact borrowed from someone else" (Joseph Gibaldi, *MLA Handbook for Writers of Research Papers*, Fifth edition. New York: MLA, 1999, p. 30). It is a form of theft and fraud. Borrowing from someone else, by the way, also includes taking and not acknowledging words and ideas from your friends or your parents. Put another way, any assignment with your name on it signifies that you are the author—that the words and ideas are yours—with any exceptions indicated by source citations and, if you're quoting, by quotation marks.

Knowing what plagiarism is, however, doesn't guarantee that you'll know how to avoid it. Is it okay, for example, to cobble together a series of summaries and paraphrases in a paragraph, provided you include the authors in a bibliography at the end of the paper? Or how about if you insert a single footnote at the end of the paragraph? The answer is that both are still plagiarism, because your reader can't tell where your thinking starts and others' thinking stops. As a basic rule of thumb, *"Readers must be able to tell as they are reading your paper exactly what information came from which source and what information is your contribution to the paper"* (Christine A. Hult, *Researching and Writing Across the Curriculum*. Boston: Allyn and Bacon, 1996, p. 203). More on this later.

WHY DOES PLAGIARISM MATTER?

A recent survey indicated that 53 percent of Who's Who High Schoolers thought that plagiarism was no big deal (Sally Cole and Elizabeth Kiss, "What Can We Do About Student Cheating?" *About Campus*, May–June 2000, p. 6). So why should institutions of higher learning care about it? Here are two great reasons:

- Plagiarism poisons the environment. Students who don't cheat get alienated by students who do and get away with it, and faculty can become distrustful of students and even disillusioned about teaching when constantly driven to track down students' sources. It's a lot easier, by the way, than most students think for faculty to recognize language and ideas that are not the student's own. And now there are all those search engines provided by firms like Turnitin.com that have been generated in response to the Internet paper-mill boom. Who wants another cold war?

■ Plagiarism defeats the purpose of going to college, which is learning how to think. You can't learn to think by just copying others' ideas; you need to learn to trust your own intelligence. Students' panic about deadlines and their mis-understandings about assignments sometimes spur plagiarism. It's a good bet that your professors would much rather take requests for help and give extra time on assignments than have to go through the anguish of confronting students about plagiarized work.

So, plagiarism gets in the way of trust, fairness, intellectual development, and, ultimately, the attitude toward learning that sets the tone for a college or university community.

FREQUENTLY ASKED QUESTIONS (FAQS) ABOUT PLAGIARISM

Is it still plagiarism if I didn't intentionally copy someone else's work and present it as my own; that is, if I plagiarized it by accident?
Yes, it is still plagiarism. Colleges and universities put the burden of responsibility on students for knowing what plagiarism is and then making the effort necessary to avoid it. Leaving out the quotation marks around someone else's words or omitting the attribution after a summary of someone else's theory may be just a mistake—a matter of inadequate documentation—but faculty can only judge what you turn in to them, not what you intended.

If I include a list of works consulted at the end of my paper, doesn't that cover it?
No. A works-cited list (bibliography) tells your readers what you read but leaves them in the dark about how and where this material has been used in your paper. Putting one or more references at the end of a paragraph containing source material is a version of the same problem. The solution is to cite the source at the point that you quote or paraphrase or summarize it. To be even clearer about what comes from where, also use what are called in-text attributions. See the next FAQ on these.

What is the best way to help my readers distinguish between what my sources are saying and what I'm saying?
Be overt. Tell your readers in the text of your paper, not just in citations, when you are drawing on someone else's words, ideas, or information. Do this with phrases like "According to X . . ." or "As noted in X . . ."—so-called in-text attributions.

Be overt. Tell your readers in the text of your paper, not just in citations, when you are drawing on someone else's words, ideas, or information.

Are there some kinds of information that I do not need to document?
Yes. Common knowledge and facts you can find in almost any encyclopedia or basic reference text generally don't need to be documented (that is,
John F. Kennedy became president of the United States in 1960). This
distinction can get a little tricky because it isn't always obvious what is and
is not common knowledge. Often, you need to spend some time in a discipline before you discover what others take to be known to all. When in
doubt, cite the source.

When in doubt, cite the source.

*If I put the information from my sources into my own words, do I still need to
include citations?*
Yes. Sorry, but rewording someone else's idea doesn't make it your idea.
Paraphrasing is a useful activity because it helps you to better understand
what you are reading, but paraphrases and summaries have to be documented
and carefully distinguished from ideas and information you are representing
as your own.

*If I don't actually know anything about the subject, is it okay to hand in a paper
that is taken entirely from various sources?*
It's okay if (1) you document the borrowings and (2) the assignment called
for summary. Properly documented summarizing is better than plagiarizing, but most assignments call for something more. Often comparing and
contrasting your sources will begin to give you ideas, so that you can have
something to contribute. If you're really stumped, go see the professor.

You will also reduce the risk of plagiarism if you consult sources after—
not before—you have done some preliminary thinking on the subject. If
you have become somewhat invested in your own thoughts on the matter,
you will be able to use the sources in a more active way, in effect, making
them part of a dialogue.

*Is it plagiarism if I include things in my paper that I thought of with another
student or a member of my family?*
Most academic behavior codes, under the category called "collusion,"
allow for students' cooperative efforts only with the explicit consent of the
instructor. The same general rule goes for plagiarizing yourself—that is,
for submitting the same paper in more than one class. If you have questions about what constitutes collusion in a particular class, be sure to ask
your professor.

*What about looking at secondary sources when my professor hasn't asked me to?
Is this a form of cheating?*
It can be a form of cheating if the intent of the assignment was to get you
to develop a particular kind of thinking skill. In this case, looking at others' ideas may actually retard your learning process and leave you feeling
that you couldn't possibly learn to arrive at ideas on your own.

Professors usually look favorably on students who are willing to take the time to do extra reading on a subject, but it is essential that, even in class discussion, you make it clear that you have consulted outside sources. To conceal that fact is to present others' ideas as your own. Even in class discussion, if you bring up an idea you picked up on the Internet, be sure to say so explicitly.

HOW TO CITE SOURCES

In general, you will be expected to follow a formalized style of documentation. The two most common are the MLA style, which uses the author-work format, and the APA style, which uses the author-date format. Most writing handbooks (compilations of the rules of grammar and punctuation, available at most bookstores) contain detailed accounts of documentation styles. In addition, you can access various websites that will provide most (though not all) of this information. (See "Citations Guides on the Web" earlier in this chapter.)

The various styles differ in the specific ways that they organize the bibliographical information, but all of them share the following characteristics:

1. They place an extended citation for each source, including the author, the title, the date, and the place of publication, at the end of the paper. These end-of-text citations are organized in a list, usually alphabetically.
2. They insert an abbreviated citation within the text, located within parentheses directly following every use of the source. Usually this in-text citation consists of the author's name and either the page (in MLA) or date (in APA). In-text citations indicate in shorthand form in the body of your paper the source you are using and direct your readers to the complete citation located in a list of references at the end of the paper or report.
3. They distinguish among different kinds of sources—providing slightly differing formulas for citing books, articles, encyclopedias, government documents, interviews, and so forth.
4. They have particular formats for citing electronic sources of various kinds, such as CD-ROMs, the Internet, and online journals and databases. These citations replace the publication information typically provided for text references to printed material with what is called an *availability statement*, which provides the method of accessing the source. This statement should provide the information sufficient to retrieve the source.

You have probably already discovered that some professors are more concerned than others that students obey the particulars of a given documentation style. Virtually all faculty across the curriculum agree, however, that *the most important rule for writers to follow in documenting sources is formal consistency.* That is, all of your in-text citations should follow the same abbreviated format, and all of your end-of-text citations should follow the same extended format.

Once you begin doing most of your writing in a particular discipline, you may want to purchase or access on the Internet the more detailed style guide adhered to by that discipline. Because documentation styles differ not only from discipline to discipline but also even from journal to journal within a discipline, you should consult your professor about which documentation format he or she wishes you to use in a given course.

Here are a few basic examples of in-text and end-of-text citations in both MLA and APA form, followed by a brief discussion of the rules that apply.

1. Single author, MLA style

In-text citation: The influence of Seamus Heaney on younger poets in Northern Ireland has been widely acknowledged, but Patrick Kavanagh's "plain-speaking, pastoral" influence on him is "less recognized" (Smith 74).

"(Smith 74)" indicates the author's last name and the page number on which the cited passage appears. If the author's name had been mentioned in the sentence—had the sentence begun "According to Smith"—you would include only the page number in the citation. Note that there is no abbreviation for "page," that there is no intervening punctuation between name and page, and that the parentheses precede the period or other punctuation. If the sentence ends with a direct quotation, the parentheses come after the quotation marks but still before the closing period. Also note that no punctuation occurs between the last word of the quotation ("recognized") and the closing quotation mark.

End-of-text book citation: Douglas, Ann. *Terrible Honesty: Mongrel Manhattan in the 1920s.* New York: Farrar, Straus, and Giroux, 1995.

End-of-text article citation: Cressy, David. "Foucault, Stone, Shakespeare and Social History." *English Literary Renaissance* 21 (1991): 121–33.

MLA style stipulates an alphabetical list of references (by author's last name, which keys the reference to the in-text citation). This list is located at the end of the paper on a separate page and entitled "Works Cited."

Each entry in the "Works Cited" list is divided into three parts: author, title, and publication data. Each of these parts is separated by a period from the others. Titles of book-length works are italicized, unless your instructor prefers underlining. (Underlining is a means of indicating italics.) Journal citations differ slightly: article names go inside quotations, no punctuation follows the titles of journals, and a colon precedes the page numbers.

2. Single author, APA style

In-text citation: Studies of students' changing attitudes towards the small colleges that they attend suggest that their loyalty to the institution declines steadily over a four-year period, whereas their loyalty to individual professors or departments increases "markedly, by as much as twenty-five percent over the last two years" (Brown, 1994, p. 41).

For both books and articles, include the author's last name, followed by a comma, and then the date of publication. If you are quoting or referring to a specific passage, include the page number as well, separated from the date by a comma and the abbreviation "p." (or "pp.") followed by a space. If the author's name has been mentioned in the sentence, include only the date in the parentheses immediately following the author's name.

In-text citation: Brown (1992) documents the decline in students' institutional loyalty.
End-of-text book citation: Tannen, D. (1991). *You just don't understand: Women and men in conversation.* New York: Ballantine Books.
End-of-text article citation: Baumeister, R. (1987). How the self became a problem: A psychological review of historical research. *Journal of Personality and Psychology, 52,* 163–176.

APA style requires an alphabetical list of references (by author's last name, which keys the reference to the in-text citation). This list is located at the end of the paper on a separate page and entitled "References." Regarding manuscript form, the first line of each reference is not indented, but all subsequent lines are indented three spaces.

In alphabetizing the references list, place entries for a single author before entries that he or she has co-authored, and arrange multiple entries by a single author by beginning with the earliest work. If there are two or more works by the same author in the same year, designate the second with an "a," the third a "b," and so forth, directly after the year. For all subsequent entries by an author after the first, substitute three hyphens followed by a period [---.] for his or her name. For articles by two or more authors, use commas to connect the authors, and precede the last one with a comma and an ampersand [&].

The APA style divides individual entries into the following parts: author (using initials only for first and middle names), year of publication (in parentheses), title, and publication data. Each part is separated by a period from the others. Note that only the first letter of the title and subtitle of books is capitalized (although proper nouns would be capitalized as necessary).

Journal citations differ from those for books in a number of small ways. The title of a journal article is neither italicized (nor underlined) nor enclosed in quotation marks, and only the first word in the title and subtitle is capitalized. The name of the journal is italicized (or underlined), however, and the first word and all significant words are capitalized. Also, notice that the volume number (which is separated by a comma from the title of the journal) is italicized (or underlined) to distinguish it from the page reference. Page numbers for the entire article are included, with no "p." or "pp.," and are separated by a comma from the preceding volume number. If the journal does not use volume numbers, then "p." or "pp." is included.

HOW TO INTEGRATE QUOTATIONS INTO YOUR PAPER

An enormous number of writers lose authority and readability because they have never learned how to correctly integrate quotations into their own writing. The following guidelines should help.

1. **Acknowledge sources in your text, not just in citations.** *When you incorporate material from a source, attribute it to the source explicitly in your text—not just in a citation.* In other words, when you introduce the material, *frame* it with a phrase such as "according to Marsh" or "as Cartelli argues."

Although it is not required, you are usually much better off making the attribution overtly, even if you have also cited the source within parentheses or with a footnote at the end of the last sentence quoted, paraphrased, or summarized. If a passage does not contain an attribution, your readers will not know that it comes from a source until they reach the citation at the end. Attributing up-front clearly distinguishes what one source says from what another says and, perhaps more important, what your sources say from what you say. Useful verbs for introducing attributions include the following: notes, observes, argues, comments, writes, says, reports, suggests, and claims. Generally speaking, by the way, you should cite the author by last name only—as "Cartelli," not as "Thomas Cartelli" or "Mr. Cartelli."

2. **Splice quotations onto your own words.** *Always attach quotations to some of your own language; don't let them sit in your text as independent sentences with quotation marks around them.* You can normally satisfy this rule with an attributive phrase—commonly known as a tag phrase—that introduces the quotation.

Always attach quotations to some of your own language; don't let them sit in your text as independent sentences with quotation marks around them.

According to Paul McCartney, "All you need is love."

Note that the tag phrase takes a comma before the quote.

Alternatively you can splice quotations into your text with a setup: a statement followed by a colon.

Patrick Henry's famous phrase is one of the first that American school-children memorize: "Give me liberty, or give me death."

The colon, you should notice, usually comes at the end of an independent clause (that is, a subject plus verb that can stand alone), at the spot where a period normally goes. It would be incorrect to write "Patrick Henry is known for: 'Give me liberty, or give me death.'"

The rationale for this guideline is essentially the same as that for the previous one: if you are going to move to quotation, you first need to identify its author so that your readers will be able to put it in context quickly.

Spliced quotations frequently create problems in grammar or punctuation for writers. Whether you include an entire sentence (or passage) of quotation or just a few phrases, you need to take care to integrate them into the grammar of your own sentence.

One of the most common mistaken assumptions is that a comma should always precede a quotation, as in "A spokesperson for the public defender's office demanded, 'an immediate response from the mayor.'" The sentence structure does not call for any punctuation after "demanded."

3. **Cite sources after quotations.** *Locate citations in parentheses after the quotation and before the final period.* The information about the source appears at the end of the sentence, with the final period following the closing parenthesis.

> A recent article on the best selling albums in America claimed that "Ever since Elvis, it has been pop music's job to challenge the mores of the older generation" (Hornby 168).

Note that there is normally *no punctuation* at the end of the quotation itself, either before or after the closing quotation mark. A quotation that ends either in a question mark or an exclamation mark is an exception to this rule, because the sign is an integral part of the quotation's meaning.

> As Hamlet says to Rosencrantz and Guildenstern, "And yet to me what is this quintessence of dust?" (2.2.304-05).

See the section entitled "How to Cite Sources" earlier in this chapter for the appropriate formats for in-text citations.

4. **Use ellipses to shorten quotations.** *Add ellipsis points to indicate that you have omitted some of the language from within the quotation.* Form ellipses by entering three dots (periods) with spaces in between them, or use four dots to indicate that the deletion continues to the end of the sentence (the last dot becomes the period). Suppose you wanted to shorten the following quotation from a recent article about Radiohead by Alex Ross:

> The album "OK Computer," with titles like "Paranoid Android," "Karma Police," and "Climbing Up the Walls," pictured the onslaught of the information age and a young person's panicky embrace of it (Ross 85).

Using ellipses, you could emphasize the source's claim by omitting the song titles from the middle of the sentence:

> The album "OK Computer" . . . pictured the onslaught of the information age and a young person's panicky embrace of it (Ross 85).

In most cases, the gap between quoted passages should be short, and in any case, you should be careful to preserve the sense of the original. The standard joke about ellipses is apposite here: A reviewer writes that a film "will delight no one and appeal to the intelligence of invertebrates only, but not average viewers." An unethical advertiser cobbles together pieces of the review to say that the film "will delight . . . and appeal to the intelligence of . . . viewers."

5. **Use square brackets to alter or add information within a quotation.** Sometimes it is necessary to change the wording slightly inside a quotation in order to maintain fluency. Square brackets indicate that you are altering the original quotation. Brackets are also used when you insert explanatory information, such as a definition or example, within a quotation. Here are a few examples that alter the original quotations cited above.

> According to one music critic, the cultural relevance of Radiohead is evident in "the album 'OK Computer' . . . [which] pictured the onslaught of the information age and a young person's panicky embrace of it" (Ross 85).

> Popular music has always "[challenged] the mores of the older generation," according to Nick Hornby (168).

Note that both examples respect the original sense of the quotation; they have changed the wording only to integrate the quotations gracefully within the writer's own sentence structure.

D. HOW TO PREPARE AN ABSTRACT

There is one more skill essential to research-based writing that we need to discuss: how to prepare an abstract. The aim of the nonevaluative summary of a source known as an abstract is to represent a source's arguments as fairly and accurately as possible, not to critique them. Learning how to compose an abstract according to the conventions of a given discipline is a necessary skill for academic researched writing. Because abstracts differ in format and length among disciplines, you should sample some in the reference section of your library or via the Internet to provide you with models to imitate. Some abstracts, such as those in *Dissertation Abstracts*, are very brief—less than 250 words. Others may run as long as two pages.

Despite disciplinary differences, abstracts by and large follow a generalizable format. The abstract should begin with a clear and specific explanation of the work's governing thesis (or argument). In this opening paragraph, you should also define the work's purpose, and possibly include established positions that it tries to refine, qualify, or argue against. What kind of critical approach does it adopt? What are its aims? On what assumptions does it rest? Why did the author feel it necessary to write the work—that is, what does he or she believe the work offers that other sources don't? What shortcomings or misrepresentations in other criticism does the work seek to correct?

You won't be able to produce detailed answers to all of these questions in your opening paragraph, but in trying to answer some of them in your note taking and drafting, you should find it easier to arrive at the kind of concise, substantive, and focused overview that the first paragraph of your abstract should provide. Also, be careful not to settle for bland, all-purpose generalities in this opening paragraph. And if you quote there, keep the selections short, and remember that quotations don't speak for themselves.

In sum, your aim in the first paragraph is to define the source's particular angle of vision and articulate its main point or points, including the definition of key terms used in its title or elsewhere in its argument.

Once you've set up this overview of the source's central position(s), you should devote a paragraph or so to the source's *organization* (how it divides its subject into parts) and its *method* (how it goes about substantiating its argument). What kind of secondary material does the source use? That is, how do its own bibliographic citations cue you to its school of thought, its point of view, its research traditions?

Your concluding paragraph should briefly recount some of the source's conclusions (as related to, but not necessarily the same as, its thesis). In what way does it go about culminating its argument? What kind of significance does it claim for its position? What final qualifications does it raise?

Here, as a model, is a good example of an abstract:

Abstract of "William Carlos Williams," an essay

by Christopher MacGowan

in *The Columbia History of American Poetry*,

pp. 395–418, Columbia University Press, 1993.

MacGowan's is a chronologically organized account of Williams' poetic career and of his relation to both modernism as an international movement and modernism as it affected the development of poetry in America. MacGowan is at some pains both to differentiate Williams from some features of modernism (such as the tendency of American writers to write as well as live away from their own cultural roots) and to link Williams to modernism. MacGowan argues, for example, that an essential feature of Williams's commitment as a poet was to "the local—to the clear presentation of what was under his nose and in front of his eyes" (385).

But he also takes care to remind us that Williams was in no way narrowly provincial, having studied in Europe as a young man (at Leipzig), having had a Spanish mother and an English father, having become friendly with the poets Ezra Pound and H. D. while getting his medical degree at the University of Pennsylvania, and having continued to meet important figures in the literary and art worlds by making frequent visits to New York and by traveling on more than one occasion to Europe (where Pound introduced him to W. B. Yeats, among others). Williams corresponded with Marianne Moore, he continued to write to Pound and to show Pound some of his work, and he wrote critical essays on the works of other modernists. MacGowan reminds us that Williams also translated Spanish works (ballads) and so was not out of contact with European influences.

Williams had a long publishing career—beginning in 1909 with a self-published volume called *Poems* and ending more than fifty years later with *Pictures from Brueghel* in 1962. What MacGowan emphasizes about this career is not only the consistently high quality of work, but also its great influence on other artists (he names those who actually corresponded with Williams and visited with him, including Charles Olson, Robert Creeley, Robert Lowell, Allen Ginsberg, and Denise Levertov). MacGowan observes that Williams defined himself "against" T. S. Eliot—the more rewarded and internationally recognized of the two poets, especially during their lifetimes—searching for "alternatives to the prevailing mode of a complex, highly allusive poetics," which Williams saw as Eliot's legacy (395). MacGowan depicts Williams as setting himself "against the international school of Eliot and Pound—Americans he felt wrote about rootlessness and searched an alien past because of their failure to write about and live within their own culture" (397).

◀ ASSIGNMENT: A Research Sequence

The traditional sequence of steps for building a research paper—or for any writing that relies on secondary materials—is summary, comparative analysis, and synthesis. The following sequence of four exercises addresses the first two steps as discrete activities. (You might, of course, choose to do only some of these exercises.)

1. *Compose a relatively informal prospectus,* in which you formulate your initial thinking on a subject before you do more research. Include what you already know about the topic, especially what you find interesting, particularly significant, or strange. This exercise will help to deter you from being overwhelmed by and absorbed into the sources you will later encounter.

2. *Conduct a "what's going on in the field" search, and create a preliminary list of sources.* This exercise is ideal for helping you to find a topic or, if you already have one, to narrow it. The kinds of bibliographic materials you consult for this portion of the research project will depend on the discipline within which you are writing. Whatever the discipline, start in the reference room of your library with specialized indexes (such as the *Social Sciences Index* or the *New York Times Index*), book review indexes, specialized encyclopedias and dictionaries, and bibliographies (print version or CD-ROM) that will give you an overview of your subject or topic. If you have access to databases through your school or library, you should also search them. (See the section in this chapter entitled "Electronic Research: Finding Quality on the Web.")

   The "what's going on in the field" search has two aims:

   - To survey materials in order to identify trends—the kinds of issues and questions that others in the field are talking about (and, thus, find important)

   - To compile a bibliography that includes a range of titles that interest you, that could be relevant to your prospective topic, and that seem to you representative of research trends associated with your subject (or topic)

   You will not be committed at this point to pursuing all of these sources but rather to reporting what is being talked about. You might also compose a list of keywords (such as Library of Congress headings) that you have used in conducting your search. If you try this exercise, you will be surprised how much value there is in exploring indexes *just for titles,* to see the kinds of topics people are currently conversing about. And you will almost surely discover how *narrowly* focused most research is (which will get you away from global questions).

   Append to your list of sources (a very preliminary bibliography) a few paragraphs of informal discussion of how the information you have encountered (the titles, summaries, abstracts, etc.) has affected your thinking and plans for your paper. These paragraphs might respond to the following questions:

   a. In what ways has your "what's going on in the field" search led you to narrow or shift direction in or focus your thinking about your subject?

b. How might you use one or more of these sources in your paper?

c. What has this phase of your research suggested you might need to look for next?

3. *Write an abstract of an article (or book chapter)* from your "what's going on" exercise that you think you might use in your final paper. Use the procedure offered in the preceding section, "How to Prepare an Abstract." Aim for two pages in length. If other members of your class are working on the same or similar subjects, it is often extremely useful for everyone to share copies of their abstracts. Remember that your primary concern should lie with representing the argument and point of view of the source as fairly and accurately as possible.

Append to the end of the abstract a paragraph or two that addresses the question, "How has this exercise affected your thinking about your topic?" Objectifying your own research process in this way will help to move you away from the cut-and-paste–provide-only-the-transitions mode of writing research papers.

4. *Write a comparative summary of two reviews of a single source.* Most writers, before they invest the significant time and energy required to study a book-length source, take the much smaller amount of time and energy required to find out more about the book. Although you should always include in your final paper your own analytical summary of books you consult on your topic, it's extremely useful also to find out what experts in the field have to say about the source.

Select from your "what's going on" list one book-length source that you've discovered is vital to your subject or topic. As a general rule, if a number of your indexes, bibliographies, and so forth, refer you to the same book, it's a good bet that this source merits consulting.

Locate two book reviews on the book, and write a summary that compares the two reviews. Ideally, you should locate two reviews that diverge in their points of view or in what they choose to emphasize. Depending on the length and complexity of the reviews, your comparative summary should require two or three pages.

In most cases, you will find that reviews are less neutral in their points of view than are abstracts, but they always do more than simply judge. A good review, like a good abstract, should communicate the essential ideas contained in the source. It is the reviewer's aim also to locate the source in some larger context, by, for example, comparing it to other works on the same subject and to the research tradition the book seeks to extend, modify, and so forth. Thus, your summary should try to encompass how the book contributes to the ongoing conversation on a given topic in the field.

Append to your comparative summary a paragraph or two answering the question "How has this exercise affected your thinking about your topic?"

Obviously, you could choose to do a comparative summary of two articles, two book chapters, and so forth, rather than of two book reviews. But in any event, if you use books in your research, you should always find a means of determining how these books are received in the relevant critical community.

The next step, if you were writing a research paper, would involve the task known as *synthesis*, in which you essentially write a comparative discussion that includes more than two sources. Many research papers start with an opening paragraph that synthesizes prevailing, perhaps competing, interpretations of the topic being addressed. Few good research papers consist only of such synthesis, however. Instead, writers use synthesis to frame their ideas and to provide perspective on their own arguments; the synthesis provides a platform or foundation for their own subsequent analysis.

It is probably worth adding that bad research papers fail to use synthesis as a point of departure. Instead, they line up their sources and agree or disagree with them. To inoculate you against this unfortunate reflex, review the sections entitled "Six Strategies for Analyzing Sources" (especially "Strategy 4: Find Your Own Role in the Conversation") and "Strategies for Writing and Revising Research Papers" in Chapter 12. ▶

GUIDELINES FOR FINDING AND CITING SOURCES

1. Citing sources isn't just about acknowledging intellectual or informational debts; it's also a courtesy to your readers, directing them how to find out more about the subjected cited.

2. Before you settle in with one author's book-length argument, use indexes and bibliographies and other resources to achieve a broader view.

3. Given that the accessibility of Internet research had made it more difficult to distinguish reliable and authoritative information from fraudulent initiations, domain named ending in ".edu" and ".gov" usually offer more reliable choices than the standard ".com."

4. When professors direct you to do bibliographic research, they usually are referring to research done with indexes; these are available in print, online, and CD-ROM formats.

5. In evaluating a website about which you don't know much, try "backspacing" a URL to trace back to its authorship or institutional affiliation. Place the cursor at the end of the URL, backspace to the last slash, and press enter.

6. Avoid sacrificing your authority by incorrectly splicing quotation into your own discussions. For example, always attach a quotation to some of your own language; never let it stand as its own sentence in your text. Attribution — "According to Dickson" — before the quote fulfills this function nicely.

7. One of the best ways of getting to know an important source during the research process is to compose an abstract of it, from 250 words to two pages. A good abstract aims to summarize the governing argument, organization and method as fairly and accurately as possible.

Nine Basic Writing Errors and How to Fix Them

Quick Take

This chapter appears at the end of the book not because grammar is unimportant, but because the end of the book is a convenient place for you to consult when you have questions about correctness and the so-called rules of writing.

There is more to thinking about grammar than the quest for error-free writing, as Chapter 11 on sentence style demonstrates, with its emphasis on how to analyze writers' syntactical choices and how to think about the relationship between a writer's style and his or her characteristic ways of thinking. Studying the nine basic writing errors one at a time, whether in a class or on your own, will enable you to find your way around in a sentence more easily, and thus, to build better sentences yourself.

The first part of this chapter, "Why Correctness Matters," makes the case for learning to recognize a pattern of error in your drafts and learning to prioritize the most serious problems, creating a hierarchy of error, rather than treating (and worrying about) all errors equally and all at the same time. Achieving grammatical correctness is a matter of both knowledge—how to recognize and avoid errors—and timing: when to focus on possible errors.

Thereafter, the chapter offers a quick-hit guide to punctuation—the five basic signs covered in two pages—followed by discussion of the nine most important grammar errors to avoid:

- **Sentence fragments**
- **Comma splices and fused (run-on) sentences**
- **Errors in subject–verb agreement**
- **Shifts in sentence structure (faulty predication)**
- **Errors in pronoun reference**
- **Misplaced modifiers and dangling participles**
- **Errors in using possessive apostrophes**
- **Comma errors**
- **Spelling/diction errors that interfere with meaning**

For each of these, the chapter offers a definition with examples, and then talks you through how to fix it—with a little "test yourself" section at the end.

As the chapter nears its end, you will find a brief "Glossary of Grammatical Terms" (four pages long) that defines and illustrates many of the key terms we have used earlier in the chapter and throughout the book. Do you know the difference between a clause and a phrase? It's a useful distinction to know when you're building sentences to last.

The chapter concludes with a grammar and style quiz, followed by chapter review guidelines and an answer key.

A. WHY CORRECTNESS MATTERS

This chapter addresses the issue of grammatical correctness and offers ways of recognizing and fixing (or avoiding) the most important errors. The first guideline in editing for correctness is to *wait* to do it until you have arrived at a reasonably complete conceptual draft. We have delayed until the end of the book our consideration of technical revisions precisely because if you get too focused on producing polished copy right up front, you may never explore the subject enough to learn how to have ideas about it. In other words, it doesn't make sense for you to let your worries about proper form or persuasive phrasing prematurely distract you from the more important matter of having something substantial to polish in the first place. Writers need a stage in which they are allowed to make mistakes and use writing to help them discover what they want to say. But at the appropriate time— the later stages of the writing process—editing for correctness becomes very important.

When a paper obeys the rules of grammar, punctuation, and spelling, it has achieved *correctness*. Unlike editing for style, which involves you in making choices between more and less effective ways of phrasing, editing for correctness locates you in the domain of right or wrong. As you will see, there are usually a number of ways to correct an error, so you are still concerned with making choices, but leaving the error uncorrected is not really a viable option.

Correctness matters deeply because your prose may be unreadable without it. If your prose is ungrammatical, not only will you risk incoherence (in which case your readers will not be able to follow what you are saying) but also you will inadvertently invite readers to dismiss you. Is it fair of readers to reject your ideas because of the way you've phrased them? Perhaps not, but the fact is they often will. A great many readers regard technical errors as an inattention to detail that also signals sloppiness at more important levels of thinking. If you produce writing that contains such errors, you risk not only distracting readers from your message but also *undermining your authority* to deliver the message in the first place.

B. THE CONCEPT OF BASIC WRITING ERRORS (BWEs)

You get a paper back, and it's a sea of red ink. But if you look more closely, you'll often find that you haven't made a million mistakes—you've made only a few, but over and over in various forms. This phenomenon is what the rhetorician Mina Shaughnessy addressed in creating the category of "basic writing errors," or BWEs. Shaughnessy argues that in order to improve your writing for style and correctness, you need to do two things:

- Look for a *pattern of error,* which will require you to understand your own logic in the mistakes you typically make.
- Recognize that not all errors are created equal, which means that you need to *address errors in some order of importance*—beginning with those most likely to interfere with your readers' understanding.

Not all errors are created equal: begin with those most likely to interfere with your readers' understanding.

The following BWE guide, "Nine Basic Writing Errors and How to Fix Them," that we have composed reflects Shaughnessy's view. First, it aims to teach you how to recognize and correct the basic kinds of errors that are potentially the most damaging to the clarity of your writing and to your credibility with readers. Second, the discussions in the guide seek to help you become aware of the patterns of error in your writing and discover the logic that has misled you into making them. If you can learn to see the pattern and then look for it in your editing and proofreading—expecting to find it—you will get in the habit of avoiding the error. In short, you will learn that your problem is not that you can't write correctly but simply that you have to remember, for example, to check for possessive apostrophes.

Our BWE guide does not, as we've mentioned, cover *all* of the rules of grammar, punctuation, diction, and usage, such as where to place the comma or period when you close a quotation or whether or not to write out numerals. For comprehensive coverage of the conventions of standard written English, you can consult one of the many handbooks available for this purpose. Our purpose is to provide a short guide to grammar—one that identifies the most common errors, provides remedies, and offers the logic that underlies them. This chapter's coverage of nine basic writing errors and how to fix them will help you eliminate most of the problems that routinely occur. We have arranged the error types in a hierarchy, moving in descending order of severity (from most to least problematic).

WHAT PUNCTUATION MARKS SAY: A "QUICK-HIT" GUIDE

These little signs really aren't that hard to use correctly, folks. A few of them will be treated in more specific contexts in the upcoming discussion of BWEs, but here are the basic rules of punctuation for the five basic signs.

The **period** [.] marks the end of a sentence. Make sure that what precedes it is an independent clause; that is, a subject plus verb that can stand alone.

The period says to a reader, "This is the end of this particular statement. I'm a mark of closure."

Example: Lennon rules.

The **comma** [,] separates the main (independent) clause from dependent elements that modify the main clause. It also separates two main clauses joined by a conjunction—known as a compound sentence. Information that is not central to the main clause is set off in a comma sandwich. The comma does *not* signify a pause.

The comma says to the reader, "Here is where the main clause begins (or ends)," or "Here is a break in the main clause." In the case of compound sentences (containing two or more independent clauses), the comma says, "Here is where one main clause ends, and after the conjunction that follows me, another main clause begins."

Examples: Lennon rules, and McCartney is cute.

Lennon rules, although McCartney is arguably more tuneful.

The **semicolon** [;] separates two independent clauses that are not joined by a conjunction. Secondarily, the semicolon can separate two independent clauses that are joined by a conjunction if either of the clauses already contains commas. In either case, the semicolon both shows a close relationship between the two independent clauses that it connects and distinguishes where one ends and the other begins. It is also the easiest way to fix comma splices (see "BWE 2" on page 356).

The semicolon says to the reader, "What precedes and what follows me are conceptually close but grammatically independent and thus equal statements."

Example: Lennon's lyrics show deep sympathy for the legions of "Nowhere Men" who inhabit the "Strawberry Fields" of their imaginations; McCartney's lyrics, on the other hand, are more upbeat, forever bidding "Good Day, Sunshine" to the world at large and "Michelle" in particular.

The **colon** [:] marks the end of a setup for something coming next. It provides a frame, pointing beyond itself, like a spotlight. The colon is quite dramatic, and unlike the semicolon, it links what precedes and follows it formally and tightly rather than loosely and associatively. It usually operates with dramatic force. It can frame a list to follow, separate cause and effect, or divide a brief claim from a more expanded version of the claim. The language on at least one side of the colon must be an independent clause, though both sides can be.

The colon says to the reader, "Concentrate on what follows me for a more detailed explanation of what preceded me" or "What follows me is logically bound with what preceded me."

Examples: *Rubber Soul* marked a change in The Beatles' song-writing: the sentimentality of earlier efforts gave way to a new complexity, both in the range of their subjects and the sophistication of their poetic devices.

> Nowhere is this change more evident than in a sequence of songs near the album's end: "I'm Looking Through You," "In My Life," "Wait," and "If I Needed Someone."

The **dash** [—] provides an informal alternative to the colon for adding information to a sentence. Its effect is sudden, of the moment—what springs up impulsively to disrupt and extend in some new way the ongoing train of thought. A **pair of dashes** provides an invaluable resource to writers for inserting information within a sentence. In this usage, the rule is that the sentence must read coherently if the inserted information is left out. (Note that to type a dash, type two hyphens with no space between, before, or after. This distinguishes the dash from a hyphen [-], which is the mark used for connecting two words into one.)

The dash says to the reader, "This too!" or, in the case of a pair of them, "Remember the thought in the beginning of this sentence because we're jumping to something else before we come back to finish that thought."

> **Examples:** For all their loveliness, the songs on *Rubber Soul* are not without menace—"I'd rather see you dead little girl than to see you with another man."
>
> In addition to the usual lead, rhythm, and bass guitar ensemble, *Rubber Soul* introduced new instruments—notably, the harpsichord interlude in "In My Life," the sitar spiraling though "Norwegian Wood"—that had not previously been heard in rock'n'roll.

NINE BASIC WRITING ERRORS AND HOW TO FIX THEM

If you're unsure about some of the terms you encounter in the discussions of BWEs, see the "Glossary of Grammatical Terms" at the end of this chapter. You'll also find brief "Test Yourself" questions interspersed throughout this section. Do them: it's easy to conclude that you understand a problem when you are shown the correction, but understanding is not the same thing as actively practicing. There's an appendix to this chapter that contains answers to these sections, along with explanations.

BWE 1: Sentence Fragments The most basic of writing errors, a *sentence fragment*, is a group of words punctuated like a complete sentence but lacking the necessary structure: it is only part of a sentence. Typically, a sentence fragment occurs when the group of words in question (1) lacks a subject, (2) lacks a predicate, or (3) is a subordinate (or dependent) clause.

To fix a sentence fragment, either turn it into an independent clause by providing whatever is missing—a subject or a predicate—or attach it to an independent clause upon which it can depend.

Noun Clause (No Predicate) As a Fragment

> A world where imagination takes over and sorrow is left behind.

This fragment is not a sentence but rather a noun clause—a sentence subject with no predicate. The fragment lacks a verb that would assert something about the subject. (The verbs "takes over" and "is left" are in a dependent clause created by the subordinating conjunction "where.")

Corrections

A world *arose* where imagination takes over and sorrow is left behind. [new verb matched to "a world"]

She entered a world where imagination takes over and sorrow is left behind. [new subject and verb added]

The first correction adds a new verb ("arose"). The second introduces a new subject and verb, converting the fragment into the direct object of "she entered."

Verbal As a Fragment

Falling into debt for the fourth consecutive year.

"Falling" in the preceding fragment is not a verb. Depending on the correction, "falling" is either a verbal or part of a verb phrase.

Corrections

The company was falling into debt for the fourth consecutive year. [subject and helping verb added]

Falling into debt for the fourth consecutive year *led the company to consider relocating.* [new predicate added]

Falling into debt for the fourth consecutive year, *the company considered relocating.* [new subject and verb added]

In the first correction, the addition of a subject and the helping verb "was" converts the fragment into a sentence. The second correction turns the fragment into a gerund phrase functioning as the subject of a new sentence. The third correction converts the fragment into a participial phrase attached to a new independent clause. (See the section entitled "Glossary of Grammatical Terms" and look under "verbal" for definitions of "gerund" and "participle.")

Subordinate Clause As a Fragment

I had an appointment for 11:00 and was still waiting at 11:30. Although I did get to see the dean before lunch.

"Although" is a subordinating conjunction that calls for some kind of completion. Like "if," "when," "because," "whereas," and other subordinating conjunctions (see the "Glossary of Grammatical Terms"), "although" *always* makes the clause that it introduces dependent.

Corrections

I had an appointment for 11:00 and was still waiting at *11:30, although* I did get to see the dean before lunch. [fragment attached to preceding sentence]

As the correction demonstrates, the remedy lies in attaching the fragment to an independent clause on which it can depend (or, alternatively, making the fragment into a sentence by dropping the conjunction).

Sometimes writers use sentence fragments deliberately, usually for rhythm and emphasis or to create a conversational tone. In less formal contexts, they are generally permissible, but you run the risk that the fragment will not be perceived as intentional. In formal writing assignments, it is safer to avoid intentional fragments.

TEST YOURSELF: FRAGMENTS

There are fragments in each of the following three examples, probably the result of their proximity to legitimate sentences. What's the problem in each case, and how would you fix it?

1. Like many other anthropologists, Margaret Mead studied non-Western cultures in such works as *Coming of Age in Samoa*. And influenced theories of childhood development in America.
2. The catastrophe resulted from an engineering flaw. Because the bridge lacked sufficient support.
3. In the 1840s the potato famine decimated Ireland. It being a country with poor soil and antiquated methods of agriculture.

A Note on Dashes and Colons

One way to correct a fragment is to replace the period with a dash: "The campaign required commitment. Not just money." becomes "The campaign required commitment—not just money." The dash offers you one way of attaching a phrase or dependent clause to a sentence without having to construct another independent clause. In short, it's succinct. (Compare the correction that uses the dash with another possible correction: "The campaign required commitment. It also required money.") Moreover, with the air of sudden interruption that the dash conveys, it can capture the informality and immediacy that the intentional fragment offers a writer.

You should be wary of overusing the dash as the slightly more presentable cousin of the intentional fragment. The energy it carries can clash with the decorum of formal writing contexts; for some readers, its staccato effect quickly becomes too much of a good thing.

One alternative to this usage of the dash is the colon. It can substitute because it also can be followed by a phrase, a list, or a clause. As with the dash, it must be preceded by an independent clause. And it, too, carries dramatic force because it abruptly halts the flow of the sentence.

The colon, however, does not convey informality. In place of a slapdash effect, it trains a light on what is to follow it. Hence, as in this sentence you are reading, it is especially appropriate for setting up certain kinds of information: explanations, lists, or results. In the case of results, the cause or action precedes the colon; the effect or reaction follows it.

Let us quickly review the other legitimate use of the dash: to enclose information within a sentence. In this use, dashes precede and follow the information, taking the role usually assigned to commas. Consider the following example:

> Shortly before the election—timing its disclosures for maximal destructive effect—the candidate's campaign staff levied a series of charges against the incumbent.

Note that if the information within the dashes is omitted, the sentence still reads grammatically.

BWE 2: Comma Splices and Fused (or Run-On) Sentences   A comma splice consists of two independent clauses connected ("spliced") with a comma; a fused (or run-on) sentence combines two such clauses with no conjunction or punctuation. The solutions for both comma splices and fused sentences are the same.

1. Place a conjunction (such as "and" or "because") between the clauses.
2. Place a semicolon between the clauses.
3. Make the clauses into separate sentences.

All of these solutions solve the same logical problem: they clarify the boundaries of the independent clauses for your readers.

Comma Splice

He disliked discipline, he avoided anything demanding.

Correction

Because he disliked discipline, he avoided anything demanding. [subordinating conjunction added]

Comma Splice

Today most TV programs are violent, almost every program is about cops and detectives.

Correction

Today most TV programs are violent; almost every program is about cops and detectives. [semicolon replaces comma]

Because the two independent clauses in the first example contain ideas that are closely connected logically, the most effective of the three comma-splice solutions is to add a subordinating conjunction ("because") to the first of the two clauses, making it depend on the second. For the same reason—close conceptual connection—the best solution for the next comma splice is to substitute a semicolon for the comma. The semicolon signals that the two independent clauses are closely linked in meaning. In general, you can use a semicolon where you could also use a period.

The best cures for the perpetual comma splicer: recognize the difference between independent and dependent clauses and get rid of the "pause theory" of punctuation.

The best cures for the perpetual comma splicer are to learn to recognize the difference between independent and dependent clauses and to get rid of the "pause theory" of punctuation. All of the clauses in our two examples are independent. As written, each of these should be punctuated not with a comma but rather with a period or a semicolon. Instead, the perpetual comma splicer, as usual, acts on the "pause theory": because the ideas in the independent clauses are closely connected, the writer hesitates to separate them with a period. And so the writer inserts what he or she takes to be a shorter pause—the comma. But a comma is not a "breath" mark; it provides readers with specific grammatical information, in each of these cases mistakenly suggesting there is only one independent clause separated by the comma from modifying information. In the corrections, by contrast, the semicolon sends the appropriate signal to the reader: the message that it is joining two associated but independent statements. (Adding a coordinating conjunction such as "and" would also be grammatically correct, though possibly awkward.)

> A comma is not a "breath" mark; it provides readers with specific grammatical information about where independent and dependent clauses are.

Fused Sentence

The Indo-European language family includes many groups most languages in Europe belong to it.

Correction

The Indo-European language family includes many groups. Most languages in Europe belong to it. [period inserted after first independent clause]

You could also fix this fused sentence with a comma plus the coordinating conjunction "and." Alternatively, you might condense the whole into a single independent clause.

Most languages in Europe belong to the Indo-European language family.

Comma Splices with Conjunctive Adverbs

Quantitative methods of data collection show broad trends, however, they ignore specific cases.

Sociobiology poses a threat to traditional ethics, for example, it asserts that human behavior is genetically motivated by the "selfish gene" to perpetuate itself.

Corrections

Quantitative methods of data collection show broad trends; however, they ignore specific cases. [semicolon replaces comma before "however"]

Sociobiology poses a threat to traditional ethics; for example, it asserts that human behavior is genetically motivated by the "selfish gene" to perpetuate itself. [semicolon replaces comma before "for example"]

Both of these examples contain one of the most common forms of comma splices. Both of them are compound sentences—that is, they contain two independent clauses. (See the section entitled "The Compound Sentence" in Chapter 11.) Normally, connecting the clauses with a comma and a conjunction would be correct; for example, "Most hawks hunt alone, but osprey hunt in pairs." In the preceding two comma splices, however, the independent clauses are joined by transitional expressions known as conjunctive adverbs. (See the "Glossary of Grammatical Terms.") When a conjunctive adverb is used to link two independent clauses, it *always* requires a semicolon. By contrast, when a coordinating conjunction links the two clauses of a compound sentence, it is *always* preceded by a comma.

In most cases, depending on the sense of the sentence, the semicolon precedes the conjunctive adverb and has the effect of clarifying the division between the two clauses. There are exceptions to this general rule, though, as in the following sentence:

The lazy boy did finally read a *book, however;* it was the least he could do.

Here "however" is a part of the first independent clause and qualifies its claim. The sentence thus suggests that the boy was not totally lazy, because he did get around to reading a book. Note how the meaning changes when "however" becomes the introductory word for the second independent clause.

The lazy boy did finally read a *book; however,* it was the least he could do.

Here the restricting force of "however" suggests that reading the book was not much of an accomplishment.

TEST YOURSELF: COMMA SPLICES

What makes each of the following sentences a comma splice? Determine the best way to fix each one and why, and then make the correction.

1. "Virtual reality" is a new buzzword, so is "hyperspace."
2. Many popular cures for cancer have been discredited, nevertheless, many people continue to buy them.
3. Elvis Presley's home, Graceland, attracts many musicians as a kind of shrine, even Paul Simon has been there.
4. She didn't play well with others, she sat on the bench and watched.

BWE 3: Errors in Subject–Verb Agreement   The subject and the verb must agree in number, a singular subject taking a singular verb and a plural subject taking a plural verb. Errors in subject–verb agreement usually occur when a writer misidentifies the subject or verb of a clause.

Agreement Problem

Various kinds of vandalism has been rapidly increasing.

Correction

Various kinds of vandalism *have* been rapidly increasing. [verb made plural to match "kinds"]

When you isolate the grammatical subject ("kinds") and the verb ("has") of the original sentence, you can tell that they do not agree. Although "vandalism" might seem to be the subject because it is closest to the verb, it is actually the object of the preposition "of." The majority of agreement problems arise from mistaking the object of a preposition for the actual subject of a sentence. If you habitually make this mistake, you can begin to remedy it by familiarizing yourself with the most common prepositions. (See the "Glossary of Grammatical Terms," which contains a list of these.)

Agreement Problem

Another aspect of territoriality that differentiates humans from animals are their possession of ideas and objects.

Correction

Another aspect of territoriality that differentiates humans from animals *is* their possession of ideas and objects. [verb made singular to match subject "aspect"]

The subject of the sentence is "aspect." The two plural nouns ("humans" and "animals") probably encourage the mistake of using a plural verb ("are"), but "humans" is part of the "that" clause modifying "aspect," and "animals" is the object of the preposition "from."

Agreement Problem

The Republican and the Democrat both believe in doing what's best for America, but each believe that the other doesn't understand what's best.

Correction

The Republican and the Democrat both believe in doing what's best for America, but each *believes* that the other doesn't understand what's best. [verb made singular to agree with subject "each"]

The word "each" is *always* singular, so the verb ("believes") must be singular as well. The presence of a plural subject and verb in the sentence's first independent clause ("the Republican and the Democrat both believe") has probably encouraged the error.

TEST YOURSELF: SUBJECT–VERB AGREEMENT

Diagnose and correct the error in the following example.

The controversies surrounding the placement of Arthur Ashe's statue in Richmond was difficult for the various factions to resolve.

A Note on Nonstandard English

The term "standard written English" refers to language that conforms to the rules and conventions adhered to by the majority of English-speaking writers. The fact is, however, that not all speakers of English grow up hearing, reading, and writing standard written English. Some linguistic cultures in America follow, for example, a different set of conventions for subject–verb agreement. Their speakers do not differentiate singular from plural verb forms with a terminal "–s," as in standard English.

She walks home after work.

They walk home after work.

Some speakers of English do not observe this distinction, so that the first sentence becomes:

She walk home after work.

These two ways of handling subject–verb agreement are recognized by linguists not in terms of right versus wrong but rather in terms of dialect difference. A *dialect* is a variety of a language that is characteristic of a region or culture and is sometimes unintelligible to outsiders. The problem for speakers of a dialect that differs from the norm is that they can't always rely on the ear—on what sounds right—when they are editing according to the rules of standard written English. Such speakers need, in effect, to learn to speak more than one dialect so that they can edit according to the rules of standard written English in situations where this would be expected. This often requires adding a separate proofreading stage for particular errors, like subject–verb agreement, rather than relying on what sounds right.

BWE 4: Shifts in Sentence Structure (Faulty Predication)   This error involves an illogical mismatch between subject and predicate. If you continually run afoul of faulty predication, you might use the exercises in a handbook to drill you on isolating the grammatical subjects and verbs of sentences, because that is the first move you need to make in fixing the problem.

Shift

In 1987, the release of more information became available.

Correction

In 1987, more *information* became available *for release*. [new subject]

It was the "information," not the "release," that "became available." The correction relocates "information" from its position as object of the preposition "of" to the subject position in the sentence; it also moves "release" into a prepositional phrase.

Shift

The busing controversy was intended to rectify the inequality of educational opportunities.

Correction

Busing was intended to rectify the inequality of educational opportunities. [new subject formulated to match verb]

The *controversy* wasn't intended to rectify, but busing was.

TEST YOURSELF: FAULTY PREDICATION

Identify and correct the faulty predication in this example:

The subject of learning disabilities is difficult to identify accurately.

BWE 5: Errors in Pronoun Reference   There are at least three forms of this problem. All of them involve a lack of clarity about whom or what a pronoun (a word that substitutes for a noun) refers to. The surest way to avoid difficulties is to make certain that the pronoun relates back unambiguously to a specific word, known as the antecedent. In the sentence "Nowadays appliances don't last as long as they once did," the noun "appliances" is the antecedent of the pronoun "they."

Pronoun–Antecedent Agreement
A pronoun must agree in number (and gender) with the noun or noun phrase that it refers to.

Pronoun Error

It can be dangerous if a child, after watching TV, decides to practice what they saw.

Corrections

It can be dangerous if *children,* after watching TV, *decide* to practice what *they* saw. [antecedent (and verb) made plural to agree with pronouns]

It can be dangerous if a child, after watching TV, decides to practice what *he or she* saw. [singular pronouns substituted to match singular antecedent "child"]

The error occurs because "child" is singular, but its antecedent pronoun, "they," is plural. The first correction makes both singular; the second makes both plural. You might also observe in the first word of the example—the impersonal "it"—an exception to the rule that pronouns must have antecedents.

TEST YOURSELF: PRONOUN–ANTECEDENT AGREEMENT

What is wrong with the following sentence, and how would you fix it?

Every dog has its day, but all too often when that day happens, they can be found barking up the wrong tree.

Ambiguous Reference
A pronoun should have only one possible antecedent. The possibility of two or more confuses relationships within the sentence.

Pronoun Error

Children like comedians because they have a sense of humor.

Corrections

Because children have a sense of humor, *they* like comedians. [subordinate "because" clause placed first, and relationship between noun "children" and pronoun "they" tightened]

Children like comedians because *comedians* have a sense of humor. [pronoun eliminated and replaced by repetition of noun]

Does "they" in the original example refer to "children" or "comedians"? The rule in such cases of ambiguity is that the pronoun refers to the nearest possible antecedent, so here "comedians" possess the sense of humor, regardless of what the writer may intend. As the corrections demonstrate, either reordering the sentence or repeating the noun can remove the ambiguity.

TEST YOURSELF: AMBIGUOUS REFERENCE

As you proofread, it's a good idea to target your pronouns to make sure that they cannot conceivably refer to more than one noun. What's wrong with the following sentences?

1. Alexander the Great's father, Philip of Macedon, died when he was twenty-six.
2. The committee could not look into the problem because it was too involved.

Broad Reference

Broad reference occurs when a pronoun refers loosely to a number of ideas expressed in preceding clauses or sentences. It causes confusion because the reader cannot be sure which of the ideas the pronoun refers to.

Pronoun Error

As a number of scholars have noted, Sigmund Freud and Karl Marx offered competing but also at times complementary critiques of the dehumanizing tendencies of Western capitalist society. We see this in Christopher Lasch's analysis of conspicuous consumption in *The Culture of Narcissism*.

Correction

As a number of scholars have noted, Sigmund Freud and Karl Marx offered competing but also at times complementary critiques of the dehumanizing tendencies of Western capitalist society. We see *this complementary view* in Christopher Lasch's analysis of conspicuous consumption in *The Culture of Narcissism*. [broad "this" clarified by addition of noun phrase]

The word "this" in the second sentence of the uncorrected example could refer to the fact that "a number of scholars have noted" the relationship between Freud and Marx, to the competition between Freud's and Marx's critiques of capitalism, or to the complementary nature of the two men's critiques.

Beware "this" as a pronoun: it's the most common source of broad reference. The remedy is generally to avoid using the word as a pronoun. Instead, convert "this" into an adjective, and let it modify some noun that more clearly specifies the referent: "this complementary view," as in the correction or, alternatively, "this competition" or "this scholarly perspective."

TEST YOURSELF: BROAD REFERENCE

Locate the errors in the following examples, and provide a remedy for each.

1. Regardless of whether the film is foreign or domestic, they can be found in your neighborhood video store.
2. Many experts now claim that dogs and other higher mammals dream; for those who don't own such pets, this is often difficult to believe.

A Note on Sexism and Pronoun Usage

Errors in pronoun reference sometimes occur because of a writer's praiseworthy desire to avoid sexism. In most circles, the following correction of the preceding example would be considered sexist.

It can be dangerous if a child, after watching TV, decides to practice what *he* saw.

Though the writer of such a sentence may intend "he" to function as a gender-neutral impersonal pronoun, it in fact excludes girls on the basis of gender. Implicitly, it also conveys sexual stereotypes (for example, that only boys are violent, or perhaps stupid, enough to confuse TV with reality).

The easiest way to avoid the problem of sexism in pronoun usage usually lies in putting things into the plural form, because plural pronouns ("we," "you," "they") have no gender. (See the use of "children" in the first correction of the pronoun–antecedent agreement example.) Alternatively, you can use the phrase "he or she." Many readers, however, find this phrase and its variant, "s/he," to be awkward constructions. Another remedy lies in rewriting the sentence to avoid pronouns altogether, as in the following revision.

It can be dangerous if a child, after watching TV, decides to practice *some violent activity portrayed on the screen.*

BWE 6: Misplaced Modifiers and Dangling Participles   Modifiers are words or groups of words used to qualify, limit, intensify, or explain some other element in a sentence. A misplaced modifier is a word or phrase that appears to modify the wrong word or words.

Misplaced Modifier

At the age of three he caught a fish with a broken arm.

Correction

At the age of three *the boy with a broken arm* caught a fish. [noun replaces pronoun; prepositional phrase revised and relocated]

The original sentence mistakenly implies that the fish had a broken arm. Modification errors often occur in sentences with one or more prepositional phrases, as in this case.

Misplaced Modifier

According to legend, General George Washington crossed the Delaware and celebrated Christmas in a small boat.

Correction

According to legend, General George Washington crossed the Delaware *in a small boat* and *then* celebrated Christmas *on shore.* [prepositional phrase relocated; modifiers added to second verb]

As a general rule, you can avoid misplacing a modifier by keeping it as close as possible to what it modifies. Thus, the second correction removes the implication that Washington celebrated Christmas in a small boat. When you cannot relocate the modifier, separate it from the rest of the sentence with a comma to prevent readers from connecting it to the nearest noun.

You can avoid misplacing a modifier by keeping it as close as possible to what it modifies.

A dangling participle creates a particular kind of problem in modification: the noun or pronoun that the writer intends the participial phrase to modify is not actually present in the sentence. Thus, we have the name dangling participle: the participle has been left dangling because the word or phrase it is meant to modify is not there.

Dangling Participle

After debating the issue of tax credits for the elderly, the bill passed in a close vote.

Correction

After debating the issue of tax credits for the elderly, *the Senate passed the bill* in a close vote. [appropriate noun added for participle to modify]

The bill did not debate the issue, as the original example implies. As the correction demonstrates, fixing a dangling participle involves tightening the link between the activity implied by the participle ("debating") and the entity performing that activity ("the Senate").

TEST YOURSELF: MODIFICATION ERRORS

Find the modification errors in the following examples and correct them.

1. After eating their sandwiches, the steamboat left the dock.
2. The social workers saw an elderly woman on a bus with a cane standing up.
3. Crossing the street, a car hit the pedestrian.

BWE 7: Errors in Using Possessive Apostrophes   Adding *'s* to most singular nouns will make them show possession, for example, the plant*'s* roots, the accountant*'s* ledger. You can add the apostrophe alone, without the "s," for example, to make plural nouns that already end with "s" show possession: the flowers*'* fragrances, the ships*'* berths (although you may also add an additional "s").

Apostrophe Error

The loyal opposition scorned the committees decisions.

Corrections

The loyal opposition scorned the *committee's* decisions.

The loyal opposition scorned the *committees'* decisions. [possessive apostrophe added]

The first correction assumes there was one committee; the second assumes there were two or more.

Apostrophe Error

The advisory board swiftly transacted it's business.

Correction

The advisory board swiftly transacted *its* business. [apostrophe dropped]

Unlike possessive nouns, possessive pronouns ("my," "your," "yours," "her," "hers," "his," "its," "our," "ours," "their," "theirs") *never* take an apostrophe.

TEST YOURSELF: POSSESSIVE APOSTROPHES

Find and correct any errors in the following sentence.

The womens movement has been misunderstood by many of its detractors.

BWE 8: Comma Errors   As with other rules of punctuation and grammar, the many that pertain to comma usage share an underlying aim: to clarify the relationships among the parts of a sentence. Commas separate the parts of a sentence grammatically. One of their primary uses, then, is to help your readers distinguish the main clause from dependent elements, such as subordinate clauses and long prepositional phrases. They do not signify a pause, as was discussed under "BWE 2."

Comma Error

After eating the couple went home.

Correction

After *eating,* the couple went home. [comma added before independent clause]

The comma after "eating" is needed to keep the main clause "visible" or separate; it marks the point at which the prepositional phrase ends and the independent clause begins. Without this separation, readers would be invited to contemplate cannibalism as they move across the sentence.

Comma Error

In the absence of rhetoric study teachers and students lack a vocabulary for talking about their prose.

Correction

In the absence of rhetoric *study,* teachers and students lack a vocabulary for talking about their prose. [comma added to separate prepositional phrase from main clause]

Without the comma, readers would have to read the sentence twice to find out where the prepositional phrase ends—with "study"—in order to figure out where the main clause begins.

Comma Error

Dog owners, despite their many objections will have to obey the new law.

Correction

Dog owners, despite their many *objections,* will have to obey the new law. [single comma converted to a pair of commas]

A comma is needed after "objections" in order to isolate the phrase in the middle of the sentence ("despite their many objections") from the main clause. The phrase needs to be set off with commas because it contains additional information that is not essential to the meaning of what it modifies. (Dog owners must obey the law whether they object or not.) Phrases and clauses that function in this way are called *nonrestrictive.*

The test of nonrestrictive phrases and clauses is to see if they can be omitted without substantially changing the message that a sentence conveys ("Dog owners will have to obey the new law," for example). Nonrestrictive elements always take two commas—a comma "sandwich"—to set them off. Using only one comma illogically separates the sentence's subject ("dog owners") from its predicate ("will have to obey"). This problem is easier to see in a shorter sentence. You wouldn't, for example, write "I, fell down." As a rule, commas virtually never separate the subject from the verb of a sentence. (Here's an exception: "Ms. Taloora, a high fashion model, watches her diet scrupulously.")

Comma Error

Most people regardless of age like to spend money.

Correction

Most *people,* regardless of *age,* like to spend money. [comma sandwich added]

Here commas enclose the nonrestrictive elements; you could omit this information without significantly affecting the sense. Such is not the case in the following two examples.

Comma Error

People, who live in glass houses, should not throw stones.

Correction

People *who live in glass houses* should not throw stones. [commas omitted]

Comma Error

Please return the library book, that I left on the table.

Correction

Please return the library *book that* I left on the table. [comma omitted]

It is incorrect to place commas around "who live in glass houses" or a comma before "that I left on the table." Each of these is a *restrictive clause*—that is, it contains information that is an essential part of what it modifies. In the first sentence, for example, if "who live in glass houses" is left out, the fundamental meaning of the sentence is lost: "People should not throw stones." The word "who" is defined by restricting it to "people" in the category of glass-house dwellers. Similarly, in the second example the "that" clause contributes an essential meaning to "book"; the sentence is referring to not just any book but to a particular one, the one "on the table."

So remember the general rule: if the information in a phrase or clause can be omitted—if it is nonessential and therefore nonrestrictive—it needs to be separated by commas from the rest of the sentence. Moreover, note that nonrestrictive clauses are generally introduced by the word "which," so a "which" clause interpolated into a sentence takes a comma sandwich. ("The dinner, which I bought for $20, made me sick.") By contrast, a restrictive clause is introduced by the word "that" and takes no commas.

TEST YOURSELF: COMMA ERRORS

Consider the following examples as a pair. Punctuate them as necessary, and then briefly articulate how the meanings of the two sentences differ.

1. The book which I had read a few years ago contained a lot of outdated data.
2. The book that I had read a few years ago contained a lot of outdated data.

BWE 9: Spelling/Diction Errors That Interfere with Meaning Misspellings are always a problem in a final draft, insofar as they undermine your authority by inviting readers to perceive you as careless (at best). If you make a habit of using the spellchecker of a word processor, you will take care of most misspellings. But the problems that a spellchecker won't catch are the ones that can often hurt you most. These are actually diction errors—incorrect word choices in which you have confused one word with another that it closely resembles. In such cases, you have spelled the word correctly, but it's the wrong word. Because it means something other than what you've intended, you end up misleading your readers. (See "Shades of Meaning" in Chapter 10.)

The best way to avoid this problem is to memorize the differences between pairs of words that are commonly confused with each other but that have distinct meanings. The following examples illustrate a few of the most common and serious of these errors. Most handbooks contain a glossary of usage that *cites* more of these *sites* of confusion.

Spelling/Diction Error: "It's" Versus "Its"

Although you can't tell a book by its' cover, its fairly easy to get the general idea from the introduction.

Correction

Although you can't tell a book by *its* cover, *it's* fairly easy to get the general idea from the introduction. [apostrophe dropped from possessive and added to contraction]

"It's" is a contraction for "it is." "Its" is a possessive pronoun meaning "belonging to it." If you confuse the two, *it's* likely that your sentence will mislead *its* readers.

Spelling/Diction Error: "Their" Versus "There" Versus "They're"

Their are ways of learning about the cuisine of northern India besides going their to watch the master chefs and learn there secrets—assuming their willing to share them.

Correction

There are ways of learning about the cuisine of northern India besides going *there* to watch the master chefs and learn *their* secrets—assuming *they're* willing to share them. [expletive "there," adverb "there," possessive pronoun "their," and contraction "they're" inserted appropriately]

"There" as an adverb normally refers to a place; "there" can also be used as an expletive to introduce a clause, as in the first usage of the correction. (See the discussion of expletives under "Cutting the Fat" in Chapter 11.) "Their" is a possessive pronoun meaning "belonging to them." "They're" is a contraction for "they are."

Spelling/Diction Error: "Then" Versus "Than"

If a person would rather break a law then obey it, than he or she must be willing to face the consequences.

Correction

If a person would rather break a law *than* obey it, *then* he or she must be willing to face the consequences. [comparative "than" distinguished from temporal "then"]

"Than" is a conjunction used with a comparison, for example, "rather X than Y." "Then" is an adverb used to indicate what comes next in relation to time, for example, "first X, then Y."

Spelling/Diction Error: "Effect" Versus "Affect"

It is simply the case that BWEs adversely effect the way that readers judge what a writer has to say. It follows that writers who include lots of BWEs in their prose may not have calculated the disastrous affects of these mistakes.

Correction

It is simply the case that BWEs adversely *affect* the way that readers judge what a writer has to say. It follows that writers who include lots of BWEs in their prose may not have calculated the disastrous *effects* of these mistakes. [verb "affect" and noun "effects" inserted appropriately]

In their most common usages, "affect" is a verb meaning "to influence," and "effect" is a noun meaning "the result of an action or cause." The confusion of "affect" and "effect" is enlarged by the fact that both of these words have secondary meanings: the verb "to effect" means "to cause or bring about"; the noun "affect" is used in psychology to mean "emotion or feeling." Thus, if you confuse these two words, you will inadvertently make a meaning radically different from the one you intend.

TEST YOURSELF: SPELLING/DICTION ERRORS

Make corrections as necessary in the following paragraph.

Its not sufficiently acknowledged that the behavior of public officials is not just an ethical issue but one that effects the sale of newspapers and commercial bytes in television news. When public officials don't do what their supposed to do, than their sure to face the affects of public opinion—if they get caught—because there are dollars to be made. Its that simple: money more then morality is calling the tune in the way that the press treats it's superstars.

C. GLOSSARY OF GRAMMATICAL TERMS

adjective   An adjective is a part of speech that usually modifies a noun or pronoun, for example, *blue, boring, boisterous.*

adverb   An adverb is a part of speech that modifies an adjective, adverb, or verb, for example, *heavily, habitually, very.* The adverbial form generally differs from the adjectival form via the addition of the ending "–ly"; for example, *happy* is an adjective, and *happily* is an adverb.

clause (independent and dependent)   A clause is any group of words that contains both a **subject** and a **predicate**. An **independent clause** (also known as a **main clause**) can stand alone as a sentence. For example,

> The most famous revolutionaries of this century have all, in one way or another, offered a vision of a classless society.

The subject of this independent clause is "revolutionaries," the verb is "have offered," and the direct object is "vision." By contrast, a **dependent** (or **subordinate**) **clause** is any group of words containing a subject and verb that cannot stand alone as a separate sentence because it depends on an independent clause to complete its meaning. The following sentence adds two dependent clauses to our previous example:

> The most famous revolutionaries of this century have all, in one way or another, offered a vision of a classless society, *although* most historians would agree *that* this ideal has never been achieved.

The origin of the word "depend" is "to hang": a dependent clause literally hangs on the independent clause. In the preceding example, neither "although most historians would agree" nor "that this ideal has never been achieved" can stand independently. The "that" clause relies on the "although" clause, which in turn relies on the main clause. "That" and "although" function as **subordinating conjunctions**; by eliminating them, we could rewrite the sentence to contain three independent clauses:

> The most famous revolutionaries of this century have all, in one way or another, offered a vision of a classless society. Most historians would agree on one judgment about this vision: it has never been achieved.

comma splice   A comma splice consists of two independent clauses incorrectly connected (spliced) with a comma. See "BWE 2."

conjunction (coordinating and subordinating)   A conjunction is a part of speech that connects words, phrases, or clauses, for example, *and, but, although*. The conjunction in some way defines that connection: for example, *and* links; *but* separates. All conjunctions define connections in one of two basic ways. Coordinating conjunctions connect words or groups of words that have equal grammatical importance. The coordinating conjunctions are *and, but, or, nor, for, so,* and *yet*. Subordinating conjunctions introduce a dependent clause and connect it to a main clause. Here is a partial list of the most common subordinating conjunctions: *after, although, as, as if, as long as, because, before, if, rather than, since, than, that, though, unless, until, when, where, whether,* and *while*.

conjunctive adverb   A conjunctive adverb is a word that links two independent clauses (as a conjunction) but that also modifies the clause it introduces (as an adverb). Some of the most common conjunctive adverbs are *consequently, furthermore, however, moreover, nevertheless, similarly, therefore,* and *thus*. Phrases can also serve this function, such as *for example* and *on the other hand*. When conjunctive adverbs are used to link two independent clauses, they always require a semicolon:

> Many pharmaceutical chains now offer their own generic versions of common drugs; however, many consumers continue to spend more for name brands that contain the same active ingredients as the generics.

When conjunctive adverbs occur within an independent clause, however, they are enclosed in a pair of commas, as is the case with the use of *however* earlier in this sentence.

coordination   Coordination refers to grammatically equal words, phrases, or clauses. Coordinate constructions are used to give elements in a sentence equal weight or importance. In the sentence "The tall, thin lawyer badgered the witness, but the judge interceded," the clauses "The tall, thin lawyer badgered the witness" and "but the judge interceded" are coordinate clauses; "tall" and "thin" are coordinate adjectives.

dependent clause (see *clause*)

direct object   The direct object is a noun or pronoun that receives the action carried by the verb and performed by the subject. In the sentence, "Certain mushrooms can kill you," "you" is the direct object.

gerund (see *verbals*)

fused (or run-on) sentence   A fused sentence incorrectly combines two independent clauses with no conjunction or punctuation. See "BWE 2."

independent clause (see *clause*)

infinitive (see *verbals*)

main clause (see *clause*)

noun   A noun is a part of speech that names a person (*woman*), place (*town*), thing (*book*), idea (*justice*), quality (*irony*), or action (*betrayal*).

object of the preposition (see *preposition*)

participle and participial phrase (see *verbals*)

phrase   A phrase is a group of words occurring in a meaningful sequence that lacks either a subject or a predicate. This absence distinguishes it from a clause, which contains both a subject and a predicate. Phrases function in sentences as adjectives, adverbs, nouns, or verbs. They are customarily classified according to the part of speech of their key word: "over the mountain" is a **prepositional phrase**; "running for office" is a **participial phrase**; "had been disciplined" is a **verb phrase**; "desktop graphics" is a **noun phrase**; and so forth.

predicate   The predicate contains the verb of a sentence or clause, making some kind of statement about the subject. The predicate of the preceding sentence is "contains the verb, making some kind of statement about the subject." The simple predicate—the verb to which the other words in the sentence are attached—is "contains."

preposition, prepositional phrase   A preposition is a part of speech that links a noun or pronoun to some other word in the sentence. Prepositions usually express a relationship of time (after) or space (above) or direction (toward). The noun to which the preposition is attached is known as the object of the preposition. A preposition, its object, and any modifiers comprise a prepositional phrase. "*With* love *from* me *to* you" strings together three prepositional phrases. Here is a partial list of the most common prepositions: *about, above, across, after, among, at, before, behind, between, by, during, for, from, in, into, like, of, on, out, over, since, through, to, toward, under, until, up, upon, with, within,* and *without.*

pronoun   A pronoun is a part of speech that substitutes for a noun, such as *I, you, he, she, it, we,* and *they.*

run-on (or fused) sentence   A run-on sentence incorrectly combines two independent clauses with no conjunction or punctuation. See "BWE 2."

sentence   A sentence is a unit of expression that can stand independently. It contains two parts, a **subject** and a **predicate**. The shortest sentence in the Bible, for example, is "Jesus wept." "Jesus" is the subject; "wept" is the predicate.

sentence fragment   A sentence fragment is a group of words incorrectly punctuated like a complete sentence but lacking the necessary structure; it is only a part of a sentence. "Walking down the road" and "the origin of the problem" are both fragments because neither contains a **predicate**. See "BWE 1."

subject　The subject, in most cases a noun or pronoun, names the doer of the action in a sentence or identifies what the predicate is about. The subject of the previous sentence, for example, is "the subject, in most cases a noun or pronoun." The simple subject of that sentence—the noun to which the other words in the sentence are attached—is "subject."

subordination, subordinating conjunctions　"Subordination" refers to the placement of certain grammatical units, particularly phrases and clauses, at a lower, less important structural level than other elements. As with coordination, the grammatical ranking carries conceptual significance as well: whatever is grammatically subordinated appears less important than the information carried in the main clause. In the following example, the 486-based personal computer is subordinated both grammatically and conceptually to the Pentium-based PC:

> Although 486-based personal computers continue to improve in speed, the new Pentium-based PC systems have thoroughly outclassed them.

Here "although" is a **subordinating conjunction** that introduces a subordinate clause, also known as a **dependent clause**.

verb　A verb is a part of speech that describes an action (*goes*), states how something was affected by an action (*became angered*), or expresses a state of being (*is*).

verbals (participles, gerunds, and infinitives)　Verbals are words derived from verbs. They are verb forms that look like verbs but, as determined by the structure of the sentence they appear in, they function as nouns, adjectives, or adverbs. There are three forms of verbals.

An **infinitive**—composed of the root form of a verb plus *to* (*to be, to vote*)—becomes a verbal when it is used as a noun ("*To eat* is essential"), an adjective ("These are the books *to read*"), or an adverb ("He was too sick *to walk*").

Similarly, a **participle**—usually composed of the root form of a verb plus "–ing" (present participle) or "–ed" (past participle)—becomes a verbal when used as an adjective. It can occur as a single word, modifying a noun, as in *faltering negotiations* or *finished business*. But it also can occur in a participial phrase, consisting of the participle, its object, and any modifiers. Here are two examples:

> *Having been tried and convicted*, the criminal was sentenced to life imprisonment.

> *Following the path of most resistance*, the masochist took deep pleasure in his frustration.

"Having been tried and convicted" is a participial phrase that modifies "criminal"; "Following the path of most resistance" is a participial phrase that modifies "masochist." In each case, the participial phrase functions as an adjective.

The third form of verbal, the **gerund**, resembles the participle. Like the participle, it is formed by adding "–ing" to the root form of the verb, but unlike the participle, it is used as a noun. In the sentence "Swimming is extraordinarily aerobic," the gerund "swimming" functions as the subject. Again like participles, gerunds can occur in phrases. The gerund phrases are italicized in the following example: "*Watching a film adaptation* takes less effort than *reading the book* from which it was made."

When using a verbal, remember that although it resembles a verb, it cannot function alone as the verb in a sentence: "Being a military genius" is a fragment, not a sentence.

◀ ASSIGNMENT: Grammar and Style Quiz

Here is an error-laden paragraph to rewrite and correct by making changes in grammar and punctuation as necessary. You may need to add, drop, or rearrange words, but do not add any periods. That way, you will be able to test yourself on your ability to use commas plus conjunctions, semicolons, colons, and dashes rather than avoid these options by separating each independent clause into a simple sentence. The quiz also contains a few stylistic problems addressed in Chapters 10 and 11. A discussion of the errors and how to fix them can be found in the Appendix to this chapter.

[1]   It is a fact that fraternities and sororities are a major part of student life at the

[2]   university, students are preoccupied with pledging. This is not approved of by

[3]   most members of the faculty, however, they feel helpless about attacking them.

[4]   Perceiving that the greek societies are attractive to the students but at the same

[5]   time encouraging anti-intellectualism, it is not an issue that can be addressed

[6]   easily. The student, who wants to be popular and cool feels that he should not

[7]   talk in class, because interest in academics or having ideas outside class is

[8]   uncool. Its more important to pledge the right house then being smart. If the

[9]   administration would create alternatives to Greek life such as a honors program

[10] students lives would be more enriched. Although for now raising the cumulative

[11] grade point necessary to pledge and remain active would be a good start.

[12] Contrary to the University's stance against gender discrimination Greek life

[13] perpetuates gender stereotypes; for example, the dances at each house for

[14] freshman women but not men. Some of the best students agree with this but

[15] mistakenly believes that most faculty endorse the system. ▶

GUIDELINES FOR REVISING FOR CORRECTNESS

1. In correcting grammar, seek to discover the patterns of error in your writing, and unlearn the logic that has led you to make certain kinds of errors recurrently.

2. Check the draft for errors that obscure the boundaries of sentences: fragments, comma splices, and run-ons. Begin by isolating the simple subject and predicate in the main clause(s) of every sentence (to make sure they exist); this check will also help you to spot faulty predication and errors in subject–verb agreement. Then, check to see that each independent clause is separated from others by a period, a comma plus coordinating conjunction, or a semicolon.

3. Check your sentences for ambiguity (the potential of being read in more than one way) by deliberately trying to misread them. If your sentence can be read to mean something other than what you intended, the most common causes are misplaced and dangling modifiers and errors in pronoun reference.

4. Fix errors in pronoun reference and misplaced modifiers by making sure that every pronoun has only one clear antecedent and that every modifying word or phrase is placed as close as possible to the part of the sentence it modifies.

5. Avoid dangling modifiers by being sure that the noun or pronoun being modified is actually present in the sentence. Avoid broad reference by adding the appropriate noun or noun phrase after the pronoun "this." (You can greatly improve the clarity of your prose just by avoiding use of the vague "this," especially at the beginnings of sentences.)

6. Check that commas are separating dependent clauses, long prepositional phrases, or other modifying elements from the main clause. A comma is not a pause; its function is to help readers locate your sentence's main (independent) clause(s).

7. Enclose nonrestrictive modifiers placed between the subject and predicate of a sentence in a pair of commas or—for more emphasis—in a pair of dashes. A nonrestrictive modifier is a phrase, often beginning with "which," that can be deleted from the sentence without changing the sentence's meaning.

Chapter 14 Appendix
Answer Key (with Discussion)

TEST YOURSELF SECTIONS

Test Yourself: Fragments

Original example: Like many other anthropologists, Margaret Mead studied non-Western cultures in such works as *Coming of Age in Samoa.* And influenced theories of childhood development in America.

Problem: The second sentence is actually a fragment, a predicate in need of a subject.

Possible correction: Like many other anthropologists, Margaret Mead studied non-Western cultures (in such works as *Coming of Age in Samoa*) in ways that influenced theories of childhood development in America.

Comment: There are many ways to fix this example, but its original form leaves ambiguous whether the fragment refers only to "Mead" or to "many other anthropologists" as well. The correction offered includes the other anthropologists in the referent and diminishes the emphasis on Mead's book by placing it within parentheses. Although the correction uses a subordinating "that" to incorporate the fragment into the first sentence, it keeps this information in an emphatic position at the end of the sentence.

Original example: The catastrophe resulted from an engineering flaw. Because the bridge lacked sufficient support.

Problem: The second sentence is actually a dependent clause; "because" always subordinates.

Possible correction: The catastrophe resulted from an engineering flaw: the bridge lacked sufficient support.

Comment: Because the colon has causal force, this is an ideal spot to use one, identifying the "flaw."

Original example: In the 1840s the potato famine decimated Ireland. It being a country with poor soil and antiquated methods of agriculture.

Problem: The second sentence is actually a fragment, a subject plus a long participial phrase.

Possible correction: In the 1840s the potato famine decimated Ireland, a country with poor and antiquated methods of agriculture.

Comment: The cause of this kind of fragment is usually that the writer mistakenly believes that "being" is a verb rather than a participle that introduces a long phrase (modifying "Ireland" in this case). It would also be correct simply to change the period to a comma in the original sentence.

Test Yourself: Comma Splices

Original example: "Virtual reality" is a new buzzword, so is "hyperspace."

Problem: This is a comma splice—both clauses are independent, yet they are joined with a comma.

Possible correction: "Virtual reality" is a new buzzword; so is "hyperspace."

Comment: Because the clauses are linked by association—both naming buzzwords—a semicolon would show that association. A writer could also condense the clauses into a simple sentence with a compound subject, for example, "Both 'virtual reality' and 'hyperspace' are new buzzwords."

Original example: Many popular cures for cancer have been discredited, nevertheless, many people continue to buy them.

Problem: A comma splice results from the incorrectly punctuated conjunctive adverb "nevertheless."

Possible correction: Many popular cures for cancer have been discredited; nevertheless, many people continue to buy them.

Comment: Without the semicolon to separate the independent clauses, the conjunctive adverb could conceivably modify either the preceding or the following clause. This problem is usually worse with "however."

Original example: Elvis Presley's home, Graceland, attracts many musicians as a kind of shrine, even Paul Simon has been there.

Problem: This is a comma splice—the two independent clauses are linked by a comma without a conjunction. The problem is exacerbated by the number of commas in the sentence; the reader cannot easily tell which one is used to separate the clauses.

Possible correction: Elvis Presley's home, Graceland, attracts many musicians as a kind of shrine—even Paul Simon has been there.

Comment: Although one could justly use a semicolon here, the dash conveys the impromptu effect of an afterthought.

Original example: She didn't play well with others, she sat on the bench and watched.

Problem: Because the second clause develops the first one, a writer might think that it is dependent on the first; conceptually, yes, but grammatically, no.

Possible correction: She didn't play well with others; she sat on the bench and watched.

Comment: If the writer wanted to link the two clauses more tightly, a colon would be appropriate instead of the semicolon.

Test Yourself: Subject–Verb Agreement

Original example: The controversies surrounding the placement of Arthur Ashe's statue in Richmond was difficult for the various factions to resolve.

Problem: The grammatical subject of the main clause ("controversies") is plural; the verb ("was") is singular.

Possible corrections: The controversies surrounding the placement of Arthur Ashe's statue in Richmond were difficult for the various factions to resolve (or, The controversy . . . was).

Comment: An error of this kind is encouraged by two factors: the distance of the verb from the subject and the presence of intervening prepositional phrases that use singular objects, either of which a writer might mistake for the grammatical subject of the main clause.

Test Yourself: Faulty Predication

Original example: The subject of learning disabilities is difficult to identify accurately.

Problem: The predicate matches the object of the preposition ("learning disabilities") rather than the subject of the main clause ("subject").

Possible correction: Learning disabilities are difficult to identify accurately.

Comment: Omitting the abstract opening ("The subject of") enables the predicate ("are") to fit the new grammatical subject ("disabilities").

Test Yourself: Pronoun–Antecedent Agreement

Original example: Every dog has its day, but all too often when that day happens, they can be found barking up the wrong tree.

Problem: The plural pronoun "they" that is the grammatical subject of the second clause does not have a plural antecedent in the sentence.

Possible correction: Every dog has its day, but all too often when that day happens, the dog can be found barking up the wrong tree.

Comment: If a writer vigilantly checks all pronouns, he or she will identify the intended antecedent of the pronoun "they" to be the singular "dog" and revise accordingly. The sentence would still be incorrect if the pronoun "it" were used instead of the repeated "dog," because "it" could refer to the nearest preceding noun, "day."

Test Yourself: Ambiguous Reference

Original example: Alexander the Great's father, Philip of Macedon, died when he was twenty-six.

Problem: A reader can't be sure whether "he" refers to Alexander or to Philip.

Possible correction: Alexander the Great's father, Philip of Macedon, died at the age of twenty-six.

Comment: The correction rewords to remove the ambiguous pronoun. This solution is less awkward than repeating "Philip" in place of "he," though that would also be correct.

Original example: The committee could not look into the problem because it was too involved.

Problem: A reader can't be sure whether "it" refers to "the committee" or to "the problem."

Possible correction: The committee was too involved with other matters to look into the problem.

Comment: As with the previous example, rewording to eliminate the ambiguous pronoun is usually the best solution.

Test Yourself: Broad Reference

Original example: Regardless of whether the film is foreign or domestic, they can be found in your neighborhood video store.

Problem: The plural pronoun "they" does not have a plural antecedent in the sentence.

Possible correction: Regardless of whether the film is foreign or domestic, it can be found in your neighborhood video store.

Comment: Although the sentence offers two options for films, the word "film" is singular and so, as antecedent, requires a singular pronoun ("it"). It is probably worth noting here that "it" would still be correct even if the original sentence began, "Regardless of whether the film is a foreign film or a domestic film." The rule for compound subjects that use an either/or construction is as follows: the number (singular or plural) of the noun or pronoun that follows *or* determines the number of the verb. Compare the following two examples: "Either several of his aides *or* the *candidate is* going to speak" and "Either the candidate *or* several of his *aides are* going to speak."

Original example: Many experts now claim that dogs and other higher mammals dream; for those who don't own such pets, this is often difficult to believe.

Problem: The referent of the pronoun "this" is unclear. Precisely what is "difficult to believe"—that mammals dream or that experts would make such a claim?

Possible correction: Many experts now claim that dogs and other higher mammals dream; for those who don't own such pets, this claim is often difficult to believe.

Comment: Often the best way to fix a problem with broad reference produced by use of "this" as a pronoun is to convert "this" to an adjective—a strategy that will require a writer to provide a specifying noun for "this" to modify. As a rule, when you find an isolated "this" in your draft, ask and answer the question "This what?"

Test Yourself: Modification Errors

Original example: After eating their sandwiches, the steamboat left the dock.

Problem: This is a dangling participle—the grammar of the sentence conveys that the steamboat ate their sandwiches.

Corrections: After the girls ate their sandwiches, the steamboat left the dock. Or, After eating their sandwiches, the girls boarded the steamboat, and it left the dock.

Comment: The two corrections model the two ways of remedying most dangling participles. Both provide an antecedent ("the girls") for the pronoun "their." The first correction eliminates the participial phrase and substitutes a subordinate clause. The second correction adds to the existing main clause ("steamboat left") another one ("girls boarded") for the participial phrase to modify appropriately.

Original example: The social workers saw an elderly woman on a bus with a cane standing up.

Problem: Misplaced modifiers create the problems in this sentence, which implies that the bus possessed a cane that was standing up. The problem exemplified here is produced from the series of prepositional phrases—"*on* a bus *with* a cane"—followed by the participial phrase "standing up," which is used as an adjective and intended to modify "woman."

Possible correction: The social workers saw an elderly woman on a bus. She was standing up with the help of a cane.

Comment: Writers often try to cram too much into sentences, piling on the prepositions. The best remedy is sometimes to break up the sentence, a move that usually involves eliminating prepositions, which possess a sludgy kind of movement, and adding verbs, which possess more distinct movement.

Original example: Crossing the street, a car hit the pedestrian.

Problem: The dangling participle ("Crossing the street") does not have a word to modify in the sentence. The sentence conveys that the car crossed the street.

Possible corrections: Crossing the street, the pedestrian was hit by a car. Or: As the pedestrian crossed the street, a car hit him.

Comment: The first solution brings the participial phrase closest to the noun it modifies ("pedestrian"). The second converts the participial into the verb ("crossed") of a dependent "as" clause and moves "pedestrian" into the clause as the subject for that verb. As in the "steamboat" example, one correction provides an appropriate noun for the participial phrase to modify, and the other eliminates the participle.

Test Yourself: Possessive Apostrophes

Original example: The womens movement has been misunderstood by many of its detractors.

Problem: The possessive apostrophe for "womens" is missing. The trickiness here in inserting the apostrophe is that this word is already plural.

Possible correction: The women's movement has been misunderstood by many of its detractors.

Comment: Because the word is already plural, it takes a simple "–'s" to indicate a movement belonging to women—not "–s'" (womens').

Test Yourself: Comma Errors

Original paired examples: The book which I had read a few years ago contained a lot of outdated data.

The book that I had read a few years ago contained a lot of outdated data.

Problem: In the first example, the modifying clause "which I had read a few years ago" is nonrestrictive: it could be omitted without changing the essential meaning of the sentence. Therefore, it needs to be enclosed in commas—as the "which" signals.

Possible correction: The book, which I had read a few years ago, contained a lot of outdated data.

Comment: The second example in the pair is correct as it stands. The restrictive clause, "that I had read a few years ago," does not take commas around it because the information it gives readers is an essential part of the meaning of "book." That is, it refers to not just any book read a few years ago, as in the first example in the pair, but rather specifies the one containing outdated data. "The book that I had read a few years ago" thus functions as what is known as a *noun phrase.*

Test Yourself: Spelling/Diction Errors

Original example: Its not sufficiently acknowledged that the behavior of public officials is not just an ethical issue but one that effects the sale of newspapers and commercial bytes in television news. When public officials don't do what their supposed to do, than their sure to face the affects of public opinion—if they get caught—because there are dollars to be made. Its that simple: money more then morality is calling the tune in the way that the press treats it's superstars.

Problems: The paragraph confuses the paired terms discussed under "BWE 9." It mistakes
"its" for "it's" before "not sufficiently."
"effects" for "affects" before "the sale."
"their" for "they're" before "supposed."
"than" for "then" before "their sure."
"they're" for "their" before "sure."
"affects" for "effects" before "of public opinion."
"its" for "it's" before "that simple."
"then" for "than" before "morality."
"it's" for "its" before "superstars."

Possible correction: It's not sufficiently acknowledged that the behavior of public officials is not just an ethical issue but one that affects the sale of newspapers and commercial bytes in television news. When public officials don't do what they're supposed to do, then they're sure to face the effects of public opinion—if they get caught—because there are dollars to be made. It's that simple: money more than morality is calling the tune in the way that the press treats its superstars.

Comment: If you confuse similar words, the only solution is to memorize the differences and consciously check your drafts for any problems until habit takes hold.

GRAMMAR AND STYLE QUIZ

The answers offered here are not exclusive—the only ways to correct the problems. In some cases, we have offered various satisfactory remedies, and as previously noted, a few of the suggested revisions—marked by a bullet—address editing for style (Chapters 10 and 11) rather than editing for correctness.

Line 1

- There are no grammatical errors per se, but "It is a fact that" is a wordy expletive that should be cut.

Line 2

- There is a comma splice between "university" and "students": insert a semicolon as the preferred option.
- "This," beginning the next sentence, is a broad reference and should be converted into an adjective, with a noun or noun phrase added, such as "This preoccupation" or "This dominance by Greek societies."
- In addition, a writer might recast the passive verb into the active: "Most faculty members do not approve of . . ."

Line 3

- There is a comma splice after "faculty": insert a semicolon.
- The antecedent of the pronoun "them" is ambiguous: substitute a noun such as "the Greeks."

Line 4

- "Perceiving" is a dangling participle: either recast to include a subject in a dependent clause (such as "Because most faculty members perceive") or insert "most faculty members" as a referent for the participle before "it" in Line 5.
- Capitalize "Greek."

Line 5

- Fix faulty parallelism: introduce the second item ("encouraging anti-intellectualism") with another "that" ("but at the same time that they encourage").
- The "it is" (an expletive) creates problems with broad reference. If Line 4 has been changed by eliminating the participle (using some version of the "Because most faculty members feel" option), recast the main clause. For example, following "anti-intellectualism," the sentence might read, "this issue cannot be addressed easily." If Line 4 has retained the participial phrase, then the revision would need to read something like "most faculty members believe that this issue cannot be addressed easily."

Line 6

- The "who" clause is restrictive: the comma must be dropped.
- The "he" is sexist: use "he or she," or change the number—to "Students who want ... feel that they."

Line 7

- Fix faulty parallelism: change "interest in" to "be*ing* interested in" so as to match "hav*ing* ideas."

Line 8

- Possessive "Its" should be the contraction "It's."
- Temporal "then" should be the comparative "than."
- Fix faulty parallelism: change "being" to "to be" to match "to pledge."

Line 9

- Change "a honors" to "an honors."
- Insert commas around the nonrestrictive modifying phrase "such as an honors program": these will separate it from both the long introductory dependent "if" clause that precedes it and the main clause that follows.

Line 10

- Make "students" a plural possessive: "students' lives."
- The "more enriched" is arguably wordy: "richer" is leaner.
- "Although" is a subordinating conjunction that creates a sentence fragment. The easiest solution is to cut it, though a writer could also attach the entire "although" clause to the previous sentence, using a comma or dash.

Line 11

- This is part of the fragment that began in Line 10.

Line 12

- Fix the possessive: make it "University's."
- Fix the case of the noun: make it "university's."
- Place a comma after "discrimination" to separate the long introductory modifying phrases from the main clause.

Line 13

- The semicolon is incorrect, because the sentence does not contain two independent clauses. A colon is better than a dash here, though both are technically correct.

Line 14

- Most rhetoricians consider "freshman" sexist: substitute "first-year."
- The use of "this" is another egregious case of broad reference (ask, "Agree with *this what?*). The best solution is probably to rewrite this part of the sentence to clarify the meaning. For example, make it "Some of the best students object to Greek life in these terms and oppose the administration's handling of the Greeks . . . "

Line 15

- Fix subject–verb agreement: make it "some . . . believe."

Here is how one corrected version of the quiz might look:

> Fraternities and sororities are a major part of student life at the university: students are preoccupied with pledging. Most faculty members do not approve of this dominance by Greek societies; however, they feel helpless about attacking the Greeks. Because faculty members perceive that the Greek societies are attractive to the students but at the same time that they encourage anti-intellectualism, this issue cannot be addressed easily. The student who wants to be popular and cool feels that he or she should not talk in class, because being interested in academics or having ideas outside class is uncool. It's more important to pledge the right house than to be smart. If the administration would create alternatives to Greek life, such as an honors program, the students' lives would be richer. For now, raising the cumulative grade point necessary to pledge and remain active would be a good start to solving the problem of Greek domination. Contrary to the university's stance against gender discrimination, Greek life perpetuates gender stereotypes: for example, the dances at each house for first-year women but not men. Some of the best students object to Greek life in these terms and oppose the administration's handling of the Greeks. But many of these same students mistakenly believe that most faculty members endorse the system.

CREDITS

This page constitutes an extension of the copyright page. We have made every effort to trace the ownership of all copyrighted material and to secure permission from copyright holders. In the event of any question arising as to the use of any material, we will be pleased to make the necessary corrections in future printings. Thanks are due to the following authors, publishers, and agents for permission to use the material indicated.

Chapter 1. Page 34: Freewrite on a scene from the film *Good Bye, Lenin!* by Sarah Kersh. Reprinted by permission of the author.

Chapter 2. Page 49: "Brooklyn Heights, 4:00 A.M." by Dana Ferrelli. Reprinted by permission of the author. **Page 66:** *Hua dan*: The Dance of Values in the Beijing Opera, reprinted by permission of the author. **Page 71:** Marketing the Girl Next Door: A Declaration of Independence? reprinted by permission of the author.

Chapter 3. Page 84: *The Dancers*, by Sarah Kersh. Pen and ink drawing, 6" × 13.75." Used by permission of Sarah Kersh. **Page 100:** "Playing by the Antioch Rules?" by Eric Fassin, *The New York Times*, December 26, 1993, p. 11. Copyright © 1993 by The New York Times Co. Reprinted by permission.

Chapter 4. Page 122: Excerpt from student paper on *The Tempest*, reprinted by permission of the author.

PHOTO CREDITS

Chapter 3. Page 78: Figure 3.1. REUNION DES MUSEES NATIONAUX, ART RESOURCE, NY. James Abbott McNeil Whistler. *Arrangement in Gray and Black No 1: Portrait of the Artist's Mother*, 1871.

Chapter 5. Page 151: Figure 5.4. ©Jeff Widener/AP

Chapter 6. Page 179: Figure 6.5. SCALA/ART RESOURCE, NY. Diego Rodrigues Velazquez. *Las Meninas*. 1656.

INDEX